POLICING HUMAN RIGHTS

CLARENDON STUDIES IN CRIMINOLOGY

RECENT TITLES IN THIS SERIES:

Respect and Criminal Justice
Watson

Neighbourhood Policing: The Rise and Fall of a Policing Model
Innes, Roberts, Lowe, and Innes

Respectable Citizens – Shady: Practices The Economic Morality of the Middle Classes
Farrall and Karstedt

Advocates of Humanity: Human Rights NGOs in International Criminal Justice
Lohne

Intimate Crimes: Kidnapping, Trust, and Gangs in Mexico City
Ochoa

Police Community Support Officers: Cultures and Identities within Pluralized Policing
O'Neill

Last Chance for Life: Clemency in Southeast Asian Death Penalty Cases
Pascoe

Police Unlimited: Policing, Migrancy, and the Values of Bureaucracy
Mutsaers

Policing Human Rights

Law, Narratives, and Practice

RICHARD MARTIN
Assistant Professor, Department of Law, London School of Economics

OXFORD
UNIVERSITY PRESS

OXFORD
UNIVERSITY PRESS

Great Clarendon Street, Oxford, OX2 6DP,
United Kingdom

Oxford University Press is a department of the University of Oxford.
It furthers the University's objective of excellence in research, scholarship, and education by publishing worldwide. Oxford is a registered trade mark of Oxford University Press in the UK and in certain other countries

First Edition published in 2021

Impression: 3

Published in the United States of America by Oxford University Press
198 Madison Avenue, New York, NY 10016, United States of America

British Library Cataloguing in Publication Data
Data available

Library of Congress Control Number: 2021933260

ISBN 978–0–19–885512–5

DOI: 10.1093/oso/9780198855125.001.0001

Printed and bound in the UK by
TJ Books Limited

For my parents,
Brian and Suzanne

General Editors' Preface

The *Clarendon Studies in Criminology series* aims to provide a forum for outstanding theoretical and empirical work in all aspects of criminology and criminal justice, broadly understood. The Editors welcome submissions from established scholars, as well as excellent PhD work. The Series was inaugurated in 1994, with Roger Hood as its first General Editor, following discussions between Oxford University Press and Oxford's Centre for Criminological Research. It is edited under the auspices of three centres: the Institute of Criminology at the University of Cambridge, the Mannheim Centre for Criminology at the London School of Economics and the Centre for Criminological Research at the University of Oxford. Each supplies members of the Editorial Board and, in turn, the Series General Editor or Editors.

Policing Human Rights: Law, Narratives and Practice is an exceptional piece of scholarship which brings together two hugely important criminological topics: human rights and policing. This book explores how human rights and policing practices inform one another from the introduction of new human rights policy to its application in interactions between the police and the public. This detailed analysis of how human rights are interwoven into policing culture and consciousness is set against the backdrop of the experience of the Police Service of Northern Ireland, a pioneer of human rights-based police reform, which has situated the UK Human Rights Act 1998 at the centre of its ethos.

This book draws on an unprecedented wealth of original information regarding the experiences of police officers navigating their duty to both protect and respect human rights in Northern Ireland. This includes information gathered through extensive interviews and focus groups with over one hundred police officers representing a spectrum of different ranks and responsibilities, as well as members of the Policing Board which is tasked with monitoring their compliance with the Human Rights Act; information acquired by observing police practices in a range of contexts, including community policing via Neighbourhood Police Teams and strategic enterprises by Tactical Support Groups; and information collected through analysis of official police documents, video-archived sessions between the public and the Policing Board and local newspaper articles covering more than a decade of police work.

This wealth of information is applied to understanding the experience of police officers as human rights practitioners, and their assimilation, perception and application of human rights principles in their police work. The book explores these experiences across a range of key contexts, including police training; routine neighbourhood policing; tactical police initiatives; public order policing, especially in the context of large events such as parades and protests; arrest and police custody. In doing so, the book demonstrates how policing is governed by human rights, and how human rights are at the core of police work.

Within this rich depiction of the general relationship between human rights and policing practices, the book presents the potent example of a police service which has adopted the upholding of human rights as a key facet of its work, status and identity, and a fundamental apparatus to effectively serve a fragmented society at its most volatile and vulnerable. In doing so, this book shows how the culture of policing has been radically altered by the introduction of human rights as a core element of how and why it functions, and the resulting expectations for police practice. It explores in detail how police officers make sense of their new obligations to defend and uphold human rights and apply this in the situations they encounter day to day. It also analyses the success of policies in redefining police culture, their translation into police training and the extent to which they shape approaches to policing at street level.

Policing Human Rights addresses topics of interest to a wide audience and will appeal to those interested in policing and human rights – academics, practitioners and politicians alike. Academically, it will be of most interest to criminologists, socio-legal scholars, sociologists, anthropologists and scholars in the field of transitional justice interested in security, democracy, policing and ethno-political division in post-conflict societies. Practically, it will be of interest most especially to police officers and agencies, and lawyers specializing in human rights and public law. Politically it will be of particular interest to policymakers, legal advisors and non-governmental organizations invested in human rights or police reform.

Such broad appeal ensures this book will make a significant contribution to literature on policing and human rights specifically, as well as regulatory practices more generally. As General Editors, we are delighted to welcome *Policing Human Rights: Law, Narratives, and Practice* into the *Clarendon Studies in Criminology series*.

Kyle Treiber and Loraine Gelsthorpe
Institute of Criminology, University of Cambridge
December 2020

Acknowledgements

Writing this book has been a humbling experience. There are many people to thank and debts still to return. I hope to convey such thanks in person where I can, but for now, let me mention a few people and institutions in particular. First and foremost, I am grateful to the Police Service of Northern Ireland (PSNI), particularly the senior officers who approached the project with warm curiosity, open-mindedness and a commitment to learn amongst the busyness and demands of their important work. To the numerous policemen and women of the PSNI I interviewed, chatted with and observed, my thanks to you for your generosity in taking the time and effort to share your working lives and entertain my questions about human rights in a frank and thoughtful manner. I appreciate the PSNI's feedback on the research at various stages, most recently at Queen's University Belfast's Human Rights Centre (2019) and with team leaders and senior officers from the PSNI's Tactical Support Group in Belfast (2020).

The fieldwork on which the book is based took me back to my native Northern Ireland for over a year during which I visited an array of police stations, training facilities and constituency offices scattered across the country. This fieldwork and the years surrounding it, alongside various conferences and workshops, were a costly enough enterprise made possible by the generous funding of the Economic and Social Research Council (ESRC) which I am very grateful for.

Looking back, I can see that the doctoral project that inspired the book has been following me around several different institutions, probably for too long in fact, but the book has undoubtedly benefited from my early career road trip. It began at Oxford's Centre for Criminology, which was a wonderful host and community in which to study. To be surrounded by such a bright, engaged and talented group of people was both a real pleasure and a source of inspiration. Many thanks to Ben Bradford for his enduring optimism and good humour which kept me afloat as I bobbed around in a sea of data and drafts during the doctorate, and who helped me to think more deeply about an empirical analysis of legitimacy. So too would I like to extend my special thanks to John Topping (QUB) for his feedback on various half-thoughts and working ideas as the project developed and for keeping me abreast of the latest developments and debates over many coffees in Belfast.

I am also very thankful to the many other colleagues, friends and interested readers who kindly commented on draft chapters at various stages, including Julia Viebach, Kieran McEvoy, Ian Loader, Heather Hamill, Sarah Turnbull, Karl Laird, Alpa Parmar, Paul Nolan and Brian and Suzanne Martin. I am especially grateful to Alyson Kilpatrick, the former human rights legal advisor to the Policing Board, for her encouragement and advice throughout the project, and also for reading parts of the book and sharing her insights. Alyson has served as an exemplar of what professional, independent and constructive human rights oversight of the police can, and ought to, look like. So too am I thankful to the Faculty of Law of the University of New South Wales, which kindly hosted me for a term as a visiting researcher, where I was able to gain fresh perspectives on my empirical data and benefit from the feedback of staff and students.

Perhaps my most loyal readers of all have been the members of Oxford's weekly Human Rights Research Group that Sandra Fredman so kindly invited me to be part of some five years ago. Thank you Sandy for encouraging my socio-legal spin on human rights and prompting me to think harder about the human rights paradigm itself. I am extremely grateful to the Research Group for their detailed feedback on drafts, but more generally, for their good company and encouragement over the years. My thanks, in particular, to Meghan Campbell, Helen Taylor, Victoria Myandazi, Tom Lowenthal, Ndjodi Ndeunyema, Jason Brickhill, Nomfundo Ramalekana, Max Harris, Mónica Olaya, Tristan Cummings, Farah Raza, Rishika Sahgal and Gauri Pillai.

The doctorate began its metamorphosis into a manuscript during my postdoctoral positions, and the finished product is all the better for its exposure to colleagues and students at the LSE's Department of Law (2017–2019) and Oxford's Bonavero Institute of Human Rights (2019–2020). My thanks especially to Conor Gearty and Peter Ramsay at the LSE, and Michael Molavi, Lucia Zedner and Liora Lazarus at Oxford, for their sage advice and encouragement at important junctures.

To the friends I have made along the way – and the older ones I managed to keep! – this is a an opportunity to say a huge thanks to you all for your humour, support and kindness over the years, in particular: Harry Anisson, Johan Boucht, Meghan Campbell, Tim Carson, John Croker, Matt Davies, Andrew Faul, Luigi Gariglio, Alice Gerlach, Rory Kelly, Karl Laird, Callum Montgomery, Thomas McDowell, Miguel Molavi, Cian Ó'Concubhair, Jim Talbert, Leila Tai, Laura Tilt, Marion Vannier, Willem van dan Berg, Rachel Wechsler and Kate West.

To my family, but especially my parents, Suzanne and Brian, to whom I dedicate the book, to my brother, Patrick, and to my uncle, Richard, and aunt, Marie: a heartfelt thank you for all the love, encouragement and support you have shown me, and for sharing the values that matter in life through your words and deeds. So too have I had the pleasure of getting to know Martin and Hildegund, who have been so generous and fun, never short of a wise word, good story and hearty meal. Finally, to Julia. As if your own professional life was not full enough, you have read and heard much more than anyone should about the contents of this book, alongside a soundtrack too often punctuated with various gripes about research, writing, jobs etc. Your great reserves of kindness and patience, wit and wisdom mean so very much: love and thanks, as always.

Finally, I am thankful to The Modern Law Review and Wiley for permission to reproduce in Chapter 3 material that first appeared in amended form in 'Ethno-National Narratives of Human Rights: The Northern Ireland Policing Board' (2020) *Modern Law Review* 83(1) 91-127, and Bloomsbury Publishing for permission to re-use select material from Chapters 7 and 8 published in 'A "Culture of Justification"? Police Interpretation and Application of the Human Rights Act 1998' in J. Varuhas. and S. Stark (eds), *The Frontiers of Public Law* (Oxford, Hart Publishing, 2019).

Richard Martin
Oxford, March 2021

Table of Contents

List of Figures and Table

Figures

Table

List of Authorities

CASES

Al Fayed and Others v Commissioner of Police of the Metropolis [2004] EWCA Civ 1579
Alford v Chief Constable of Cambridgeshire [2009] EWCA Civ 100
Armstrong v Chief Constable of West Yorkshire [2008] EWCA Civ 1582
Associated Provincial Picture Houses Ltd. v Wednesbury Corporation [1948] 1 KB 223
Austin and Another v Commissioner of the Metropolis [2009] UKHL 5
Austin and Others v UK (App nos 39692/09, 40713/09 and 41008/09) ECHR 459 (15 March 2012)
B and others v Chief Constable of Police Service of Northern Ireland [2015] EWHC 3691
B v Chief Constable of Hampshire Constabulary [2015] EWHC 1238
Belfast City Council v Miss Behavin' Ltd [2007] UKHL 19
Bank Mellat Her Majesty's Treasury (No 1) [2013] UKSC 38
Bare v IBAC [2015] 48 VR 129
Bukta and Others v Hungary (App no 25691/04) ECHR 610 (17 July 2007)
Castles v Secretary to the Department of Justice [2010] 28 VR 141
Commissioner of Police of the Metropolis vDSD [2018] UKSC 11
Castorina v Chief Constable of Surrey [1996] (*Times* 15 June 1988)
Cumming v Chief Constable of Northumbria Police [2003] EWCA Civ 1844
DPP v L and S [1998] CO/3682/98
DSD and NBV v Commissioner for the Metropolis [2014] EWHC 436
DB v Chief Constable of Police Service of Northern Ireland [2017] UKSC 7
De Freitas v Permanent Secretary of Ministry of Agriculture, Fisheries, Lands and Housing [1999] 1 AC 69
Douiyeb v Netherlands (App no 31464/96) ECHR 67 (4 August 1999)
Dumbell v Roberts [1944] 1 All ER 326
Fáber v Hungary (App no 40721/08) ECHR 2026 (24 July 2012)
Finucane v UK (App no 29178/95) 37 EHRR 29 (1 October 2003)
Fitzpatrick and Others v Commissioner of Police of the Metropolis [2012] EWHC 12 (QB)
Frumkin v Russia (App no 74568/12) ECHR 64 (12 January 2016)
Fox, Campbell & Hartley v UK (App nos 12244/86, 12245/86 and 12383/86) ECHR 27 (30 August 1990)
G v Federal Republic of Germany [1989] 60 DR 25
Gillan and Quinton v UK (App no 4158/05) ECHR 28 (12 January 2010)
Handyside v UK (App no 5493/72) ECHR 5 (7 December 1976)
Hayes v Chief Constable of Merseyside [2011] EWCA Civ 911
Huang v Secretary of State for the Home Department [2007] 2 AC 167
Jordan v UK (App no 24746/94) ECHR 327 (4 May 2001)
Kaya v. Turkey (App no 22535/93) ECHR 129 (28 March 2000)
Keegan v UK (Application no. 28867/03) ECHR 764 (18 July 2006)
Kelly and Others v UK (App no 30054/96) ECHR 29 (4 May 2001)
Kavala v Turkey (App no 28749/18) ECHR 898 (10 December 2019)
Khlaifia and Others v Italy (App no 16483/12) ECHR 757 (15 December 2016)
Kontrová v Slovakia (App no 7510/04) ECHR (31 May 2007)
Kudrevičius and Others v Lithuania (App no 37553/05) ECHR 1310 (26 November 2013)

Laporte, R (on the application of) v Chief Constable of Gloucestershire [2006] UKHL 55
MC v Bulgaria (App no 39272/98) ECHR 651 (4 December 2003)
McCann and Others v UK (App no 18984/91) ECHR 31 (27 September 1995)
McKerr v UK (App no 28883/95) ECHR 329 (4 August 2001)
McShane v UK (App no 43290/98) ECHR 465 (28 May 2002)
Murray v UK (App no 18731/91) ECHR 3 (8 February 1996)
O'Hara v Chief Constable of the Royal Ulster Constabulary [1996] UKHL 6
O'Hara v UK (App no 37555/97) ECHR 598 (16 October 2001)
O v Commissioner for the Metropolis [2011] EWHC 1246
Öllinger v Austria (App no 76900/01) ECHR 665 (29 June 2006)
Opuz v Turkey (App no 34401/02) ECHR 870 (9 June 2009)
Osman v UK (App no 23452/94) ECHR 101 (28 October 1998)
Oya Ataman v Turkey (App no 74552/01) ECHR 493 (5 December 2006)
Parker v Chief Constable of Essex [2017] EWHC 2140 (QB)
P.F. and E.F. v UK (App no 28326/09) ECHR 2015 (23 November 2010)
Plattform 'Ärzte Für Das Leben' v Austria (App no 10126/82) ECHR 15 (21 June 1998)
R (A) v Chief Constable of Kent Constabulary [2013] EWCA Civ 1706
R (Elgizouli) v Secretary of State for the Home Department [2020] UKSC 10
R (Osborn) v The Parole Board [2013] UKSC 61
R (Moos and McClure) v Commissioner of Police of the Metropolis [2012] EWCA Civ 12
R (Roberts) v Commissioner of the Metropolis [2015] UKSC 79
R (SB) v Governors of Denbigh High School [2006] UKHL 15
R v. Secretary of State for the Home Department, Ex parte Daly [2001] UKHL 26
Re Alexander and Others [2009] NIQB 20
Re DB's Application [2014] NIQB 55
Re DB's Application [2014] NICA 56
Re E (a child) (AP) (Northern Ireland) [2008] UKHL 66
Re Parsons [2003] NICA 20
Richardson v Chief Constable of West Midlands Police [2011] EWHC 773 (QB)
Salmon v Chief Constable of the Police Service of Northern Ireland [2013] NIQB 10
Shanaghan v UK (App no 37715/97) ECHR 330 (4 May 2001)
Shields v CC of Merseyside [2010] EWCA Civ 1281
Stankov and the United Macedonian Organization Ilinden v Bulgaria (App nos 9221/95 and 29225/95) ECHR 563 (2 October 2001)
Stepuleac v Moldova (App no 8207/06) ECHR 897 (6 November 2007)
S, V and A v Denmark [2018] (App nos 35553/12, 36678/12 and 36711/12) ECHR 353 (22 October 2018)
Tagayeva and Others v Russia (App no 26562/07) ECHR 354 (13 April 2017)
Wilding v Chief Constable of Lancashire [1995] CA, unreported 22 May 1995
Wood v Commissioner of Police for the Metropolis [2009] EWCA Civ 414
Ziliberberg v Moldova (App no 61821/00) ECHR 51 (1 February 2005)

STATUTES

Charter of Human Rights and Responsibilities Act 2006 (Victoria)
Convention for the Protection of Human Rights and Fundamental Freedoms
Human Rights Act 1998
Human Rights Act 2004 (ACT)
Human Rights Act 2019 (Queensland)

Policing and Crime Act 2017
Police and Criminal Evidence Act 1984
Police and Criminal Evidence (Northern Ireland) Order 1989
Police (Northern Ireland) Act 2000
Protection of Freedoms Act 2012
Public Order Act 1986
Public Order (Northern Ireland) Order 1987
Public Processions (Northern Ireland) Act 1998
Serious Organized Crime and Police Act 2005
Terrorism Act 2000

List of Abbreviations

AEP	Attenuated Energy Projectiles
CAJ	Committee on the Administration of Justice
CDO	Civilian Detention Officer
CJNI	Criminal Justice Inspection Northern Ireland
DUP	Democratic Unionist Party
ECHR	Convention for the Protection of Human Rights and Fundamental Freedoms
ECtHR	European Court of Human Rights
ESRC	Economic and Social Research Council
GFA	Good Friday Agreement
HET	Historical Enquiries Team
HIU	Historical Investigations Unit
HMIC	Her Majesty's Inspectorate of Constabulary
HRA	Human Rights Act 1998
ICP	The Independent Commission on Policing for Northern Ireland
IRA	Irish Republican Army
JCHR	Joint Committee on Human Rights
LIB	Legacy Investigation Branch
NGO	Non-governmental organization
NIHRC	Northern Ireland Human Rights Commission
NIPB	Northern Ireland Policing Board
PACE	Police and Criminal Evidence Act 1984/ Police and Criminal Evidence (Northern Ireland) Order (1989)
PONI	Office of the Police Ombudsman for Northern Ireland
PSNI	Police Service of Northern Ireland
RUC	Royal Ulster Constabulary
SDLP	Social Democratic and Labour Party
SF	Sinn Féin
TSG	Tactical Support Group
UUP	Ulster Unionist Party

PART I

Setting the Scene

Introduction

Righting Policing

Prologue

It was a drizzly morning in early September 2016. I broke from Belfast's rush-hour traffic and turned onto the Crumlin Road in the north of the city. This road is a wide one. It buffers two communities whose divisions reflect the competing histories, politics and identities that still define Northern Ireland to this day. It can feel like there is no end to the commemorations marking one event or another in the country's conflict-ridden past. The morning's event was significant for local policing and, on reflection, a fitting close to over a year of fieldwork in Northern Ireland. The event attracted senior police, politicians, lawyers, academics, community activists and non-governmental organizations. The Land Rovers of the Police Service of Northern Ireland (PSNI) lined the side-street leading up to the event's venue: the Crumlin Road Gaol. The Gaol once housed infamous prisoners whose acts of terrorism, criminality or politics (depending on one's viewpoint) played a role in sustaining the country's thirty-year armed conflict (1968–1998). But today, gathered in its newly refurbished function room, were former Royal Ulster Constabulary (RUC) policemen turned senior police officers, former Republican prisoners turned elected politicians, the Committee on the Administration of Justice, a long-standing criminal justice non-governmental organization established at the height of the conflict and the Northern Ireland Human Rights Commission, itself a product of the country's 1998 peace settlement.

It was in this setting, before these audiences, that the PSNI and the Northern Ireland Policing Board (the Policing Board) chose to celebrate over a decade of human-rights inspired policing in Northern Ireland. The event was carefully choreographed. A series of video clips were projected onto the Crumlin Road Gaol's white

Policing Human Rights. Richard Martin, Oxford University Press. © Richard Martin 2021.
DOI: 10.1093/oso/9780198855125.003.0001

walls and various faces of policing's recent past appeared, from former Chief Constable Sir Hugh Orde to former Policing Board's legal advisor Sir Keir Starmer. Each praised the efforts made to incorporate human rights in local policing and encouraged their successors to continue the good work. On a make-shift stage, the PSNI's Chief Constable was joined by both the Policing Board's Chairperson and its human rights legal advisor. A local BBC News anchor managed the flow of questions from the audience to the stage: the Committee on the Administration of Justice asked for guarantees that human rights monitoring would continue; a member of Sinn Féin wanted to know the Chief Constable's views on the proposed repeal of the Human Rights Act 1998 (HRA); the Police Federation asked why more wasn't being said about officers' human rights. Unionist politicians were notably absent from the event.

The Chief Constable, George Hamilton, proudly reaffirmed the PSNI's commitment to human rights and articulately responded to questions about police decision-making using the language of the HRA. 'As a police officer' he said, 'human rights protect me, my family and my community and I think that it is something to be cherished.' In an authoritative tone, he traced the European Convention on Human Rights (ECHR) to its British drafters in the 1950s and reminded the audience of the fundamental freedoms it sought to safeguard in post-war Europe. The Policing Board's legal advisor, Alyson Kilpatrick, steered a middle course, asserting her independence from both the Policing Board and PSNI. Whereas the Chief Constable linked human rights to post-war Europe, Kilpatrick reminded the audience of the significance of human rights closer to home. She alluded to the abuse of rights throughout the country's conflict and, more positively, the concrete commitment to human rights made in the 1998 peace settlement. Kilpatrick applauded the PSNI's commitment to and compliance with human rights, based on her year's review. She went as far as to state that even if the HRA was repealed, the PSNI would still operate with a rights-based approach: 'it's become so natural to them'. If anything, Kilpatrick's frustration lay with the cynical political narratives tarnishing human rights.

Such an event must have been hoped for, but surely could not have been envisaged, by the Independent Commission on Policing (the Independent Commission) when it published its blueprint for a 'new beginning' for policing in Northern Ireland in 1999. As

Loader and Mulcahy (2003: 39), citing Unger (1987), have observed, the police are a social institution 'made and imagined'. The police service the Commission imagined for post-conflict Northern Ireland was one defined by human rights – this was the Commission's 'central proposition':

> We recommend a comprehensive programme of action to focus policing in Northern Ireland on a human rights-based approach. We make a number of specific recommendations … but the achievement of such an approach goes beyond a series of specific actions. It is more a matter of the philosophy of policing, and should inspire everything that a police service does. It should be seen as the core of this report. (ICP, 1999: 20)

This vision was unashamedly ambitious. It would require police officers to master the technicalities of human rights law but also to internalize human rights as *the* purpose of their work: '[officers] should perceive their jobs in terms of the protection of human rights' (ICP, 1999: 21). It was the apparent success in making this vision real, of re-orientating the police around human rights, that local audiences had gathered in Crumlin Road Gaol to reflect upon and celebrate, but also to debate – and of which I, as a fledgling researcher, was trying hard to make sense. I scribbled down some initial impressions in the Gaol's car park before driving home, half-thoughts left lingering, questions still to be answered, a story yet to be told.

This book is an endeavour to make sense of and critically examine the legal, social and cultural dynamics of human rights on display in condensed, but vivid, form that morning at the Crumlin Road Gaol. In doing so, it seeks to better understand how and why police officers performing different aspects of policing, operating in distinct regulatory sites and enacting their own identities and experiences, come to encounter and engage with human rights law in their everyday work. By way of its concepts, methods and style of analysis, the book aspires to embrace criminology's interdisciplinary spirit, drawing on concepts from criminology itself, as well as law, anthropology, sociology and organizational studies, to illuminate the empirical realities of human rights law. It offers a series of empirical findings and conceptual insights that expose how human rights law functions in modern policing, and the histories, imaginations, visions and values police officers' express in narratives, sensemaking and practices of routine police work. In the chapters that follow I take the reader on a tour of four sites of policing: the public forums host to 'official' police narratives, routine policing, public order policing and police custody. But before embarking on this tour, I want to consider this emergence of human rights as a normative vision and regulatory basis for police reform far beyond Northern Ireland, and to draw out the various issues this throws up for scholars of human rights and criminal justice.

The Arrival of Human Rights on the Police Scene

The sketch of the Crumlin Road Gaol reflects, in miniature, an endeavour taking place worldwide: to implement and enforce human rights as guiding principles with which to discuss and critique, and ultimately to oversee and protect, the citizen's relationship with the state. Fundamentally, human rights offer a non-utilitarian counterweight to social and political questions. The state's interference with interests captured in the legal cocoon of human rights must be carefully justified according to limitation clauses attached to rights which set out the legitimate aims and means such interference must be limited to. Born out of the horrors of the Second World War, the incorporation of human rights into constitutional texts was to provide 'the individual or the minority with the shield to be used against a possible tyranny or rights by the majority' (Barak, 2012: 22). The last half century has now witnessed 'an apparently ceaseless and expanding process of international human rights standard-setting through an almost kaleidoscopic proliferation of instruments and treaties' (Grear, 2012: 19). The Universal Declaration of Human Rights, adopted in 1948, is the normative source of over 200 international human rights instruments, most notably the two international covenants on human rights signed in 1966,[1] and has given life to a proliferation of new constitutions that include judicially enforceable bills of rights in post-colonial societies and established democracies (Hoffmann, 2012). The power of police to crucially protect, but also fatally undermine, these freshly formalized rights prompted a swathe of international initiatives to align policing more closely to human rights norms. Pioneering events like the UN Division of Human Rights conference on the 'Role of the Police in the Protection of Human Rights',

[1] The International Covenant on Civil and Political Rights and the International Covenant on Economic, Social and Cultural Rights.

held in Canberra in 1963,[2] were to set in motion the extension to police and law enforcement agencies of the human rights principles and ever-more detailed standards contained in international codes of conduct, training documents and ethical principles.[3]

At the domestic level, human rights have become a 'new agenda in policing' (Neyroud and Beckley, 2013), even 'the most important development in law for policing' (Dixon, 2007). The codification of international human rights law in domestic constitutions standards has raised hopes of fostering a 'culture of justification'. Individuals are no longer to be seen as subjects of executive power reliant on a cluster of residual liberties, or mere service-users of the administrative state, but as holders of distinct claim-rights that the state must respect. Expressed in its strong form by Mureinik (1994) in the South African context, a culture of justification is the opposite of a 'culture of authority' in that it requires every exercise of public power to be fully justified, with cogent arguments and powers of persuasion replacing fear and coercion. Public authorities such as the police, in exercising their power, should not merely refrain from unreasonable decisions, they should reflect upon, consider and account for how their decisions impact on individuals' legally recognized rights – and where an interference with human rights arises, authorities ought to provide a legitimate basis and proportionate means for doing so. Rash, muddled or ignorant decisions will not do; authorities must offer reasoned and rational arguments, capable of persuading relevant audiences of their justification (Cohen-Eliya and Porat, 2011).

The core human rights principles of legality, necessity and proportionality lie at the heart of this notion of a culture of justification. As a threshold requirement, the principle of *legality* requires

[2] For reflections on this conference and an event to mark its anniversary, see Hambly (2014) and Bronitt, O'Brien and Bull (2014).

[3] Some the most notable examples include: the UN Code of Conduct for Law Enforcement Officials, UN Human Rights and Law Enforcement: A Trainer's Guide on Human Rights for the Police; Basic Principles on the Use of Force and Firearms by Law Enforcement Officials; United Nations Body of Principles for the Protection of all Persons under any form of Detention or Imprisonment; United Nations Declaration of Basic Principles of Justice for Victims of Crime and Abuse of Power; European Union Codes of Police Ethics Recommendation; Council of Europe Parliamentary Assembly Declaration on the Police; the European Convention on Human Rights and Fundamental Freedoms; and the Human Rights Act 1998 (see further Goold, 2016: 226–7; Kilpatrick, 2018: 124–34).

that police have a legal basis for the power they are exercising that interferes with an individual's recognized rights. Whether the interference is justified will depend on the particular formulation of the right itself. Most notable here are qualified rights in the ECHR (Articles 8–11) that permit interference where it is justified according to two legal principles, which serve as a device for determining the weight to be attached to competing interests and values as a matter of law (Barak, 2012: 131). The first, *necessity*, concerns the particular outcomes that police action seeks to achieve. To be lawful, such actions must seek to achieve one of the criteria listed in the Convention right that is engaged. The second, *proportionality*, concerns the relationship between this purpose and the means of achieving it. In order for police activity to be 'proportionate', the police measure or activity must be shown to be: (i) rationally connected to the objective pursued; (ii) no more than necessary to achieve the protected interest; (iii) fair – that there is a fair balance being struck between the right of the individual and the right of the community.[4] It is the subtle weighing and structuring of competing interests that mark the particular contribution of a human rights approach to decision-making (Campbell, Ashworth and Redmayne, 2019: 46–7).

Human rights principles and standards, and the idea of a 'culture of justice', have become weighty pillars of landmark police reforms in post-conflict societies, including South Africa (Hornberger, 2010) and a number of Western Balkan states (Collantes-Celador and Schwandner-Sievers, 2019), as well as in policing initiatives and efforts to improve ethical standards and the accountability of police in Central Europe, Canada, England and Wales, and the Australian states of Victoria, Queensland and Australian Capital Territory.[5] Within the UK specifically, the introduction of the HRA at the turn of the millennium has made

[4] See especially *Bank Mellat v Her Majesty's Treasury (No 1)* [2013] UKSC 38, Lord Sumption at [20] and *De Freitas v Permanent Secretary of Ministry of Agriculture, Fisheries, Lands and Housing* [1999] 1 AC 69, Lord Clyde at p. 80. For commentary, see in particular Barak (2012), and in the context of criminal justice more specifically, Campbell, Ashworth and Redmayne (2019), pp. 46–9.

[5] In these states, police, as public authorities, must give 'proper consideration' to human rights in decision-making. See the Charter of Human Rights and Responsibilities Act 2006 (Victoria), section 38(1); Human Rights Act 2019 (Queensland), section 58(1)(b); and Human Rights Act 2004 (ACT), section 40B(1)

it 'unlawful for a public authority to act in a way which is incompatible with a Convention right' (section 6 of the HRA). Indeed, leading proponents of the HRA championed the impact this provision could have in promoting a 'culture of justification' and thus purposeful, well-reasoned consideration of human rights principles in the routine decision-making of public authorities, not least the police (Irvine, 1998; Klug and Starmer, 2005). Since 2000, the UK has witnessed the introduction of a host of statutory schemes that have anchored the legal regulation of police powers in human rights concepts of *legality*, *necessity* and *proportionality*. Just some of the many possible examples include the use of covert intelligence (Regulatory Investigatory Powers Act 2000), the powers of arrest and authorization detention (Serious Organized Crime and Police Act 2005) and pre-charge bail (Policing and Crime Act 2017). Beyond these legislative initiatives, Her Majesty's Chief Inspectorate of Constabulary's (2009, 2011) critical nationwide review of the policing of the G20 protests in London 2009 has served to reinforce human rights law in public order training, as well as how operations are planned and conducted.

The Research Scene

A central concern of policing scholarship has been the exercise of routine police power and discretion, in particular the impact this has on the rights and liberties of the poor, marginalized and powerless. This is born out of a scholarly curiosity in how and why police go about their work, but also a political concern about the deployment and distribution of police coercive power (Loader and Mulcahy, 2003: 41–2). The focus has tended be on the use or abuse of specific police powers, but particularly stop and search, with human rights featuring as one part of a broader inquiry of police legitimacy, culture and discrimination (see e.g. Bowling and Phillips, 2007; Crawford, 2008; Skinns, 2011; Bradford, 2017). Public order policing, in particular, has seen a swell in empirical studies, stimulated in part by Her Majesty's Inspectorate of Constabulary's (HMIC) critical review of public order policing (HMIC, 2009, 2011), which examined 'negotiated

(b). For a more general discussion of policing and human rights in Australia, see Bronitt, O'Brien and Bull (2014).

management' and dialogue models of crowd management and, relatedly, the risks of 'strategic incapacitation' of protestors (see e.g. Gorringe et al., 2012; Stott, West and Radburn, 2018; Gilmore, Jackson and Monk, 2019). Similarly, research on police custody has fruitfully explored how routine police practices impact on the vulnerability of detained persons (Dehaghani, 2016), execute migration policies (Parmar, 2019) and contribute to the pains of detention in police custody (Skinns and Wooff, 2020). So too have policing scholars ventured into the unchartered territory of undercover police work to shine a rare spotlight on the authorization and deployment of clandestine tactics used in covert investigations and the organizational sub-cultures that accompany this (Loftus and Goold, 2012; Loftus, Goold and Mac Giollabhuí, 2016).

It is remains rarer, though, to find work emanating from either criminal justice or human rights scholarship with an in-depth focus on human rights law and discourse as the object of empirical study. In his review of the available literature, Goold has remarked on the relative paucity of empirical research on human rights law and discourse and its relationship with policing:

> [T]here are very few empirical studies that focus specifically on the question of policing and rights, or the barriers to effective human rights policing. As a result, we know little about how the police understand human rights, how the police's institutional and working cultures shape individual's responses to those rights ... These are all areas that need to be the subject of further research. (Goold, 2016: 236)

A few specific examples illustrate this well. When it comes to public order policing, despite human rights featuring as a core element of HMIC's analysis and the reforms, typically only passing reference is made to human rights in recent studies. Similarly, only limited attention has been paid to how human rights concepts that underpin the Police and Criminal Evidence Act 1984 (PACE), which have been the grounds for legal challenges, animate police custody in the two decades since the introduction of the HRA. In the rare instances where human rights law is foregrounded, the discussion is often practitioner-focused, taking on a more descriptive and programmatic approach that presents, at times, an overly simplistic success/failure dichotomy of human rights, usually associated with specific police reform initiatives or policies (see Lindholt et al., 2003; Uildriks, 2005; Crawshaw, Cullen and Williamson, 2007; Neyroud and Beckley, 2013; Goodman-Delahunty, Beckley and Martin, 2014).

There are some exceptions, though, that hint at the promise of a more critical, sociologically engaged inquiry of human rights. Such works include Hornberger's (2011) anthropological account of rights reform and police violence in South Africa, and Wahl's (2013) critical analysis of a human rights training programme for police officers in North India. Within England and Wales, the impact of the HRA has attracted only a few empirical studies. Drawing on a small sample of officers involved in covert policing, Bullock and Johnson (2012) described officers as having little substantive knowledge, even basic awareness, of the rights granted by the HRA. They found little evidence to suggest that police work had fundamentally changed, that practices were attuned to questions of rights or that internal processes had made 'human rights a weighty principle of police work' (Bullock and Johnson, 2012: 632–3). In their ethnographic work of covert policing, Loftus, Goold and Mac Giollabhuí (2016) were similarly unconvinced that officers had developed a greater respect for the right to private and family life of those placed under surveillance, despite the introduction of the Regulatory Investigatory Powers Act 2000 (RIPA). They concluded RIPA 'essentially confirmed the legality of covert surveillance and became a framework through which officers justified and documented their decision-making, thereby protecting them from internal and external criticism' (Loftus, Goold and Mac Giollabhuí, 2016: 642). In the context of street-policing, Pearson, Rowe and Turner's (2018) ethnographic work found officers to be broadly aware of the HRA yet remarkably poor at actively considering human rights principles like 'necessity' and 'proportionality' when determining whether or not to make arrests.

The general dearth of empirical research on human rights law, discourse and practice in contemporary policing is especially notable if we pause and compare it with the rich debates and substantive insights that the introduction PACE generated. Writing during this high-water mark for law and policing research, Dixon (1996: 289) described how '[t]he impact of PACE is one of the most controversial issues in British criminology'. Great debate rumbled between the rule sceptics (McConville et al., 1991), who emphasized the salience of police culture and informal 'working rules' over the law, the rule optimists (Baldwin and Kinsey, 1982), who posited that in the right organizational setting and legal format rules could temper police behaviour and the rule-critics (McBarnet, 1981), who argued it was the very substance of law which enabled and legitimated illiberal police practices. This might be explained, in part, by the shift towards normative accounts of rule compliance in the booming police legitimacy scholarship, which speaks the language of procedural justice, social alignment and group identity, not human rights or legal regulation (Bradford and Jackson, 2016; Trinkner et al., 2017). So too might it reflect a general disinterest in codified human rights in English culture (Loader, 2007), linked to the common law's own preference for civil liberties (Hunt, 1999). Perhaps it is also a reflection of a wider debate over what it means to 'do human rights criminologically' – with the legal field emerging as a particular fault line with respect to how, if at all, human rights ought to be researched, analysed or adopted by criminologists (Murphy and Whitty, 2013: 568–9).

The sustained interest in, and adoption of, human rights in police reform, rhetoric and regulation gives rise to two fundamental sets of questions, yet to be seriously addressed. The first set of questions raises conceptual and methodological issues. Can we meaningfully engage with (human rights) law beyond the established 'insider' approach associated with doctrinal analysis? And if we can, what does this mean for how we understand what human rights law is and who the members of its interpretive community are? What insights and approaches from the social sciences might aid us in the task of explaining how human rights law is understood in settings beyond the court? In addressing such questions, there is much to be gained, it would seem, from bringing criminological and human rights scholarship into much closer conversation than is usually the case. Human rights scholars are recognizing ever more 'the necessary in interdisciplinarity of this most law-orientated of subjects' (Meckled-García and Çali, 2006; Douzinas and Gearty, 2012: 10). This reflects the growing acceptance of the 'dynamic network of cross references' between law, politics and society, including that human rights law requires moral and cultural foundations it cannot generate itself (Hoffmann, 2012: 83, 95; Fredman, 2013). So too are criminologists engaging with human rights more closely and critically than ever before (Murphy and Whitty, 2013). Studies include the practical operation of human rights in the criminal justice system (e.g. Goold and Lazarus, 2007; Amatrudo and Blake, 2014) but also rich accounts of the vernacular of human rights in local discourses of crime, security and politics (e.g. McEvoy, 2003; Rock, 2004; Loader, 2007).

The questions in the second set, which relate closely to the first, are empirical and concern the form, functions and features of human rights law in police practice. How is human rights law incorporated into organizational narratives or oppositional discourses, and understood, interpreted and applied by officers? How do internal structures, workplace pressures and associated coping strategies affect officers' interaction with, and perceptions of, rights-based standards and principles? How do officers use, resist or reinterpret human rights and associated policies, practices or discourse? What features of sub-cultures across police ranks and roles influence how officers experience, engage with and apply human rights? How might human rights become not only a tool to critique police but also 'a means to ameliorate and consolidate legitimacy' (Hornberger, 2010: 262)? Again, in approaching these questions, there are significant insights to be drawn from the sociology of policing and human rights research. The former includes the role of law in policing (Dixon, 1997; Smith, 1998; Ericson, 2007), as well as formal and informal accountability (Chatterton, 1979; Waddington, 1994; Campeau, 2015) and the interplay between police culture, officers' coping strategies and their working practices (Waddington, 1999; Loftus, 2009; O'Brien-Ollinger, 2016). The latter offers rich accounts of how contested, adaptive and dynamic human rights are as a legal and political project (Gearty, 2006; Douzins, 2012), and how the realization of human rights protections are conditional on various facets of social life and local cultures (Çali and Meckled-García, 2006; McInerney-Lankford, 2018).

Policing Human Rights

The book aspires to provide some tentative answers to the two sets of closely related questions just outlined. In doing so, the chapters that follow offer a sociologically inspired, empirically grounded, account of human rights law in policing, using the Police Service of Northern Ireland as an organizational case study. The fruits of this labour are a series of substantive insights and associated arguments that tell the story of how and why officers' encounter, and engage with, human rights law in the various ways they do in contemporary police work. The findings of the book are based on extensive fieldwork with the PSNI, including interviews and focus groups with over one hundred police officers from over twenty police stations and five departments that I conducted in Northern Ireland between September 2014 and December 2016. This is supplemented by interviews with members of the Northern Ireland Policing Board; short periods of observation with Neighbourhood Policing Teams, the Tactical Support Group and police training sessions; video archives of thirty-nine public sessions of the Policing Board; local newspaper archives; and official documents of the PSNI and the Northern Ireland Policing Board.

It is argued that an empirical account of human rights law – that is, to grasp the performances, philosophies and practices that animate human rights in policing – ought to be advanced using a sociological approach to law that is genuinely interdisciplinary. That is to say, if we are to fully grasp the understandings, interpretations and practices that animate the empirical realities of human rights law, we ought to seek inspiration from concepts taken from sociology, anthropology and organizational studies, as well as criminology. While recognizing human rights as emanating from, and relating to, established legal principles and standards, the book seeks to uncover how and why human rights law comes to be socially constituted, organizationally conditioned and practically interpreted and applied in policing. Such a project entails reflecting on, and critically engaging with, what Cotterrell (1997: 100) has described as the 'discursive closure' of law – that is, the established 'conception of law as a distinct discourse, possessing its own integrity, its own criteria of significance and validation, its own means of cognition and constituting objects of which it speaks'. This is something I attempt in Chapter 1, in which I propose a sociological approach to human rights law, comprised of three foundations – *vernaculars*, *sensemaking*, *practices* – that then provide the conceptual bedrock for the rest of the book.

In seeking to advance a sociological analysis of human rights law in policing, the book embraces what has been termed a 'naturalistic' perspective of law's interpretation and application in organizations (Manning, 1986; Hawkins, 1992, 2002). This is to conceive of an organization like the police as being 'responsive to its environment, while its members are viewed as people with their own values, needs, expectations and agendas, rather than as dispassionate individuals all working coherently to achieve a set of organizational goals' (Hawkins, 1992: 26). Such an approach is distinct from positivistic analyses, which too often risk an 'oversimplified and monochrome picture' of organizational decision-makers that casts them as actors rationally weighing up isolated legal issues in a framework guided and constrained solely by legal rules (Hawkins, 2002: 29). Focusing on the numerous settings in which legal decisions are made, a naturalistic approach concerns itself instead with sensemaking and interpretation of the law by organizational actors set within the wider social field in which they contextualize and apply the law (Hawkins, 2002: 30). Police officers' attitudes towards, and engagements with, human rights law, like decisions more generally, are 'not made in a vacuum, but in a broader context of demands and expectations arising from the environment' they inhabit (Hawkins, 2002: 31). It is in this spirit of inquiry that the book adopts *in situ* analyses that take seriously the organizational, social and cultural dynamics that provide structure and meaning to how officers encounter and engage with human rights law. This involves paying closer attention to micro- and meso-level processes that contribute to human rights narratives, sensemaking and practices than is typically the case in the existing policing scholarship (Merry, 2017).

Adopting the PSNI as the case study within which to pursue these *in situ* analyses, I invite the reader inside an organization often cited as a 'world leader' in adopting a human rights approach to policing (Bayley, 2008; English, 2016; Kilpatrick, 2018) and which has proven to be of great interest to police reformers and policymakers across the world. In the aftermath of the country's conflict (1968–1998), policing underwent one of the world's most ambitious and contested reform programmes. The 'central proposition' at the heart of the reforms was a 'human rights approach' to policing, resulting in: a new police oath and code of ethics incorporating the ECHR; extensive training in fundamental principles and standards of human rights; a statutory duty on the newly created Policing Board to monitor police compliance with the HRA 1998; and the recruitment of a specialist in-house human rights lawyer by the PSNI. Since 2005, the PSNI has introduced over 200 human rights recommendations (PSNI, 2016a: 3) and attracts police leaders, oversight bodies, policymakers and students from across the world who are keen to learn from its story. If the lofty ideals of international human rights law treaties or the performance indicators of multi-million-pound reform projects are to be achieved anywhere, many commentators will point you in the direction of the very police service and associated bodies on show that morning at the Crumlin Road Gaol. The PSNI thus serves as a highly instructive case study precisely because it has gone to unprecedented lengths to foster and sustain a human rights-based approach to policing that has been imagined in so many international treaties, reform efforts and regulatory schemes.

The case study of the PSNI also, of course, raises the question of how generalizable the book's findings are for other jurisdictions where police reforms have neither been as politically pressing or as organizationally advanced. And this is made more complex still by Northern Ireland's post-conflict society, which is animated by lively local rights discourse (Curtis, 2014) and extensive legal safeguards following a legacy of rights abuses by the state (Harvey, 2001). Just some of the features that distinguish policing in Northern Ireland from many other contexts include the legacy of an armed conflict, marked ethno-national divisions in society and politics, start-stop devolved government and a terrorist threat level labelled as 'severe'. For the reader visiting Northern Ireland for the first time in the book, the chapters will reveal the enduring legacy of these conflict-related issues and their impact on 'high' and 'low' policing (Brodeur, 2010). Attending to the local culture and politics of Northern Ireland is vital in order to properly grasp, and account for, the subtle dynamics that animate police work and which interact with human rights vernaculars, sensemaking and practices. That said, readers will also encounter core elements of police work and practices that appear across the world (public order policing, police custody and neighbourhood policing), legal principles and standards common to jurisdictions where international human rights law standards apply (especially in the UK and EU), and workplace pressures, operational demands and sub-cultural traits that will be familiar in many police organizations. The lessons that might be drawn from the case study is something I reflect upon more critically in the Conclusion, but the generalizability of the Northern Ireland case study is also something I would encourage readers from other jurisdictions to reflect upon throughout the book, drawing on their own expertise.

The story I tell in the chapters ahead is of a police service in which senior officers are trying to sustain human rights as a central narrative to explain the work, status and identity of the PSNI in a divided society. How the official police narrative is received by local political parties and oversight bodies tells us much about the condition of human rights, politics and policing in Northern Ireland today. Equally, how police officers interpret and apply the legal standards of human rights offers valuable insights into human rights as a regulatory framework and an ethics of power in policing. The accounts in the book are grounded in human stories of the officers who have come to inhabit its chapters: the outlooks, experiences and understandings of policemen and women empowered by, as well as burdened with, the responsibility to police under the mantra of human rights. These are voices rarely heard in the police scholarship, not least because of the traditional reluctance of the police in Northern Ireland to allow researchers access to the sites of work explored in the book. Before sketching an outline of the book, and explaining its sociological approach in the next chapter, I want to first locate the case study of the PSNI within the Northern Irish context, which will help make sense of the local policing and human rights debates that resurface in the chapters ahead.

In the Shadow of the Past: Policing, Human Rights and the Condition of Northern Ireland

Ethno-national vantage points have long served as the lens through which policing is understood, interpreted and debated in Northern Ireland. This is a region of the UK that has long sat uneasily on the right shoulder of Ireland. For centuries, the population has been divided over whether one identifies as a member of the Protestant majority or Catholic minority. Yet religion is really a proxy for the community one is born into, rather than the church one attends (Bryan, 2000: 12). Many Protestants have a sense of being British, allied to a preference for retaining the constitutional link between Northern Ireland and Great Britain (Unionism). Many Catholics, on the other hand, have stronger cultural and historical ties to Ireland and desire to, at some point in the future, reunite Northern Ireland with the Republic of Ireland (Nationalism). This division has rumbled since at least the sixteenth century, when settlers from Scotland and England first arrived in Ulster as part of an effort to 'Anglicize' this part of the island of Ireland (Bardon, 2012). Policing was intimately bound up with the colonial project in Ireland and the formation of the Northern Irish State after the partition of Ireland in 1921. The RUC, almost exclusively Protestant in composition, was the coercive arm of a Unionist state that had, from its very inception, promoted a social and economic order that discriminated against Catholics in politics, housing, education, industry and culture (Hillyard, 1998; McKittrick and McVea, 2012).

The late 1960s witnessed the mobilization of a diversity of Catholic groups and communities against the disadvantage and discrimination they faced under the umbrella of the civil rights movement. The brutality of the RUC's response to the largely peaceful protests of the civil rights movement in late 1968 signalled a steep decline in the relationship between the RUC and Catholic communities. This was followed by the well-documented failure of the RUC to protect civil rights demonstrators from a violent ambush by Loyalist counter-protestors at Burntollet Bridge in January 1969 and the further clashes between police and the residents of Derry's Bogside, a Catholic enclave of the city. By the early 1970s, widespread rioting had broken out across parts of Derry and Belfast. The Provisional Irish Republican Army (IRA) emerged as the defenders of the Catholic communities subjected to increasing hostility and violence by the British Army which followed in the wake of the introduction of internment without trial in August 1971. Protestant vigilante groups soon grew into paramilitary groups to protect their own communities from the Provisional IRA (McKittrick and McVea, 2012). Fuelled by the internment of thousands of Catholics and the tragic events of Bloody Sunday in 1972,[6] the Provisional IRA grew in its numbers and violence. Paramilitary groups and security forces were drawn into sharp conflict with one another, a situation that would last for several decades (Hillyard, 1988; Hadden, 2012).

A stream of litigants exercised their right of petition to the European Court of Human Rights (ECtHR) during the conflict that ensued (1969–1998), seeking to remedy injustices and curb the violence and excesses of the security forces (McEvoy, 2000; Dickson,

[6] The British Army shot dead thirteen unarmed civil rights campaigners in Derry in January 1972. In 2010, the Saville Inquiry published its damning findings into the incident, provoking former Prime Minister David Cameron to issue an apology for the actions of the armed forces.

2010; Turner, 2017). Such hope often proved optimistic. The ECHR proved to be an underwhelming instrument for protecting the human rights of suspects detained and questioned at the hands of the police and army (Dickson, 2010). Nonetheless, the RUC's human rights record remains the topic of ongoing contestation. The complaints levelled at the RUC include: the abuse of officers' special powers of search, arrest and detention under the Northern Ireland (Emergency Provisions) Act 1973; allegations of a 'shoot to kill' policy in police and army counter-terrorism operations in the early 1970s; police brutality against suspects held at designated police interrogation centres, as well as against Republican protestors; and police collusion with Loyalist paramilitaries in the murder of Catholics, including inadequate investigation of deaths where state informers were involved (see Committee on the Administration of Justice (CAJ), 1988; Human Rights Watch, 1997; Dickson, 2000, 2010; Office of the Police Ombudsman for Northern Ireland (PONI), 2007, 2016). The danger, stress and bereavement police officers faced on and off duty (Brewer and Magee, 1991: chapter 6) may contextualize, but cannot excuse, the human rights abuses still coming to light to this day.

Policing had become one of the most emotive, controversial parts of the bitter conflict that killed 3,600 people and injured 40,000 (McKittrick and McVea, 2012). As a key part of the Good Friday Agreement (GFA), signed in 1998, the political parties agreed that peace brought an 'opportunity for a new beginning to policing in Northern Ireland with a police service capable of attracting and sustaining support from the community as a whole'.[7] The Independent Commission on Policing (ICP) was established in 1998 as part of the GFA. The Commission's panel of experts, chaired by Conservative Peer Lord Chris Patten, embarked on the formidable task of re-imaging Northern Irish policing. The Commission's consultation attracted over 10,000 people at its public meetings and over 2,500 written submissions (ICP, 1999: 11). Acutely aware that police partisanship was a central fault line during the conflict, the Commission's recommendations proposed: a revived commitment to community policing; greater accountability through the Policing Board and local District

[7] The Agreement brought an end to the country's armed conflict. It was signed by Northern Ireland's political parties (with the exception of the Democratic Unionist Party) and the British and Irish governments after extensive negotiations.

Policing Partnerships; a recruitment quota to increase the number of Catholic officers; and, of course, a 'human rights approach' to policing. After considerable political debate, the Commission's proposals were enacted in the Police (Northern Ireland) Act 2000 and reform began in earnest in November 2001 when the RUC was disbanded and replaced by the PSNI (Shearing, 2000; Ellison and Mulcahy, 2001; Murphy, 2013: chapter 4).

If the PSNI was 'made and imagined' for a peacetime society, the one it actually polices today is a negative kind of peace, characterized by the absence of conflict rather than the presence of reconciliation. Two decades have passed since the GFA but the chasm between Unionism and Nationalism remains. A tribal ethno-nationalism pervades local politics (moderate parties have been electorally decimated), levels of segregation are alarmingly high (just 7 per cent of pupils attend Protestant–Catholic integrated schools) and Catholics still out-score Protestants in nearly every measure of social deprivation (Wilson, 2016). This is a society yet to reach a shared sense of its history and, crucially, its conflict. The following statement, released by the political parties after failure to agree on mechanisms for 'dealing with the past' in 2013, sums up the present state of affairs all too well:

> We cannot yet agree on the causes of the conflict, a mutual understanding of those events, or even at times the terminology to describe them. Indeed, the period of violence up to 1998 is variously termed a war, a conflict, or the troubles. (Northern Ireland Executive, 2013: 21)

In the absence of an overarching transitional justice framework (Bell, 2002; cf. McEvoy and Bryson, 2016; Turner, 2017: chapter 6), the state's positive duty arising under Article 2 of the ECHR to investigate conflict-related deaths lies with the PSNI. This Article 2 duty requires the state to conduct full and effective investigations into the circumstances of controversial deaths caused directly or indirectly by state actors.[8] To this end, the PSNI established a £60 million in-house investigation unit – the Historical Enquiries

[8] See generally *McCann and Others v UK* (App no 18984/91) ECHR 31 (27 September 1995); *Kaya v. Turkey* (App no 22535/93) ECHR 129 (28 March 2000). In the Northern Irish context specifically, see *Jordan v UK* (App no 24746/94) ECHR 327 (4 May 2001); *Kelly and Others v UK* (App no 30054/96) ECHR 29 (4 May 2001); *McKerr v UK* (App no 28883/95) ECHR 329 (4 August 2001). The ECtHR identified four requirements that an Article 2 compliant investigation must satisfy: independence from those implicated in the events; effective in the sense of being capable of bringing those responsible to justice; a prompt response

Team, now the Legacy Investigation Branch – to address victims' families concern and compile reports for them, as well as to re-examine the prospect of prosecution in cases where sufficient evidence arose (Lundy, 2009; Criminal Justice Inspection Northern Ireland (CJINI), 2013). Half of the PSNI's major investigation teams and legal department are working exclusively on historical cases (PSNI, 2015a). The PSNI's handling of these cases, particularly the impartiality of its officers, has been subject to sustained criticism from victims' families and politicians (Lundy, 2009; HMIC, 2013, 2015).

The PSNI's chief officers have expressed deep frustration and growing concern at the toxicity these legacy issues are having on policing and have strongly encouraged politicians to relieve the PSNI of its investigatory burden (*Belfast Telegraph*, 2017c). The former Chief Constable George Hamilton's (2015) position was especially clear: 'I will not allow this organization [the PSNI] to become the scapegoat for political failure to reach an agreement on this critical issue of the past'. A package of new measures and bodies to address the legacy of the conflict was proposed in the Stormont House Agreement (December 2014). The agreement between the British and Irish governments and five political parties in the Northern Ireland Executive would see the establishment of initiatives including an International Commission for Information Retrieval, an Oral History Archive and an Implementation and Reconciliation Group (see McEvoy and Bryson, 2016). Most significant for the PSNI, though, would be the creation of the Historical Investigations Unit, which would take responsibility for investigating conflict-related deaths. At the time of writing, the Stormont House Agreement remains unimplemented due to wider political disputes between Sinn Féin and the Democratic Unionist Party, but also specific concerns over the balance of cases relating to state versus non-state actors that would be subject to review by the Historical Investigations Unit (News Letter, 2017b).

The contemporary interplay between policing, the legacy of the conflict and human rights can be seen more broadly too. As Figure 0.1 illustrates, public satisfaction with the PSNI is high but remains consistently lower amongst Catholics than Protestants. The reasons for this extend beyond the activities of police to issues of

by the investigating authorities; a sufficient element of public scrutiny of the investigation or its results (*Jordan* at [106–9]). For legal commentary see especially Ní Aoláin (2002) and Anthony and Mageean (2007).

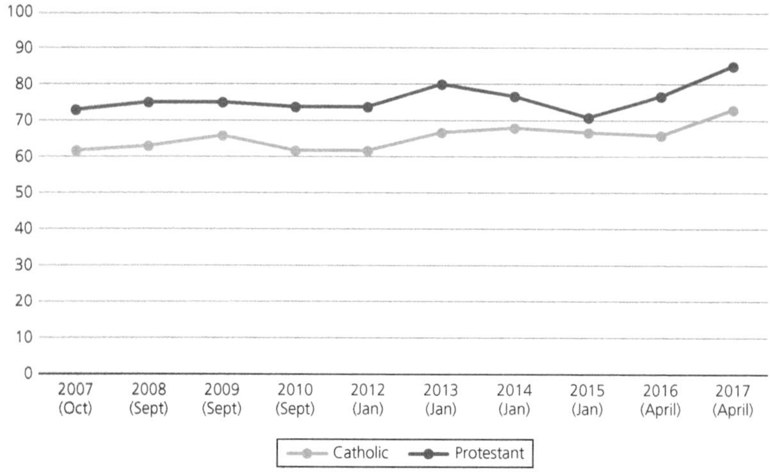

Figure 0.1 Percentage of People who are Very/Fairly satisfied the PSNI Treat Members of the Public Fairly in Northern Ireland as a Whole

Compiled by the author using data from the Policing Board's omnibus surveys

community diversity and cross-community interaction (Bradford et al., 2019). The past also lives on in the form of thousands of annual Loyalist parades, hundreds of which raise tensions as they pass by Republican neighbourhoods. In policing these events, the PSNI is thrust into the centre of local disputes. Human rights have been proffered as the best tool for resolving the competing demands of marchers, residents, and local businesses (Quigley, 2002; Strategic Review of Parading, 2008). Finally, the PSNI is not only faced with the threat of Dissident Republican terrorists, but also Loyalist paramilitaries, which still operate in some housing estates. Between 2006 and 2015 there were 787 punishment beatings, 11,000 shootings and bombings and 3,899 forced evictions (Wilson, 2016). Despite not being state actors bound by human rights law, whether paramilitaries should nevertheless be critiqued and condemned using the praxis of human rights law standards is a long-running debate (McEvoy, 2003; Felner, 2012).

The prominence of human rights is a remarkable feature of Northern Ireland's political discourse, reflecting the legacy of the past just outlined but also the outworking of the rights-inspired peace settlement (Turner, 2017: 103–13). An entire chapter of the

GFA was dedicated to human rights, in which signatories affirmed 'their commitment to the mutual respect, the civil rights and the religious liberties of everyone in the community'. This encouraged a series of legal initiatives and institutional arrangements that were implemented to cement human rights law into Northern Ireland's post-conflict society. These included: the incorporation of the ECHR into domestic law through the HRA; the restriction on the legislative competence of the Northern Ireland Assembly to introduce bills incompatible with the ECHR; and the establishment of the Northern Ireland Human Rights Commission to review the adequacy and effectiveness of law and practice relating to the protection of human rights. Writing in a period of post-Agreement optimism in 2001, Harvey (2001: 263) described how:

> there has been a marked increase in the deployment of rights discourse in Northern Ireland since its adoption. Interests which in the past would have been constructed in different terms are now being reinvented in the language of rights.

Fifteen years later, Harvey's (2015, 2017) writing bears a more cautious tone. Not only has Brexit shaken the foundations of the GFA, the last decade has exposed the susceptibility of human rights to ethno-national appropriation. This was strikingly illustrated in the Northern Ireland Human Rights Commission's (NIHRC) determined efforts to introduce a Bill of Rights for Northern Ireland. Three draft Bills were published between 2001 and 2005 and a civic forum was created in 2008, comprising twenty-eight members from politics and civil society. After much debate within the forum, the process stalled. Of the forty substantive rights proposed by the NIHRC, only three enjoyed (qualified) cross-party (Nationalist–Unionist) agreement. Unionists argued for a restrictive bill of rights, Nationalists wanted an expansive one; Unionists preferred non-discrimination, Nationalists insisted on substantive equality; Nationalists championed socio-economic rights, Unionists rejected them because they undermined parliamentary sovereignty (Harvey and Schwartz, 2009). A strong brand of social conservativism in Northern Ireland has also sparked heated political and legal debate over the compatibility of the country's prohibitions on same-sex marriage and abortion with domestic and international human rights standards (de Londras, 2017). The PSNI is a vocal contributor to Northern Ireland's human rights discourse. Having invested great energy in reforming itself on the basis of human rights and having been forced to confront its legal responsibilities arising from ECHR standards – most notably in policing parades as well as historical investigations – the PSNI has its own human rights narrative to contribute to contemporary Northern Irish society. It is rare to hear a speech by the Chief Constable or encounter a public session of the Policing Board where mention is not made of human rights.

The Arrangement of the Book

To the aid the reader as they progress through the book's Parts, a summary of the four sites of policing in the book, the source of data relied upon in each and their order of appearance is set out in Figure 0.2. The following chapter further sets the scene by introducing the components of the sociological approach to human rights law the book seeks to advance. The substantive chapters begin in Part II. They reveal how human rights law is socially constituted and made sense of by different actors, deconstructing how and why it becomes imbued with the visions, values and agendas of the particular actors whose professional worlds come into contact with it. Infused with both the PSNI's organizational self-conceptions of human rights – legality, ethics, accountability – and political parties' ethno-national divisions, rights contestations can be understood as a form of what Curtis (2014) has described as 'war by other means': a vernacular for continuing, rather than resolving, debates over national belonging, cultural expression and state repression. Despite the PSNI's determined efforts to make real the Independent Commission's vision of a technical and cultural commitment to human rights, the politics of policing remains infused with historical rights discourses, the legacy of policing and conceptions of the imperfect peace.

Chapter 2 asks how and why human rights have become such an integral part of the official PSNI narrative over the last decade. The reason, I argue, lies in the apparent power of human rights to cool down, if not neutralize, political tensions, debates and controversies that still animate 'high' policing (Brodeur, 1983) in the country. The apparent allure of human rights lies in its capacity to promote the PSNI's ethical credentials, neutrality and accountability to high-level audiences – politicians, oversight bodies and the media – that remain acutely attuned to signals of

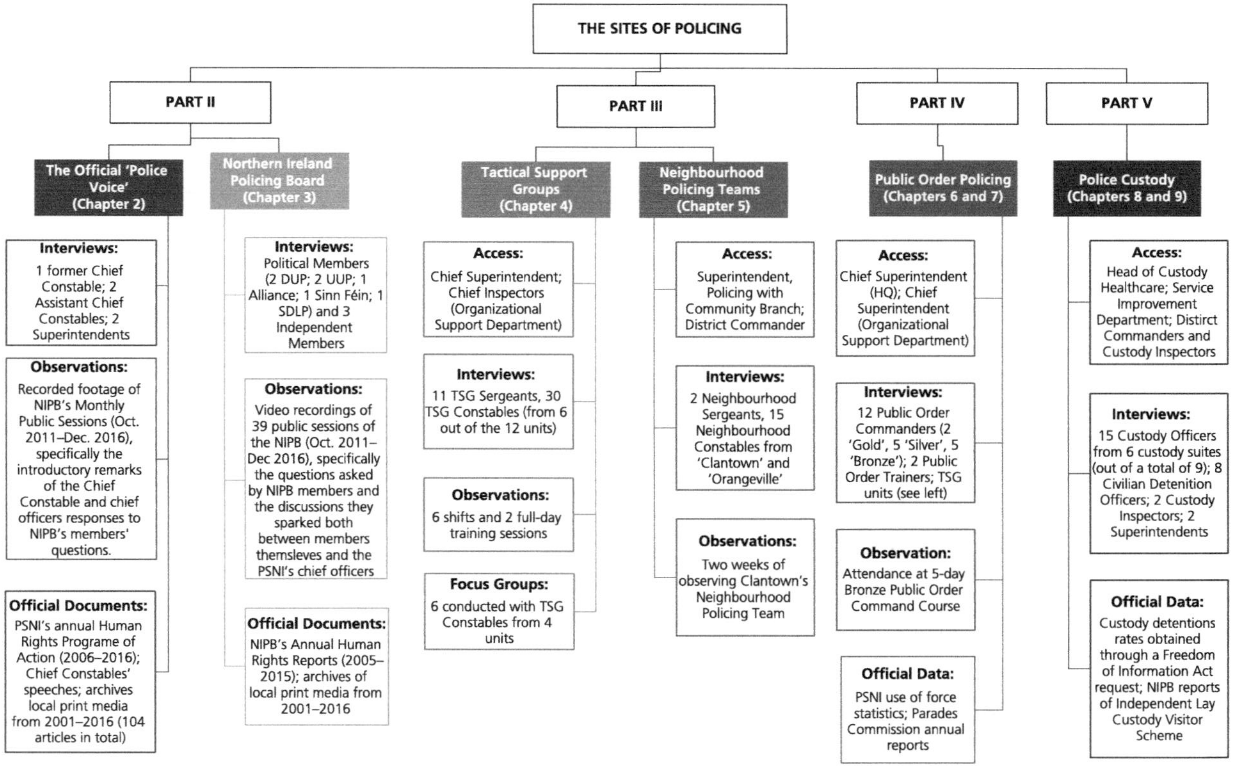

Figure 0.2 Sites of Policing

police partisanship or impropriety. For the PSNI's chief officers, the human rights reforms that they have worked hard to embed within the organization have rehabilitated the PSNI's moral authority to comment on matters of politics, transition and peace in Northern Ireland. I identify three central properties that comprise this official narrative. Each of these, I argue, contributes to a purported vision of the PSNI as worthy of endorsement by elite audiences. The extent to which these claims are accepted, or even recognized, by the general public remains debatable but I argue that the very ability of the police to mount and sustain this narrative lies in its 'authorization' by powerful audiences that contribute to local debates over policing in Northern Ireland.

Chapter 3 turns to the Policing Board as a further site in which to examine alternative developments and deployments of human rights captured in the official accounts of local political parties. The Policing Board is presented as an arena where the demands of human rights law meet the much broader and contested understandings of human rights in local political discourse. Beyond its extensive powers to appoint and dismiss chief officers and to set police targets and priorities, the Policing Board is bestowed with a statutory duty to monitor the performance of the police in complying with the HRA. Drawing on a content analysis of video footage of thirty-nine monthly public sessions of the Policing Board, as well as in-depth interviews with representatives of the political parties who sit, or sat, on the Policing Board, I compare the attitudes and agendas of Unionist and Nationalist political members towards human rights oversight. I argue that regardless of the statutory duty to monitor policing based on the standards of the HRA, for political members on the Policing Board, human rights are a vessel harbouring deep sentiments and concerns at the heart of which are competing histories of the conflict, legacies of policing and understandings of Northern Ireland's imperfect peace. The narratives expressed on the Policing Board swirl around, and at times directly contradict, the PSNI's official narrative and further demonstrate the elasticity of human rights to fit the visions of different actors.

But what about the policemen and women of the PSNI, who are themselves drawn from this same society? How do they receive, interpret and understand the properties of human rights expounded by chief officers and taught to them in training? How responsive are occupational cultures and organizational priorities to the loud, but deeply contested, human rights narratives that swirl around the PSNI? These questions are answered in Part III, which examines routine policing as experienced by the Tactical Support Group and Neighbourhood Policing Teams. Consistent with an exploration of human rights as vernacular, socially constructed amidst everyday life and workplace demand, in Part III I draw upon the concept of 'sensemaking'. I use these to capture the relationship between the micro- and meso-levels generally, but more specifically the social interaction between officers' biographies, experiences, cultural resources and organizational settings that affect officers' understanding of human rights.

Chapter 4 adopts Hughes' (1958) concept of 'dirty work' to introduce the occupational context within which Tactical Support Group officers were making sense of human rights as a vernacular of police work. With this conceptual scaffolding in place, I proceed to identify and examine a series of counter-narratives officers attached to human rights as a normative vision for policing and a regulatory standard in their everyday work. It is argued that officers made sense of human rights so as to bring order to the complexity and ethical challenges they faced, to foster their own self-legitimacy and to defend against challenges to the policing legacy in Northern Ireland. This required officers to reinterpret and modify the official rights narrative in various ways, such that its substance varied even if it served similar sensemaking purposes of the official narrative with respect to fostering self-esteem and maintaining self-legitimacy. As a result of their sensemaking, the very idea of what human rights *are* became more fluid for junior officers, less tethered to the properties of human rights *law* echoed in the official police narrative. Consistent with a social constructivist style of analysis, human rights came to be understood and experienced less as an external, imposed, distinct entity but as an 'embedded and emergent feature of social life' (Ewick and Sibley, 1998: 22).

Chapter 5 extends the analysis of sensemaking to the Neighbourhood Policing Teams whose task is to maintain good relations in communities where trust in policing remains a challenge. The chapter critically engages with the two analytical bridges constructed by the PSNI and the Policing Board to discursively connect human rights with community policing. Having introduced the two towns where the fieldwork was conducted, I explore how officers encountered, and responded to, the lay lexicons of rights that confronted them within communities and in their experience of local policing, juxtaposing these with the official rights narrative of the PSNI's chief officers. Occupationally rooted in these neighbourhoods, officers had to maintain ongoing relationships with key influencers, make compromises and respond to local demands. The chapter reveals how officers felt human rights to be remote from their daily work. It could not adequately account for, or make sense of, officers' relationships with and activities in communities.

The second half of the book continues to explore the relationship between human rights and policing, focusing on human rights law standards and principles that take a pronounced form in the regulation of public order policing (Part IV) and police custody (Part V). These Parts will examine more closely in these two realms of police work how a police officer performs as a kind of human rights 'practitioner' – that is, a professional actor required to bring a resolution to a specific factual issue through understanding, engaging with and applying the law. The emphasis thus shifts from officers' socialization in human rights and sensemaking narratives, to how officers have interpreted and applied human rights law, and its associated statutory standards, as a series of principles and body of rules regulating police officers' decision-making. In each of the two sites of policing, I reveal how organizational structures and roles, variations in the types and influence of police sub-cultures and the presence of external accountability (closely linked to perception of 'in-the-job trouble') best explain how and why human rights law is having a greater impact in public order policing than in police custody. This variation cannot, I argue, be explained by the substantive law alone, which, in both sites, grants police considerable operational discretion.

Chapter 6 reveals how the strong institutionalization of human rights in the policing of parades and protests in Northern Ireland is not a product of senior officers' own internal practices and processes, closely monitored by the Policing Board. I introduce and develop the idea of the PSNI's public order 'script'. The script can be thought of as the organization's carefully constructed template for managing public order events, especially contentious parades and protests. This script is written and promoted by public order commanders who are acutely aware of the political sensitivities of parades and protests and the formal oversight they face in policing them. In the material form of operational plans and briefing documents, the script is communicated to frontline officers – often the Tactical Support Group (TSG) – who are tasked with performing the police operation according to the script. The chapter examines the social and legal context within which it is written and performed. I then proceed to trace in detail the production, promotion and delivery of human rights law as an integral part of the police script, before analysing how public order commanders came to acquire the knowledge and expertise needed to become human rights scriptwriters and decision-makers. This hints at a movement away from the kinds of 'common sense' understandings described in Part III, to a more legalistic, technical one, suited to the responsibilities commanders' shoulder and the formal audiences they address.

Chapter 7 demonstrates how the police script is performed in practice, based primarily on commanders' accounts, PSNI use of force data and two legal challenges concerning the PSNI's handling of public order events. Re-engaging with Waddington's (1994) seminal study of public order police commanders, I demonstrate how the overriding goal of commanders remains that of minimizing the likelihood of 'in the job trouble' arising from contentious parades. I argue, *contra* Waddington, that commanders did not perceive (human rights) law as an impediment to the planning and carrying out of police operations, but rather as a crucial tool for avoiding possible 'trouble'. Commanders were acutely aware of the ramifications their decision-making had for the parade and protest groups involved, as well as their own professional standing within the organization. In some circumstances, human rights law offered concrete standards to apply, but in others it could structure but not definitively resolve how competing rights ought to be balanced. Within this discretionary space, commanders operated in the shadow of the law: they took instructions from their lawyer, incorporated human rights principles and case law into the police script and articulated their decisions using rights terminology.

Part V provides the final site of study: police custody. This is a frenetic but focused site of everyday interpretation and application of legal safeguards by rank-and-file officers that impacts heavily on individuals' rights. Chapter 8 reveals why the rights-inspired safeguards under PACE, given effect in domestic law to Article 5 of the ECHR (right to liberty), had significantly less impact on junior-ranking custody officers responsible for authorizing suspects' detention. Chapter 9 explores how the procedural safeguards in PACE that purport to protect the suspect's right to liberty have fared in the face of organizational pressure to detect and 'clear up' crime. Drawing on recent case law from the High Court and Divisional Court of Northern Ireland and the Court of Appeal of England and Wales, I reveal how the safeguards have been only loosely protected by the courts. Adopting the three procedural safeguards to structure the analysis in the chapter, I reveal how officers apply, dismiss, interpret and reconstruct these rights-based standards. Custody officers described being routinely presented with arrests that fell short of the (judicially watered down) legal standards designed to protect individuals' rights. A target-driven culture that pressurized officers to make arrests was cited by custody officers as the greatest threat to individuals' right to liberty in police custody.

Chapter 9 exposes the organizational pressures and cultural allegiances that animated legal decision-making in police custody. It reveals custody officers' own accounts of how they managed the 'booking-in' process when suspects were brought into custody to be detained on the request of arresting officers. Custody officers described how they assisted arresting officers to reach the legal threshold required for the arrest and detention of suspects by using certain ploys. Custody officers navigated their way through the pressures of their job using various modes of adaption – the ploys that enabled them to ease the pressures emergent from their role. The eagerness of response officers to arrest and detain suspects was something custody officers could understand, even if they felt it was driven too often by performance targets and organizational demands rather than basic principles of fairness or the precept of necessity. Softened by a cultural affinity to their fellow junior officers and freed by the relative absence of meaningful accountability from solicitors, lay visitors or judges, custody officers found themselves succumbing to the pressure to detain. In law and in practice, the individual's right to liberty at this entry point of the criminal justice system appeared more fictional than real. Custody officers knew this and regretted it but felt powerless to respond to the structural and cultural pressures they faced.

The concluding chapter brings the book to a close by reflecting on the sociological account of human rights law advanced across its chapters. It reconsiders the values of this approach and its potential for future studies of the operation of human rights law within and surrounding the criminal justice system. Adopting

Ewick and Sibley's (1998) notion of the common place of law in everyday life, I then draw together the four substantive parts of the book to recapitulate how and why officers came to be 'before', 'with' and 'against' human rights law. Finally, I consider what lessons might be drawn out of the Northern Ireland case study for scholars, policymakers, governments, police leaders and community groups keen to make real the human rights ideals, principles and standards so prominent in international law and reform initiatives. What conditions might facilitate, encourage and contribute to human rights reform of policing? And what role might legal regulation play in fostering compliance with human rights?

1

Towards a Sociological Approach to Human Rights Law

> At the heart of all foundational discourse lies an argument about the potential validity of human rights in different fora, whereas legal discourse is premised on a validity that must always already be given. As a result, the question of foundations has always also been a question of ownership. It is a question of who may speak for human rights under what authority. And it has brought forth a long-standing contest between human rights lawyers, foundational thinkers of human rights – moral philosophers, anthropologists, historians, etc. – and simple 'users' of the language, on who is the principal owner of the discourse. By and large, the lawyers can so far be said to have been resoundingly victorious. (Hoffmann, 2012: 83)

What are human rights? For political theorists this is to invite a discussion of the grounding of a special kind of moral claim, be it through concepts of agency and autonomy (Gewirth, 1982), dignity (Gilbert, 2018) or capabilities (Nussbaum, 1997). Those of us who are lawyers, though, will likely respond with greater ease. Human rights can be understood as a body of international law born out of the Universal Declaration of Human Rights, further codified in international treaties, like the ECHR, and incorporated in domestic constitutional statutes, as well as reflected in, and emergent from, the common law itself.[1] Having sourced this set of legally recognized rights, we then look to the case law for judicial determination of the scope and substance of each right;

[1] See, for instance, Lord Reed in *R (Osborn) v The Parole Board* [2013] UKSC 61, at [56]–[63], Lord Mance in *R (Kennedy) v The Charity Commission* [2014] UKSC 20, at [46] and [133] and Lord Kerr in *R (Elgizouli) v Secretary of State for the Home Department* [2020] UKSC 10, at [107] and [124].

Policing Human Rights. Richard Martin, Oxford University Press. © Richard Martin 2021.
DOI: 10.1093/oso/9780198855125.003.0002

examine how emerging standards fit with first principles or sit with established lines of authority; identify exceptions to general rules and apply settled, or sometimes shifting, legal tests.[2] It is the dominance of this legal conception of human rights that has overwhelmingly reserved the study of human rights for lawyers (Çali and Meckled-García, 2006; Freeman, 2011; O'Byrne, 2012). This is similarly the case when it comes to human rights and policing, at least in the UK context. The subject is comprised of works that skilfully review the judgments of domestic and international courts (e.g. Starmer, Strange and Whitaker, 2002; Emerson, Ashworth and McDonald, 2012), exemplifying a doctrinal style analysis that examines the internal consistency and normative appeal of judicial determination of rights (e.g. Fenwick, 2009; Mead, 2009; Ashworth, 2014).

This book takes as its starting point a legal conception of what human rights 'are' and returns to it throughout as a basis from which to critically engage with officers' understandings, interpretation and applications of human rights. But the argument I introduce here and develop in the chapters that follow is that the established conception of human rights law as contained within judicial institutions and crafted by legal actors, and the doctrinal methods associated with this conception, can stand in the way of a richer, fuller grasp of human rights law in policing. To survey court judgments alone would result in a pale and partial conception of human rights in policing, not least given Northern Ireland's post-conflict context. This raises the question, asked too infrequently in human rights legal research, as to what sociological concepts and methods might be adopted to capture and critique the impact of legal norms in the cultural contexts, political climates and organizational settings in which they are implemented (McInerney-Lankford, 2018: 47–55). This calls on us, I think, to confront and consider more critically what Cotterrell (1997: 100) has described as the 'discursive closure' of law – that is, an established 'conception of law as a distinct discourse, possessing its own integrity, its own criteria of significance and validation, its own means of cognition and constituting objects of which it speaks'. At the same time, we ought to remain mindful of the regulatory force of the law, its authoritative interpretation by

[2] For a detailed account of how doctrinal analysis compares with socio-legal research see especially McCrudden (2006) and Goodman (2018).

courts and the interaction between statutory provisions, frontline decision-makers and courts' supervisory roles.

An overarching argument of the book, which connects its parts, is an epistemological one: if we are to fully grasp the routine understandings, interpretations and practices that animate human rights law in policing, we ought to explore and experiment with a sociological approach to law which incorporates insights from policing scholarship on the likes of legal regulation (Dixon, 1997), divided societies (Brewer and Magee, 1991) and police culture (Waddington, 1999; Reiner, 2010). In sketching out what such a sociological approach to human rights law might look like, in this chapter I introduce the three conceptual foundations adopted and outline the research methods deployed in the book. The first of these is how human rights law comes to be adopted and deployed as '*vernacular*' beyond traditional legal forums and judicial audiences in order to both legitimate and challenge police power. The second is human rights law as a set of principles and standards that officers are socialized in, and engage in '*sensemaking*' of, amidst their sub-cultures, everyday routines and organizational demands. The third is how human rights law comes to be '*practiced*' by officers in specific roles in so far as they are professional actors required to bring a resolution to a specific factual issue through understanding, engaging with and applying human rights law principles and standards. Collectively, these features comprise the book's sociological approach to human rights law.

Reconsidering 'Legal Closure'

Criminologists are engaging with human rights more creatively and critically than ever, both in the subject matter they are examining and the research methods they are deploying. But as Murphy and Whitty (2013: 570) have observed, a fault line exists on 'the role of law ... and more specifically, the legalization of rights'. This divides the legally orientated scholars, interested in the operation of human rights law in the criminal process, legal mechanisms and institutions (see e.g. Lazarus and Goold, 2007, 2019; Amatrudo and Blake, 2014; Campbell, Ashworth and Redmayne, 2019), and the more sociologically minded, concerned with cultural and political accounts of human rights far beyond law as an institutionalized doctrine (e.g. McEvoy, 2003; Rock, 2004; Loader, 2007). In explaining the sociological approach to human rights law that

I advance in this book, it is worth thinking a bit more about how and why this fault line emerges within criminologists. As Murphy and Whitty (2013) astutely observe, an explanation for this lies in the plurality of disciplinary, methodological and normative approaches that an engagement with academic criminology's history would likely reveal. But so too, I think, is there a more fundamental issue, often left unspoken, concerning the very nature of what (human rights) law is and thus what it might mean to study it using social scientific as well as doctrinal methods. This issue, and its implications for researching human rights law, can be meaningfully engaged with through the jurisprudential notion of 'legal closure'.

Legal closure refers to an established, if ever-more contested (McCrudden, 2006), conception of law as 'a self-sufficient or self-contained sphere of reasoning, practice, or discourse' (Cotterrell, 1997: 91; see also McInerney-Lankford, 2018: 49). Versions of legal closure animate leading accounts of law in western philosophy. Take, for example, Dworkin's account of law as a discursive realm, observing morality, politics and society in its own terms, Kelsen's pure theory of law as distinct and irreducible with its own mode of cognition, or Teubner's (1988) and Luhmann's (2004) autopoiesis theory, in which law's language is distinct, only capable of receiving scrambled signals from its neighbouring systems. In these leading accounts, law is cast as a basic discipline with 'a distinct discourse, possessing its own integrity, its own criteria of significance and validation, its own means of cognition and constituting objects of which it speaks' (Cotterrell, 1997: 100). Rooted in the positivist tradition, law is judged on its own terms, derives its authority from its autonomy and only encounters a degree of indeterminacy in 'hard cases' (see, in particular, Turner, 2017: 60–4 on legal closure in the transitional justice context). According to this understanding, human rights law similarly operates through a binary legal code of legal/illegal, violation/non-violation. Human rights law retains its integrity by removing ambivalence from human rights discourse: 'it radically reduces its complexity, and it renders it institutionally decidable and, thus, enforceable' (Hoffmann, 2012: 84). This leaves us facing a distinct, autonomous legal knowledge, 'a special logic of law to be understood only through specialized legal training and experience' (Cotterrell, 1997: 95). We think 'like a lawyer' or we do not. To suggest we might engage with human rights law sociologically begins to sound more like a misunderstanding to be avoided than an opportunity to be grasped.

The fault line within criminology over how – as well as how closely – to engage with human rights *law*, as I see it, reflects two orientations towards legal closure. On the one hand, there are those who consider the legalistic, hegemonic and western-centric nature of human rights as fatal shortcomings (Murphy and Whitty, 2013: 570). To rely too heavily on human rights *law* is to risk fastening oneself into the straitjacket of the law, to narrow one's inquiry before it might properly begin. Loader (2007), for example, calls for a distinctly non-legal analysis of the 'cultural life' of human rights, grounded in political and lay vernacular of rights and security. In the transitional justice context, McEvoy has warned of the seduction of positivistic legal analysis that forecloses questions from law's neighbouring disciplines that lawyers 'should be both *asking* and *asked*' (McEvoy, 2007: 417). This is especially so, it is argued, with respect to human rights law: 'the translation of rights discourse into the legalese of international standards "thins out" the wider political, social and cultural complexities of conflicted societies' (McEvoy, 2007: 418–19). Such concerns are not, of course, confined to criminology alone. They mirror a stream of critical human rights scholarship which has, itself, warned of the intellectual perils of unmooring human rights law too far from its moral and cultural foundations (Hoffman, 2012) and sought to alleviate an impending 'crisis of legalism' by insisting on space for political debate and democratic institutions in the protection of human rights (Gearty, 2006: chapter 3). The latter, in particular, is a response to a kind of legal closure in which human rights law comes to be legitimated on the basis that it precedes, or is somehow above, politics 'as reflective of a truth beyond politics to which politics ought to be subject' (Gearty, 2006: 72).

On the other hand, legally minded and doctrinally trained human rights and criminal justice scholars might offer the rejoinder that law's autonomy from neighbouring disciplines is both proper and real. Indeed, the study of human rights in particular is dominated by legal analysis (Çali and Meckled-García, 2006; Andreassen, Sano and McInerney-Lankford, 2018). It might be thought *proper* in the sense that closure enables law as a discipline to self-characterize and self-define itself as a discipline and practice. This enables lawyers to focus on what the subject of their trade is and what their toolkit requires. So too, of course, is law's intellectual validity gained from the status, influence and authority conveyed by its technicalities, and a professional prowess exhibited by its trained craftspeople (Cotterrell, 1997: 96, 106). Reflecting on 'the apparently almost complete blindness to the potential relevance of legal issues in much social science research', McCrudden (2006: 646) suggests one explanation is that academic law 'may seem too intimidating and technical, too specific, too detailed' to have much to offer. In respect of human rights specifically, An-Na'im (2012: 111) observes that while social scientists might enrich our study of it 'there is the risk that they might ignore or misinterpret applicable legal norms'. Legal closure is discursively real in so far as the judiciary is often legitimated – whether in formal judgments or extra-judicial speeches – on the basis that the court's constitutional task of applying the law is closed off from policy issues or political judgments which are the proper business of the executive. Some human rights practitioners, meanwhile, underscore the importance of legal closure for realizing real change precisely because of authoritative international treaties and texts containing binding commitments that are backed by formal institutions and oversight mechanisms (Donnelly, 2006; McInerney-Lankford, 2009).

In sum, the 'strongly defined positions on legalism' said to constitute a fault line in academic criminology when it comes to human rights (Murphy and Whitty, 2013: 568) might be understood as reflecting a much more general, and long-held, conception of law as a 'closed' system that one is either 'inside' or 'outside' of. This can, however, lead to research specialisms that risk creating blind spots that inhibit the acknowledgment and engagement with the empirical reality of human rights law (Murphy and Whitty, 2013: 580). For doctrinal lawyers who take an 'internal' perspective that privileges legal coherence, there can be a tendency to proceed to make assumptions 'about the importance, influence and legitimacy of the law' and neglect the role and significance of 'external' social features in understanding law (McInerney-Lankford, 2018: 41–3). For sociologically orientated criminologists, there is a risk of under-playing how the substance, authority and institutions of law do affect how individuals and groups relate to one another in social settings (Zedner, 2011: 279), as well as how legal standards influence what is possible for organizations to achieve, especially in regulatory settings (McCrudden,

2006: 649). But what if human rights law could be reconceived not as a fault line to be skirted around, purposefully avoided or blindly leapt across, but consciously and curiously examined? What I propose, and proceed to apply in the chapters that follow, is a sociological approach to human rights law that strives to appreciate the variation, complexity and influence of legal doctrine while paying close attention to the real-world social settings in which (human rights) law is invoked, encountered and engaged with. Let me briefly flesh out the intellectual source of such an approach, before considering the specific features of it that are developed in the book.

A sociological approach to (human rights) law is premised on the idea that law is not as secure, autonomous or unified as traditional accounts suggest – and that the interdisciplinary-minded lawyer (or the legally minded criminologist for that matter) can, with curiosity and perseverance, place doctrinal insights and skills of analysis in meaningful proximity to social scientific theories and methods. Conceptually, law is an institutionalized doctrine of rules, regulations, concepts and modes of reasoning, but these are rationalized practices of state control that enlist a plurality of actors and which structure the social world (Cotterrell, 1998: 192). This interconnection between the legal and social realm has a wide-ranging intellectual tradition of its own – from Weber and Durkheim, to Ehrlich and Petrazycki – but at its core, the sociology of law is *sociological* because, as Cotterrell (1998: 191) suggests, it foregrounds the need to reinterpret law systematically and empirically as a social phenomenon, capturing the diverse ways in which participants themselves think about the social world in legal terms. This calls for an empirical project of illumination: 'showing through systematic behavioural studies what law as institutionalized doctrine means in the varied local contexts of social life where its ultimate value and significance must be judged' (Cotterrell, 1997: 296; 1998, 181–6). The commitment is to asking 'how law might be *reinterpreted* and so reimagined and reshaped consistently with its social character' (Cotterrell, 1998: 188).

In the context of human rights law, taking a sociological approach is to show an alertness to three developments in particular: the form that law takes, the actors involved and the modes of legal regulation. First, the semantic formulation of human rights law is particularly significant. Human rights are open-textured and thus capable of hosting a range of interpretations in particular contexts. Being 'realistic' about human rights law is to acknowledge that human rights do not provide a basis for a fully fleshed out vision of morality or philosophy (Greer, 2009). Even in the context of the ECHR, one of the world's most sophisticated protection regimes, determining the scope, content and restrictions on rights requires the injection of values circulating around, not necessary within, law's discursive system; values 'must be formulated elsewhere and brought to discussions of rights' (Wilson, 2006: 78). But again, recognizing law as an institutionalized doctrine is to appreciate that human rights law is based on some degree of consensus, developed over time, across societies, shaped by legal practices and rules of interpretation (Fredman, 2013). This is not to doubt the malleability, contestability and conditionality of human rights soon to be developed. Rather social meanings, interpretations and applications of human rights are cast in the shadow of legal doctrine that is open-textured but nonetheless constitutionally determined by powerful institutional actors, most significantly, the senior judiciary (Scheinin, 2017).

Second, law's community of interpretation in which legal ideas are formed, applied and enforced is growing in diversity. A sociological approach to law seeks to broaden the perspectives of the various participants in legal processes, practices and forms of knowledge beyond the forms of law familiar to lawyers (Cotterrell, 1998: 187–8, 191). It is the case, today, for example, that:

> Modern pressure groups of many kinds, and such occupational groups as journalists, police, social and public administration specialists, regulators, and social scientists, have contributed, for very varied reasons, to policy critique of law in a dialogue with government and regulators. It seems that much more is said about law, and by much more diverse groups of commentators, than in the recent past. (Cotterrell, 1997: 105)

When it comes to human rights specifically, the last few decades alone have witnessed the emergence of a 'bricolage' of human rights institutions, which invite, if not require, actors beyond law's established cohort of judges and lawyers to engage with human rights (de Witte, 2012). Examples include human rights legislative committees, dedicated commissions and non-governmental organizations (Pegram, 2010; Kavanagh, 2015). It is within these institutions that politicians, policymakers, civil servants and activists have joined law's 'interpretive community'. This institutional landscape commands closer attention to the social dynamics, visions and agendas that are brought to bear on human rights law – something increasingly recognized in both doctrinal and socio-legal studies of human rights law, including strands of criminal justice scholarship produced by lawyers (see e.g. Lazarus and Goold, 2007, 2019; Campbell, Ashworth and Redmayne, 2019; Lazarus, 2020).

Third, and relatedly, there is increasing diversity and complexity of modern regulation, but especially the shift from command-and-control styles of regulation to internal, self-regulation of actors by way of statutory duties, ethical frameworks and organizational reforms (McCrudden, 2005; Fredman, 2012). The focus of the book is on particular modes of regulation relating to human rights law, but other significant examples include the emergence and evolution of legal self-regulation across the criminal justice system, including sentencing guidelines for judges, codes of guidance for Crown Prosecutors or Codes of Ethics for police officers in England and Wales, Northern Ireland and the Republic of Ireland (see further Campbell, Ashworth and Redmayne, 2019: chapter 3). Keeping pace with such regulatory developments requires us to pay growing attention to the political, social, cultural and occupational conditions within which principles and standards of both hard and soft law are interpreted and applied. The idea of a 'specifically legal form of argument, reason or interpretation is challenged by the range of modern state regulation with its varying methods, diverse sites of practice, and indefinite boundaries' (Cotterrell, 1997: 284). Extending this to human rights specifically, it comes to be 'made up of distinct discourses' that are 'constituted by a host of actors, practices and institutions, which do not necessarily speak the same dialect (of human rights), yet provide the space within which human rights discourse unfolds' (Hoffmann, 2012: 95).

A sociological approach to law does not require adherence to any specific social science or discipline, distinct method or theoretical outlook. It is transdisciplinary and inclusive (Cotterrell, 1998: 177, 187). Let us now turn to examine three concepts taken from anthropology, organizational studies and law respectively that I have drawn on to bring substance to the sociological approach to human rights law I apply in the chapters of the book that follow.

Human Rights as a 'Vernacular' of Policing

A core agenda of legal anthropology has been to explore the conditions and limitations of the varieties of legal closure. In post-conflict societies like Northern Ireland, the idea of law as a discursively closed system, speaking its own language and distinct from the extra-legal environment (Teubner, 1988; Verschraegen, 2002) is challenged by the very fact that law and legal arenas are sites of struggle political actors use 'to "own" the direction of transition' (McEvoy, 2000; Bell, 2012). In post-conflict Northern Ireland, this has included the legislation on the right of ex-combatants to work in public institutions (McEvoy and White, 1998; Hearty, 2016), the statutory definition of a 'victim' of the conflict (Moffett, 2016), and, most recently, questions over legal amnesties. McEvoy (2007) has challenged those of us working at the crossroads of law, politics and transitional justice to pursue a 'thicker' conception of legalism. Such a conception can, I think, be arrived at through an interdisciplinary analysis that reflects critically on the actions, motivations, assumptions and power relations which influence actors. It is in this spirit that I want to reach into social constructivist accounts from anthropology to gather some ideas that might enable us to better capture the contingent, contested nature of human rights law within the social realm.

Extending beyond, while not disinterested in, international and domestic law, legal anthropologists have sought to explore how social actors discuss, interpret, dismiss or expand human rights claims (Riles, 2006; Wilson, 2006; Goodale and Merry, 2007; Merry, 2017). This has, most interestingly, involved a shift from well-worn debates over the universality versus cultural relativism of human rights to the practice of human rights: 'on where and how human rights concepts and institutions are produced, how they circulate, and how they shape everyday lives and actions' (Merry, 2006a: 39). A particular focus of this project has been the 'vernacularization' of rights, that is, how the vocabulary of international human rights law is learnt, translated and adopted by local actors within and beyond domestic institutions (Merry, 2006b; Curtis, 2014). Referred to in the literature as human rights 'talk', 'language' or 'claims'(McEvoy, 2003; Wilson, 2007; Curtis, 2014), the subject of enquiry is 'the coteries of concepts, practices and experiences through which human rights have meaning at different levels – levels which are prior to and go beyond the merely legal' (Goodale, 2006: 490). In particular, Wilson (2006: 78) has called for greater attention to be paid to 'the social forms that coalesce in and around formal rights practices and formulations, and that are usually hidden in the penumbra of the official political process'. In advancing what we might refer to as the 'social life' of human rights, Wilson (2006) suggests the value of charting a trajectory of rights claims, including its performative dimension, in sites of political contestation, asking: 'How do various social actors understand the various claims, immunities, privileges, and liberties articulated in the language of human rights? How do they apply or reject them? And what do they hope to achieve in doing so?'

There are, I think, three elements lurking within Wilson's call to action that, once drawn out further, offer helpful analytical waypoints to inform and structure the analysis of human rights as a vernacular of policing. The first is the impact that the given historical context has in structuring the ambit and style of human rights contestation involving social actors. The plurality of interpretations of human rights arises in large part from its open-textured norms. Yet it would be wrong to suppose that rights offer a neutral vernacular open to all or that rights-based contests operate on a level playing field (Bartholomew and Hunt, 1990). Rights claim-making is often more culturally and institutionally accessible (or meaningful) for particular social groups based on their historical legacies and legal status. Dominant groups and institutions routinely 'police the boundaries of prevailing rights constructions' to sustain status quo relationships and interests, thereby 'killing off' rights claims 'bubbling up' from less powerful or marginalized groups (McCann, 2014: 245). Similarly, the very rights that are nowadays enjoyed by some, and actively campaigned for by others, will almost certainly be a crystallization of past political struggles – struggles which may have shaped the institutional architecture and established norms within which contemporary debates over rights take place (Bartholomew and Hunt, 1990).

Situated within its historical context, human rights as a vernacular secondly provides an articulation of a much wider array of interests, fears and aspirations that find expression through rights 'talk'. Rather than being 'closed' off from outside systems, human rights as a vernacular is a means of expressing social and political ideas (McCann, 2014). Jackson (2007), for example, has documented how the campaign of indigenous activists in Colombia for a 'right to culture' acted as a framework for a host of issues ranging from bilingual education to customary healthcare. Just as human rights can serve as a vessel for expressing broader sentiments and ideologies, so too is it bound up with, and contingent upon, broader discursive resources and normative traditions (McCann, 2014: 248). In the context of the security and rights discourse in political and public culture in England, for instance, Loader (2007) has detected the interlocking properties that explain why rights claims can be 'so routinely and carelessly regarded within English public culture'. With closer hermeneutic attention, Loader (2007: 28) suggests we can appreciate how human rights are 'intimately and inescapably entangled with people's hopes, fears and fantasies concerning the trajectory of their own lives, and that of the political community which they inhabit'. This suggests the value of deconstructing the vernacular of rights to hear associated ideas entangled within it.

The third element pertains to how human rights can be used by groups to actively construct claims with the hope of achieving legal gains in specific fields. This is reflected in the literature which has analysed how social movements seek to elevate human rights claims into formal rights recognized in law (Bartholomew and Hunt, 1990). When framed in rights terminology, political and social causes become easier for the law and its legal actors to 'hear', opening up the possibility for judicial recognition or legislative enactment (Wilson, 2007). This is well illustrated in North America, where campaigners have coupled rights discourse with high-profile constitutional litigation as a principal weapon in progressive struggles for democratic rights (Fudge and Glasbeek, 1992). Examples include challenges brought by trade unions before the appellate courts in an attempt to have their right to act as a collective unit recognized and litigation initiated in US courts by members of the LGBT movement (Goldberg, 2015). Legal recognition is the sign of victory for rights activists because it removes vulnerable claims and aspirations from the 'rough-and-tumble of politics, turning them into substantive rights enforceable in court' (Gearty, 2006: 62; Wilson, 2007: 352).

In sum, this threefold dimension of the 'social life' of human rights seeks to capture the dynamics animating the reception, interpretation, engagement and deployment of human rights – that is to say, how social actors in specific settings act upon human rights typically presented as a body of formally recognized principles and standards. The framework is an aid to pursuing what Curtis refers to as a 'measured critique' of rights discourse; one which rightly avoids scrutiny or dismissal of rights talk for its hints of politicization but seeks instead to understand the politics that can 'direct or suffuse rights discourse and its reception' (Curtis, 2014: 216). Crucially, and perhaps worth drawing out more explicitly, the 'social life' of human rights is based on an epistemology of legality as being socially constructed. As masterfully demonstrated by Ewick and Sibley (1998: chapter 3), such an understanding casts law as an embedded and emergent feature of social life. But to be clear, such an account does not deny that the purposes, ideals and doctrines of law are not a major part of its social construction, rather it suggests that they are not the *whole* experience and representation of law (Ewick and Sibley, 1998: 22–3; Sibley, 2005: 336).

The PSNI is a vocal contributor to Northern Ireland's human rights discourse. Having invested great energy on human rights reform and required to confront its legal responsibilities arising from ECHR standards – most notably in policing parades as well as historical investigations – the PSNI has its own human rights narrative to contribute to contemporary Northern Irish society. Seldom is a high-profile speech made by the Chief Constable where mention is not made of human rights. As Harvey (2015: 61) further noted in his recent review of human rights and criminal justice in Northern Ireland:

> Fluency in the language of human rights (particularly the ECHR) is programmatically and strategically wise for anyone wishing to progress within the institutional contexts of policing and justice.

It is this vernacular of human rights – the legal descriptors, formulations and modes of regulation it implies, as well as the political and cultural conditions that give meaning to it – that I set out to examine in the first two chapters of the book. It is an endeavour to present and analyse the official and unofficial narratives of human rights in policing; to grasp the motivations of the policing actors and to lay bare the histories, imaginations, visions and values they express through human rights law.

Human Rights, Socialization and Sensemaking

The familiar task for policing scholars is to try to explain the social processes by which the visions, strategies and practices of police reform interact with the agency, personalities and experiences of officers. Such an endeavour plunges us into deeper sociological waters that involve the interaction of micro, meso and macro levels of analysis, and more fundamentally, the enduring issue of agency and structure, of free will and determinism in everyday life (Ewick and Sibley, 1998: chapter 3). Within studies of police reforms, the deployment of Bourdieu's concepts of 'field' and 'habitus' have been popular devices for framing officers' relationships with one another and their organizations, as well as the local actors and communities they encounter (Chan, 1996, 2007; Blaustein, 2015; O'Brien-Ollinger, 2016; O'Neill, 2019). For others, service has been found in Schütz's (1953) concepts of 'recipes' and 'schemes of experience' (Brewer and Magee, 1991) and Goffman's (1959) dramaturgical metaphors of 'front' and 'back' stages of self (Manning, 1977; Hornberger, 2011) as heuristics for how and why people behave the way they do. What connects these studies and the conceptual devices they deploy is a social constructivist understanding of police behaviour and decision-making. Consistent with this epistemological approach I draw upon two related, but under-used, concepts: 'socialization' and 'sensemaking'. I use these to capture the relationship between the micro- and meso- levels generally, but more specifically the social interaction between officers' biographies, experiences, cultural resources and organizational settings that affect officers' understanding of human rights.

Socialization is a process whereby actors are inducted into the norms and rules of a community through social interactions that lead newcomers and novices to endorse expected ways of thinking, feeling and acting (Checkel, 2005: 804; see also Johnston, 2001: 494). Studies of socialization span academic disciplines and worldly institutions. Most relevant for our purposes here is the core idea of the 'internalization' of norms, which can be understood as the desired end-point of norm socialization, arrived at when actors' identities, roles and understandings align with those of the institution (Johnston, 2001). This process involves actors adopting what in another context Hart (1961) has described as a 'critical reflective attitude' to an authority and its requests. Where the attitude is a positive one, the actor comes to believe that obedience to the authority is morally right. This marks a shift from a 'logic of consequences' to a 'logic of appropriateness', whereby pro-organizational behaviour becomes 'just the right thing to do' (Johnston, 2001: 495). It is surely this kind of internalization that the police reformers had in mind when promoting a human rights approach as a 'culture' and 'philosophy' of policing and which, as we will see in Chapter 2, is described by chief officers as 'part of our psyche; it is how we think, weigh up options and ultimately make decisions'. As yet to be incorporated into this analysis, however, is a mechanism for explaining how socialization takes place: how the meso-level of the police organization and the micro-level of the individual officer might be connected, even mutually dependent.

Such a mechanism ought to help identify and illuminate the factors affecting the extent to which human rights law principles and standards – presented in training, policies, reports, briefings etc. – influenced officers' internalization of human rights. Significant insight can, I think, be gained by deploying the concept of 'sensemaking' as a process of interpretation and meaning production whereby individuals and groups reflect on phenomena and thus 'enact (create) the social world, constituting it through verbal descriptions which are communicated to and negotiated with others' (Brown, Stacey and Nandhakumar, 2008: 1038). Sensemaking is prompted by interruptions or discrepancies in our social worlds, often arising out of occasions of ambiguity or uncertainty, which challenge core facets of our identity, our taken-for-granted understandings and the organization to which we belong. At its heart, sensemaking is grounded in identity construction. It 'is a search for plausibility and coherence, that is reasonable and memorable' that 'maintains the self while resonating with others' (Brown, Stacey and Nandhakumar, 2008: 1038). The need for self-enhancement, self-efficacy and self-consistency motivates sensemaking and influences the substance of the self-identity individuals create (Weick, 1995: 20). And this meaning-making process, tied up with identity, is ongoing. It embodies past experiences and expectations, it is constructed retrospectively, and is focused on, and structured by, the cues people notice, extract and develop from their organizational setting and cultural context (Weick, 1995: chapter 2).

According to institutional theorists, organizations themselves are the most significant shapers of junior members' 'sensemaking' and subsequent socialization. The institutional perspective emphasizes the power of senior managers to articulate and disseminate powerful storylines that produce a 'discrete, regular, generalized and uninterrupted' way of understanding that is adopted by group members (Humphreys and Brown, 2002: 439). However, a more persuasive analysis of organizational sensemaking, consistent with a sociological approach to law, is proffered by a social constructionist lens that integrates human action and structural constraint. Organizations do play a role in priming, editing and triggering sensemaking (Weber and Glynn, 2006: 1640), especially during turbulent periods of reform (Chan, 2007). Without collective narratives, personal stories would be rendered unintelligible and uninterpretable (Ewick and Sibley, 1998: 243). But, crucially, even in the face of great reform and institutional re-imaginings, people retain a significant capacity to 'read and author their own reality and thus oppose centralizing impositions' (Humphreys and Brown, 2002: 424). The identity-constitutive stories told by organizations impinge upon the social identities, occupational lives and daily routines of their participants. Individuals are bestowed with an 'intrinsic ability to interact with their own thoughts, and, therefore, to draw new distinctions, imagine new things, and employ metaphor, metonymy, and mental imagery' (Tsoukas and Chia, 2002: 574). Individual and organizational narratives thus 'overlap, interweave, distance and disassociate', with the consequence that organizations are not monolithic, constrained by the sole official voice, but polyphonic, comprising simultaneous, contradictory dialogues (Humphreys and Brown, 2002: 439).

A great deal of sensemaking is expressed, disseminated and reified in the form of narratives or stories (Weick, 1995; Ewick and Sibley, 1998). This reflects the social interactions involved in constructions of self and work, but also the particular function narratives perform as a means of organizing the richness, the messiness of human interaction (Bruner, 1991: 4). As described by Weick (1995: 128), 'when people punctuate their own living into stories, they impose a formal coherence on what is otherwise a flowing soup'. Stories are the product of editing, authored with the benefit of hindsight, often guided by some felt outcome. Stories can offer a means by which to reduce emotional disruption and repair self-esteem (Weick, 1995: 128–9). Storytelling plays an especially important role in making interruptions, challenges and surprises manageable for police officers (van Hulst, 2013, 2020; O'Neill, 2019). Narratives become a medium for conveying lessons of experiential learning, the crafts of their trade and local knowledge of the 'patches' they patrol (Shearing and Ericson, 1991; van Hulst and Ybema, 2020). Scholars of sensemaking thus pay close attention to individual, as well as organizational, narratives (Weick, 1995: 39).

As illustrated in a voluminous body of scholarship, police culture is a rich resource in officers' sensemaking efforts (Chan, 2007; Loftus, 2009). Culture informs, supports and provides cues for the sensemaking processes triggered by external changes that induce members to re-evaluate aspects of their organizational identity (Weick, 1995; Ravasi and Schultz, 2006: 433). An established corpus of work has identified a series of traits described as cultural in the sense that they form accepted practices, rules and principles, as well as taken-for-granted rationales and belief, which are situationally applied (Manning, 1989: 360). Police culture is often portrayed as a series of values or attitudes, acquired through on-the-job socialization, and capable of predicting routine behaviour and decision-making (Campeau, 2015: 669). Simultaneously 'explained and condemned' (Waddington, 1999), these traits include officers' sense of mission, cynicism, suspicion, isolation, conservatism, machismo and racial prejudices (see Loftus, 2009; O'Neill, 2019; Bowling, Reiner and Sheptycki, 2019: chapter 8). Just how far these cultural features determine police action, rather than act as a discursive outlet or coping mechanism, is debatable (O'Brien-Ollinger, 2016: 210–11; O'Neill, 2019: 17–20). So too has the conceptual template of police culture authoritatively recapitulated by Reiner in various editions of *The Politics of Policing* risked creating what Sklansky (2007) has described as 'cognitive burn-in', whereby it serves 'as a collective imprint in how we think about the topic which can divert our attention from new directions and emergent trends' (Campeau, 2015: 671).

In Part III, I attempt to take Campeau's (2015) sage advice on board and move away from reifying established approaches to police culture that often re-identify already well-known values and attitudes of officers towards everyday aspects of their working lives, and reveal how features of police culture might be used as a resource to make sense of their occupational lives. The salience of police culture here lies in how it stimulates, informs and supports officers' sensemaking of human rights. How people define and experience themselves is influenced by activities and beliefs grounded in, and interpreted using, cultural assumptions and values (Hatch and Schultz, 2002: 25) Officers spend considerable time and energy constructing accounts of their routine work to bring meaning, coherence and integrity to it, with the key audience for such justifications often being themselves and their fellow officers. The phenomena being made sense of is human rights. Officers' sensemaking takes places against the established official, legalistic narrative of human rights, analysed in Chapter 2, constructed by chief officers and expressed through formal police training, policies, procedures, oversight and briefings, but ultimately this is made sense of through informal socialization which encompasses aspects of police sub-culture.

Police as 'Practitioners' of Human Rights

The third conceptual foundation of the book suggests we can meaningfully make sense of officers performing specific police roles and responsibilities in liberal democracies as 'practitioners' of human rights law – that is, as professional actors required to bring a resolution to a specific factual issue through understanding, engaging with and applying human rights law principles and standards. Rather than tracing how human rights are socially constituted by officers – how they make sense of, talk about and deploy it – this conceptual starting point focuses more on how officers interpret and apply human rights law in their decision-making in regulatory settings, although social dynamics are a part of such settings. In this narrow sense, then, officers are practitioners in so far as they are actively engaging with human rights standards and – as is no doubt the case in law firms, courtrooms and legislative committees – such engagement involves individuals with varying levels of knowledge, information and competency, surrounded by local cultures and workplace habits, in situations that are often stressful, unpredictable and time-limited but where a decision must be made.

An immediate and entirely understandable response to the conceptualization of police officers as 'practitioners' of human rights might well be a healthy dose of scepticism that legal principles or standards of authority might guide or be actively considered by officers, as well as cynicism about the willingness of police to respect and protect rights, given the infamous features of public culture said to influence officers' exercise of discretion. More fundamentally, the structural inequalities and institutionalized prejudices that mark the societal status quo mean that in fulfilling the core mandate of order maintenance and in the symbolic performance of authority, the police as an organization is antithetical to rights. I seek to engage with, incorporate and develop these critical insights at various points in the book. But at a conceptual level, I consider these consistent with, rather than counter to, a conceptualization of police as 'practitioners' of human rights law. Practice concerns the activity itself, both the 'application or use of an idea, belief, or method' – interpreting and applying human rights law principles and standards – and the repetition of this activity 'so as to acquire or maintain proficiency in it' (Oxford English Dictionary). From a normative standpoint, to endorse or reject, to like or dislike the practitioner's particular method or the outcome of their interpretation and application, is to evaluate the *qualities* of this *activity*.

In fleshing out this conceptualization, it is helpful to turn once more to the legal scholarship. As Cotterrell remarked over two decades ago, engagement with, and application of, the law is no longer – if it ever was – the sole preserve of lawyers and judges: 'Law's community of interpretation is not one but many'; as such Cotterrell continued, '[l]egal theory must explore ... the possibilities for rational interpretation within such communities' (Cotterrell, 1997: 289). The domestication of the ECHR through the Human Rights Act 1998 has expanded the scope and significance of human rights law's interpretive community in the UK. Beyond equipping the courts with a new interpretive tool to smooth out incompatibilities in primary and subordinate legislation (section 3) and the power to declare primary legislation incompatible with a Convention right (section 4), the HRA also requires public authorities to play their part in domestic human rights protection. The HRA makes it 'unlawful for a public authority to act in a way which is incompatible with a Convention right' (section 6). Leading proponents of the HRA championed the impact this provision could have in promoting a 'culture of justification': the purposeful and well-reasoned consideration of human rights principles in the routine decision-making of public authorities (Irvine, 1998; Klug and Starmer, 2005).

In order to comply with section 6 of the HRA, police policies and procedures must be compliant with the Articles of the ECHR, but so too must everyday activities and decisions of police officers respect human rights law principles and standards, as interpreted and applied by the domestic and Strasbourg courts. As decided by the House of Lords in the leading case of *Denbigh High School*, the sole concern of domestic courts is whether the decision the authority arrived at violates a Convention right: what matters is the 'practical outcome, not the quality of the decision-making process that led to it'.[3] A public authority's failure to reason its way to a conclusion using Convention standards and principles is no basis for unlawfulness under section 6(1) of the HRA. Crucially, however, where a public authority is conscious of, or addresses its mind to, the Convention in arriving at its decision, the House of Lords held that it will 'attribute due weight to that conclusion'.[4] The court will be 'inherently less likely' to disagree with the public authority's decision where there has been proper consideration of the Convention,[5] and 'a challenger's task will be the harder' where the authority has 'conscientiously paid attention to all human rights considerations'.[6]

The concept of deference in public law has particular significance for the police given the expertise of officers making challenging operational decisions. The courts have proven willing to defer to the operational expertise of police when determining whether or not interferences with Convention rights are lawful. Deference is the relative weight the court will give police decision-makers when conducting their own proportionality assessment of whether Convention rights have been unlawfully interfered with. Lord Carswell in *Re E (a child) (AP) (Northern Ireland)*,[7] quoting Lord Bingham in *Huang*,[8] explained that such deference is part of the 'ordinary judicial task of weighing up the competing

[3] Lord Bingham, *R (SB) v Governors of Denbigh High School* [2006] UKHL 15, at [31].

[4] Lord Rodger, *Belfast City Council v Miss Behavin' Ltd* [2007] UKHL 19, at [26].

[5] Lord Neuburger, ibid., at [91].

[6] Lord Bingham, *Denbigh* (n 3), at [31].

[7] *Re E (a child) (AP) (Northern Ireland)* [2008] UKHL 66.

[8] *Huang v Secretary of State for the Home Department* [2007] 2 AC 167.

considerations on each side'.[9] In *E*, the police were, Lord Carswell stated, 'uniquely placed' by virtue of their experience and intelligence 'to make a judgment on the wisest course to take' in dealing with riotous situations in urban areas.[10] So too has deference been formulated in spatial terms as an 'area of discretionary judgment' within which courts will be alert to the situational exigencies that face decision-makers, as stated by Lord Kerr SCJ in *Re DB*:

> A definite area of discretionary judgment must be allowed the police. And a judgment on what is proportionate should not be informed by hindsight. Difficulties in making policing decisions should not be underestimated, especially since these frequently require to be made in fraught circumstances.[11]

Whichever formulation deference takes, its existence underscores the importance of understanding how police arrive at decisions and form judgments which have the potential to influence the court's own assessment of proportionality. Even beyond the specific rights contained in the ECHR, as outlined in the Introduction, numerous statutory schemes that grant and govern police powers come to be heavily influenced by the human rights principles of 'necessity' and 'proportionality'.

Drawing this analysis together, the agents of interpretation and application of human rights standards and principles are not confined to lawyers or judges: they are neighbourhood constables deciding whether there is a positive duty to intervene in a situation of grave danger per the right to life (Article 2 of the ECHR); Custody Officers assessing whether the legal threshold of 'necessity' has been met to justify taking away a person's liberty (Article 5 of the ECHR); they are public order commanders balancing protest groups' right to assemble and express their views (Articles 9 to 11 of the ECHR) against the interference with the rights of business owners and local residents who have the right to family and private life (Article 8 of the ECHR); armed officers determining whether the 'absolute necessity' threshold has been met to use potentially lethal force (Article 2 of the ECHR). These core aspects of police work require officers to understand, interpret and apply human rights law standards, as pronounced in court judgments,

[9] Lord Carswell, in *E*, at [58].
[10] Ibid.
[11] *Re DB's Application* (2017) UKSC 7, at [76] (my emphasis).

and principles, such as those governing the weighing of competing rights and the interests of the public. To describe the police as human rights practitioners is to seek to better acknowledge and understand officers as an emergent but poorly understood member of a legal community tasked with interpreting and applying human rights law principles and standards.

To be clear though, in proposing there is much to be gained from acknowledging this legal reality, it is not to suggest officers are, or ought to be seen as, human rights technicians or activists, let alone campaigners or advocates. Within many jurisdictions that are signatories to international human rights law treaties, police exercise immense power in ways that not only respect, protect and fulfil rights but also violate, diminish and disregard them, especially when it comes to ethnic minority and marginalized communities that risk being 'over-policed and under-protected' (Muir, quoted in Home Office, 1999: 313). With communities' fraught, and at times deadly, interactions with police ringing out loudly from names – Rodney King, George Floyd, Stephen Lawrence, Jean Charles de Menezes, Adama Traoré – and places – Brixton, Drumcree, Ferguson, Minneapolis – it would be misguided to suggest the emergence of international human rights law and its implementation into domestic safeguards over the last half century has somehow transformed the core tenets of the police function or officers' working practices or assumptions. In the UK alone, cultural and organizational challenges remain if human rights are to be foregrounded in routine policing (Bullock and Johnson, 2012; Pearson, Rowe and Turner, 2018). This is to reinforce, not to overlook, the great responsibility officers have, particularly in self-regulatory contexts, to perform their practice with integrity and to be well-trained and resourced to skilfully do so.

In assessing the role police play as 'practitioners' of human rights law in Northern Ireland, a useful starting point has been the Policing Board's annual human rights reports, produced by the Policing Board's legal advisors, which offer a detailed appraisal of technical points of the PSNI's compliance with HRA. In particular, the reports provide a valuable legal analysis of the latest legislation and case law and how the PSNI's formal policies and procedures have incorporated them. What these reports do not do, though, is offer a detailed empirical exploration or conceptual analysis of officers' own conceptions, interpretations and applications of human rights or the interplay between human rights law, politics and practice. So, whilst these reports are an immensely informative and practical guide for police and oversight bodies, they do not tell us, as an academic audience, much at all about the internal workings, personalities and cultures that animate police as human rights practitioners. This is what I seek to do in Parts IV and V, drawing on interviews, focus groups and short periods of observation with a range of officers, performing distinct types of police work, in different operational and regulatory contexts, engaging with particular human rights law standards.

Research Methods

The book's empirical findings draw on extensive fieldwork, which relied on semi-structured interviews, focus groups and short periods of observation with officers from PSNI departments, in addition to desk-based analysis of relevant case law from the domestic courts and the ECtHR, statutory provisions, annual reports of the RUC (1990–2001), PSNI (2001–2016) and the Policing Board (2003–2017), published minutes of the Policing Board's Performance Committee and PSNI official policies and procedures (publicly available). In addition, I conducted a content analysis of local newspapers, sourced using the Factiva database and based on articles in circulation in Northern Ireland from 2000 to 2018 that included the terms 'human rights' and 'PSNI' (*N*=387). Each article was read in full. From this dataset, a sub-set of articles (*n*=104) was identified as directly relevant because each article contained elements of the PSNI's or political parties' human rights discourse. This sub-set of articles was coded. A full breakdown of the fieldwork component of the research can be found in Table 1.1. The specific areas of operational policing were carefully selected based on my review of the Policing Board's human rights monitoring reports, the relevant case law and meetings with senior officers. The areas were chosen to capture the variety of possible ways human rights might be interpreted and applied in police occupational roles and regulatory contexts.

The majority of the fieldwork took place between September 2014 and September 2015, and was supplemented with several more interviews with senior officers to clarify initial findings from November to December 2016. Research across police departments, spread throughout twenty locations in Northern Ireland over the course of a year, was a logistical challenge but, in the

Table 1.1 Overview of the Fieldwork

	Role/Rank/Event	Sample	Duration	Dates
Semi-structured Interviews	Policing Board members		40–120 mins	May 2015–November 2016
	Alliance	1		
	Democratic Unionist Party	2		
	Sinn Féin	1		
	Social Democratic and Labour Party	1		
	Ulster Unionist Party	2		
	Independent members	3		
	Legal advisors	2		
	Tactical Support Groups		18–104 mins	November–December 2014
	Inspectors	2		
	Sergeants	8		
	Constables	17		
	Neighbourhood policing		22–114 mins	May–June 2015
	Constables	13		
	Sergeants	2		
	Public order commanders		53–215 mins	September 2014–December 2015
	Gold (Asst CC)	2		
	Silver (Chief Superintendent)	5		
	Bronze (Chief Inspector)	5		
	Public order trainers/tactical advisors/human rights trainer	3	45–139 mins	February–May 2015
	Police custody		23–105 mins	August–September 2015
	Custody officers	15		
	Civilian detention officers	8		
	Custody inspectors	2		

continued

Table 1.1 *Continued*

	Role/Rank/Event	Sample	Duration	Dates
	Custody superintendent	2		
	Chief officers		59–108 mins	December 2014–May 2015
	Chief Constable	1		
	Assistant Chief Constable	2		
Focus Groups	Tactical Support Groups		25–128 mins	
	Group A (constables)	3		April 2015
	Group B (constables)	3		May 2015
	Group C (constables, sergeant)	3		May 2015
	Group D (constables)	4		June 2015
	Group E (constables)	2		June 2015
	Group F (sergeants)	3		June 2015
	Probationary constables	5	45 mins	June 2015
Observations	Video recording of public sessions of the Northern Ireland Policing Board		39×, 1 hour each	October 2011–December 2016
	Five-day public order bronze command course		30 hours	June 2015
	Public order training day courses		7 hours	February 2015
	Level 1 (TSGs)		7 hours	March 2015
	Level 2 (Public Order Units)		6 hours	May 2015
	Multi-unit public order training day and six shifts with Tactical Support Groups		30 hours	November 2014–June 2015
	Neighbourhood policing in Clantown	N/A	2 weeks	May 2015
	Student officer training	N/A	10 hours	17 August–11 September 2015

(continued)

Table 1.1 *Continued*

	Role/Rank/Event	Sample	Duration	Dates
	Official events:			
	Launches of Policing Board's Annual Human Rights (Belfast)			25 March 2014
				20 February 2015
	Northern Ireland Policing Board (NIPB) Conference 'Reflecting and Refocusing: 15 years on'			7 September 2016
				3 November 2016

end, I managed to conduct interviews and focus groups involving over one hundred officers in over twenty sites. Some officers were curious about me, the research and how I had managed to get access to the PSNI. The overwhelming majority were generous with their time, keen to tell me about their work and were notably frank in the accounts they shared with me. I spent most time with a TSG unit who were particularly welcoming and keen to help; after dropping in and out of the station over several months, my presence was rarely remarked on. I produced a short report of some of the research findings for the police shortly after the fieldwork and presented further reflections on my findings to officers in March 2019.

In securing research access, I had face-to-face meetings with senior officers from the PSNI's Service Improvement Department. In these meetings I introduced the project and was put in contact with other senior officers responsible for the specific departments within which I wanted to conduct the fieldwork. Having held subsequent meetings with these senior officers, I then met with team leaders and supervisors within the departments. These meetings involved providing an outline of the research project, its purposes and the safeguards in place to protect officers' anonymity and the handling of the data. Supervisors then inquired whether any officers in their team would be willing to participate in the research, with copies of the research outline, participant information and consent form attached to emails. I met with those officers who were willing to take part in the research project in order to conduct the research interviews. There is a risk that officers might feel some pressure to take part in the research if their team leader encourages them to do so. I managed this by reiterating to the participants that they should feel no such obligation to take part. It was overwhelmingly the case, though, that officers were keen to express their views and experiences and seemed to appreciate having their perspective listened to. Almost all interviews and focus groups were audio recorded and every officer was promised anonymity: officers have been given pseudonyms and geographical locations are not included.

Gaining and sustaining research access can take energy, commitment and goodwill on the part of the researcher and the organization being researched. The police in Northern Ireland are not, traditionally at least, well-known for their ease of access to researchers. And indeed, the situation seemed far from promising when I first began scouting out the prospects of doing research with the PSNI. Nonetheless, with help from local connections, I secured a meeting with a senior officer from the PSNI's Service Improvement Department. Brokering access was undoubtedly assisted by the fact that the senior officers were recent graduates of master's programmes and some had completed research projects of their own. There were social factors at work too that helped in securing access, with it becoming apparent in conversations with some senior officers that we had attended the same school and lived or socialized in nearby neighbourhoods. It was agreed from the outset that the research should be useful and not damage public confidence in the PSNI. So too did I sense a confidence in senior officers that the PSNI's human rights compliance was something to be proud of – that there was a positive story to be told. I was put in contact with the senior officers responsible for each department and conducted my own follow-up meetings with them. These meetings were an opportunity for me to prove my credentials, get a sense of issues or sensitivities within each department and incorporate topics of interest to them into the research design where practicable.

How the various officers I met, interviewed and observed in conducting the fieldwork made sense of me, and how this affected what they shared, is difficult to know specifically. I am a

Belfast-born, small 'P' Protestant, middle-class, grammar-school educated young man. In so far as these characteristics align with a positive vision of Northern Irish identity amongst police officers, my being this way likely helped build rapport with my participants. I met several officers with whom I had mutual friends or acquaintances, who attended the same school or who socialized in similar places as I did. Officers quite naturally assumed I would be from a Northern Irish university, so on hearing I was at the University of Oxford I occasionally received amusing comments, curiosity or reservation, to which I usually responded with a healthy dose of local humour. That said, my Northern Irish accent has softened after years spent studying in England; at times, I sensed some officers trying to discern whether or not I really *was* a local. As someone born and part-raised in Northern Ireland, I am all too aware that when it comes to the questions one asks, the analysis one undertakes and the conclusions one arrives at, ethno-national allegiances, real or perceived, matter: Protestant or Catholic, Unionist or Nationalist, Loyalist or Republican, British, Irish or Northern Irish. Too often such binaries matter far more than they ought to and determine far more than they should. But they are, nevertheless, labels emergent from personal and collective identities; they speak to deeper entanglements of history, of experience, of loss, of belonging, of ideas – and thus lay claim to their own truths. In writing this book, I have shared its chapters with audiences near and far, in the hope that the feedback I have received will help to expose and unsettle my own biases and to remedy overly partial accounts. Just how successful this endeavour has been is for the reader to judge.

Two slightly different styles of interviewing and coding were adopted for Parts II–III and IV–V to reflect the three particular conceptual foundations discussed earlier in this chapter. When it came to conducting interviews with participants for Parts II–III of the book, the aim was to elicit and explore official vernaculars and sensemaking practices respectively. To capture how human rights law was understood, made sense of and deployed by each participant in their particular role or workplace, and for what purpose, I encouraged participants to reflect on how they encountered, engaged with and understood the references to human rights law in their work as police officers, or in the case of Chapter 3, members of the Policing Board. I began interviews and focus groups by encouraging officers to tell me about what a typical day looked like, what they enjoyed about their work as well as the everyday pressures they faced, and the kinds of interactions they had with colleagues and communities. In their answers, officers produced narrative accounts which had 'their own legitimacy as part of the world-views of the individuals involved' (Mulcahy, 1994: 416). It is this 'world-view', as it relates to human rights and policing, I was interested in, more than the assessment of the 'validity' of accounts (see also Loader and Mulcahy, 2003: 61–2). This style of narrative analysis, which focuses on meaning in content, is distinct from discourse analysis which pays very close attention to elements and forms of speech (Drisko and Maschi, 2016: 82).

In researching and analysing Parts IV–V of the book, the focus was on the police as a form of human rights 'practitioner'. Participants were thus purposefully selected because they worked most closely with a legal conception of human rights – either commanders planning and conducting public order operations that required close attention to human rights law standards or Custody Officers who were formally receiving and informally reviewing arrests, and applying the core statutory safeguards protecting the suspect's right to liberty. The starting point in interviews and the subsequent analysis thus shifted from officers' socialization in human rights and sensemaking narratives to human rights law as a series of principles and standards relating to officers' decision-making. This was reflected in the types of questions I asked participants because they were premised on an a priori understanding of bodies of human rights law that specifically applied to their area of police work. I was keen to gauge officers' awareness of the legal standards and principles, how they became (or did not become) familiar with them, how they interpreted and applied them and how human rights law came to be connected to formal (or informal) modes of internal and external regulation. The questions in these interviews were more explicit in connecting human rights and legal standards and prompting officers to recall from their own experiences what the 'law in action' looked like. The same focus on the legal standards, drawn from the case law of domestic courts and the ECtHR and statutory provisions, informed the coding of the data and the subsequent analysis of it. I transcribed the data during and after the fieldwork. I coded the data, concentrating on the frequency, form and substance of participants' discussion of human rights law, 'focusing on key words and offering possible explications of their broader and more complex meanings as constructions of social reality' (Cunningham, 1992: 1352). I began by using NVivo to code the data but ultimately found it more intuitive and accessible to work in Microsoft Word, highlighting and commenting upon the text, then transferring the text into an Excel document which was formatted according to the themes arrived at.

Conclusion

In this chapter, I have sought to set out a sociological approach to human rights law that challenges what has been labelled an 'insider/outsider' perspective of the law (see McCrudden, 2006). This can, I think, enable us to come to approach the legal dimension of human rights not as a fault line to be skirted around, purposefully avoided or blindly leapt across, but consciously and curiously examined. This is best achieved by combing insights from the sociology of law with the methods, concepts and ideas from criminology, anthropology, sociology and organizational studies. At the same time, it requires a willingness on the behalf of criminologists to become more familiar, perhaps even more confident, in engaging with, incorporating and critiquing the statutes, treaties, law reports and scholarship that makes up the field of human rights (Zedner, 2011: 279). In the four substantive parts of the book that follow, the aim is to examine how human rights law interacts with officers' routine practices, the way they talk about and make sense of their working world and the social and organizational structures within it. In pursuit of this, I draw on works from law, anthropology, criminology and organizational studies to make sense of human rights law in policing as a *vernacular* used in official discourse (Part II), as a subject of *sensemaking* for officers performing routine policing (Part III) and as a body of principles and standards interpreted and applied by officers as *practitioners* (Parts IV–V). Collectively, these concepts offer us a way into, and a means of making sense of, the variety of ways in which officers encounter human rights law in different sites of police work.

PART II

Official Vernaculars: The Politics of Rights

2

The Official Police Voice

The task of this opening substantive chapter is to trace how and why human rights law has come to be such an integral and sustained feature of the PSNI's official narrative. The reason, I argue, lies in the apparent power of human rights discourse to cool down, even if not quite neutralize, political tensions, debates and controversies that still animate 'high-level policing' (Brodeur, 1983) in the country. The seeming appeal of human rights lies in its capacity to promote the PSNI's ethical credentials, neutrality and accountability to high-level audiences that remain acutely attuned to signals of police partisanship or impropriety. For the chief officers, the human rights reforms that they have worked hard to embed within the organization (Murphy, 2013) have rehabilitated the PSNI's moral authority to comment on matters of politics, transition and peace in Northern Ireland. That is, not only have human rights become a central strand of the official voice of chief officers, the reforms on which this narrative is based has helped chief officers reclaim the 'police voice': 'the power to "name", diagnose and classify social problems' (Loader and Mulcahy, 2003: 226). To frame this chapter's analysis of the PSNI's official vernacular of human rights, I draw upon and gently rework Bottoms and Tankebe's (2012, 2013) 'dialogic' model of legitimacy to better account for the conditional nature of power and legitimation. Doing so enables us to better identify and account for the dynamic struggles in which rights-based claims are deployed as part of efforts to frame, or even resolve, contemporary political and public debates.

The interpretive project in this chapter goes beyond the legal to expose the social and political origins and consequences of human rights law as a legitimating discourse for powerful actors like the police – something which has been observed as an increasing trend, but rarely examined empirically in any great depth (see

Policing Human Rights. Richard Martin, Oxford University Press. © Richard Martin 2021.
DOI: 10.1093/oso/9780198855125.003.0003

Gearty, 2006: 60). I begin by introducing the concept of police legitimation and illustrate how Bottoms and Tankebe's dialogic model might be recrafted to better capture power dynamics in Northern Ireland. I use this modified notion of legitimation to frame the chapter's analysis of the construction, expression and deployment of human rights as a legitimating narrative of policing to high-level audiences. By closely examining chief officers' forewords and speeches, as well as their public responses to questions at the Policing Board's public session, I identify three central properties that define this official vernacular, which are human rights as *legality*; as *an ethics of power*; and as *accountability*. Each of these major strands of the police voice, I argue, contribute to a purported vision of the PSNI as worthy of endorsement by elite audiences. The extent to which these claims are accepted, or even recognized, by the general public remains debatable but I argue that the very *ability* of the police to mount and sustain this human rights narrative lies in its 'authorization' by powerful audiences that contribute to local debates over policing in Northern Ireland.

Legitimation, the Official Voice and Influential Audiences

Bottoms and Tankebe (2012, 2013) have rightly called for greater attention to be given to the role and perspective of the police as 'power-holders', the possessors of a particular type of authority. In an effort to promote a richer account of empirical legitimacy, Bottoms and Tankebe draw on the works of Weber (1968) and Raz (2009), which posit that authorities rarely, if ever, rely on coercion alone to achieve support and compliance from the public. Rather, authorities seek to cultivate a belief in the minds of those they govern that the power they wield is morally justifiable. Accordingly, Bottoms and Tankebe propose a 'dialogic and relational' conceptualization of legitimacy which emphasizes its 'interactive character': power-holders make claims to legitimate authority, which are responded to by one or more audiences, and these responses may motivate power-holders to re-adjust their claims. This relatively simple, yet fundamental, claim will be familiar to sociologists and political scientists, based as it is on the established works of Weber (1968) and Beetham (1991). But in the field of enquiry cultivated by criminal justice researchers, power-holders and their 'claims' have generally received less attention.[1] The relative infancy of the 'dialogic' approach to legitimacy makes it a fertile concept with which to creatively engage in light of the existing research.[2] I suggest that the dialogic approach ought to be developed in two ways to properly account for, and explain, police legitimation in the context of politics and accountability.

The first relates specifically to the act of legitimation: the material practices that power-holders engage in to make, enhance or cultivate moral authority of their power in the eyes of subordinates, as well as themselves (Barker, 2001). Bottoms and Tankebe (2013: 69–72) single out two modes of legitimation as particularly significant in the context of policing: *cultural legitimation* (the cultural markers that symbolize the special status of police, such as distinct police uniforms, marked vehicles, ceremonial graduations and funerals) and *performative legitimation* (the effective and performance of primary police functions, most notably maintenance of a just social order). Although both are worthy of further exploration, Bottoms and Tankebe, have, I think, overlooked a third mode of legitimation: *discursive legitimation*. Cultural and performative legitimation are rituals or acts that can be studied through close observation of the everyday work of officers and their reflexive accounts. Discursive legitimation takes its most pronounced form, I think, in what Loader and Mulcahy have termed the 'corporate police voice' (Loader and Mulcahy, 2001: 43; cf. Shiner, 2010); that is, a strategically constructed and carefully deployed narrative that can be pieced together from official documents and chief officers' remarks in public, as well as research interviews.

The discursive expression of legitimacy is well captured in the works exploring how police and criminal justice agencies deploy 'storylines' (McLaughlin and Murji, 1998), 'narratives' (Cote-Lussier, 2013), 'histories' (Mulcahy, 2000) and 'visions' (Mulcahy,

[1] For a rare exception see McEvoy and Schwartz's (2015) assessment of the shaping of the judicial role during the Northern Irish conflict. Though the dialogic approach of Bottoms and Tankebe is not discussed, their analysis of the public, political and legal 'audiences' the judiciary 'performed' to is similar in tone.

[2] For an extended analysis and elaboration of the dialogic model of legitimacy, see Martin and Bradford (2019).

1999) to defend their reputations and identities. Scholarship over the last decade has evidenced how the police attentively, and at times anxiously, seek to cultivate, manage and defend a corporate 'reputation' or 'brand' through professionalized and centralized public relations and media units – an enterprise undoubtedly bound up with the wider project of institutional legitimation. Empirical research in both the UK (Mawby, 2002, 2010) and Australia (Lee and McGovern, 2013) involving staff from police media units, for example, has found that the concept of legitimacy is 'central to understand the motivations of police media work and some of the themes through which respondents describe their work' (Lee and McGovern, 2013: 107). The veracity of such discourses is secondary to the ideological work they do in constructing a vision capable of eliciting support from public audiences (McLaughlin and Murji, 1998: 397).

A powerful example of discursive legitimation in the Northern Irish context is Mulcahy's (1999, 2000; Mulcahy and Ellison, 2001) astute deconstruction of the determined strategies of the RUC to cultivate legitimacy. The dual demands of institutional stability and organizational self-esteem prompted the RUC to respond to these challenges to the moral authority of its power with the careful, strategic cultivation and deployment of 'organizational memories' during the conflict (Mulcahy, 2000). Expressed in the RUC's publications and annual reports, this official discourse promoted the commitment, bravery and sacrifice of its officers, the hidden community support for policing and the RUC's commitment to accountability. Similarly, the language of professionalism was consciously deployed as a discursive tool to enhance legitimacy and reinforce the British government's conflict management approach of 'containment' and 'normalization'. Professionalism was conveyed through the specific language of 'consent' and 'service' which were 'mobilised to maximise the force's positive self-conception, minimise its problems, and side line its critics' (Mulcahy and Ellison, 2001: 286).

Locating the official police voice alongside political cultures, social change and institutional tensions prompts a second extension of Bottoms and Tankebe's dialogic model of legitimacy: the role of elite actors as influential audiences that can, in fact, be constitutive of legitimating discourses. Bottoms and Tankebe (2013: 65) acknowledge that police 'will need to legitimate themselves upwards (to state or national governing bodies)', but they offer very little about the role of other power-holders as core audiences for legitimation, capable of affecting the production, content and cultivation of legitimacy claims. And yet we know police organizations are routinely drawn into contact with, rely upon, and direct their voice towards other elite actors, including politicians (Loader and Mulcahy, 2003; Murray and Harkin, 2017), oversight bodies (Campau, 2015), courts (Bronitt and Stenning, 2011) and the media (Ericson, Baranek and Chan,1989; Mawby 2010; Lee and McGovern, 2013). More generally, Barker (2001: 51) argues that rulers themselves are the principal audience for legitimation and, when recognition is sought from others, it is most often from 'the rulers' own immediate associates, institution, or community'. Powerful institutions in society are not simply audience members being addressed in a legitimacy dialogue, but are constitutive of the very power held by criminal justice agencies, like police or prisons, and in turn, the claims they are capable of plausibly cultivating.

It is necessary, then, for the dialogic model of legitimacy to account for the contingent nature of power-holders' legitimation which necessarily implicates other societal power-holders. To this end, there is much to be found in the theoretical insights of Berger and Zelditch (1998). Berger and Zelditch offer an account of the legitimacy of power that is embedded within social controls that facilitate, mediate and limit actions between power-holders. Berger and Zelditch (1998: chapter 12) write that the 'exercise of authority is actually a matter of the coordinated action of a system of actors, not a dyadic relation between a superior and subordinate'. To account for hierarchies of power in society, they distinguish between two levels of support for authorities: first, support by peers or superiors of an authority (authorization); and second, support by peers of a subordinate over whom that authority is exercised (endorsement). For a directive by an authority to be executed, and before it is considered for possible endorsement by a subordinate's peers, it must be backed by the actions (authorization) of others. Accordingly, '[l]egitimacy will normatively regulate power if, and only if, it is true that others will not back invalid directives. Thus, normative regulation of powers lies in the effect of validity on authorization and endorsement by a complex system of others' (Berger and Zelditch, 1998: 269).

Introducing this role of other elites to a power-holder, specifically through their 'authorization' of an authority's directives/

requests, is to acknowledge the conditional nature of power-holder claims vis-à-vis other power-holders, something which is currently absent in Bottoms and Tankebe's theoretical analysis. Powerful actors in society are not simply another member of 'the audience' that power-holders appeal to, but rather a key component in the very ability to assert and substantiate a claim to legitimacy. An authority needs 'authorization' from other powerful actors in society in order to proceed to seek 'endorsement' from a broader audience, such as the public. Applying this to police legitimation, political actors, oversight bodies and criminal justice agencies are not merely audiences, but integral to the very power dynamics that enable police organizations to assert and substantiate legitimacy claims. This is an idea we will return to for closer consideration in the final section of this chapter. Before we get there, I want to first explore the material form of the PSNI's official human rights narrative, specifically the human rights reporting scheme the Independent Commission's reforms inspired, the key individuals involved in this scheme and their respective motivations. The chapter will then identify the legitimating properties chief officers have come to associate human rights with. These properties reveal the PSNI's official visions and ideals of human rights, which will be returned to and critically examined in the context of routine policing in Part II of the book.

Listening to the Official Voice: The Construction of Human Rights

The vernacular of human rights articulated by the PSNI was first heard during a series of specialist conferences in 2001 as chief officers, sharing platforms with lawyers and academics, mooted how best to achieve the Independent Commission's human rights vision for policing (Cramphorn, 2001; Kinkaid, 2001).[3] Inspired by the Council of Europe's own programme for human rights policing, as

[3] There was no mention made of human rights in the RUC's annual reports from 1990–1998. It was first raised in the RUC's annual report in 1998/9 in the reporting of a conference hosted by the Chief Constable, and organized by the RUC's Community Affairs department, 'to celebrate the 50th Anniversary of the Universal Declaration of Human Rights and to demonstrate the Royal Ulster Constabulary's commitment to safeguarding the human rights of all members of the community' (RUC, 1999: 63).

well as the Independent Commission's recommendations, reform processes soon got underway. An Assistant Chief Constable was given responsibility for leading introducing the human rights recommendations in the Independent Commissions' Report, serving as the organizations 'human rights champion', a symbolic move to demonstrate just how seriously the organization was taking human rights. Specifically, the PSNI recruited an in-house human rights lawyer as well as a human rights training advisor; human rights training packages were rolled out across the PSNI with new determination; an oath of allegiance to uphold human rights was introduced; and work began on a police Code of Ethics inspired by the ECHR. These specific reforms were, of course, just one part of the massive organizational change that took place from 2001 to 2007. The PSNI's senior management sought to satisfy the hundreds of Independent Commission recommendations, with their progress carefully monitored by a specially appointed Oversight Commissioner (see Murphy, 2013: chapter 4).

It was from 2003 onwards that the PSNI's official human rights narrative rose to prominence. This was due in large part to the introduction of the Policing Board's human rights monitoring framework, devised by Sir Keir Starmer, an eminent human rights barrister, in co-ordination with the PSNI (Starmer, 2007; Rea and Masefield, 2014). The Policing Board, itself a product of the Independent Commission-inspired reforms, was bestowed with a statutory duty (the first of its kind in the UK) to ensure the police complied with the HRA. The PSNI agreed to allow the Policing Board's legal advisors to access police training, policies and operations in order for them to assist the Policing Board in fulfilling its statutory human rights monitoring duty. The principles guiding this approach were that the legal advisors' oversight ought to consider the whole of policing, both positive and negative; encourage a positive dialogue with the PSNI, addressing issues as they arose; and not be retrospective, focusing on contemporary police practices (Starmer and Gordon, 2005). The oversight scheme's dialogic aspirations were clear from its reporting framework: the legal advisors publish their findings and recommendations based on their year-round observations in the Policing's Board's Annual Human Rights Report. This Report is then responded to by the PSNI in their own annual Human Rights Programme of Action.

Keen to demonstrate its progress in achieving the Independent Commission's human rights reforms, the PSNI allowed the

Policing Board's legal advisors extensive access to what had long been a closed, secretive police organization (Mulcahy, 2000). In one interview with former PSNI Chief Constable Sir Hugh Orde (2002–2007), it became clear how strikingly important the Policing Board and its legal advisors – as 'high' policing (Brodeur, 1983) audiences – were throughout this period of reform:

I would have the Ombudsman, the Policing Board, the human rights advisors – they were allowed to go wherever they wanted, in at these briefings, seats at the front row, they had input in these briefings. It was a very different way of policing. Culturally that was seen as pretty seismic because you had to convince people outside who doubted that we were absolutely delivering change. And that was critical, they had to be convinced something was different ... It required relentless energy and relentless pressure to deliver the change in fairly quick time, against a series of oversight bodies of which Keir Starmer and the human rights stuff was critical. (Sir Hugh Orde, interview, 15 December 2014)

The symbolism of the PSNI's Programmes of Action, as formal documents approved by chief officers, is captured in the Chief Constable's opening remarks in one of the early Programmes:

The production of this Report is another indication of the Police Service of Northern Ireland's commitment to develop further the ideal of a human rights-based approach to policing ... Its production is intended to demonstrate to the Policing Board, and to the wider community, the Police Service of Northern Ireland's commitment to engage with others to improve on a continuous basis. (PSNI, 2007: 5)

The institutional dialogue between the Policing Board and PSNI continues to this day. A decade and a half of reporting now provides us with a rich archive of the 'police voice', but its sheer endurance also says something telling about the perceived utility of human rights long after the reform process has run its course. It would appear from recent Programmes of Action that chief officers still feel a strong need to prove their organization's credentials to elite audiences. The Programmes of Action, we are told, remain a 'public declaration and demonstration of our commitment to human rights' (PSNI, 2014a: 3) and are 'not just about the publication of our policies and procedures; it is about telling our story' (PSNI, 2015a: 4). Notably, this narrative is imbued with increasing organizational self-confidence; it is a story of progress, of success. Writing in their reports, chief officers proclaim how human rights are 'well established in our current working practices and policies, we are widely acknowledged as international leaders in this area' (PSNI, 2011: 2), and that the implementation of over 200 Policing Board recommendations is 'testament to PSNI's commitment to ensuring … a positive human rights culture and awareness' (PSNI, 2014a: 3).

In recent years, the official police voice has taken on a pronounced oratory form too. It is heard in chief officers' responses to members of the Policing Board at its monthly public sessions, often to allay politicians' concerns over covert intelligence, public order policing or investigations into conflict-related deaths. Chief officers have also used other public forums to promote their rights narrative, most notably the launch of the Policing Board Annual Human Rights Report, which is typically a high-profile event centred around a panel discussion with the Chief Constable, Policing Board members and its legal advisors. Reflecting the PSNI's growing ownership of rights discourse, the former Chief Constable Hamilton has even delivered speeches at human rights conferences in Belfast, including the keynote speech at the Northern Irish Human Rights Consortium (Hamilton, 2014a; 2016a; 2016b). The audiences at these events reveal to whom this rights narrative is addressed: local NGOs, politicians, academics, oversight bodies and other chief officers. In the following section, I want to look more closely at the particular properties of human rights – the ideals, commitments, associated principles – which are foregrounded by chief officers to help make it an attractive narrative with which to appeal to high-level audiences and recover a societal position from which the PSNI can 'act and judge' (Hornberger, 2011: 3) in post-conflict Northern Ireland.

Interpreting the Official Voice

Narratives shift across time, location and audience, and subtle changes may reveal an understating of, and sensitivity to, political events or institutions (Payne, 2008). There are three core properties of human rights that chief officers routinely returned to in their public narrative: human rights (i) as legality, emphasizing officers' compliance with legal rules and court-authorized standards; (ii) as an ethics of power, alluding to police culture and officers' morality; and (iii) as accountability, underscoring how open the organization was to outside scrutiny. Using a set of discursive techniques explored in the sections that follow, chief officers engaged in what Little (1996) has described in the context of legal discourse as 'characterization'. This refers to the reframing of a dispute on terms favourable to the speaker, which can entail dodging one formulation of a dispute in favour of another one. It is premised, ultimately, on the idea that people can derive various perceptions from the same set of facts, circumstances or events. Reframing is a kind of rhetorical manoeuvring around obstacles and towards strategic goals (Little, 1996: 379–8). It is argued that chief officers sought to discursively construct and project three dimensions of human rights as part of an effort to defend the PSNI and enhance its legitimacy in the eyes of elite audiences. Let us critically examine these three dimensions drawn from human rights.

Human Rights as Legality

Legality goes to the heart of the rule of law in democratic societies – no person or authority, no matter how powerful, ought to be above the law. The actors wielding state power should be subject to formally enacted, publicly accessible laws, applied in an impartial manner. This notion of legality as rule-boundedness is a particularly significant antecedent of audience legitimacy, understood in the empirical sense of a felt obligation to obey the command of an authority (Beetham, 1991). Writing in the context of policing, Ericson (1996: 203) has argued that legitimacy often depends on the police's ability 'to make convincing claims that they are acting in an orderly manner, in accordance with established morality, procedure and hierarchy'. As such, questions focus around procedural propriety and legal compliance with formal rules. But simpler still, Ericson (2007) suggests there is a common sense component to legality: the good police officer, just like the good citizen, is the person who acts in accordance with agreed-upon rules. It is what explains 'why, when people are called upon to account for what they did, they often present their actions as having simply followed the rules' (Ericson, 2007: 369).

Faced with accusations of partisan policing, especially by politicians at Policing Board meetings, chief officers have routinely sought refuge in this notion of legality as rule-boundedness. In the words of former PSNI Chief Constable Matt Baggott (2012): 'I am making quite clear that my job is to apply the law and to be impartial ... I cannot get involved in discussions that are beyond the law ... '. By frequently emphasizing the existence of legal rules in their official narrative, chief officers have sought to convince high-level audiences that police are cognizant of, and compliant with, formal rules. These claims are strengthened by the rhetorical authority drawn from legal 'form' (Hastrup, 2003) and 'sources' (Ericson, 1996) such as international conventions and court rulings. Rhetorical discourse is reactive, similar to how an answer derives from a question. The following extract illustrates the specific legal 'forms' and 'sources' in the context of public meetings of the Policing Board. By way of immediate context, earlier that day the Nationalist Social Democratic and Labour Party had accused the PSNI of refusing to disclose the identity of the suspected killers of a Catholic man murdered during the conflict because the suspects had, in fact, been RUC informers at the time (*BBC News*, 2015a). In his opening speech, the Chief Constable sought to fend off accusations, deploying the narrative of legality in its fullest form:

> I want to respond to the front page of one of our local papers today, which states that a policing board member believes the PSNI are shielding murderers. Let me be clear, *in a liberal democracy such as ours, no-one is above the law*. Board members, I assume, are aware of *the legislation that we as a police service operate*, including the Police Act, the Human Rights Act, the European Convention on Human Rights and the Regulation of Investigatory Powers Act. (Public Session, NIPB, Feb 2015)

This account brings into play the characterization technique Little (1996: 383–4) describes as the 'expanding universe', whereby the relevant context surrounding the dispute is purposefully enlarged so as to introduce additional dimensions that dilute the strength of the initial claim. Here, the principle of legality, as the foundation stone of liberal democracies, is coupled with a list of statutory bases for police powers to shift the discussion into a normative context in which it appears absurd that such an accusation could be well-founded.

So too has the combination of rule-bound compliance with authoritative 'sources' been deployed to proffer a definitive answer to concerns raised by Republican communities, as well as researchers, over the high rate of stop and search, especially of young men in socially deprived areas and Republican neighbourhoods (Hearty, 2017: 232–4; Topping and Bradford, 2020). This extract captures the tenor of the PSNI's official discourse:

> *I accept that there are many who would argue that stop and search[es]... are an unnecessary infringement of human rights.* Believe me, I wish we did not need these powers but the facts remain that we are required to use them in order to keep people safe. *The UK Supreme Court has ruled that, used properly, the powers are lawful.* (Chief Constable Hamilton, 2016b)

The rhetorical manoeuvre here is not about reframing the context but rather directly confronting the claim that stop and search powers are being abused head on, and then using the device of 'flipping' to achieve a favourable outcome for the speaker (Little, 1996: 390). The manoeuvre begins by the former Chief Constable identifying some common ground, however narrow (recognizing concerns that stop and search infringes human rights) but then turning this rights-based critique on its head by citing the judgment of the UK Supreme Court in *(R)Roberts v Commissioner of the Metropolis*.[4] In *Roberts*, the court held that section 60 of the Criminal Justice and Public Order Act 1994 (stop and search without reasonable grounds of suspicion) was a lawful interference with Article 8 of the ECHR. Provided the power of suspicionless stop and search was used 'properly'– reasons are given by the officer so as to enable the court to determine whether the exercise of the power was 'necessary' for the purposes of preventing disorder or crime – it *was* lawful. As a discursive strategy, the former Chief Constable alluded to the essence of the Supreme Court's reasoning to support – on the basis of human rights law – suspicionless stop and search, which has been critiqued by Republican communities as an infringement of human rights and as a disruption tactic used to target legitimate opponents of the post-GFA status quo (Hearty, 2017: 233).

A further feature of the PSNI's official discourse that emerges from a careful reading of the chief officer's official texts, speeches and responses to questions of the Policing Board is what Cotterrell (1997) has referred to as 'legal closure'. As discussed in the book's Introduction, the heart of legal closure is the 'conception of law as a distinct discourse, possessing its own integrity, its own criteria of significance and validation' (Cotterrell, 1997: 91). The rhetorical power of legal closure derives from the claim that 'law is self-standing and irreducible or that it has an independent integrity which is normally unproblematic, natural,

[4] *(R) Roberts v Commissioner of the Metropolis* [2015] UKSC 79.

or self-generated' (Cotterrell, 1997: 91). Human rights law – as a standard that purports to regulate the discretionary space within which police can be accused of ethno-political partisanship – has been heavily deployed to close off critiques of one of the most politicized areas of policing in Northern Ireland: the investigation of conflict-related deaths. Nationalist political parties have been forthright in expressing concern over the commitment of the PSNI's specialist unit (the Legacy Investigation Branch) to fair and impartial investigations of killings by security forces. As we shall see in Chapter 3, at the Policing Board's public sessions, Sinn Féin have consistently alleged the police are failing their obligation, per Article 2 of the ECHR (the right to life), to ensure an effective investigation into deaths. The PSNI have responded with their own counter-narrative of Article 2, used to bracket off these concerns as distinctly *legal* ones, and which, as a consequence, are framed as requiring technical answers by lawyers and judges, not politicians:

> I have on a number of occasions sought legal advice as to my obligations and independence when it comes to investigating the past … The precise extent of the investigative obligations arising from Article 2 of the European Convention on Human Rights is a complicated and developing issue, the final determination of which can only be made by the courts. There are a number of ongoing judicial proceedings in this area, and I look forward to the legal clarity that these will bring. But, while we wait for judicial clarity, the current legal advice is that PSNI's Legacy Investigations Branch is Article 2 compliant. (Chief Constable Hamilton, 2016b)

In response to criticisms over delay in the disclosure of material to coronial inquests, the PSNI have reminded politicians of the police duties under Articles 2 and 8 of the ECHR to consider the impact of disclosure on individuals whose identities might be revealed by the material. The police narrative elevates such concerns to questions of law – the police are merely agents of the coroner with strict legal duties as captured in the words of PSNI Deputy Chief Constable Drew Harris (2016):

> There is always a decision to be taken about whether to advance a case. In large part, it comes down to our Article 2 and Article 8 responsibilities. The Article 2 responsibilities that we have concerning individuals *weigh heavily on us* and place an obligation, at times, *to engage, in effect, in a legal argument* … I know that we get a lot of bad media and it has

sapped public confidence in certain areas of the coronial process, but we are there as agents of the coroner, working for the coroner in delivering an ECHR-compliant inquest.

The technique of characterization on display here has been described by Little (1996: 386) as belonging to the 'rival components' model. The Deputy Chief Constable accepts the impetus of the problem – that disclosure of information to the coroner's court is an issue – but shifts the balance that his political opponent has placed on the interests at stake. The speaker emphasizes the rights of the police informant or source to remain alive and safe, thus presenting the issue of disclosure as a defining feature of the issue at hand, which complicates what is presented by Republican politicians as purposeful obstruction of the coronial process on the part of the PSNI (as we will see in Chapter 3).

To be clear, there is no doubt there are real legal duties arising from Articles 2 and 8 of the ECHR that the PSNI must, and do, take seriously. What is significant is how strongly this legal discourse features in the remarks and statements before non-legal audiences. While the PSNI may well be 'engaging, in effect, in a legal argument', the legal argument itself exhibits what Kennedy (1991: 97) refers to as 'nesting' – that is the reproduction, within a legal solution, of the policy conflict the solution was supposed to settle. The rights framework brings structure to the process of balancing release of information to the coroner and the safety of the source of that information, but still requires a weighting of interests to be made by senior officers – and it is this weighting that critics are attempting to probe further. More critically, the PSNI's discursive deployment of human rights as legality risks conveying, in the minds of sceptical observers, what Cohen (2001: 22) calls 'interpretive denial': the speaker conceiving something is 'happening' but that this ought to be recast in a different way if it is to be 'properly understood'. The PSNI's narrative re-interprets the debate over conflict-related investigations as one concerning the legal criteria of Article 2 ECHR investigations, rather than the broader issue of state responsibility for harms caused during the conflict.

The heavy recourse to legal discourse by the PSNI in their official voice risks crowding out other ways of understanding harm and recompense arising from the conflict (cf. Kennedy, 2002; Gearty, 2006: 84). As argued by O'Barr and Conley, alienation arises from a legal formulation being used to 'define the problems of ordinary people in ways that may have little meaning for them, and to offer remedies that are unresponsive to their needs as they see them' (quoted in Cunningham, 1992: 1301). The PSNI's resort to legality risks distracting from the wider societal and budgetary debates that surround information retrieval, access to justice and the need for a more institutionally joined-up process for dealing with legacy issues (McEvoy and Bryson, 2016). The characterizations on display in the official discourse have generated cynicism and suspicion amongst some communities. In the context of legacy investigations, there have been very real concerns and disappointment for some victims' families arising from organizational and bureaucratic failures within the PSNI's Historical Enquiries Team identified by Her Majesty's Inspectorate of Constabulary (HMIC). Investigations carried out by HMIC discovered former RUC officers reviewing and overseeing cases where the state was suspected of having been involved in the deaths, and different investigatory practices in cases where the state was involved (army or police) compared to non-state involvement cases, with the former receiving more favourable treatment and safeguards (HMIC, 2013). As expanded on in Chapter 3, the resort to Article 2 as a central response in the face of such criticisms can be interpreted by some communities as reflecting a 'legal system without an anchor' (Little, 1996: 402), where police, like lawyers, can adopt obfuscatory and dilatory strategies to present the law or facts in such a way as to support their case.

Human Rights as an 'Ethics of Power'

The PSNI's chief officers portray human rights as a set of moral principles to which the organization has wilfully, and proudly, bound itself to. Chief officers keenly convey rights as *the* ethical framework guiding the work of police officers and tempering their power. Writing forewords to the Programmes of Action, chief officers insist the PSNI's commitment to human rights extends beyond legal compliance to reflect the organization's morality – indeed, it's very identity – as an organization: 'human rights is part of our culture; ingrained in how things are done' (PSNI, 2013a: 2) and 'it is not only in the DNA of policing ... it is also part of our psyche; it is how we think, weigh up options and ultimately make decisions' (PSNI, 2015a: 3). In fulfilling their duty to protect the public, which requires officers to, for example, use their powers of arrest or stop and search, chief officers describe human rights as 'a practical framework through which we can use these powers with the consent and confidence of our community' (Chief Constable Hamilton, 2014a). Drawing on Hornberger's (2010: 263) analysis of the 'ethical in action', it is clear ethics here are not being deployed in the philosophical sense of 'open-ended, undetermined deliberation over what is good and just' but instead as 'a practical means for following a more or less predetermined moral course of action' (2010: 263).

As Wallach (2005) has argued, there is a 'constitutive ambiguity' at the heart of human rights as an ethical framework because it seeks to constrain powerful institutions, yet to be effective the same institutions must be prepared to invest in, and commit to, that framework. The PSNI have sought to evidence this self-commitment, frequently reminding audiences that their Code of Ethics: 'serves as [our] discipline code ... It integrates the European Convention on Human Rights in police practice, acting as the standard that must be reached and against which officers can be judged' (PSNI, 2009: 1). As will be illustrated in Chapter 4, it was apparent that frontline officers were, in fact, only faintly aware of the ECHR references in the Code and tended to view it cynically as a 'stick to beat them with' should something go wrong. Yet, for the purposes of appealing to elite outside audiences, the Code remains a tangible, heavily endorsed document. In a similar vein, the PSNI has continued to remind readers of the role of the chief officer who acts as the 'Champion for Human Rights' – something that, public audiences are told, is undertaken 'with great enthusiasm' (PSNI, 2007: 6).

The notion of a police 'ethics of power' as a legitimation strategy has a longer history in Northern Ireland. The morality implicit in accounts of officers' bravery and risk in the face of grave danger featured prominently in the RUC's official narrative. This emphasized the great sacrifice RUC officers made, risking life and limb to protect communities and counter paramilitary insurgents (Mulcahy, 2000). The themes of sacrifice and morality were expressed through the 'Roll of Honour', which appeared in the RUC's annual reports and listed the names of the RUC officers killed in the preceding year, and memorials to RUC officers that hung on the walls of many stations (Mulcahy, 2000: 76). Traces of moral distinction between the police and paramilitaries can be heard in the official police voice today through human rights specifically as a kind of 'ethics of power' directly relevant to the operational challenges posed by the small but dangerous remnants of the Provisional IRA. Human rights, as *the* ethical identifier of the PSNI, are expressed by the distinction chief officers make between the morality of the police officers compared to those involved in terrorist activity in Northern Ireland. Chief officers describe how the PSNI delivers a 'professional policing service' in the face of 'a number of dangerous violent Dissident Republicans [who] are actively planning attacks on police ... These groups care nothing for Human Rights or human lives' (PSNI, 2015a: 5). The 'often untold' story, according to former Chief Constable Hamilton (2014a), is the bravery of his officers who 'display a dignity and respect for human life that is entirely absent in the actions of those who are willing to take life'. This story, though, is one firmly on display in physical form *within* the organization itself today. The organizational memory of morality and professionalism lives on in the garden of remembrance housed at the PSNI's headquarters in Belfast and in the memorials that I saw hanging in the backstage areas of police stations I visited, with rows of faces of RUC officers displayed under the title, 'Our Murdered Colleagues'.

In promoting human rights as an 'ethics of power', established and alleged human rights abuses committed by the RUC during the conflict stand as a potential ethical spoiler which must be navigated around by the PSNI in order to establish a convincing account in the eyes of its critics (O'Rawe, 2005). For a significant number of Republican communities, the legacy of policing is one that is defined by RUC oppression, discrimination, mistreatment of suspects and even collusion with Loyalist paramilitaries. Such experiences, memories and stories are not easily cast aside; they jar with the storyline told by chief officers, many of whom were former RUC officers. The furthest the police voice goes is to hint at a 'historic relationship' with communities and their 'real or perceived' concerns. Sceptical audiences should, the PSNI insists, be re-assured by its commitment to human rights today, as evidenced in the following excerpts:

I accept that given the historic relationship between police and some communities we still have more work to do to secure that confidence which is so necessary for policing with consent. Policing with human rights as the bedrock of our approach is an effective, and right, means of breaking down barriers and building trust. (PSNI Programme of Action, 2015–16: 3)

Our policing history has taught us a lot ... Real or perceived, the inappropriate or blunt use of police powers such as stop and search; vehicle check points; and house searches can cause unease, anger and distrust in the community. Human rights are all the more important in such challenging circumstances. (Chief Constable Hamilton, 2014a)

The idea of 'legal closure' – law as a discursively closed system, speaking its own language and distinct from the extra-legal environment – is challenged acutely in post-conflict societies by the very fact that law and legal arenas are sites of struggle which political actors use to 'own' the direction of transition (McEvoy, 2000; Bell, 2012). The rehabilitative potential of the law in transitional contexts surely lies in part in the willingness of state actors to acknowledge their wrongdoing and the moral deficiencies of the laws they enforced in the past (O'Rawe, 2007: 218). Despite the Independent Commission's exclusive focus on a 'new beginning' for policing and its insistence that human rights were at the core of its report, it could not explain why this was so. Indeed, there is a notable ahistoricism at the heart of the Commission's report:

We do not, in this report, make judgments about the extent to which the RUC may or may not have been culpable in the past of inattention to human rights or abuse of human rights ... we were not charged in our terms of reference to make judgments about the past. (ICP, 1999: 18)

Similarly, the Policing Board settled exclusively on the PSNI's, not the RUC's, compliance with human rights standards – a decision more understandable given the limits of their statutory duty and their need to ensure a working relationship with the PSNI (Starmer, 2007). The most extensive account of the RUC's human rights abuses remains scattered across academic commentary rather than any shared understanding, let alone accepted account, of policing during the conflict.

This pragmatic, forward-looking assessment of rights has meant acknowledgement of past wrongdoing has not been required. The PSNI thus has a degree of discursive space within which to cultivate and promote a human rights narrative largely untarnished by the reputation of its predecessor (Mulcahy, 2000). And yet it seems significant in that the reforms inspired by the Independent

Commission were felt by many RUC officers at the time to be the ultimate act of betrayal; capitulation to Nationalist pressure on the British government (Lawther, 2010). The oath of office, stating that officers would respect human rights, was particularly resented because of a perception that it implied officers had failed to do so in the past (Hillyard and Tomlinson, 2000). In this narrative of human rights as an 'ethics of power', it makes sense, therefore, that the Independent Commission is rarely acknowledged as the source of human rights. Instead, greater significance tends to be attached to the HRA, which shared a similar birthday to the ICP report:

> People always look to Patten and, yes, it had a huge impact but I would argue *the Human Rights Act had a bigger impact on policing* in that for the first time you had clear parameters. Sometimes that's lost in the whole Patten era. (Former Assistant Chief Constable Peter Sheridan quoted in *Irish News*, 2008a; emphasis added)

> The protection of human rights has always been at the core of policing. The introduction of the Human Rights Act 1998 in October 2000 served to formalise this in a way that had not before existed. (PSNI Programme of Action, 2008: 2)

By laying emphasis on the HRA – a statute having effect across the UK – the official police voice plays down the unique need of the Independent Commission's rights reform of the police and what is perceived by some officers as an implicit critique of the RUC. In preserving an acceptable self-understanding and identity, human rights are recast as something that were always part of policing, even if they were talked about less in the past. This is a theme we will return to examine more closely in Chapter 3 in the context of what I refer to as the 'old guard'. For now, though, the prominence of the official police voice, but especially reliance on legal characterization and the morality of its predecessor organization, emphasizes the value of the Oral History Archive proposed as part of the Stormont House Agreement as a forum for airing the complex and, likely contradictory, experiences and narratives of those involved in, as well as impacted by, the activities of the conflict's state and non-state actors. As argued by McEvoy and Bryson (2016: 83–8), this ought to offer an opportunity for victims and survivors from across all walks of life to 'tell their stories in full and in context, at a time and place that best suits needs'. In the meantime, the PSNI's official narrative does not go uncontested politically by Nationalist and Republican members of the Policing Board. As we shall see in Chapter 3, these members have proven to be quick to adopt oppositional frames to challenge the very human rights credentials chief officers are so keen to publicly promote.

The act of legitimation involves individual power-holders rationalizing and ethically interpreting their authority in a way that is often specific and personal, rather than abstract or structural (Barker, 2001: 33). A core part of legitimation is thus 'making sense of power … to those who exercise power' (Luckman in Barker, 2001: 37). This notion of endogenous legitimation helps, I think, to shine light on some of the encounters I had with the senior officers who contributed to the official police voice. It seemed, at times, that the narratives of success they articulated were as much for them as for me. I was told how integral human rights principles were to the PSNI's training and operations: 'you're getting genuine commitment and not just compliance' insisted Superintendent Dan. It was equally common to hear favourable comparisons made between the PSNI and other forces: 'certainly, in UK terms, we've embedded a human rights culture beyond many, if not all, police services', claimed Chief Superintendent Alan. In some interviews, officers pulled documents from their desk drawers, proudly thumbing at references to the ECHR and case law. A similar rhetorical flourish was shown by Eddie, a likeable, sharp-witted Superintendent who had experienced the turbulent transition from RUC to PSNI:

> I would be *small 'c' Conservative politically*, but the effect this has had on me [human rights reform] is that the prospect of the current Conservative government taking its signature off the European Convention terrifies me; I think it would be such a bad decision. My daughter's a law student, she's studying it academically, and she finds it *remarkable that a police officer would be so wedded to it*, but what in actual fact it gives us is twelve simple rules to apply to any decision you make, and of those twelve, you know, they're the big twelve, of those twelve, three or four will be directly impacted by it, and if *you know in your own heart* that you are compliant with that – this is going to sound grandiose – but you can stand there and think, I'll see you in Strasbourg. Literally, *I will see you in Strasbourg, because I'm confident right through.*

In this account, Eddie gestures towards the features of cop culture that one would think ought to orient officers away from, rather than closer to, an affinity with human rights –their crime control mentality, resistance to rules, a cynical and conservative reading of events (Bowling, Reiner and Sheptycki, 2019). And yet for Eddie, a senior officer and firearms commander, human rights provided him with a powerful explanation for – a means of understanding – the powers he has and the authority he wields in his command district; he can stand confident, knowing in his 'own heart' that he's acting in accordance with a set of ethical guidelines. Eddie's account is perhaps one example of a category of PSNI officer that Lawther (2010: 470) has termed the 'modernizers' – the higher-ranking officers keen to promote the PSNI, and to make sense of themselves, as a progressive group that reflects twenty-first century policing values, of which human rights compliance is one. Just how far legitimation through human rights travelled down through the ranks to frontline officers is a matter we will turn to in detail in Chapter 3.

Human Rights as Accountability

The assertion of accountability was a central component of the RUC's legitimating narrative, especially when faced with major scandals or scrutiny (Mulcahy, 2000). The issue was, however, that such accountability seemed sorely lacking when and where it was needed most. The Police Authority, tasked with overseeing the RUC in undoubtedly challenging circumstances, was, as Walsh (2018: 618) argues, characterized by its 'timidity, invisibility and subservience to central government and the Chief Constable'. The Authority's reluctance to investigate controversial police policies or assert its independence compounded many Nationalist's distrust towards the RUC's integrity, impartiality and restraint. Times have changed. In the wake of the Independent Commission's reform, it is often remarked by PSNI Chief Constables – quite rightly – that their police service is one of 'the most scrutinised in the world'. The oversight bodies include: the Policing Board; the Police Ombudsman; Police and Community Safety Partnerships; the Criminal Justice Inspectorate for Northern Ireland; Her Majesty's Inspectorate of Constabulary; the Northern Ireland Human Rights Commission; and the Northern Ireland Assembly's Committee for Justice. The Policing Board is particularly influential. It is unique in the UK and Ireland because it brings together representatives of political parties and civil society to sit as a body with the collective task of holding the PSNI to account (Rea and Masefield, 2014).

The notion of accountability has been strongly interwoven into the PSNI's official narrative of rights, but the difference is that accountability arrangements are more rigorous, which stands in sharp contrast to the lack thereof during the conflict (Mulcahy, 2000). Since its inception, the PSNI has reiterated its openness to reform and accountability to sceptical audiences, particularly political and community leaders and the Oversight Commission that monitored the implementation of the Independent Commission's reforms. The PSNI has consistently emphasized the oversight of the Policing Board's human rights legal advisor, who carries out meetings, observations and audits of police practice year-round. In the forewords of the PSNI's Programmes of Action, chief officers proudly remind readers of the 'unrestricted access' (PSNI, 2008a: 3) and 'spirit of openness' (PSNI, 2010: 3) the PSNI has shown the legal advisors, demonstrating that '[a]s a service we have repeatedly shown ourselves open to change' (PSNI, 2007: 3). Reflecting on their positive relationship with the Policing Board's legal advisors, and thanking them for their 'informed critique' (PSNI, 2008a: 3) and 'constructive criticism' (PSNI, 2007: 3), senior officers conclude that the PSNI is 'perhaps one of the most accountable organizations in these islands' (Chief Constable Hamilton, 2016a).

Given such a heightened level of police oversight, it is unsurprising that the PSNI has been quick to be held to account in light of operational or organizational shortcomings. High profile issues in recent years have included: the police approach to serious public disorder, especially the Flag Protests (discussed in detail in Chapter 6); the failure to disclose sensitive material to the Police Ombudsman, resulting in a threat of legal challenge (Kearney, 2014); the rehiring of former RUC officers on temporary contracts (seen by Nationalists as undermining the ICP's reforms) (McDonald, 2012); and, as mentioned, the controversy surrounding the administration and impartiality of the PSNI's investigation into conflict-related deaths (Lundy, 2009, 2011; HMIC, 2013, 2015). However, the PSNI has sought to neutralize these public critiques by welcoming critical reports and feedback because it helps the organization to 'raise the standard' (PSNI, 2008a: 2). After all, 'the implementation of human rights is a constant process; it is a job that is never truly complete; and therefore something to which we cannot reduce our efforts' (Chief Constable Hamilton, 2016b).

A common technique deployed by chief officers to ward off criticism at public meetings of the Policing Board is to remind audiences of the presence of strong accountability mechanisms. Several excerpts are illustrative of the general approach. In response to the HMIC's critical report into the Legacy Investigation Branch's compliance with Article 2 of the ECHR, the then Chief Constable sought to reassure the Policing Board of the police efforts to improve in light of its recommendations.

> [A]t the request of the Policing Board, the framework was properly examined by HMIC, who gave a very damning report on the work of HET and they also said, here's 20 things you can do to put it right. We have done our 19, it's done, if there's flaws in the framework, we've fixed them from an HMIC perspective and that's why *I'm trying to convince you* we're doing our level best, with good faith, to deliver for these victims who are still hurting today. (Chief Constable Hamilton, 2014b)

Those who make arguments, whether they are sincere or manipulative in nature, do so to influence others (Little, 1996: 392). The very motivation behind the narrative is brought to the surface in this extract with the Chief Constable's explicit reference to 'I'm trying to convince you'. A further strategy deployed when chief officers faced criticism relating to historical matters has been to re-emphasize the improvements that have been made in accountability measures over the last two decades. This is well-illustrated in the following response of former Assistant Chief Constable Will Kerr to a question asked by a Sinn Féin representative at a public meeting of the Policing Board. The substance of the question arose from a news story which reported that weapons seized by RUC forensic teams during the conflict had been returned to communities and had been used in murders carried out by Loyalist paramilitaries:

> There's a range of covert elements that are *used the world over, and we're no different* ... the only reassurance I can give you is that anything we do in that covert space is subject to the most onerous, the most rigorous human rights based accountability framework ... perhaps the difference between the process and the accountability and oversight now compared to the process that was applied in the past is that *there are very significant audit trails about what decisions are made, the proportionality and*

necessity of those decisions and those records are openly available to either the Oversight Surveillance Commissioner or the Police Ombudsman. (Public Session, NIPB, June 2015)

Here, accountability as human rights is used to defend against a mixture of organizational criticism through temporal containment ('accountability has improved in recent years'), self-correction ('we are doing our best to implement recommendations'), the relative normality of invasive powers ('police worldwide use covert surveillance and informants') and hints of legality too ('the proportionality and necessity of those decisions'). Collectively, this discursive construction amounts to what Cohen (1996) refers to as 'partial acknowledgement'. Without attacking the source, evading the context or outright denying the alleged event, the speaker projects that he or she is taking allegations seriously without the reputational damage that would flow from full acknowledgment and apology for this incident having occurred.

The appeal to accountability is particularly powerful because the PSNI recognize the potential that oversight bodies have to shape the dominant narratives that swirl policing, and thus to reinforce (or discredit) the claims that comprise the PSNI's human rights discourse. On hearing that most young people did not understand the role of the Police Ombudsman and Policing Board, Chief Constable Hamilton publicly called on them at the event at Crumlin Road Gaol to 'sell their wares' and increase their profile because the public needed to know the police were being held to account in this manner. On other occasions, Chief Constable Hamilton (2016b) has called on the Policing Board oversight to 'breathe confidence' into its Legacy Investigations Branch, linking with a general theme expressed by senior officers before the Policing Board:

For PSNI, human rights provide a practical framework through which we can use our policing powers while the *rigorous accountability structures* of the Policing Board and the Police Ombudsman ensure that we exercise these powers with the confidence and consent of the community.

By binding high-level policing actors into their rights narrative, chief officers invite other institutional voices to speak up, knowing they can help strengthen the official PSNI narrative. It is to these influential audiences that we turn now.

Influential Audiences: 'Authorizing' Human Rights Narratives

With the properties of the PSNI's official human rights narrative now identified and examined I want to complete this chapter's analysis of human rights as a mode of discursive legitimation by returning to Berger and Zelditch's (1998: 268) crucial insight that legitimacy is better conceptualized as a 'coordinated system of action, not a dyadic relation between a superior and subordinate'. In the context of Northern Ireland, this system is comprised of a web of local accountability bodies, politicians and the media. We will return to explore how the PSNI's rights narrative has been received by political audiences in the next chapter; the focus here is on how the Policing Board and local media, as particularly influential actors, have affected the very ability of the police to construct and maintain human rights as a legitimating narrative. In Berger and Zelditch's terms, the Policing Board and the local media have 'authorized' the PSNI to proffer human rights claims.

The incorporation of other power-holders into models of legitimation, drawing on Berger and Zelditch's notion of 'authorization', remains consistent with Weber's account of legitimacy as concerned with audiences' beliefs in the right of an authority to issue commands. Weber recognized that the power of ideas relies on them being 'carried' by influential groups and organizations in society (Kalberg, 2002). These 'carriers' of ideas have the power to define the situation and motivate subordinates to respond accordingly. Weber identified self-interest as a significant factor motivating actors' judgments as to whether to respond in a way that contributes to a legitimate order (Weber, 1968: 36). The ideas that most influence actors are those that align with their interests. The connection between ideas and interests, Weber suggests, is affected by 'elective affinities': the sets of social factors or mentalities which are related to, and tend to gravitate towards, one another (Gerth and Mills, 1946: 62). 'Elective affinities', Löwry argues, can prompt actors to enter into relationships of reciprocal attraction, influence and reinforcement (Löwry in McKinnon, 2010). Such relationships can serve to uphold the legitimacy claims of elite actors. This account, inspired by Berger and Zelditch's model and consistent with Weber's insights, is brought to life in the Northern Irish policing context.

The Policing Board has been central to developing and sustaining the human rights oversight process the PSNI proudly adhere to, but senior officials from the Policing Board have also played a role in reinforcing the PSNI's narrative of ethics and accountability. Most strikingly, Chairpersons of the Policing Board have been an important 'carrier' in the form of their forceful defences in national newspapers of the PSNI's commitment to human rights in the face of political critiques. In 2001, Policing Board Deputy Chairperson Denis Bradley penned a direct challenge in the *Irish Times* to Sinn Féin's refusal to support the PSNI because of the refusal of former RUC in the PSNI to swear the human rights oath (Bradley, 2001). Bradley, a Nationalist, acknowledged the importance of the oath but insisted great work was underway to ensure a cultural commitment to human rights in policing. In 2013, Policing Board Chairperson Anne Connolly wrote in the *Belfast Telegraph* in response to Unionists' criticism that human rights were preventing the PSNI from dealing with public disorder more assertively. Mirroring the PSNI's own narrative, Anne Connolly (2013) insisted the 'PSNI's approach to public order policing has been nationally and internationally commended ... Senior PSNI officers have said that the Human Rights Act provides officers with a clear framework for making difficult and challenging decisions'.

The motivation for these public remarks invites us to consider the Policing Board's own obligations to the PSNI. That is, the Policing Board has a statutory duty to oversee the police in such a way that promotes police effectiveness and efficiency, co-operation with the public and impartial policing (section 3 of the Police (Northern Ireland) Act 2000). Indeed, when the PSNI has made progress in areas like human rights reform, the Policing Board has acknowledged its corporate role to publicly commend and support such progress (Rea and Masefield, 2014). Particularly significant, though, is the Policing Board's investment of considerable resources and reputational esteem in devising and maintaining the flagship human rights monitoring scheme it introduced with the help of its first legal advisor, Keir Starmer; indeed, the Policing Board's own legitimating narrative is bound up with human rights too (Rea and Masefield, 2014: 275–300). International visitors to the Board have been invited to its public session, shown the

Annual Human Rights Reports and introduced to their legal advisor (Bushe, 2006). The Policing Board has bound its own institutional reputation to its ability to be an effective player in police oversight, especially in human rights compliance, which has made it receptive and willing to authorize the PSNI's positive human rights narrative, especially the theme of accountability.

Most influential in authorizing the PSNI's human rights claim-making, though, has been the 'authorization' of the Policing Board's human rights legal advisors.[5] As symbols of human rights legality and exacting oversight, the advisors serve as a vital source of external praise. They have identified areas of concern in their annual reports but have coupled this with consistent praise of the PSNI's commitment to human rights, their determined application of legal standards and openness to oversight. At high-profile events, the advisors have further reinforced the properties of ethics and legality, describing to politicians, community leaders and local NGOs how officers' references to rights are not just 'empty words trotted out for purposes of police oversight bodies' but had 'become so natural to them' (Kilpatrick, 2016). Similarly, former legal advisor Jane Gordon has publicly congratulated the PSNI for doing 'more than any other police force in the United Kingdom to achieve human rights compliance' and assisting 'in breaking down the traditional closed culture of policing' (Gordon quoted in Rea and Masefield, 2014: 291).

The Policing Board has its own divisive politics, which is something we will consider in Chapter 3. Yet in different and unexpected ways, disputes between political parties have, at times, served to reinforce the PSNI narrative. The moderate Nationalist political party, the SDLP, broadly supported the police reforms, endorsed the PSNI and took their seats on the Policing Board. Their political rival, the Republican Party Sinn Féin, refused to recognize the PSNI until 2007. During this period, the SDLP sought to convince its Nationalist base that its support for policing was justified. To the PSNI's benefit, it did so by highlighting how successful the police reforms had been. The SDLP's representative on the Policing Board, for instance, cited expert opinions on the 'excellent progress' the PSNI had made (Attwood, 2004). At the other end of the spectrum, Unionist politicians on the Policing

[5] Of which there have been four: Sir Keir Starmer (2003–2007); Jane Gordon (2003–2008); Alyson Kilpatrick (2008–2017); John Wadham (2019–).

Board have supported the PSNI in the face of Nationalist criticism. Notably, they have dismissed human rights critiques over the use of stop and search (*News Letter*, 2010), public order tactics (*Belfast Telegraph*, 2011a) and the retention of suspects' DNA samples (*BBC News*, 2009). Rejecting Sinn Féin's criticism of PSNI training, use of force and discipline, the Democratic Unionist Party (DUP) retorted: '[i]nstead of pushing these issues, they [Sinn Féin] should recognize that there's a wider consensus in support of what police are doing at a human rights level' (Jeffrey Donaldson quoted in *News Letter*, 2007).

The second high-level policing 'carrier' that has been significant in enabling the PSNI to mobilize a convincing human rights narrative has been the local print media. The distorted, sensationalist and often inaccurate reporting of human rights law by the print media in the UK is well-known (Mead, 2019). Generally, though, local newspapers have been willing to produce relatively balanced, if not positive, reporting on human rights and policing.[6] As demonstrated by Figure 2.1, there has been consistent coverage of human rights and the PSNI in the print media circulating in Northern Ireland. As Figure 2.2 further illustrates, the vast majority of this coverage is by the three main local newspapers (the *Irish News*, typically Nationalist in its readership, and the *Belfast Telegraph* and the *Belfast News Letter*, typically Unionist in its readership). Collectively, this coverage has included the reporting of international conferences hosted by the PSNI and Policing Board (*Irish News*, 2005; *Belfast Telegraph*, 2006). Furthermore, there has been coverage, particularly in the earlier years of reform, of the launch of the Policing Board's annual reports, citing the positive remarks of the Policing Board's legal advisors just mentioned, most notably the publication of the first annual report in 2005, which generated significant media attention, as indicated in Figure 2.1. Substantively, there has been sustained reporting on issues including the introduction of the Taser (*Irish News*, 2008b), the policing of public disorder (e.g. *Belfast Telegraph*,

[6] In some cases, the media has demonstrated how conditional its authorization is. For example, an opinion piece appeared in the *Irish News* (Emerson, 2014) strongly rejecting the PSNI's claim that it could not intervene in illegal protests or disclose material to Coroners inquests due to Article 2. The article dismissed this as 'officialdom justifying decisions that seem rather convenient to itself by marrying the Human Rights Act with conjectural fatalities'.

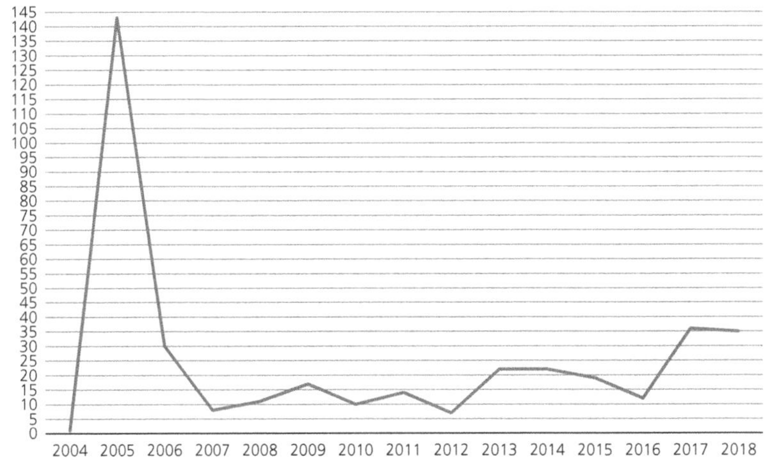

Figure 2.1 References to 'Human Rights' and the 'PSNI' in Newspapers Circulated in Northern Ireland

2013) and stop and search (e.g. *Belfast Telegraph*, 2010). The long-recognized symbiotic nature of the police–media relationship (Chibnall, 1975; Mawby, 2010) helps to explain why the PSNI is often given an opportunity to defend their actions or decisions in these articles, alongside the remarks of politicians and community leaders. Police sources, after all, fulfil the media's institutional imperatives of 'impartiality, balance and objectivity' of reporting and grounding stories 'in authoritative statements from accredited sources' (Hall et al., 1978).

Particularly significant seems the willingness of newspapers to publish the opinions of, and interviews with, chief officers. This has given the PSNI an important outlet for its claims of legal, ethical and accountable policing to reach wider audiences. Former Assistant Chief Constable Sheridan, once the most senior Catholic officer in the PSNI), wrote in local newspapers to reassure communities about police use of informers, expressed using human rights as accountability and legality discourse (Sheridan, 2006, 2007). And in recent years, it has become a rite of passage for new Chief Constables to give extended interviews with local journalists. The former Chief Constable Matt Baggott was quick to roll out the official narrative, describing how he was 'massively impressed that human rights in all decision making, in all training

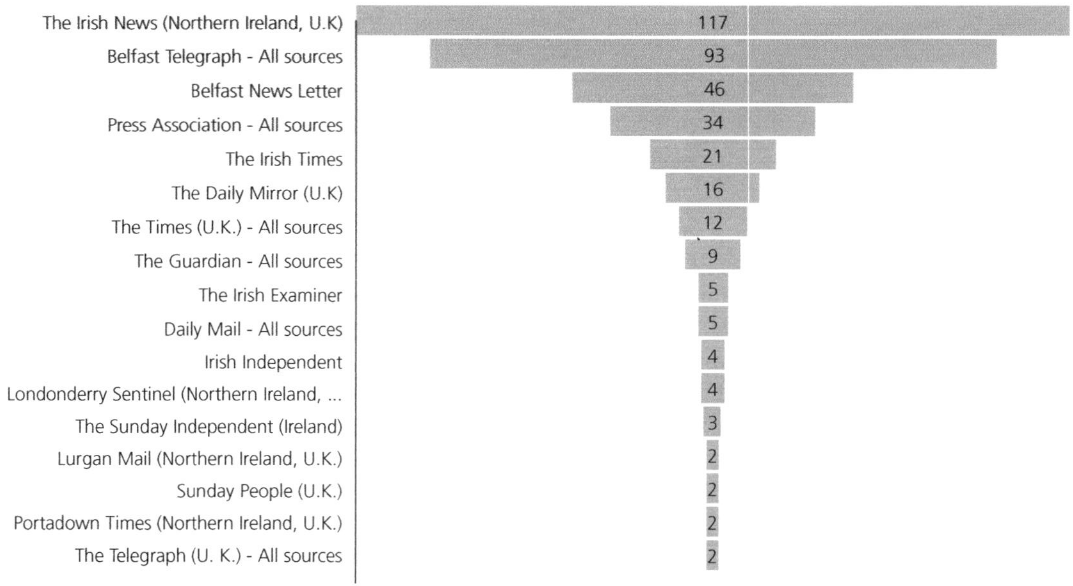

Figure 2.2 Newspaper Sources Mentioning 'Human Rights' and the 'PSNI'

is absolutely fundamental to what people do here. I am not just impressed. I am amazed' (quoted in *News Letter*, 2010). Likewise, former Chief Constable George Hamilton used his interview to reassure readers of his own ethical commitment: '[t]he human rights framework will be right at the centre of my leadership of this organization' (quoted in Kilpatrick, 2014).

Conclusion

The human rights reform of the PSNI which followed the Independent Commission has been the subject of rigorous oversight and much acclaim, with the Policing Board consistent in their praise since their monitoring began over a decade ago. But as this chapter has demonstrated, the oversight of, and compliance with, human rights law has not simply been confined to technical reports, closed meetings or court judgments. In fact, at a time in the UK when human rights are often the first thing to be politically side-lined in the face of terrorist attacks or fear of suspect communities (Lazarus and Goold, 2019), the PSNI's official narrative is defined by its loud, proud, public commitment to rights. Indeed, reflecting on the 'barren cultural soil' in which human rights are said to be planted in England, Loader concludes that the promotion of human rights is likely to depend on social movements and liberal professionals resistant to 'the seductive claims of strong rulers bearing the promise of security' (Loader, 2007: 41). The Northern Irish situation, however, illustrates the malleability of human rights to be adopted by powerful state actors like the police, and for human rights to be imbued with the police's visions and ideals, and put to work for their political ends.

The human rights properties of ethics, legality and accountability have been drawn out and deployed by chief officers to re-establish the police in Northern Ireland's post-conflict society. A good senior officer, like a good advocate, knows to choose a characterization that will resonate with their audience, even if the characterizations adopted will never achieve universal appeal; the aim is to adopt widely appealing principles that audiences will at least be tempted to embrace (Little, 1996: 394). The elevation of human rights beyond a mere regulatory scheme and into a sustained official narrative by chief officers is best explained by its allure as a legitimating language in what remains a fraught political environment. Elite policing audiences – the oversight commission, the Policing Board, the Police Ombudsman, the Northern Ireland Office – have been keen to see and hear progress on the human rights reforms which were the 'central proposition' of the Independent Commission's report. But even beyond the initial years of the reforms in the early to mid-2000s, human rights have continued to be adopted as a way of 'doing', but also *talking* about policing; a discursive device with which to regain the legitimacy to commentate on matters of crime control, social order and dealing with the past. By constantly invoking its commitment to these human rights properties of ethics, legality and accountability before powerful 'authorizers' or 'carriers', chief officers are striving to prove to others, as well as themselves, that the PSNI *is* the legitimate provider of order and security in Northern Ireland. Specifically, it is trying to convince those audiences who will listen that, notwithstanding the RUC's legacy, the PSNI, as an institution born out of the peace process, does possess a voice worthy of classifying, diagnosing and interpreting contemporary problems (Loader and Mulcahy, 2003: 226). These problems include the legacy of the conflict which the PSNI is forced to confront and, at times, provide imperfect answers to, as outlined in the Introduction.

How the core characterizations of human rights that animate the PSNI's official human rights vernacular – ethics, legality, accountability – resonate with internal police audiences is a central theme returned to throughout the book. As we continue to explore the various sites of police work and the regulatory formats, pressures and cultures particular to each, I will show how these properties are rejected, endorsed, applied or adapted in light of frontline officers' roles and the practical issues they face in their everyday work, as well their own personalities and life experiences. Before turning to these internal audiences, though, I want to explore more fully a powerful external audience identified in this chapter, the Policing Board. If, as a corporate body, the Policing Board was a significant 'authorizer' and 'carrier' of the PSNI's official human rights narrative, the situation becomes more complicated when we account for the divergent views of the political members that sit on the Policing Board. By doing so, we can arrive at a fuller understanding of how political audiences in receipt of the PSNI's official rights narrative have grappled with such claims. So too do the competing narratives that emerge serve to properly situate the book within the contemporary contestations over human rights in Northern Ireland. Let us now look more closely at this local politics of human rights and policing.

3

The Policing Board

Ethno-Political Tenors

> [T]he challenge for my organization, charged with the delivery of policing in a peace building society, is that at times, the universal nature of human rights is ignored, and the focus becomes solely on an interpretation of 'my' human rights or the human rights of 'my community'. (Former PSNI Chief Constable George Hamilton, 2014)

The Policing Board sits at the heart of the intersection between human rights law and politics. As a corporate body, the Policing Board has a statutory duty to monitor police compliance with the HRA. Yet, as a group of individuals, its members are drawn from the same political and civic spheres that remain divided over the role and relevance of human rights in the country's post-conflict society. In the absence of empirical research, important questions about this pioneering model of human rights oversight remain unanswered. Have the imperatives of police reform and public confidence in the police for the survival of the peace process insulated the Board from the political tribalism and institutional instability that beset the first decade of devolution in Northern Ireland? Alternatively, have the Board's political members' perceptions and interpretations of its statutory human rights duty been heavily mediated by ideas of Northern Ireland's past, the peace process and the necessity for police reform in the first place? In this chapter, I answer these questions to expose the tensions that animate political discussion of human rights and policing in Northern Ireland, and discern the beliefs, sentiments and fears that might explain this. I draw on video footage of thirty-nine monthly public sessions of the Policing Board (October 2011 to December 2016), as well as in-depth interviews with representatives of the

Policing Human Rights. Richard Martin, Oxford University Press. © Richard Martin 2021.
DOI: 10.1093/oso/9780198855125.003.0004

political parties who sit, or sat, on the Policing Board, to compare the attitudes and agendas of Unionist and Nationalist political members towards a human rights-based oversight of policing.

In this chapter, I argue that regardless of the Policing Board's statutory duty to monitor policing based on the standards of the HRA, for the political members on the Policing Board, human rights are a vessel harbouring deep sentiments and concerns at the heart of which are competing histories of the conflict, legacies of policing and understandings of Northern Ireland's imperfect peace. These narratives swirl around, and at times directly contradict, the official police voice, further demonstrating the elasticity of human rights to stretch to fit the visions of different actors. The examination of alternative official narratives by political parties in Northern Ireland is developed across three sections, inspired by the dimensions of the 'political life' of human rights set out in Chapter 1. These three dimensions are: the role historical context plays in structuring the ambit and style of human rights contestation involving social actors; human rights as an articulation of a much wider array of interests, fears and aspirations that find expression through rights narratives; and how human rights can be used by groups to actively construct claims with the hope of achieving legal gains in specific fields. Applying this analytical framework, I then return to the Policing Board to examine: (i) human rights and policing in its historical context; (ii) human rights as an articulation of interests, concerns and aspirations; and (iii) human rights as a resource to achieve strategic ends. I conclude by reflecting on what the divergent understandings of Unionist and Nationalist politicians mean for our understanding of human rights and the condition of policing in contemporary Northern Ireland. Let us first begin, though, by introducing the Policing Board as an oversight body with a distinctly discursive character.

The Policing Board

The Policing Board can be thought of as an arena where the demands of human rights law meet the contested understandings and perceptions of the relevance of human rights in local politics. The Policing Board replaced the Police Authority in 2001 as the public body bearing primary responsibility for holding the PSNI to account. It was carefully crafted by the ICP to take the lead role in human rights oversight. Beyond its extensive powers to appoint and dismiss chief officers (section 35 of the Police (Northern Ireland) Act 2000) and to set police targets and priorities (sections 25–26 of the Police (Northern Ireland) Act 2000), the Policing Board was bestowed with a statutory duty to 'monitor the performance of the police in complying with the HRA (section 3(3)(b)(ii) of the Police (Northern Ireland) Act 2000). Most relevant here is section 6(1) of the HRA which makes it unlawful for the PSNI, as a public authority, to act in a way that is incompatible with the ECHR. This statutory obligation is strengthened by further duties requiring the Board to issue a police Code of Ethics making 'officers aware of the rights and obligations arising out of the Convention rights' (section 52(1)(b) of the Police (Northern Ireland) Act 2000) and to produce an annual report that includes an evaluation of the performance of the police in complying with the HRA (section 57(1) of the Police (Northern Ireland) Act 2000).

The Policing Board is comprised of a representative group of individuals drawn from mainstream politics and wider civil society. Ten are 'political' members appointed from, and reflecting the composition of, the Northern Ireland Assembly; the other nine are 'independent' members, often drawn from academia, commerce and civil society, appointed by the Northern Ireland Minister of Justice. The Policing Board's membership being in its majority elected representatives was, as the ICP (1999: 30) noted, 'essential' to the Board's ability to 'command respect and credibility' thus creating 'a body whose views command respect and cannot be taken lightly by either government or police'. The Board has come to reflect the redistribution of power since the GFA, including the strong party-political expression of ethno-national identity (McGlynn et al., 2014). The mandatory power-sharing that stems from the GFA has contributed in part to a form of 'ethnic outbidding' which has witnessed moderate Unionist (Ulster Unionist Party; UUP) and Nationalist (Social Democratic and Labour Party; SDLP) parties lose significant electoral ground to their harder-line rivals – the Democratic Unionist Party (DUP) and Sein Féin (SF) respectively (McGlynn, Tonge and McAuley, 2014: 275). From 2002 to 2007 the Board continued to sit despite the suspension of the Northern Ireland Assembly and was strengthened when Sinn Féin took up their seats in 2007, having initially refused to formally endorse the PSNI.

With members having little, if any, training in human rights law, the Policing Board was swift to appoint independent counsel to act as human rights legal advisors. The advisors have proven key to fulfilling the statutory duty in two respects. First, in supplying the Board with the necessary legal advice to properly question, scrutinize and report upon the PSNI's rights compliance. This is enabled by the extensive access the PSNI has granted advisors to observe live policing operations (including public order command rooms) and police training (new recruits and annual refresher training), and review internal policies and procedures (see further Kilpatrick, 2018: 58). Second, in compiling and drafting the Board's annual human rights report. The reports rely on ECHR standards to assess fourteen core aspects of policing, based on the advisor's own assessment of the PSNI's policies and procedures, observations of live operations and training and meetings with senior officers (Starmer and Gordon, 2005). The annual reports are supplemented by the advisor's valuable thematic reports, which provide a legal analysis of important topical issues for policing, including domestic abuse, children and young people, LGBT people, the use of stop and search powers and racial hate crime. This monitoring framework has, rightly I think, been praised by Bayley (2008: 237) as 'a model of its kind ... It is the most complete on-going assessment of police adherence to human rights anywhere in the world'.

The Policing Board's Performance Committee takes specific responsibility for overseeing the PSNI's compliance with the HRA. In its private committee meetings, it receives and comments upon official reports, often from the Department of Justice, HMIC and CJINI, and probes senior officers from relevant departments on the finer details of police policies and practices. The breadth of the Committee's work in carrying out human rights oversight, and the multitude of agencies it receives evidence and reviews from, is captured in the published minutes of its monthly meetings. Since 2011, the Committee has discussed the following high profile and often politically sensitive matters concerning human rights: counter-terrorism strategy; stop and search; destruction of PSNI service weapons; the implementation of body-worn cameras; child sexual exploitation; redaction and disclosure of materials for coronial inquests; domestic abuse; covert intelligence and informants; and paramilitary attacks. In doing so, the Committee frequently relies on briefing papers, oral updates and advice from the Board's human rights legal advisor, who attends the vast majority of Committee meetings. The advisor also gives rolling updates on drafts of the Board's annual human rights report and the thematic reports, which Committee members comment and make suggestions on.

The monitoring duty requires members of the Policing Board to actively turn their attention to and engage with human rights alongside their political opponents. I want to explore, for the first time, just how connected perceptions and conceptions of this monitoring duty have been to the wider ethno-national disputes over human rights generally and policing specifically. Have the imperatives of police reform and the statutory duty served to temper political members' understandings and orientations towards human rights oversight of policing? Did political members consider human rights a helpful, even necessary, concept for making sense of, debating and regulating policing in light of their own vantage points? How was legal advice interpreted in light of the political sentiments and concerns that surround policing? In answering these questions for the first time, I do not seek to assess the internal workings of the Board itself but to explore the 'political life' of human rights that animates human rights monitoring – that is, to detect and examine the political narratives, attitudes and agendas that swirl around human rights monitoring.

The Board holds monthly public sessions, almost always in its Belfast office. A visitor to these meetings will arrive into a large, brightly lit room to find Policing Board members sitting behind tables arranged in a sweeping horseshoe. Political members sit in their Unionist-Nationalist blocs; independent members are dotted in between, perhaps signalling their own political leanings. Opposite them are the PSNI's chief officers, themselves seated in a single row, synchronized by their matching uniforms but led by their Chief Constable, who is positioned front and centre. Interested audiences, including representatives from the Police Federation and local journalists, sit in the public gallery, listening out for soundbites and stories to report. As the session gets under way, the cameras dotted around the room start rolling, the live YouTube broadcast begins, and the Twitter feed starts ticking. The sessions are an open forum for Policing Board members to express views on topical issues and ask questions of the PSNI's chief officers. Questions range from the routine (cross-border milk smuggling and road traffic accidents) to the extraordinary (police mishandling of conflict-related murders and allegations of police collusion). As the Chief Constable observed during one public session:

> On a monthly basis at this Board, more often than not, the majority of the questions we're asked by Board members are less focused on the civic policing issues that are contained within the policing plan than they are on the issues relating to our society in transition, those issues of legacy, public disorder and terrorism and so on. (Hamilton, 2015c)

In my research interviews, some participants openly acknowledged that public sessions were a 'showpiece' that were, at times, 'stage managed' by the political parties (Research Interview (2) 28 October 2016). The performative nature of these sessions made them a rich source of data, brimming with rights 'talk'. Within this discursive arena, political members gave expression to the narratives and identities they brought to bear in constructing rights claims and defences before key audiences, including their constituents, political adversaries, chief officers and the local media.

In the sections that follow, I adopt the three analytical way-points drawn from 'political life' that were first outlined in the Introduction to the book. First, the impact that the given historical context has in structuring the ambit and style of human rights contestation involving social actors. Second, human rights as an articulation of a much wider array of interests, fears and aspirations that find expression through rights 'talk'. Third, how human rights can be used by groups to actively construct claims with the hope of achieving legal gains in specific fields. Each of these offers a means of structuring the analysis and explores the key themes arising from the qualitative sources. By eliciting and examining the political narratives, frames and constructions that animate human rights oversight of policing, these sections reveal how competing histories of the conflict, legacies of policing and understandings of the country's imperfect peace animate attitudes and agendas towards the monitoring duty.

Human Rights in Context

The 'vernacularization' of rights is a helpful point of departure in making sense of how, and why, the historical context of human rights struggles in Northern Ireland during the conflict informed political members' orientations towards the monitoring duty. As suggested by Merry, the attractiveness of rights as a discursive 'frame', and thus its likelihood of being adopted and translated by social actors, depends on its compatibility with, and contribution to, the actors' prior experiences, traditions and practices (Merry, 2006a; Wahl, 2013). The 'translation' and deployment of rights discourse was central to the political heritage of Nationalism and Republicanism. The seeds of the conflict were sown in the institutional disregard for the civil and political rights of Catholics/ Nationalists by the Unionist ruling majority in the North since the partition of Ireland. As Gearty (2006: 157) observes, human rights are a rhetorical resource for the silenced and dispossessed to shout for attention and demand an end to suffering. It was in such circumstances, and to such effect, that Nationalists deployed rights frames in political speeches, campaigns and rallies to challenge the perceived abuses of the security forces during the conflict (Mageean and O'Brien, 1998). Rights discourse helped to internationalize the conflict, repackaging emergency legislation and counter-terrorist tactics as abuses of internationally recognized human rights standards (Hadden, 2012). SF in particular relied on international human rights covenants alongside their own rights translation, including the 'right to peace' and 'Irish national rights' (Mageean and O'Brien, 1998). 'Frames' are important in generating shared beliefs and defining appropriate strategies of action (Snow, 2004). For Republicans, the moral disequilibrium of rights advocacy by SF on the one hand and paramilitary violence by the IRA on the other contributed to a critical appraisal of the armed struggle, reflecting – as McEvoy (2000: 566–71) suggests – a deeper internalization of rights beyond instrumental 'framing'.

This legacy of rights-based argumentation lives on in the contemporary practices of SF and the SDLP. In research interviews and public sessions, members demonstrated what Hunt has described as human rights 'literacy' (Hunt, 2010: 607): they were quick to identify rights issues (e.g. stop and search, covert intelligence operations, collusion investigations) and articulate them using rights 'frames', and assertively challenge chief officers' own rights discourse at public sessions.[1] This 'literacy' empowered members to engage with the legalistic style of the Board's monitoring duty. As Evans and Evans suggest, the very

[1] See, e.g., Gerry O'Hara (SF) Public Session, November 2013; Gerry Kelly, (SF) Public Session, May 2014; Catriona Ruane (SF), Public Session, October 2015.

ability to identify issues as engaging human rights law is a significant step in fostering effective political oversight (Evans and Evans, 2011). At Performance Committee meetings, Nationalist members were described to me as consistently adopting rights-based argumentation, being quick to avail themselves of the Board's legal advisor (Research Interview, 12 July 2015; Research Interview (1), 1 November 2016). This helped to foster a 'culture of justification' whereby decision-makers, in this case senior police officers, became accustomed to having to justify their actions not in general or abstract terms, but according to established human rights law standards.[2]

Accountability bodies are an opportunity to contribute to a more positive, better-informed public discourse of human rights law. This is especially so for the Board given that it meets publicly and hosts annual events to launch its annual human rights report which involve local political parties, NGOs, community groups, criminal justice agencies and, of course, the PSNI. Notably, the SDLP and SF sought to use these events, as well as local media outlets, to promote, and in some instances to defend, the human rights oversight of policing conducted by the Board. Gerard O'Hara (SF) has publicly called for an 'educated process about what human rights are', criticizing the Police Federation's 'far from proper understanding of human rights' which he claimed had appeared in a newsletter to frontline officers (O'Hara, 2015). Similarly, Conall McDevitt (SDLP), writing when chair of the Performance Committee, penned a newspaper article criticizing those who 'misunderstood both the nature of rights and their application' and succumbed to 'sensationalist' misinformation and 'disingenuous and ill-informed commentary' (McDevitt, 2011). McDevitt offered a brief history of the ECHR and its salience given the conflict, reiterating a sense of Nationalists' guardianship, even ownership, of rights.

But so too can cultural traditions and political heritage serve to limit the resonance and appeal of particular 'frames' (Snow, 2004). For Unionist members, the political and cultural history of their community left them reluctant to adopt an explicitly rights-based appraisal of policing. A rights 'frame' failed to capture their established relationship with the Unionist state and the

[2] See, e.g., George Hamilton (PSNI), Public Session, March 2015; Will Kerr (PSNI), Public Session, June 2015.

RUC. After the formation of the Northern Irish state, Unionists dominated government, filled the ranks of the RUC and shaped social and cultural life; with power firmly in their hands, they rarely saw the need to protect the rights of the Nationalist minority (Cowell and Cowell, 1999: 5). Unionists had, in general, been loath to entertain Nationalists' civil rights claims, which they deemed anti-democratic attempts to gain 'special' (not equal) treatment (Cowell and Cowell, 1999). It was only in the face of evolving Anglo-Irish relations, international pressure and wariness of Nationalists' rights rhetoric that the UUP adopted rights discourse, albeit sporadically and instrumentally (Cowell and Cowell, 1999). Even then, in many Unionist circles, rights were considered a 'Nationalist agenda', being used to subvert the state and divert attention from paramilitary groups (Felner, 2012; Munce, 2014: 206–7). This was allied to a law-and-order rhetoric that portrayed rights protections as impeding the RUC's ability to counter a brutal IRA campaign: the rights abuses that did take place had been for the 'greater good' of the innocent majority (Cowell and Cowell, 1999; Bell, 2012: 224–5).

Unionists' aversion to rights discourse remains to this day. Two narratives expressed by Unionist members in interviews were particularly powerful in connecting the past with the present. First was a lingering *scepticism* towards the very idea of levelling claims against the state using rights terminology. As we shall see, this is linked to the legacy of policing, but we should not be quick to overlook this aversion to the very frame of 'human rights'. Unionist members readily admitted it was not a vernacular that they felt to be open to them to use or one for which they had an affinity.[3] This is not unique to policing; the DUP expressed a strong desire to avoid the term 'human rights' altogether during the Bill of Rights debate, suggesting that reference be made to 'guiding principles' or 'values' (Smith, McWilliams and Yarnell, 2014: 44). Second was a sustained *cynicism* of how rights claims are used by Republicans to unfairly discredit PSNI officers and sully the earnest efforts of the PSNI to investigate conflict-related

[3] A partial exception was one member who, particularly impressed by the legal advisors, grew more comfortable with the idea of human rights. They admitted, though, it had taken a while to come to terms with it: 'unless you are a lawyer, you don't understand the full ramifications ... the debates are complicated' (Research Interview, 27 April 2015).

deaths (as discussed further below). As Lundy and McGovern argue, Unionists, marked by a historical distrust of Republican politicians, have long been suspicious of 'an invariably insincere republican "articulacy"' when it came to equality, human rights and reconciliation' (Lundy and McGovern, 2008; Lawther, 2014: 79–82, 116). Echoing this feeling of distrust and sense of insincerity, a DUP interviewee insisted that as long as Republicans continue to 'abuse' human rights – that is, to use rights discourse to capture and mobilize the policing concerns of Republican communities – then:

> It sets a mood amongst unionists that it is a republican agenda and therefore, there is little or no support for the whole human rights regime ... You will not convince most, practically any, unionists, that the whole human rights thing is anything other than a republican agenda, and that's the difficulty about it all. (Research Interview (1), 28 October 2016)

This alludes to Unionists' wariness of being outmanoeuvred by the guile and tactics of SF 'agendas'. The promotion of equality and human rights protections, formal recognition of the Irish language and campaigns for truth recovery have been perceived by Unionists to be part of a Republican 'masterplan' to gradually dilute, and ultimately undermine, key core cultural and political aspects of 'Britishness' (McAuley, 2003, 2004; Lundy and McGovern, 2008; Lawther, 2014: 79–82; Turner, 2017: 125–6). The historically infused rights narratives contributed to Unionist members' aversion to human rights oversight. In the eyes of one independent member, there was an 'a priori resistance to human rights' amongst most Unionist members: 'As soon as the words human rights are mentioned a vibration enters the room. A Unionist member will put up their hand and ask why it needs to be mentioned like that. They oppose the framing of [the subject] in human rights terms' (Research Interview, 17 November 2016).

Several informants felt Unionists tended to lack the basic knowledge and understanding of human rights law which – coupled with a reluctance to improve it – deprived the Board of fuller debates as time was spent re-explaining basic principles. This was reflected in the interviews by one UUP member, who stated: 'I think it's a show, referring to the reference of any article ... it tries to imply a legalistic scenario there. If you're just referring to human rights legislation, why do you need to go beyond that?' (Research

Interview (2), 28 October 2016). In the eyes of Nationalists, on the rare occasions Unionists *did* experiment with rights 'talk', interviewees described a form of what Hornberger has labelled 'counterfeit rights' (Hornberger, 2011: 10–12) – bald claims to entitlements cloaked in rights language but detached from enforceable legal standards (e.g. 'right to march' or right of Ulster Scots to be a hate crime protected category) (Research Interview, 12 July 2015; Research Interview (1), 1 November 2016; Research Interview (2), 1 November 2016). Nationalists were quick to expose the relative rights illiteracy of their Unionists, as reflected in the words of an SDLP member:

> I think unionists misuse it because they don't understand some of it ... They talk sometimes of it in the wrong context, as if there's an absolute right to parade, to walk up the Queen's highway, they don't get it, they don't understand it to the same level. (Research Interview (2), 1 November 2016)

This 'inarticulacy' resonates with what Lundy and McGovern have previously described as an ethnic stereotype of the Unionist persona as 'plain-speaking' and 'practical-minded', belonging to the 'honest Ulsterman' (Lundy and McGovern, 2008; Lawther, 2014: 113–17). The difficulty Unionists had in translating 'plain-spoken' claims into recognized legal standards, or engaging with standards raised by Republicans, only reinforced Unionist members' suspicion and cynicism of human rights – a theme returned to in the final section of this chapter in the context of legacy issues.

Notwithstanding Unionists' reluctance to engage in, or to promote, explicitly rights-based discourse, it was apparent that members wanted, and managed, to actively engage in core aspects of the human rights monitoring. We can, I think, best make sense of this by examining two 'techniques of neutralisation' (Sykes and Matza, 1957; Maruna and Copes, 2005) that revealed themselves in interviews with DUP members. These 'motivational accounts' were effective precisely because they preserved Unionist narratives of cynicism and suspicion. The consequence was to enable DUP members to engage in the human rights oversight without, in their own minds, endorsing or promoting human rights per se. The first of these techniques is what Ashforth and Kreimer (1999: 421) refer to as 're-framing'. It involves transforming the meaning attached to tainted occupational tasks in order to render them palatable and edifying. Acutely aware of the DUP's aversion to human rights terminology, Board officials purposefully sought to reframe institutional aspects of the monitoring duty (Research Interview, 18 November 2016). The Human Rights and Professional Standards Committee was renamed the Performance Committee, and thematic reports were introduced (in addition to the annual reports). The thematic reports, despite being written by the legal advisor and based on human rights law standards, were designed to sound less rights- and more issues-focused. As an official explained in one interview, the aim was not to disguise human rights per se, but to 'try to take it out of green-[Nationalist-]tinged perspective', thus enabling Unionist members to engage more fully with their statutory monitoring duty (Research Interview, 18 November 2016).

The reframing away from an explicit reference to human rights appeared, in fact, to open up space for Unionist members to reconcile rights-based oversight with their political narratives. As captured in the words of one DUP member, the significance of the committee's name in shaping how Unionist members understood the substance (and appeal) of its oversight work should not be underestimated:

> [W]e had the choice of any of the chairmanships and that is literally why we took it – to try and take the politics out of it. Because if you look at the actual title of it, it looks at performance issues within policing. Performance issues within policing to me are day-to-day policing, how well were they actually performing their duties as a police officer – that wasn't being looked at. When I looked through the records of the committee, it was politics from start to finish and the actual issues of police performance weren't even being looked at ... So, our number one task was to turn the focus of the committee on to actual day-to-day policing. (Research Interview (1), 28 October 2016)

This reframing disconnects rights oversight from the 'politics' of policing (Republican members' concerns over stop and search, covert surveillance, conflict-related investigations) to 'ordinary' policing (crime figures, detection rates, police incivility) that Unionists felt most comfortable scrutinizing. The discursive 'turn of focus' enabled Unionists to invest in initiatives that, without explicitly referring to it, were in the spirit of human rights oversight, including: regular reviews of public complaints made against the PSNI, scrutiny of victim satisfaction regarding PSNI feedback on case progression, and thematic reports, including domestic abuse, which were emphatically endorsed by the DUP *and* SF (Research Interview, 12 July 2015; Research Interview (1), 28 October 2016; Research Interview (1), 1 November 2016).

The second technique of neutralization is a version of what Ashforth and Kreimer (1999) label 're-focusing'. Refocusing shifts attention to less tainted or problematic aspects of the frame and its associated practices (Ashforth and Kreiner, 1999: 423). A (partial) version of refocusing can be seen at work in DUP members' attitudes towards the Board's human rights legal advisor. Unionists were wary that the advisor's role advanced Republicanism's human rights 'agenda' and a legal discourse they were uncomfortable engaging with.[4] Yet Unionists readily admitted the advisor was an undeniably skilled lawyer who enabled the Board to conduct its oversight duty effectively. As one DUP member conceded, 'despite all our reservations', the advisor, had in fact, aided *their* community (Research Interview (1), 28 October 2016). First, the advisor's reports had, apparently, contradicted Nationalist complaints about discriminatory policing. DUP members recalled with pleasure how, when a positive report on PSNI practices emerged, 'it was very hard for SF or anyone from a Nationalist background to contradict the individual who they had set up to verify the evidence' (Research Interview (1), 28 October 2016). Second, according to the DUP, the advisor's evaluation of arrests made during contentious Loyalist protests in December 2012 exposed heavy-handed policing towards Loyalists (Research Interview, 13 May 2015). Members explained that this had some positive impact within Loyalist communities, yet the general narrative of cynicism proved difficult to shift. As summed up by one DUP member: 'there's an understanding in those communities "Hmm, it's not all bad" but generally in the unionist community,

[4] The Board's legal advisor, it should be noted, has stated publicly how she 'guards jealously' her independence from the political parties and has been eager to remind public audiences she is a consultant to, not an employee of, the Board. See A. Kilpatrick, Speech, Launch of Human Rights Annual Report, Crumlin Road Gaol, Belfast. 7 September 2016 (field notes, on file with author). The issue of the cost of the human rights came to a head in 2015 when the advisor's budget was classed as 'discretionary spending', and thus liable to be reduced. Alarmed by this, SF and the SDLP successfully pressured the NI Department of Justice and the Board's officials to ensure the funding remained uncut (see CAJ, 2015: 2–3).

it's still seen as a republican agenda' (Research Interview (1), 28 October 2016).

Talking through Human Rights

The second dimension of the social life of human rights captures the interactive nature of rights discourse. Far from discrete or insular, rights talk, as McCann (2014: 248) argues, is a practice 'inextricably interrelated with, contingent on and transformed by contact with other discursive resources and normative traditions'. As articulated in research interviews and expressed at the Board's public sessions, human rights discourse is intimately bound up with, and its salience tempered by, two contested issues: the legacy of policing during the conflict and the success of police reform for contemporary policing.

Policing the Conflict

The ICP explicitly avoided making 'judgments about the extent to which the RUC may or may not have been culpable in the past of inattention to human rights or abuse of human rights' (ICP, 1999: para 4.4, 18). Similarly, the Board settled on a forward-looking approach to rights oversight, focusing exclusively on contemporary policing (Rea and Masefield, 2014: 277). In the absence of a formally acknowledged or mutually agreeable account of the 'signal events' which shape communities' attitudes towards the RUC (and officers' towards communities) (Brewer and Magee, 1991), political parties have sought to reawaken and deploy communities' 'collective memories' to make sense of and inform their responses to transitional justice initiatives, including the reform of the RUC.[5] These memories draw upon and pull together individuals' experiences of policing, the state and the 'other community' to reify and privilege a version of the conflict as a 'usable past' (Lawther, 2014: 28–30; Hearty, 2017: 151–62, 226). It was collective memories of policing that human rights oversight

[5] Signal events are major controversies and scandals surrounding the RUC that 'are key markers in individuals' biographies and they become the fulcra around which experiences of and attitudes towards the security forces come to be understood, structured and articulated' (Mulcahy, 2006: 133).

stimulated and stirred, and which, in turn, informed political members' attitudes and behaviours towards it.

For Nationalists, the significance of the monitoring duty was anchored in historic accounts of abusive police practices – intimidation, brutality, detention – their communities felt themselves to have suffered. SF, in particular, have deployed emotive memories of rights abuses to motivate strategic engagement with police oversight, with the aim of ensuring such abuses never reoccur (Hearty, 2017: 151–61). Republicans' 'struggle' is in a sense embodied in SF's very appointees to the Board – for example, Gerry Kelly and Pat Sheehan, both former hunger strikers in the Maze Prison – and, as illustrated in the following section, the recounting of familiar 'signal events' of the conflict. As captured in the words of one SF member in their interview, the significance of the performance committee's oversight lies in the lessons of the past:

> [W]e're moving from a situation in my analysis where the RUC were a paramilitary police force, they saw themselves as defenders of the state, rather than defenders of the people and the law, so who guards the guards? There was nobody guarding the guards. They could do what they wanted, and they did ... If the PSNI don't understand the importance, if they go into defensive mode in relation to defending that, they're on the road to nowhere. (Research Interview, 12 July 2015)

SF's endorsement of, and keenness to fulfil, the monitoring duty marked an extension of what Hearty has described as Republicans' 'critical engagement' with the PSNI (Hearty, 2017: 155). This is characterized by a marked wariness of police powers, especially use of force, as well as the legal justifications for high-profile operations, including public order policing and legacy-related investigations. At public sessions, SF and SDLP members' questions spoke to collective memories of partisan policing, including concerns that the PSNI were wilfully ignoring the illegal activities of Loyalist paramilitaries (Delores Kelly (SDLP), Public Session, 4 July 2014), neglecting the legal safeguards in handling of police informants (Delores Kelly (SDLP), Public Session, 6 June 2014; Gerry Kelly (SF), Public Session, June 2015; Gerry Kelly (SF), Public Session, December 2014) and failing to adequately protect Nationalist communities from unlawful parades (Gerry Kelly (SF), Public Session, 29 May 2014).

For Unionists, human rights monitoring was a dimension of police reforms that sat uneasily with their strong emotional, even personal, connection with the RUC. As one DUP member stated firmly when I asked about the origins of the Board's monitoring duty: 'There's a couple of things I think we have to deal with before you bring it right up to date with what the Performance Committee is doing. The context is important' (Research Interview, 13 May 2015). Drawing attention to rights violations by the RUC had long been considered an act of betrayal towards the Unionists' own community – both real and 'imagined' communities (Lundy and McGovern, 2008; Lawther, 2014: 28–32). In grappling with the need for the monitoring duty, Unionist members drew on their own memories that resolutely guarded against the implicit, and in their view misguided, critique that the RUC was violating, rather than protecting, rights (Research Interview, 13 May 2015; Research Interview (2), 28 October 2016). This speaks directly to Lawther's (2014: 30; 2017) account of the 'living quality' of memory to defend the RUC as a noble force deserving of loyalty from the Unionist community from which its members mostly came. This 'living' memory was acted out at public sessions: Ross Hussey (UUP), a former RUC officer, and Jonathan Craig (DUP), both of whom had family members who served in the RUC, mobilized their emotive experiences of being threatened and attacked by Republican paramilitaries to defend the RUC's legacy in the face of critiques of the RUC by SF (Public Session, 25 November 2014).

Two storylines within unionism's collective memory were especially significant in downplaying their opponents' claim that rights reforms were a direct response to the RUC's abuses of power. The first, a version of Cohen's 'implicatory denial',[6] was that the moral significance of police practices and the emergency law must be weighed up against the paramilitary threat of the time. This is well-captured in the emotive words of one Unionist member who described rights protections as perfectly fine in 'normal society' but less so in the challenging context of the conflict:

I have to accept that there were things done wrong in the past, but I think history has to accept the RUC were operating under a terrorist threat,

[6] This form of denial does not assert that the event did not happen but seeks instead to 'negotiate or impose a different construction of the event from what might appear to be the case' (S. Cohen, 1993: 110). On states of denial within Unionist and loyalist communities when it comes to dealing with the past more generally see the excellent account by Lawther (2014: 32–8).

> which no other country in Europe had to face. Police officers were being shot dead in their own homes, in their places of worship and being blown to bits at the side of the road, so therefore policing had to reflect the danger of the job they were undertaking ... the Emergency Provisions were not human rights friendly, but from the basic human right of the right to life, they [RUC] had to be to deal with the circumstances they were faced with. (Research Interview (2), 28 October 2016)

It is the indeterminacy of rights, Tushnet (1984) argues, which enables this kind of 'balancing' technique. Actors can acknowledge the existence of rights, yet define them in such a way – or place in question the social surrounding – to adjust the weight of the right, thus denying its normative thrust, if not legal power (Tushnet, 1984: 1371–5). The balancing of the rights of suspects being properly outweighed by the 'greater good' (the right to life) facilitated a Unionist narrative that overlooks the role that rights abuses by security forces played in fuelling the conflict (Dickson, 2000; Lawther, 2014).

The second was a form of 'interpretive denial', which refers to claims that 'what happened is not what you think it is, not what it looks like, not what you call it' (Cohen, 2001: 7). This dismissed as 'manufactured' and 'artificial' the idea that Nationalist communities' lack of support for, and under-representation in, the RUC could be traced back to its rights abuses or discriminatory practices (Research Interview, 13 May 2015; Research Interview (1), 28 October 2016; Research Interview (2), 28 October 2016). Reviving the trope of 'behind closed doors' support for the RUC within Nationalist communities, Unionist members continued to insist Republican intimidation of Nationalists was the ultimate reason why Nationalist communities were reluctant to support or join as officers in the RUC (Hillyard and Tomlinson, 2000: 406; Mulcahy and Ellison, 2001). Consequently, the PSNI's ability to appeal to Catholic officers was not, according to Unionists, by virtue of human rights reforms or improved accountability, but Republican ceasefires and the end of SF's cynical refusal to endorse the PSNI (Research Interview, 13 May 2015). Rather than further legitimizing 'their' police force, human rights were still perceived by Unionist members as an integral part of what DUP members continued to describe as a 'political' programme of reform that betrayed the sacrifice and service to the RUC (Research Interview (1), 28 October 2016; Research Interview (2), 28 October 2016), two themes that remain core to some Unionist identities (Lawther,

2014: 131–5, 144–53). The 50:50 recruitment quota – designed to increase the proportion of Nationalist police officers – was, in particular, decried at the time as violating the rights of Unionist applicants.[7] Over fifteen years later, 60 per cent of DUP members still considered the reforms introduced following the ICP's report to have 'gone too far', while over 80 per cent still opposed the 50:50 recruitment strategy (Gomez and Tonge, 2016: 70).

The significance of the collective memories to which Unionist members clung lies in the 'blind spots' (Lawther, 2014: 164) they reinforced when it came to rights-based oversight. In interviews, members struggled to grasp, or were at least unwilling to acknowledge, the rights abuses during the conflict that underscored the need for a firm commitment to such oversight: one member suggested the landmark human rights reforms to policing were a mere concession needed to win over Republican support for policing (Research Interview (1), 28 October 2016), another suspected they were simply an extension of the rights-based approach arising from the introduction of the HRA (Research Interview, 27 April 2015), while one stated, bluntly, that only the ICP could possibly know why rights were so central to reforms (Research Interview, 13 May 2015). A 'human rights approach' to policing was not seen, therefore, as being addressed towards, or for the obvious benefit of, the Unionist community. Unionist members stopped short of dismissing the merit of the rights monitoring – it was acknowledged as encouraging 'professional policing' and could act as a 'health check' on police performance – but remained wary of suggesting it was a feature of post-conflict policing that was beyond critical appraisal. This leads us to the narratives of contemporary policing.

The power of human rights references to re-awaken these divergent legacies, and make profound disagreements audible, is captured in the extract below from the Board's public session in May 2014 in which the then Chief Constable was answering questions about the police response to protests in Belfast and

[7] See, e.g., Lady Silvia Hermon, then a member of the UUP: 'Since religious liberty and freedom from all forms of discrimination are basic essential human rights, it is totally repugnant that trainees will be selected on the basis of their religion' (HC Deb vol. 372 col. 489). The compatibility of the 50:50 recruitment scheme with the ECHR was challenged (unsuccessfully) in *Re Parsons* [2003] NICA 20. See also Harvey (2012).

PSNI commanders' decision-making. The strong assertion of the human rights credentials of the PSNI by the then Chief Constable became an emotive trigger, pivoting the discussion away from public order policing to the human rights record of the RUC and security services during the conflict. This, in turn, spiralled into competing claims of victimhood connected with paramilitary violence, with the SDLP (and DUP) condemning the violence of Republican paramilitaries inflicted on Nationalist communities.

MATT BAGGOTT [PSNI]: Across this table there's about 200 years of operational experience and a firm adherence to human rights – which you're welcome to challenge. But actually our professional opinion collectively is that actually we had to make judgments based on protection of life and safety and secondly on the advice of Queen's Counsel.

...

CATRIONA RUANE [SF]: I thought your tone was very dismissive in your answers ... I think your comment about 200 years of operational discretion and experience was quite arrogant. And you also used human rights during those 200 years and you asked us to cite them, I would respectfully suggest you listen to members of our Policing Board instead of putting them down. I would also suggest you read the countless human rights reports, not within Ireland or Britain, but internationally, during those 200 years you talked about.

...

JONATHON CRAIG [DUP]: Chief, sometimes we never fully escape the past in Northern Ireland. I started this week with the Cummins family and the murder carried out by the Republicans to that family. It is good to see that further inquiries may well bring justice for that family. I was reminded last night and this morning that violence by Republicans was not only visited on the Unionist community but also the Republican community.

...

DELORES KELLY [SDLP]: Can I just correct one point that Jonathan said. He said how he's reminded about how violence was visited on the Republican community. I have to say that the Republican movement visited violence on the Catholic Nationalist community and I believe more Catholics were murdered by the Provisional IRA than all of the other groups including state forces and Loyalist paramilitaries together. So far from being the defenders of the Catholic Nationalist community, they actually killed many of their own community. (Public Session, 29 May 2014)

In making sense of contestations like this it is important to acknowledge how discursive practices can reflect, and reproduce, understandings and experiences (Payne, 2008; Curtis, 2014). The speakers involved in these raw exchanges lived through the conflict; they were part of the very legacies that were re-affirmed and renegotiated in public sessions. Political members on both sides of the divide were heavily involved in organizations that were at war during the conflict. Sinn Féin's policing spokesman and Policing Board member, Gerry Kelly, for example, is a former member of the Provisional IRA who escaped from the Maze Prison in 1983. His then party colleague on the Policing Board, Catriona Ruane, was involved in campaigns during the conflict, including the 'Colombia Three', which argued for the return of three Irishmen who would later be convicted in their absence of training FARC insurgents in Colombia. Sitting just a few seats away at Board meetings was Ross Hussey (UUP), a retired RUC officer, and Jonathon Craig (DUP) , who has described being targeted by Republican paramilitaries during the conflict (Public Session, November 2014). These same subjectivities enveloped members' assessments of contemporary policing, a topic to which we now turn.

Contemporary Policing

Lurking within political members' orientations towards the monitoring duty were their competing assessments of the success of the police reform process and the condition of policing today. Such assessments were informed not only by collective memories but also by present-day experiences of the communities they represented. Brodeur's distinction between 'high' and 'low' policing, alluded to earlier, is especially helpful in grasping the divergent accounts of Unionist and Nationalist members. The object of 'high' policing is the protection of a specific political regime, including its state apparatus and institutions (Brodeur, 2010: 227). This form of 'political' policing often makes use of covert strategies to surveil, monitor and disrupt groups deemed by specialist police units to be threats to the state and its institutions (Brodeur, 1983: 514). 'Low' policing refers, instead, to routine street policing by local officers. Directed against persons of 'low status' with the goal of maintaining order and preventing crime, it relies principally on police visibility alone, with recourse to the use of force if required 'in the narrow context of particular incidents' (Brodeur, 2010: 182).

The police reforms were an endeavour to move away from the 'high' policing role the RUC had played. Strategies to thwart the residual paramilitary threat – covert surveillance, public order policing, counter-terrorism – were to be carefully regulated and monitored (ICP, 1999: paras 4.8, 6.38, 6.43–45; chapter 9). Similarly, a community-orientated approach to 'low' policing was designed to improve confidence in frontline policing, especially within Nationalist communities (ICP 1999: chapter 7; Topping, 2015). Official reports do attest to the PSNI's sustained engagement with, and adherence to, the vast majority of the Board's recommendations (Office of the Oversight Commissioner, 2007: 21–30; NIPB, 2015a), and survey data reveals high levels of public confidence in police effectiveness and fairness.[8] Yet the significance of 'high' policing, and the importance of the Board's monitoring of it, remained a central fault line in the political narratives of contemporary policing. Nationalist members expressed a sense that policing had improved, but a wariness of policing tactics remained, especially the use of force and counter-terrorism powers of arrest and detention. For Nationalist members, though, 'high' policing concerns arise from the continuity in composition of the PSNI from the RUC, and a fear of the reforms 'backsliding' (Research Interview, 12 July 2015; Research Interview (1), 1 November 2016).

While a significant number of officers availed themselves of the severance package offered as part of the police reforms,[9] many transferred to the PSNI. This 'institutional crossover' was particularly concentrated at senior command level, as well as 'high' policing units like covert intelligence, serious crime and public order policing (Hearty, 2017: 218–19). SDLP and SF members voiced an acute wariness of the continued influence of 'old boys' from the RUC operating as a 'dark force' within the PSNI, who 'lurked in the background' and sought to protect the RUC's role

[8] At aggregate levels, trust in the PSNI is remarkably high and differs little between Protestants and Catholics, see Bradford et al., (2019).

[9] Within fifteen months of the voluntary severance scheme beginning, a total of 1,274 officers had left the PSNI, costing a total of 48.3 million pounds (PSNI, 2002: 3, 15).

in, and style of, 'high' policing during the conflict.[10] Articulating the Republican bifurcation of 'old' and 'new' PSNI officers, a SF representative described how:

There are layers of the PSNI that don't want the truth to come out and I think they're at every level, including the most senior level, and I think there's layers of the PSNI that really want change and I think there's a battle going on there. (Research Interview, 12 July 2015)

Human rights oversight was considered crucial to confronting these 'dark forces'. The Performance Committee, in particular, was described as an opportunity to ask questions of senior officers responsible for sensitive areas such as covert surveillance and use of counter-terrorism powers. Members insisted the work of the human rights legal advisor was 'fundamental' in allowing them to accept, and if necessary challenge, the official accounts provided by senior officers (Research Interview (2), 1 November 2016, Research Interview, 12 July 2015). The advisor's professional standing, access to the PSNI and quality of work garnered a degree of respect amongst members:

I find that there are very few on the Board who don't respect her advice. Now, they respect her advice, they might try and circumvent actions from the advice, but generally I find there's quite a collegiate atmosphere in relation to her advice. (Research Interview, 12 July 2015)

Nationalist members did, however, allude to Unionist ploys that they suspected were at work behind the scenes of the Committee, either to prevent legal advice being requested in the first place or, when provided, to prevent it from being implemented in full. The existence of these ploys, and the effects they may or may not have had, is contested. What this does reveal, though, is Nationalists' continued distrust of unionists' commitment to human rights, particularly on issues of 'high' policing, and their sense that they need to be 'on guard' against 'rollback' of the human rights agenda (see also Hearty, 2017: chapter 8).

Conversely, for Unionist members, the 'institutional crossover' and sustained Protestant majority in the PSNI's composition

[10] Questions were on topics including allegations that firearms seized by the RUC during the conflict had been returned to communities (Public Session, 5 June 2015) and the refusal of former RUC officers to co-operate with conflict-related investigations (Public Session, 8 November 2014).

enabled them to continue to emotionally invest in, and reinforce their identity through, the PSNI. Dismissing the ICP's report as a 'false dawn' for policing, one DUP member insisted 'the reality is the individuals in the force never changed' (Research Interview, 17 November 2016). The transfer of loyalty from the RUC to the PSNI was apparent in public sessions, with Unionists eager to praise the work of the police and publicly defending the PSNI in the face of Nationalist members' criticism of its work or its officers.[11] A firm belief in the integrity of the PSNI's officers strengthened Unionist members' sense that the Board had little to concern itself with regarding rights oversight. The general sentiment is captured well by one UUP representative:

> I think that it's accepted that human rights are just part of everyday policing so there is no need for this continual prodding at it – it's there, it's accepted, it's ingrained into the police service … So I think that it's no longer an issue, that would be my view – it's no longer an issue. (Research Interview (2), 28 October 2016)

This was allied to a broader narrative of crime, violence and policing today. With the transfer of policing and justice powers and, at that time, a functional devolved assembly, the country was, so the narrative went, returning to a state of normality. Policing was *not*, one member insisted, 'the great battleground it once was, policing is now just mundane' (Research Interview, 27 April 2015; Research Interview (2), 28 October 2016). Issues deemed to be about human rights – composition of the police, use of force tactics, stop and search, counter-terrorism tactics – had finally been addressed. Northern Ireland was now a place where police could devote their time to 'real' crime relating to local disorder – burglary, drug dealing, domestic abuse (see also Hearty, 2015, 2018; Halliday and Ferguson, 2016). This narrative not only downplays the obvious cleavages of the conflict that remain – paramilitary punishment attacks, ongoing investigations into collusion between security forces and Loyalist paramilitaries, unresolved conflict-related deaths (see, e.g., Cory, 2004; de Silva, 2012), it

[11] e.g. Public Session, 4 July 2014; Conall McDevitt (SDLP) and Jonathan Craig (DUP), Public Session, 8 June 2012; Catriona Ruane (SF) and Jonathan Craig (DUP), Public Session, 5 October 2012. As one member stated frankly: 'I'm still biased because I'm still very proud of my association with the police, so I would therefore always be very pro-police' (Research Interview (2), 28 October 2016).

is also evidence of the disconnect between political unionism and Loyalist communities, with the latter expressing growing concern over the 'high' policing by the PSNI of contentious Loyalist parades and protests (Research Interview, 27 April 2015).

When it came to issues of 'low' policing, political members described how they could generally work constructively, even if they had divergent views on the extent to which this was *really* about human rights per se. As one Unionist member noted when discussing 'real' (as distinct from 'high') policing:

> We as politicians obviously have differing views on certain issues but we also agree on quite a lot as well, and *real policing* we will agree on, the necessity to have a police service and police service on the ground, that's eighty per cent of your discussions. (Research Interview (2), 28 October 2016; emphasis added)

What distinguished Unionists' framing was, rather, the *extent* to which oversight ought to be couched in human rights terms and thus how exacting the scrutiny needed to be, including the work of the legal advisor. Unionist members expressed concern that too great a focus on rights could inhibit officers' effectiveness in controlling crime. In the words of one DUP member, an over-emphasis on rights had led to 'absurd, perverse nonsense' (Research Interview (1), 28 October 2016) where criminals' rights were protected over those of victims and police officers. Sharing this concern, a fellow member stated: 'I think there has to be a measured approach to human rights in policing, because if the scrutiny on policing is suffocating it, well then it is actually counterproductive' (Research Interview, 13 May 2015).

Mobilizing Human Rights

Turning now to the third and final dimension of the social life of human rights, this section seeks to explore in greater detail how political members sought to mobilize (or to stall) human rights in pursuit of their political goals. It explores how Article 2 of the ECHR has been used as a legal standard by SF to critique the PSNI's investigation of conflict-related deaths and the counter-narratives adopted by Unionist members. How investigations into these killings are prioritized, by whom and for what purposes raises fundamental issues of victimhood, blameworthiness, trust and reconciliation that transitional societies must confront (Bell, 2002). In total, 3,644 people were killed as a consequence of the conflict. Specific counts vary, but the overall picture is clear: most deaths were caused by Republican paramilitaries (2,167), followed by Loyalist paramilitaries (1,115) and security forces (362) (McKittrick and McVea, 2012). To support the RUC, the British Army deployed over 300,000 soldiers to Northern Ireland between 1969 and 2007 as part of Operation Banner. The conflict claimed the lives of 1,441 serving officers, 722 of whom were killed in paramilitary attacks. British soldiers were responsible for the deaths of around 300 people during the conflict, over half of whom were civilians (House of Commons Defence Committee, 2017).

In the absence of an overarching approach to dealing with the conflict's legacy, the search for truth and justice has often come down to the determined efforts of families, NGOs, lawyers and politicians to seek answers through the criminal justice system (Lundy and McGovern, 2008). For the relatives of those killed by the security forces, there have been sustained legal campaigns to ensure that the UK fulfils its procedural obligation under Article 2 of the ECHR – that is, the positive duty to conduct full and effective investigations into the circumstances of controversial deaths caused directly or indirectly by state actors.[12] Between 2000 and 2003, relatives of victims successfully challenged the UK's compliance with the procedural obligation under Article 2 before the ECtHR, known collectively as the *McKerr* cases.[13] A striking feature of the Board's public sessions is how Article 2 has been explicitly mobilized and deployed by SF in over a quarter of the thirty-nine sessions (2011–2016) to critique the PSNI's handling of legacy-related issues. The Article 2 discourse has been

[12] *McCann and Others v UK* (App no 18984/91) ECHR 31 (27 September 1995); *Kaya v. Turkey* (App no 22535/93) ECHR 129 (28 March 2000). See, especially, Ní Aoláin (2002); Anthony and Mageean (2007).

[13] *Jordan v UK* (App no 24746/94) ECHR 327 (4 May 2001); *Kelly and Others v UK* (App no 30054/96) ECHR 29 (4 May 2001); *McKerr v UK* (App no 28883/95) ECHR 329 (4 August 2001); *Shanaghan v UK* (App no 37715/97) ECHR 330 (4 May 2001); *McShane v UK* (App no 43290/98) ECHR 465 (28 May 2002) and *Finucane v UK* (App no 29178/95) 37 EHRR 29 (1 October 2003). See, generally, Bell and Keenan (2005). The ECtHR identified four requirements that an Article 2 compliant investigation must satisfy: independence from those implicated in the events; effective in the sense of being capable of bringing those responsible to justice; a prompt response by the investigating authorities; a sufficient element of public scrutiny of the investigation or its results (*Jordan* at [106–109]).

directed at two key elements of policing relating to the legacy of the conflict.

The first is the PSNI's reluctance to disclose sensitive material to coronial inquests and the Police Ombudsman's investigations into allegations of historical misconduct by RUC officers.[14] SF accused the PSNI of failing to adhere to their Article 2 obligation to ensure effective investigations into deaths by disclosing relevant material to coronial inquests. Making reference to the legal agreement reached between the UK and the Committee of Ministers following the *McKerr* group of cases, SF argued the law was on their side:

> The families have walked a long road to Europe and back. *In fact, I was with them on that road to Europe and here in Ireland when the results came through that the European Court had ruled against the British government.* I hope you agree with me that the families deserve justice and truth and they deserve that we operate within the legal framework ... *I am asking you now to adhere to the law in relation to the European Court of Human Rights ruling and all information should be disclosed to the families* ... A very positive signal would be for you to release all the documents in relation to this to the families. When will you release all the documents to the families? (Catriona Ruane (SF), Public Session, 6 April 2012 (emphasis added)

This style of argumentation speaks to Risse and Sikkink's (1999: 11–14) notion of 'moral consciousness-raising' through which human rights gain traction in domestic struggles. Using emotions and evocative symbols to shame and isolate the state, moralistic rights discourse can be an important stage in persuading actors to confront, and justify, their actions. Connecting strongly with SF's distrust of the 'dark forces' within the PSNI and 'collective memories' of distrust towards the RUC, SF members publicly accused the PSNI of being deliberately 'obstructive' (Catriona Ruane (SF), Public Session, 6 April 2012) and of 'stalling' (Gerry O'Hara (SF), Public Session, 11 November 2013) families' determined efforts to achieve justice for their loved ones killed by the security forces.

The second target of SF's Article 2 discourse was the lack of independence and accountability of the investigatory unit the PSNI established to review conflict-related deaths. The Historical

[14] This issue was the subject of an inspection by the Criminal Justice Inspectorate of Northern Ireland, see CJINI (2016).

Enquiries Team (HET) was established by the PSNI in 2005 (Lundy, 2009; cf. Lawther, 2014: 149–53). It had a team of one hundred investigators and a budget of over £30 million to review and investigate over 3,000 unsolved murders from the period 1969–1998 (House of Commons Defence Committee, 2017). Its aim was to provide families of victims with case reports and re-examine any evidential opportunities for future prosecutions. The HET was heavily criticized by Patricia Lundy's (2009, 2011) influential research exposing its lack of accountability, independence and equal treatment of cases that raised serious concerns over the HET's compliance with Article 2 procedural standards. The review conducted by HMIC similarly found that the HET treated cases with state involvement differently and 'less rigorously' than cases where there was no state involvement, and that the involvement of former RUC and PSNI officers in state involvement cases could 'easily ... [give] rise to the view that the process lacks independence' (HMIC, 2013: 100–1). In 2014, the HET was replaced by the Legacy Investigation Branch (LIB), a smaller unit of seventy officers and staff embedded more closely within the PSNI, tasked with reviewing the remaining caseload (1130 incidents involving 1421 deaths) and resourced with an annual budget of £4.5 million (NIPB, 2019: 8).

SF consistently cited the procedural requirement under Article 2 – requiring practical independence of those investigating the state's involvement in killings – to critique the HET, in particular its reliance on former RUC officers as investigators (Gerry Kelly (SF), Public Session, 6 October 2013; Public Session, 6 December 2014). Republicans were also forthright in using their involvement with victims' groups and rights-based advocacy during the conflict to re-assert themselves as custodians of rights discourse. This was demonstrated clearly in one exchange between the PSNI and two Sinn Fein Board members during a public session of the Board, which concerned what amounted to an ineffective state investigation into deaths during the conflict for the purposes of Article 2 of the ECHR:

Chief Constable George Hamilton: I think it's really important we don't re-write history. The Article 2 compliant inquests were decisions taken by the European Court of Human Rights in relatively recent history ... It hasn't been the case that 35 and 30 years ago the police were being obstructive, it's that there was a much more superficial approach taken within the coronial system until there was a challenge which was upheld in the European Court.

Gerry Kelly (SF): With respect, if you ask the families who were not able to get the information over that long period of time, they will not be saying to you it was because of the ECHR, because it wasn't there, there was a duty before the ECHR to hand over information that was pertinent to love ones being killed.

Catriona Ruane (SF): I am disappointed in relation to the comments that you made on the shoot to kill and ECHR. I was at Strasbourg in 2000 with the families, 12 judges ruled against the British government, we had Stalker and we had Stevens, we need to be careful with the language, with the greatest of respect. (Policing Board, Public Meeting, February 2016)

It was these kinds of exchanges with the PSNI and Unionist political members that helped to instill a sense of Republican guardianship over rights – it was part of *their* struggle, it was *their* political parties that had pushed for human rights to be written into the peace agreements and it was *their* communities that had suffered at the hands of the state. This reinforces Bartholomew and Hunt's (1990) claim that rights-based argumentation is not a neutral device, capable of being lifted and deployed by anyone. Unionist politicians were not in Strasbourg supporting challenges concerning the failure to investigate deaths at the hands of security forces; it was neither their case, their cause nor their forum for doing battle.

SF's mobilization of Article 2 was met with general disdain from Unionist members, who were reluctant to acknowledge, or engage with, the issue in public sessions. The common response was to dismiss SF's Article 2 critique outright as nothing more than a 'witch-hunt' against the RUC officers who brought skill and expertise to the investigation of legacy cases (Jonathan Craig (DUP), Public Session, 13 January 2012; Ian McCrea (DUP), Public Session, 7 December 2012). Unionism, generally, has been wary that an exclusive focus on state accountability – achieved through inquests, inquiries and police investigations – is resulting in disbalance, in so far as it distracts from the death and destruction caused by paramilitary groups. The concern is that state investigations of the security services risks elevating paramilitaries killed by state actors to a 'moral equivalence' with the thousands of innocent victims and hundreds of security personnel that were killed by the IRA (Simpson, 2013; Lawther, 2014). This speaks to a Unionist 'myth of blamelessness' (Lawther, 2014: 132), characterized by a denial of responsibility for the role of the security forces in the emergence and continuance of the conflict and a sense that the sacrifice of RUC officers is being betrayed. As one DUP interviewee stated: 'For most unionists, it's [investigations into the past are] not that big a deal because, let's face it, we were not the ones generally who were going out and murdering people and causing mayhem ... they were lawful, therefore they have nothing to worry about'.

But unionism's reluctance to adopt their own human rights-based discourse has left them poorly equipped to articulate their own communities' experiences and understandings of conflict-related deaths in this political arena. A Unionist counter-narrative might begin by departing from an established conception of the duty to respect human rights as applying exclusively to state actors. Discursively, the death and injuries caused by paramilitaries could be recast as grievous violations of the interests that the likes of Articles 2 and 3 of the ECHR seek to protect. A version of this rights-based argument against non-state actors has been made by leading human rights scholar and former independent member of the Policing Board Brice Dickson, who submits, on normative grounds, that human rights ought to raise awareness of, and promote accountability for, abuses of power by paramilitary groups as well as state actors (see Dickson and Osborne, 2007:163). Doing so would challenge Republicans' abstract admission of collective wrongdoing sustained by an inward-looking narrative that serves to downplay Republican paramilitary acts, as well as intra-community violence perpetrated by militant Republicans (Hopkins, 2015; Hearty, 2017: 150–1).

As Ignatieff has argued, if human rights are to form a basis for political deliberation, it requires a consensus surrounding their value as a framework, coupled with a willingness to listen respectfully to oppositional claims (Ignatieff, 2001: 10). This entails, Fredman (2013) suggests, 'bounded deliberation', whereby actors justify their position using value-based reasoning while remaining open to persuasion; political opponents must strive to reconcile competing visions and be prepared to make painful compromises along the way. In the political rough-and-tumble of the public sessions, evaluative consensus and value-based reasoning were elusive. This excerpt illustrates how SF's use of Article 2 – drawing on the link made by the ECtHR between investigative independence and public confidence[15] – activated Unionists' discursive frames and collective memories:

JONATHAN CRAIG [DUP]: I want to make very very clear, the party [DUP] is very very content with the LIB that you are setting up … We need to nail this about Article 2 compliance: there's nothing which says this isn't Article 2 compliant. Nothing whatsoever. Some people are choosing to play politics with it and they want to send that message out that it isn't.

CATRIONA RUANE [SF]: In relation to Article 2 compliance, I have to say I respectfully disagree with Jonathan's comments in relation to that. One of the central tenets of Article 2 compliance is public confidence and I can tell you very clearly, any of the families I have met – Loughinisland, McGurks, any of the families – they do not believe that what you are establishing is Article 2 compliant. I think it's very important we understand what Article 2 compliance means.

…

ROSS HUSSEY [UUP]: I think the previous speaker should bear in mind that over 300 RUC officers lost their lives serving this country and a lot of those murders have not been resolved satisfactorily either. I think it's a disgrace once again these type of comments are being made, over 300 officers lost their lives and I find the previous comments offensive in the extreme. (Public Session, 6 December 2014)

How 'bounded' the Performance Committee's deliberation was in private sessions remains unknown, but the Board has acknowledged that the Performance Committee's members 'expressed diverging views' over the LIB's compliance with Article 2 of the ECHR (NIPB, 2014: 23). Ultimately, though, it has proven difficult for Unionists to sustain a convincing narrative of how the PSNI's legacy investigation units satisfy the procedural requirements of Article 2 in light of HMIC inspections of the HET in 2013. As discussed earlier, these inspections exposed serious issues of independence and accountability that raised objective concerns relating to Article 2 (HMIC, 2013, 2015).

The DUP has come to accept that 'these realities cannot simply be dismissed' and to support the introduction of a new, institutionally independent body to investigate conflict-related deaths

[15] See *Ramsahai v Netherlands* (2008) 46 EHRR 43, at [325]; see also *Re McQuillan* [2019] NICA 19 13, at [151–7].

(DUP, 2018, 8). This illustrates that the distillation of hard legal standards, ultimately accepted by all parties to be in play, alongside respected empirical findings, can exert a degree of 'closure' over political contestation on this issue of 'high' policing. Human rights thus came to be mobilized within the Board's institutional structures to engage with the legacy-related issues. First, on the issue of disclosure, the Performance Committee monitored the PSNI's engagement with the coronial process.[16] Second, regarding the HET/LIB's compliance with Article 2, the Performance Committee closely monitored Lundy's critical research (2009–2012) into HET and devised the terms of HMIC's subsequent inspection in 2013. Based on HMIC's report, and informed by its own legal advice, the Board declared it had no confidence in the HET and established a Working Group, chaired by Professor Brice Dickson, an independent member of the Board and an esteemed human rights scholar (Northern Ireland Committee for Justice, 2013: 5). This oversaw the implementation of HMIC's recommendations, as well as making its own recommendations based on consultation and information supplied to the Group (NIPB, 2014).

Conclusion

The second Part of the book has exposed the malleability of rights talk and its capacity to be appropriated by elite audiences and imbued with a myriad of ideas, visions, priorities and principles, directed at other high-policing audiences. The Policing Board is a deliberative arena where the statutory duty to monitor the PSNI on the basis of the HRA has collided with deep political divisions. Infused with both the PSNI's organizational self-conceptions of human rights – legality, ethics, accountability and political parties' ethno-national divisions, human rights contestations have become a form of what Curtis (2014) has referred to as 'war by other

[16] The Board's Chair wrote to the Chief Inspector of Criminal Justice in Northern Ireland setting out proposals for a formal inspection which ultimately took place in 2016, following the joint support of the Minister of Justice. The Performance Committee requested the PSNI provide a written response to the recommendations made by CJINI's inspection into the PSNI's management and disclosure of information to the coronial process (see Performance Committee minutes, 17 September 2015; 10 March 2016; 12 December 2016 (Belfast: Northern Ireland Policing Board)).

means': that is, a vernacular for continuing, rather than resolving, debates over national belonging, cultural expression and state repression. Despite the PSNI's determined efforts to make real the ICP's vision of a technical and cultural commitment to human rights, the politics of policing remains infused with historical rights discourses, the legacy of policing and conceptions of the imperfect peace. In the absence of a co-ordinated approach to 'dealing with the past', collective memories and conflict-narratives in particular continue to animate the present. Rather than bringing 'a fresh sense of urgency or moral obligation to the debate' (Gearty, 2016: 2), as human rights have done in other contexts, rights talk has stuck onto and further entrenched ethno-political divisions over the conflict, policing and rights.

It is these associations, histories and contradictions which the PSNI has been so keen to neutralize in its own rights narrative, which is at pains to promote the neutral, pro-legitimating properties of human rights as legality, ethics and accountability. But what about the policemen and women of the PSNI, who are themselves drawn from this same society? They vote for these political parties, they read the local newspapers, they tune in to radio talk shows and, ultimately, when they put on their uniforms, they are crucial symbols of a form of social order. How do these officers receive, interpret and understand the properties of human rights expounded by chief officers and taught to them in training? How porous are occupational cultures, regulatory formats and organizational priorities to the loud, but deeply contested, rights narratives that swirl around the PSNI? What are the techniques, ploys, even manipulations, that lead officers to endorse, comply or dismiss the legitimating properties of human rights that are supposed to regulate and determine their occupational lives? These are the questions to which we turn in the sites of policing explored in the remaining parts of the book.

PART III

Routine Policing: Making Sense of Rights

4

Dirty Work

The Tactical Support Group

> What are the conditions in which rules originating from the law are internalized, becoming guiding principles of conduct? … The answer is to be found in the organizational structure, the promotion, complaints and discipline systems, definitions of role and evaluation of performance, the skills, capacities, and limitations of police officers, the satisfactions and frustrations of the job, the expectations of the wider society, and the way all these influences are reflected in the culture of police working groups. (Smith, 1998: 619)

In the two chapters that follow I invite the reader into the realm of routine policing. The purpose is to capture how the PSNI's official human rights narrative is received, interpreted and internalized by junior officers, taking account of the kinds of dynamics noted by Smith. When making reference to 'routine' policing, I do so with the same duality that Brewer and Magee (1991: 55–6) had in mind in their own study of Northern Irish policing conducted in the late 1980s – that is, the ordinary, often mundane, calls for action that police officers are responding to now as I write and you read, as well as the process by which this work is 'done' and made sense of. Part III focuses on two groups of officers performing routine policing, each with their own roles, working pressures and processes, as well as organizational expectations and public interactions. This chapter devotes its analytical attention to the 'dirty work' of the Tactical Support Group (TSG) to explore how human rights were internalized amidst the social and moral taint associated with the type of police work they perform. Chapter 5 continues the exploration of human rights internalization but shifts the attention towards officers in Neighbourhood Policing

Policing Human Rights. Richard Martin, Oxford University Press. © Richard Martin 2021.
DOI: 10.1093/oso/9780198855125.003.0005

Teams responsible for maintaining good relations within communities where the 'endorsement' of policing often remains elusive.

My fieldwork with the TSG began on a cold night in the dead of November 2014. With the lashing rain pelting off my car windscreen, I steered in the direction of the parking bay inside one of Belfast's still heavily fortified police stations. As I walked across the yard, I saw the bulky figure of this TSG unit's Inspector who filled the doorway of the station that his officers had made their occupational home. Dressed in a dark jumpsuit, heavy boots and a baseball cap, he extended his arm for a firm handshake. Escaping the rain, we headed inside where I found his officers roaming the corridors, the soles of their boots squeaking on the plastic floor as they made their way between the station's gym facilities, kitchen and the briefing room where officers relaxed between their taskings. My time with the TSG would end some months later, in Spring 2015. By then I was trusted enough to let myself into the main building, knowing where to find the usual characters and having learnt when best to secure an interview or focus group. I observed training sessions, several shifts and interviewed many of their colleagues from other TSG units across the country. The TSG treated me well. They were interested in the research and curious about what I was going to write; above all, they were keen that I grasped the frustrations and challenges their work brought.

The reputation of the TSG tends to precede it. Known infamously within communities as the 'bully boys', 'riot squad' or just 'thugs', the stigma of the TSG stems primarily from its confrontational work and its paramilitary-style uniform. Its officers carry out 'tasks' on behalf of the police departments that 'bid' for the TSG's time and expertise. These tasks range from searching messy premises for weapons, drugs or paramilitary paraphernalia to counter-terrorist patrols; from policing contentious parades to physically removing non-compliant suspects from custody cells. A constable in the TSG put it bluntly: 'I think we do the dirty work of the police.' Tainted by their association with 'dirt', and further sullied by felt accusations of belligerence and ill-discipline, TSG officers remained resolute in going about their daily tasks, actively resisting the corrosive labels applied to them. It is for these reasons – their interaction with the public in confrontational situations, routine engagement with individuals' rights and sense of being occupationally misunderstood – that the TSG are such an interesting part of routine policing in Northern Ireland to examine as a form of human rights practitioner.

As will be recalled from the previous chapter's analysis, the official narrative constructed and deployed by chief officers cast human rights as a source of ethical power capable of re-establishing organizational identity and empowering chief officers to act as social commentators. The PSNI have promoted human rights as a central and enduring hallmark of contemporary policing, proffering to junior officers what Ravasi and Schultz (2006: 435) describe as 'legitimate and consistent narratives that allow them to construct a collective sense of self'. It is through the kinds of official narratives examined in Chapter 2 (human rights as legality, an ethics of power, as accountability) that the PSNI has sought to 'influence how internal and external audiences define and interpret the organization, by locating it within a set of legitimate social categories' (Ravasi and Schultz, 2006: 435). According to an institutionalist perspective, we would expect junior officers to readily adopt the PSNI's official narrative, specifically the human rights properties senior officers use to bring meaning to, and legitimate, their routine work. In sum, the official narrative operates as a social structure that seeks to influences officers' understanding of, and subsequent behaviour relating to, human rights.

The focus of this chapter's analysis is on how junior officers performing routine work *internalized* human rights, with *sensemaking* providing the process through which this took place; a process producing identity-rich, context-dependent narratives that function to foster self-enhancement, self-efficacy and self-consistency amidst occupational challenges. Sensemaking is a situated practice, taking place amidst individuals' working lives and occupational settings and drawing on resources from each. In this chapter, our focus is on the TSG, drawing on Hughes' (1958) concept of 'dirty work' to introduce the occupational context within which TSG officers were making sense of human rights as a vernacular of police work. With this conceptual scaffolding in place, I proceed to identify and examine a series of counter-narratives officers attached to human rights as a normative vision for policing and a regulatory standard in their everyday work. It is argued that officers made sense of human rights so as to bring order to the complexity and ethical challenges they faced, to foster their own self-legitimacy and to defend against challenges to the policing legacy in Northern Ireland. This entailed officers re-interpreting and modifying the official rights narrative in various ways, such that the content of the narrative varied even if it served similar sensemaking goals to the official narrative: making the complex orderly, fostering self-esteem and maintaining self-legitimacy.

Doing 'Dirty Work'

In describing his work to me as 'dirty', TSG Constable Jay struck upon the same word coined by Everett Hughes (1951, 1958) to capture occupations perceived as disgusting or degrading by influential audiences, involving tasks that are 'counter to the more heroic of our moral conceptions' (Hughes, 1958: 50). This notion of 'dirty work' is, I think, a most helpful means of capturing the site in which sensemaking took place and the need it created for order, consistency and self-esteem. Consistent with a social constructivist analysis, 'dirtiness' is neither inherent in the work itself nor those who do it, but rather conceived of as such by audiences who consider it to be physically, socially or morally tainted in some manner or another (Hughes, 1958: 199). By delegating dirty work to certain others, groups can feel clean, even superior, to the workers doing it. Such workers, in turn, take on its stigma, becoming 'tainted' by their association with it. What unites dirty workers, then, is the stigma endured from audiences external to their trade, perhaps experienced as putdowns, demeaning questions or implicit assaults on their character and self-worth (Ashforth and Kreiner, 1999: 417–18). In their attempt to resolve human problems often arising in situations of despair, deprivation or degradation, the work of police officers has been classed as a 'dirty' trade (van Maanen, 1973; Waddington, 1999). The dirtiest feature of policing has been said to be officers' routine exercise of coercive authority in circumstances of moral ambiguity (Dick, 2005), involving conduct that 'otherwise would be exceptional, exceptionable or illegal' (Waddington, 1999: 299). Developing this insight further, there are, I think, further dimensions of policing that might be seen as tainted in one way or another. This is especially so when it comes to the routine work of the TSG. The officers I spoke to gave numerous examples of the kinds of physical,[1] social and moral stigma alluded to by Hughes (1958)

[1] The TSG also experienced physically 'dirty work', however, it is less relevant than social and moral taint when it comes to thinking about the capacity

and helpfully clarified by recent work in organizational studies (Ashforth and Kreiner, 1999; Kreiner, Ashforth and Sluss, 2006; see also Löfstrand, Loftus and Loader, 2016).

The TSG firmly believed that in the eyes of many Loyalist and Republican communities, their work was not just unpopular but amoral in the sense described by Ashforth and Kreiner (1999: 415) as 'somewhat sinful or of dubious virtue'. TSG units were often deployed at contentious parades when disorder had already broken out. Donning their protective equipment that included dark jumpsuits, balaclavas, helmets and shields, the TSG became a physical yet faceless manifestation of the Parade Commission determinations that restricted the movement of communities' marches and protests (discussed in detail in Chapter 6). Having been deployed in cordons to prevent violent clashes between rival communities, officers were derided by some communities as the 'riot squad' or 'bully boys' and subject to vitriolic remarks: 'they regularly come off with things like, you know, "You should be ashamed of yourself" and "Your mother must be so proud of you" – sarcastically obviously' (TSG Constable Pauline). As TSG Constable Nathan further explained, 'we have people saying to our faces, and it's just a quote, it's not pleasant, but they call us "the Taig[2] Support Group" so they say that we would favour Nationalists because they're getting their parade re-routed' (TSG Constable Nathan). Dressed in protective uniform (body armour, balaclavas, helmets) the TSG felt de-humanized:

> I think there's a stigma attached to us that we're not approachable, you can't speak to us. Certainly, in the likes of Twaddell [north Belfast] it would be regularly heard 'Don't be speaking to them, they're just the TSG' you know, as if we're not the real police kinda thing. (TSG Constable Quin)

Many in the TSG described how they were labelled as 'Robocop', which officers interpreted to mean they were not human beings worthy of respect. This verbal and physical abuse took its toll, with many officers mentioning in interviews how morale dipped

of human rights to restore confidence in officers' moral authority in the face of challenges to it.

[2] A highly derogatory and insulting term used to describe a person who is Catholic.

after long periods of public disorder, which brought with it injuries to officers as well as long and unpredictable periods on shift.

A further source of the perceived immorality of dirty work derives from its workers' methods being 'deceptive, intrusive, confrontational, or that otherwise defy norms of civility' (Ashforth and Kreiner, 1999: 415). For the TSG, few tasks were as tainted as house searches. In their quest for incriminating evidence in suspects' homes, the TSG crossed the boundary of public and private space, at times forcefully, to encounter home-owners whose reactions ranged from hostility and aggression to confusion and despair. It was common for TSG officers to be accused of 'raiding' homes, breaking front doors and leaving behind a trail of destruction. While the TSG prided themselves on doing a professional job, the presence of ten bulky officers rummaging around only reinforced certain communities' perceptions of the TSG as 'mindless thugs'. The policemen and women of the TSG had to come to terms with the morality of these kinds of intrusive, disruptive tasks that comprised their routine work.

> Searching is a very invasive task you know, when you go to somebody's house and sometimes you force entry, you damage their door when you come in and it's maybe a family home and there's maybe kids there or elderly people there and you're coming in to basically go through every belonging that they have, all their drawers and there's nothing private at that point, we're going through everything, and it's very very invasive, so it's not surprising that you get that abuse. (TSG Constable Owen)

In addition to the perceived immorality of their work, TSG officers experienced a kind of social taint arising from regular contact with groups that are themselves stigmatized (Ashforth and Kreiner, 1999: 415; see also Löfstrand, Loftus and Loader, 2016: 307–10). As Bittner (1974: 30) observed some time ago: 'no human problem exists, or is imaginable, about which it could be said with finality that this certainly could not become the proper business of the police'. Several TSG interviewees described how they arrived in situations 'where there's a problem' (TSG Sergeant Adam), 'if things had got out of hand' (TSG Constable Jay), 'when something bad happens' (Focus Group 2) or 'to pick up the pieces' (TSG Constable Larry). Officers were expected to defuse already hostile situations (e.g. incidents in custody, riots in neighbourhoods) or to perform tasks that would likely result in confrontational encounters involving challenges to their authority (e.g.

counter-terrorist searches or patrols). As such, officers suspected that residents in communities where searches and patrols took place (often Loyalist and Republican housing estates) associated the TSG with notorious characters or streets in their locality. In other cases, officers felt criticized for being overly protective of suspected drug dealers or paedophiles because they asked angry residents not to gather around the property or refused to disclose confidential information about police investigations.

The social taint of TSG further extended to their servile relationship with their colleagues in other police departments, as well as senior management. Organizational hierarchy, coupled with tasks delegated from various police departments, meant the TSG enjoyed little, if any, autonomy to plan and conduct their daily work. TSG units followed regimented schedules devised by centralized administrators, requiring them to be at set destinations by set times: even when they arrived at local stations to be briefed by police teams, some TSG officers felt judged by their smartly dressed colleagues. As explained to me by officers in one focus group, they felt conscious of being perceived as lazy by their colleagues: 'we maybe seem for a lot of people as just sitting about and sort of doing nothing but at the end we're waiting to get briefed or we're waiting for the search to come in, so what do we do? Do we just sit in the back of the truck and hide?' (Focus Group 2). Curiously, the TSG *were* engaging in the kind of action-orientated, crime-fighting type of work – house searches, counter-terrorist patrols, public order policing – that officers consider particularly valuable (Waddington, 1999; Loftus, 2009). Yet officers still felt they were being judged by their peers, particularly response units who were swamped with full docket loads and labouring under targets while TSG officers lumbered around stations, 'resting' or 'feeding' in between their taskings. Other officers expressed concern that they were starting to lose key skills they had worked hard to gain in their initial years, from taking statements to correctly filling out forms. Wary of this predicament, and growing tired of the TSG, Constable Larry had taken his sergeants exams; he was ready to move up and on. As he explains, the 'TSG is an infantry solider, you're told go here, stand there, eat that, hit that door – don't think about it … its mind-numbing'.

Particularly galling for officers, however, was the sense that their bosses disowned TSG units when controversy arose from conducting the tasks they were instructed to carry out by senior officers. After rioting or hostile house searches, district teams were thought to be quick to apportion blame to the TSG and distance themselves from any fallout from residents, as illustrated in the following excerpt:

TSG A: I think sometimes TSG is just used as the scapegoat of policing. If something goes wrong they just blame the TSG type-thing. You're out there in your blue suits and you're obviously looking the worst side of policing for the public perception, but at the end of the day we just do what we're told, we have to act professionally as best as we can.

TSG B: It's almost a case of nobody really wants to have us and if they could get away with not having us they would, but things are still happening and they need us, so we're like a necessary evil for them [police managers]. (Focus Group 2)

Similar frustration simmered in the stories told about the TSG uniform. On one occasion, a district commander had told a TSG unit to put yellow visibility jackets on top of their blue suits to appear less threatening to communities. For officers, baking in the summer heat under yet another layer of clothing and now wearing a flammable jacket over their specially designed non-flammable suits perfectly epitomized their bosses' lack of respect for, or understanding of, the TSG. Many officers I spoke to believed their rights were subordinate to those of rioters: 'basically you're the pawns, almost like cannon fodder at times' (TSG Constable Jay). This presence of the competing priorities and pressures of 'street cops' and 'management cops' (Bowling, Reiner and Sheptckyi, 2019) is something we will return to in detail in Chapter 6, in the context of the authorization of the use of force in public order policing.

Counter-Narratives of Human Rights

In interviews, focus groups and observations with the TSG it was apparent that human rights were understood by, and registered with, officers not merely because failure to do so might result in sanction from police management or external accountability bodies. As suggested by Weick (1995: 109), an inquiry into the substance of sensemaking represents 'an attempt to learn what people "draw on" to construct roles and interpret objects'. There were subtler, more complex elements at work in how TSG officers received, processed and made sense of the PSNI's official rights narrative in the context of their 'dirty work'. This process of sensemaking coalesced around four core narratives that affected officers' socialization in rights: '*They go on about it ad nauseam*', '*It's for the bosses*', '*It's just common sense*' and '*It's what we've always been doing*'. Collectively, these narratives, informed as they were by police culture and individual experiences, provide an account of how officers were neither straightforward nor uncritical consumers or expressors of the official narrative. While officers were clearly cognizant of rights as guiding paradigm and mindful of it as organizational vernacular, ultimately their sensemaking narratives were closely bound with more experiential, identity-driven efforts to bring order to the complexity and unambiguity of aspects of the job, to foster self-legitimacy in the face of their dirty work and to defend against challenges to policing legacies.

'They Go On About It Ad Nauseam'

The roles, scripts and symbols senior officers disseminate convey official identities, expectations and frames to group members. These can, in turn, 'steer' members' everyday sensemaking in a direct but taken-for-granted manner – that is to say, they serve as the waypoints towards socialization (Weber and Glynn, 2006: 1646). Efforts to socialize officers in human rights principles and standards have taken the form of 'technologies of training courses, codes of conduct, conferences, inspection ... which do not coerce people but rather try to persuade, entice, or convince them' (Hornberger, 2010: 268). This speaks to the role police organizations can play as sense-givers, seeking to instil respect for human rights as core organizational values. As discussed in Chapter 2, the PSNI has heavily promoted human rights as key to the organization's identity – how it was 'made and imagined' – and gone to great lengths to persuade officers to internalize the basic principles of human rights. These principles range from the idea of individuals as bearers of legally enforceable rights against the police, to categories such as positive and negative duties of the police and concepts like proportionality, which – as outlined in the Introduction – govern the lawful engagement of police with qualified rights. By socializing officers, the police service's aim is for officers to internalize the basic principles of human rights by virtue of their normative appeal, rather than fear of sanction or hope of reward. The organizational processes by which officers are exposed to, receive, and process the official discourse of rights they are expected to internalize primarily arise in training sessions, operational briefings and formal documentation.

The PSNI's initial human rights training (2001–2004) attracted stinging criticism from legal commentators for being overly simplistic, inaccurate and silent on rights abuses during the conflict (see Kelly, 2002; O'Rawe, 2007; cf. Hornberger, 2011: chapter 3). Significant improvements in the training programme have since been reported, thanks in part to the careful oversight of the Policing Board's human rights legal advisors, who reviewed manuals, lesson plans and class delivery (NIPB, 2007; but see also recent concerns of 'a punitive culture more closely associated with "a pseudo-militaristic" training environment' having re-emerged, NIPB, 2019: 9). Likewise, the PSNI's specially appointed Human Rights Training Advisor helped to ensure that human rights were contextualized in an operational policing scenario and worked closely with police trainers responsible for delivery across the PSNI (NIPB, 2019: 6). With training at police college well-behind them at this stage of their careers, TSG officers continued to receive a regular dose of the HRA at bi-annual refresher training courses for firearms and personal safety protection, as well as training exercises for house searches and public order policing. There was a consensus amongst the TSG that the drum of the PSNI's official rights discourse beat loudly throughout these training sessions, as well as the official communications and documents they encountered in their everyday work: 'it's just something that's always in the background' (TSG Constable Larry); 'it's drilled into us so much' (Focus Group 1); 'it's something that applies to everything and you just have to listen to it' (TSG Constable Ben). Officers had a clear sense of the emphasis the PSNI placed on human rights, noting how it was mentioned explicitly by officers at every training session who would ask them which rights were engaged by various powers and the tactical options available to commanders in public order situations.

One experienced police trainer I interviewed described how human rights teaching had, in his eyes, evolved over the last decade, emphasizing the core knowledge he thought officers now had – and which was indeed expressed in my own interviews with them – of the human rights engaged in their routine tasks:

The pendulum went full tilt and I think it went ridiculously – everything, even in training, we had to mention human rights in every single lesson, the pendulum has come back down a bit, it's sitting at a really good spot – *you hear about death by human rights, you know, 'cause people switch off.* But realistically, *because it's been engrained*, we've got that bank of knowledge, if we're putting a lesson together, we don't have to go down and say, if we're using a baton or shield tactic, oh what human right would you infringe if you were doing that? Years ago, people would said 'You need to ask them', now we don't because you'd be aware. (Emphasis added)

I observed several public order refresher courses during which engagement with human rights by both trainers and officers was notable but brief in the course of the lesson. At one course, the morning session began with TSG units gathered in a large room. A flickering projector beamed out references to public order policy, the code of ethics and decision-making model for bleary-eyed officers to refamiliarize themselves with. Across the yard, a large hanger housed a collection of doors affixed to wooden stands, designed for practising forced entry in a manner that would prevent injury to officers or occupants. Under a large poster which bullet-pointed Article 8 of the ECHR (the right to private and family life), the trainer explained the importance of a 'graduated response' – a term officers later joked about as one of the PSNI's buzzwords, which meant officers should try opening the door before battering it down. After this session, officers, laden with protective gear, waddled to another building for a refresher in how to forcibly remove obstructive sitters from roads. Before the practical activities, they listened to another short presentation regurgitating the relevant legislative powers and PSNI policies. The trainer asked a muted audience what the relevance of the HRA was for this tactic. She reminded them that because this involved the use of force, their actions needed to have a basis in law, be necessary and proportionate to achieve the aim and thus justifiable in the face of formal scrutiny.

In interviews, officers described this lacklustre engagement as a response to human rights fatigue, rather than blind ignorance or a latent hostility towards human rights. Rather, they were fed up of hearing stock phrases like 'legality', 'proportionality' and 'necessity'. In fact, when specifically asked in interviews, I was struck by the ease with which most officers could identify how their daily tasks fell within the ECHR and the practical steps they made to respect human rights:

> It's present in everything that we do, from, you know, you stop someone in the road, there's the likes of the right to private and family life and a right to privacy, so you're not discussing your dealings with them with everybody back at base, or you're not putting that into the public domain ... Right to life is the most extreme obviously, but you know, you have your right to privacy, your right to freedom of assembly, which comes into your protest, your right to freedom of conscience and thought and religion, which comes into protests as well, and then your privacy comes into searching people and house searches as well. (TSG Constable Owen)

Significantly, this did not mean officers consciously made sense of their everyday work as policemen and women in rights terms, but rather when asked in an interview setting they could draw upon their training to explain how certain ECHR articles were engaged by their tasks and the practical steps they ought to take to respect these rights. Although this is indicative of some level of internalization of human rights, many in the TSG had reached saturation point. Indeed, according to TSG Constable Jay, 'every time it was human rights, and people basically just switched off because it's like white noise, you get so much of it and the brain can't take anymore'.

The official PSNI narrative of human rights could be further seen and heard by the TSG in their routine briefings prior to searches and public order operations. The presence of human rights in briefing packs and operational orders was very familiar. Officers explained how extracts of articles of the ECHR and core principles established in case law could be found over three or four pages in a dedicated section of the operational order disseminated to them in the immediate run up to deployment for a task or operation. The extent to which human rights was 'briefed out', and the manner in which it was done, varied depending on who was responsible for the briefing and the nature of the operation. Generally, officers recalled how only passing reference was now made to human rights, with briefing officers 'just going through the motions'. As TSG Constable Larry explains:

> As part of the briefing pack it'll generally say the search is human rights compliant and then read – 'If anyone wants to read, it's here' but generally we wouldn't ... a lot of the boys have heard it that many times we don't listen to it anymore. It's like listening to a ... on an aeroplane,

the safety brief. Do you listen to it or do you just continue reading your book, you know?

As was the case with training, officers explained that reference to the ECHR was so familiar they no longer needed the same level of detail they were given during the early years of the PSNI. As one TSG Sergeant explained: 'I'm sitting there doing an [Operational Order] at the minute and I've put human rights on it, but it's a reminder for people, they know it and they know not to step outside of it' (Focus Group 5).

The function of training documents, briefings packs and operational orders as internal regulation is something returned to in detail in Chapter 6. But for now, their significance lies less in their regulatory force than their symbolism. We can think of human rights within the '*ad nauseam*' narrative as operating as a form of what Weick (1995: 118) describes as a 'paradigm' – that is, 'standing operating procedures, shared definitions of the environments and agreed upon system of power and authority'. People are more likely to agree on the existence of the paradigm than on its specific rules or rationalized forms; but such rules and forms – training documents, briefings packs and operational orders – remain significant because they become the artefacts that symbolize a working culture and aid its transmission (Weick, 1995: 120). The '*ad nauseam*' narrative expresses officers' fatigue in constantly receiving the same artefacts that give materiality to the paradigm of human rights, but not a rejection or qualification of the paradigm itself. The shared beliefs of TSG officers will likely have been subject to periodic revision, modifying their interpretation to adapt to the progression of time and environmental changes the PSNI has experienced from the period of reform onwards. At the time of my fieldwork, I came to hear this narrative after well over a decade of sustained reference to human rights within the organization. A recurrent theme to emerge from my various discussions with officers, it captured officers' clear consciousness of the rights paradigm; a consciousness that had been fostered by the same artefactual forms that now gave rise to boredom, if not fatigue.

'It's More for the Bosses'

The PSNI as an organization and its senior officers as 'sense-givers' have heavily promoted human rights as both a basis of legality and ethics of power. These functions of human rights are salient to sensemaking in the context of the TSG's 'dirty work': could officers draw on human rights to address issues of self-esteem, as senior officers did in the context of reputational challenges in public forums? Could it aid them in navigating the web of accountability that has been spun around their working lives? Officers' answers suggested human rights were, in sensemaking terms, 'enacted' by them. Sensemaking involves the construction of the very subject under examination – that is to say, it 'highlights the action, activity and creating that lays down the traces that are interpreted and then reinterpreted' (Weick, 1995: 13). Officers did not only come to make sense of human rights as a paradigm to be read and interpreted. They also actively drew on social experiences to generate a narrative of human rights that recast it as a resource belonging to senior officers who, first, dealt in its technicalities, and second, played in its rhetoric.

With respect to the first, in their routine work, the TSG saw little need to engage with the HRA in a more detailed, legalistic sense than the general consciousness they described in the narratives just discussed. TSG officers were particularly frank in stating that they could not provide specific case names, as they suspected their public order commanders probably could. Some had heard stories of filing cabinets full of policies and procedures being wheeled into a senior officer's command room in the run up to a high-profile parade. Others assumed commanders must have been liaising with the PSNI's legal services department to help them reach decisions. In this high-pressure environment, TSG officers spoke aloud of how they imagined their bosses devising public order or search operations: 'They'll put the decision-making model up and go "Right, our thoughts on this is ... " and they will go through that. When it gets to our level, we just do it ... a lot of it I think is just for senior management, they would look at it in a lot more depth than what we would' (Focus Group 2). The products of these meetings, as recounted by the TSG, were operational orders and briefings, discussed further in Chapter 6.

Officers explained how they trusted that the PSNI – equipped with lawyers, trainers and policy teams – had verified the compliance of legislation, powers and procedures with the HRA. As frontline officers, they prioritized clear instructions on what their powers were and the limits of them, as explained by one young conscientious constable I met:

We're not human rights lawyers, I couldn't go in and tell you, you know, Article 2 right to life, I know what it enshrines but other than right to life and a few wee bits. I couldn't start to go into the article 10 and give it to you verbatim, and nor do I want to, but I know what it is, what it allows me to do and what it doesn't and who it protects and how as a police officer there's times where I potentially could breach that but it would be for a legal purpose. I know that there, but *I don't need to go into the real, you know, the real bones of it, I just need to know what I can do and what I can't do and why that's legal or why something's not legal.* I don't' need to go into [it] – I mean I've seen the full documents, there's a lot of reading in it you know. (TSG Constable Jay; emphasis added)

As Hornberger (2011: 8) has observed in the South African context, we should not overlook the fact that this legalistic understanding, technical competence and educational opportunity tends to be 'framed by and steeped in a middle-classness'. For many in the TSG, police training was the first time they had to engage with human rights, or the law for that matter, in a more sustained and focused way:

It was hard going, but again, for most of us we'd never experienced it [human rights] before and it was like being back at school, you're trying to learn algebra. It's exactly the same thing, your head's pickled. (Focus Group 3)

Few officers had positive experiences of human rights training at police college, which was invariably described as too academic and out of touch with practical skills needed 'on the ground' (see also NIPB, 2019: 10–11). Some, but not all, officers did not seem to have enjoyed the same level of education as senior colleagues, either before or since joining the PSNI, for a variety of reasons to do with class, culture, personalities and job roles. Some officers played up popular stereotypes, joking in self-deprecatory tones that police were not known to be the sharpest or brightest group, whilst others jested that they had drunk away their school days in the park or had never really been that 'academic, you know, books and stuff' (field notes, 4 February 2015). That said, officers were mindful of the need to know the legislative source of the powers they were using in case they were confronted by 'savvy' members of the public, not least Dissident Republicans, who might challenge police on the legal basis for the arrest or stop and search.

Personal biographies and social identities are key resources for sensemaking too (Brown, Stacey and Nandhakumar, 2008: 1037;

Wahl, 2013). Narratives are 'worked on' to maintain coherence and repair challenges to self-conceptions of who we *really* are. The authoring of sensemaking narratives is intimately bound up with individuals' identity generation and how it relates to organizational representations of routine work (Humphreys and Brown, 2002: 440). Take Constable Nathan, for example. We chatted at length as we sat in a police truck in North Belfast one evening during my fieldwork as we waited for a Loyalist protest to disperse. Nathan had joined the police because he hated bullies, whether it was at school decades ago or in society now. For Nathan, the police were not the bullies but rather a force for good in Northern Ireland that could protect vulnerable people from those who would prey on them within their communities – from paramilitaries to drug dealers, paedophiles to burglars. He had a strong faith, plenty of experience and a confident manner to go with it, sometimes to the irritation of his colleagues. We discussed in a later interview the topic of human rights and stop and search:

> There were challenges in the courts that what we were doing and had been doing then [suspicionless stop and search] wasn't compliant with that [Article 8 ECHR], but when they looked at it and said, 'well, actually, it is compliant all we need is a code of practice to sort of govern this, and the code of practice must be ECHR compliant'. Well then, that's what happened, but I never really had any doubt that what we were doing was the right thing, if you know what I mean ... again me as an individual officer saying to myself 'what I'm doing here is right because I'm trying to save someone's life or I'm trying to prevent this person taking somebody else's life or whatever, be it stopping a terrorist suspect or searching their house or stopping people with drugs and all the rest of it, so I never really had any moral sort of conflict in my mind that I was doing the right thing.

The power under section 44 of the Terrorism Act 2000 to stop and search a person without reasonable suspicion was held by the ECtHR to violate Article 8 because it was 'neither sufficiently circumscribed or subject to adequate legal safeguards against abuse' to comply with the 'in accordance with law' standard.[3] Nathan had some sense of the legal issue, but in sharp contrast to the PSNI's official discourse of legality analysed in Chapter 2, the

[3] See *Gillan and Quinton v UK* (App no 4158/05) ECHR 28 (12 January 2010), at [87].

morality of his power, directed as it was towards the 'bullies' in society, was never in doubt in his eyes.

There was a sense amongst TSG officers that human rights served as an important tool for bosses, but it was debatable whether it could do the same for them as constables out on the street, faced with 'dirty work'. External accountability bodies, especially the Police Ombudsman and the PSNI's internal complaints department, were felt to be lurking around every corner, just waiting for officers to slip up. The power of a good notebook entry was key to coming out on top of any investigation, or even court case, that might follow a complaint from the public. This was particularly the case if officers had resorted to the use of force. And yet few TSG officers described relying upon the language of human rights, in terms of the articles engaged or the qualifying conditions that justified interference with the right, as public order commanders did. Rather, the task was one of post-hoc rationalization using a decision-making model (Neyroud and Beckley, 2013: chapter 3) officers were taught in training (see further NIPB, 2019: 11). If an Attenuated Energy Projectile (AEP) had been fired by the TSG during a riot, sergeants described instructing the driver of their Land Rover to scribble down who fired the shot, the conditions they faced and who had been targeted. Likewise, on the rare occasion an arrest was made and officers suspected it would attract a complaint, they described how they would take great care to document salient points like the arrestee's demeanour, the threat they posed and the prior warnings given so as to fend off any future accusations about the police conduct the arrestee might make.

Turning to the rhetoric of human rights, many officers in the TSG sensed human rights were a brand owned and deployed by their bosses in the management of the politics of policing in Northern Ireland. Gesturing towards the official rights discourse examined in Chapter 2, a TSG officer remarked:

> They [the PSNI] don't want to get caught by it [human rights], it is a big hot potato, as you say, it is a big selling point to say we're human rights compliant, it's a big buzzword ... it's a great thing for the organization to turn around and say we've got it. (Focus Group 3)

In what TSG Sergeant Colin referred to as the 'goldfish bowl environment' of Northern Ireland, with all eyes focused on the PSNI, many in the TSG thought their senior officers had to be seen to be doing and saying the right things, especially when it came to building bridges with sceptical politicians or community leaders. 'It's all about image', stated TSG Constable Quin. Even if the TSG rank-and-file were not present at the Policing Board's monthly meetings or annual events, they knew from the organizational presence and the remarks of their bosses that human rights were part of the PSNI's corporate identity and official organizational message. In addition to serving as officers, they were members of Northern Irish society. They read the local papers and watched the regional news in the station or at home with their families. They saw and heard their chief officers trying to control the narrative around the usual political fissures – conflict-related deaths, parades, paramilitary shootings, and so forth.

As an internal audience in receipt of this official narrative, the TSG were not easily won over by their bosses' discursive performances. For some officers, the feeling was one of disheartenment at witnessing what they perceived to be their bosses' pandering to politicians or community leaders with dubious histories – the so-called 'bad boys' from days gone by (due to affiliations with Republican paramilitary organizations). For others, the endeavour of trying to 'appease the unappeasable' – those communities or groups (often Loyalists and Republicans) that were disillusioned with policing – was a distraction from real police work; it was politics at the expense of 'getting on with the job' of policing, regardless of how police actions were perceived. A mixture of these sentiments is expressed in the following account:

> You just have to have a look at the police officers that come on TV who are just being politicians, they don't want to offend anyone or they don't want to be seen to be going with any political side or any side that a party might align with. For us it's just pathetic really, they're supposed to be commanders, leaders of people, but they're crapping themselves about human rights when they shouldn't be, it's nothing to do with them. (Focus Group 2)

Such concerns were understandable given the public disorder in Northern Ireland shortly before the fieldwork began. This led to a significant number of injuries to police officers, long and demanding shifts and limited opportunity for rest days. It was within this context that a disconnect existed between what officers received via the official narrative and what they wanted to hear as officers doing the PSNI's 'dirty work'. Reflecting the disjuncture between 'street cops' and 'management cops' found in other studies (e.g. Foster, 2003: 212–13; Reiner, 2010: 132–4), the PSNI's official rights narrative did not resonate with the daily hardships, frustrations or successes of the TSG. There was a strong sense amongst officers that the official narrative was failing to promote the issues they saw as properly worthy of credit, such as the kinds of news items and press releases that would help repair the damage in their moral and social esteem. TSG Sergeant Colin, for example, thought the PSNI 'fell down badly on the PR front, massively in fact' because the media and communications department was not proactive enough in countering critical media narratives. He continued, 'it's a media savvy world out there, certain political groups and community associations are only too keen to hang us by the media noose, I think we should be a bit more savvy'. What 'savviness' meant was police chiefs publicly accounting for operations the TSG were involved in, leaving the communities and officers better informed about the likes of high-profile parades or protests where violence broke out. Examples included explanations of why the use of AEP was authorized, descriptions of the damage caused by rioters and appreciation of the injuries sustained by officers. TSG Constable Anthony summed it up: 'I don't think there's any harm in our organization coming out quickly to support us in quite strong words'.

It is noteworthy that the Code of Ethics – the documentary proof of the PSNI's ethical credentials which chief officers promoted so heavily (see Chapter 2) – rarely came up when I asked officers about human rights. It was not, it seemed, something that naturally came to mind or was immediately associated with human rights by most officers. When asked explicitly when the Code would be referred to or talked about, officers explained it only would be if a complaint was made against them or they were preparing for a promotion. If one of the aims of the Code was to act as 'an ethical framework' to assist and empower police officers, in almost all discussions with TSG officers this goal was lost to more cynical interpretations of the ends it served. An oft-repeated phrase was that the Code was nothing more than a 'stick to beat police with', emphasizing its disciplinary function. The Code was described as too broad and ambiguous, which made it very easy to breach. The major concern was that such ambiguity could be seized upon (unfairly) by the PSNI's complaints department or the Police Ombudsman as a way of sanctioning officers (see similarly

Ericson, 2007: 371). This was an example, some officers thought, of the complainant's rights being prioritized over those of officers who had to make split-second decisions, often relating to the use of force, in high-pressure situations.

'It's Just Common Sense'

Clifford Geertz (1975: 17–18) describes common sense as an account that strikes at the heart of a topic and is distinguishable by 'the air of simple wisdom with which it is uttered'. To pass something off as common sense in our day-to-day business is to suggest it is so obvious, banal or uncontroversial that we need not dwell upon it, let alone subject it to great analysis or debate. In interviews with the TSG, common sense was a quality that strongly influenced officers' interpretation and understanding of human rights in their occupational lives. Indeed, officers' insistence that human rights were 'just common sense' made my focus on rights an awkward line of enquiry in some interviews. I still recall one constable who stopped me mid-question as I asked in one of the focus group discussions about human rights criteria governing the use of force, a topic covered heavily in their training. The officer stated:

> I don't know, am I missing something? Whenever you're doing your training ... somebody's giving you verbals, you don't point your gun at them! They talk about lawful and proportionate and blah blah blah. To me it's common sense and it's probably common sense put on paper. (Focus Group 4)

The idea of common sense knowledge is considered so central to junior officers' understandings of their daily work that Holdaway (1986: 140) describes police culture as: 'the attitudes, beliefs and associated actions about policing that officers regard as "common sense"' (see also O'Brien-Ollinger, 2016). Greater clarity, however, is found in Brewer's (1984; Brewer and Magee, 1991) description of common sense using Schütz's (1953) ethno-methodological approach. According to Brewer (1984: 69), common sense knowledge is a 'set of beliefs, maxims, ideas and types which are often vague and contradictory' that are 'taken for granted' and become group members' 'natural attitude'. This stock of common sense knowledge derives from a process of reasoning informed by personal biographies, as well as socialization with peers. Narratives of common sense can tell us something about the reasoning and knowledge police officers learn to rely upon in managing the precarity of 'the street' (van Maanen, 1973; McNulty, 1994) and the complexity of rules, procedures and policies designed to govern their work (Holdaway, 1986; Ericson, 2007). The simple wisdom of common sense is, then, more complex.

Common sense is a cultural system; it is an organized body of considered thought based on our interpretation of the immediacies of our experiences. It tells us something about a group's culture, as well as the topic under discussion. As such, common sense has 'an ingenerate order to it capable of being empirically uncovered and conceptually formulated' (Geertz, 1975: 25). The notion that police training can simply 'deal with' common sense 'assumptions', as Grewal and Munasinghe (2016) bluntly assert, belies the depth of meaning lurking within common sense phraseology. We should, therefore, be prepared to dig a bit deeper when officers pass off human rights as simply common sense. The five properties of common sense identified by Geertz (1975: 18) – *naturalness*; *accessibleness*; *thinness*; *practicalness*; *immethodicalness* – offer a most helpful framework for unpacking the 'process of reasoning' and 'stock of knowledge' that contributed to TSG officers' sensemaking of human rights. These five properties are, in Geertz's (1975: 18) words, 'the stylistic features, marks of attitude, tonal shading that animate common sense thought', and each can be heard in pronounced form in officers' occupational narratives. Collectively, this narrative is one that, I think, can be understood as an attempt to clean the 'dirtiness' of the TSG's work in officers' own eyes by conveying themselves and their behaviour as competent and considerate, even compassionate.

In contrast to the official police voice, TSG officers' understandings were not allied to the HRA or the Independent Commission's reforms, but to officers' own humanity, to their decency as individuals. This sensemaking was allied to two related properties of common sense identified by Geertz (1975: 18, 24): *naturalness* ('matters as being what they are in the simple nature of the case … depicted as inherent in the situation, intrinsic aspects of reality, the way things go') and *accessibleness* (any person can grasp common sense conclusions and, if clearly stated, will embrace them). Human rights were commonly referred to by officers using phrases like 'they're sort of human nature … you know it's the right or the wrong thing to do without sort of having to recite the articles' (TSG Constable Quin), and 'it's generally don't be a scumbag, be an ordinary human being ... 99 people out of 100 would adhere to human rights legislation without even knowing anything about them' (TSG Constable Larry). Consequently, respect for human rights came 'automatically as a good officer' (TSG Constable Greg), something that 'general, normal, decent people would buy into' (Focus Group 1) or 'If you're any normal thinking person, you're never gonna sort of ... you know, object to any of those rights' (Focus Group 5). By detaching human rights from the HRA – appearing as it did in briefing documents, operational orders and policies – and re-attaching it to a taken-for-granted morality, officers were able to speak of the maturity and discipline they saw regularly in their colleagues. Sensemaking was thus bound up with officers' experiences performing 'dirty work' together, specifically the human qualities they inferred from each other's behaviour that served to counter the external claims that challenged their legitimacy.

Yet so too did officers readily acknowledge that the 'naturalness' and 'accessibility' of human rights was also connected in some way to its heavy organizational presence. In sensemaking terms, the perceptual cues that formed the substance of the artefacts of human rights, discussed earlier, could play an influential role in action formation (Weber and Glynn, 2006: 1649). Human rights had been translated into phrases and a mnemonic[4] by police policymakers and trainers that filtered into officers' consciousness. Thus, in explaining their practical knowledge of when they could or could not use house-search powers or tactical options in public order settings, officers struck upon a third property of common sense: *simpleness*, meaning the matter at hand is precisely what it seems and therefore 'sobriety, not subtlety, realism, not imagination, are the keys to wisdom' (Geertz, 1975: 22). The use of AEP, more commonly known outside of policing as plastic bullets, is a good example of how the use of a weapon that can result in serious injury of another citizen can be retranslated in rights terms and procedures. The use of force standards of Article 2 (discussed in Chapter 7) permit potentially lethal force only when it is *absolutely necessary* to protect life or serious injury. What did this

[4] The mnemonic 'P.L.A.N.' (Proportionate, Necessary, Accountable and Legal) was commonly referred to and appeared in the training material.

technical standard mean for officers? Echoing the view of several AEP gunners I spoke to, Constable Owen explained:

> To use potentially lethal force [such] as a baton gun there has to be an immediate threat to life or serious injury, so, the example they always use in training is if somebody is likely to throw a petrol bomb into an empty shop you can't shoot them because it's empty, you can't shoot to protect property, but if somebody's going to throw a petrol bomb into a shop where there are people in it you potentially could shoot them because there's then a threat to life or serious injury.

Through training, human rights took the form of what Weick (1995: 123–4) has described as a 'theory of action' to refer to the aggregated rules that interpret stimuli in meaningful ways in the interests of action. Using their own accessible, 'common sense' language, officers explained accurately how their training taught them to apply legal standards with their AEP rifle in hand and target in sight – to 'filter and interpret signals from the environment and tie stimuli to responses' (Weick quoting Hedberg, 1981: 7). As Constable Owen explained: 'they [police trainers] drill it into you that you aim for the belt buckle, as opposed to chest or tummy or head, so yeah, that's the main thing with shooting anybody'. It was through these kinds of practical tips that officers came to know how to err on the correct side of the law – indeed, to meaningfully internalize core human rights law standards.

Not all officers, though, were as receptive to even this type of common sense thinking. As Ericson (2007: 372) remarks, 'following a rule is a social practice against a background of taken-for-granted knowledge, assumptions and routines'. TSG Sergeant Eric, for example, was proud of having served over two decades in the police. He was a hardened man, sceptical of fresh-faced recruits who got caught up in the minutiae of 'training speak' on the use of force. Eric's personal biography had taught him the need for quick, sensible decisions in stressful situations. As such, he felt unaffected by human rights: 'I try not to think too much about it, you know? I think you've got a gut feeling, he's doing bad, you put a baton strike in and whatever'. The greatest risk, Eric thought, was younger officers walking on eggshells and not intervening to defend someone because of fear of breaching the aggressor's human rights. 'What's better', he asked, 'a minor breach of an article or preventing someone from being seriously injured?' Eric stepped outside of the human rights rubric promoted by chief officers and as understood as a matter of law. Rather than making sense of human rights as a means of structuring decision-making in fraught situations where competing rights were engaged, Eric considered the rights calculus as over-intellectualizing what could be a morally intuitive 'gut feeling' and as potentially tipping the scales in favour of the aggressor's rights at the expense of the rights of innocent parties (cf. Wahl, 2013).

A further strand of officers' common sense rights narrative marked a combination of two further properties Geertz identifies. The first is what he refers to as *practicalness*, not in the sense of being useful but in the 'folk-philosophical sense of sagacity that is involved. To tell someone, "be sensible" … to wise up: to be prudent, level-headed, keep his eye on the ball' (Geertz, 1975: 20–3). The second, which is closely connected, concerns its *immethodicalness* mode of expression in so far as 'common sense wisdom is shamelessly and unapologetically ad hoc'. It comes in epigrams, proverbs, obiter dicta, jokes, anecdotes'. Both properties are well captured in the following extract, typical of the wit and wisdom that officers used to play down human rights as typifying anything special:

> The bottom line is it's common sense, that's what a lot of these things have come from and again, from experience, you sort of think it shouldn't hinder you if you're doing your job right, with a bit of sense, using a bit of common sense. There's people here that say 'oh, this human rights, it stops us …' What is it stopping you from doing? I watched this programme the other night *Confessions of a Copper*. Did you watch it? Like you know, these guys policing in the 70s they wanted to drag people off and beat them up and pin things on them, 'oh human rights, it's all human rights now' well, thank God it's human rights now, if that's what you were up to! (TSG Constable Kevin)

Human rights were synonymous with sensible, respectful policing. Many officers jumped straight to Articles 2 and 3 of the ECHR, stating that they obviously would not kill or torture someone. Human rights were considered a 'grand way' of putting what was, in fact, 'simple, basic stuff'. As TSG Constable Greg quipped when talking to me about house searches, 'I will respect someone's right to private and family life … It's not like I'm going to run around with someone's knickers on my head, you know what I'm saying?' The stock phrase frequently used by officers was that human rights were 'About treating people the way you would like to be treated yourself' (see also Bullock and Johnson, 2012: 641–2). This rule of thumb was described as an easy way of 'keeping you right' and also reducing the chances of public complaints to the Police Ombudsman. Examples offered by officers included ensuring that suspects in custody were offered a drink of water or the chance to use the toilet on arrival, or that if the wrong house was searched by mistake by the TSG, a padlock would be put on the door and keys left at the local police station for the unfortunate home-owner.

Notably, few officers recited populist tropes heard in the tabloid media that described human rights as aiding defendants, failing victims and protecting criminals (cf. O'Rawe, 2005: 947). Further still, despite many officers coming from Unionist/Protestant backgrounds, none described human rights as being part of a 'Republican agenda' in the same way as the Unionist Policing Board members referenced in Chapter 3 did. TSG officers did associate human rights with the claims of chief officers and made easy reference to its heavy organizational presence, alluding to the institutional perspective of organizations as significant sense-givers. But crucially, neither the properties of ethics, legality and accountability, nor the narratives of Nationalist politicians or the scepticism of Unionist politicians, were present in TSG officers' own accounts of human rights. For most TSG officers, respect for human rights was a core but unremarkable part of policing; neither exciting nor of great concern to them. The cumulative effect of these 'common sense' properties was, on the one hand, to downplay the elevated status of human rights in the official police voice, casting human rights as something ordinary, typical, not worthy of making such a big deal about. But on the other hand, this sensemaking narrative of human rights as common sense, coupled with its constant presence – the '*ad nauseam*' narrative – has, it would seem, fostered and served to embed a distinct rights consciousness and grasp of core standards.

'It's What We've Always Been Doing'

The narrative of 'nothing's changed' belonged principally to a group of officers who we might label the 'old guard'. The essence of the narrative is captured in the words of one such member of the TSG when I asked about what impact he thought the introduction of human rights in the early 2000s had had on officers at the time:

> I've been in the police before they brought in all the human rights training and your job hasn't changed any. You have the legislation there, it was what we were doing before, only now there is legislation there to ensure that's what we're doing, if you know what I mean? You're still a police officer doing your job and if you were doing it properly you wouldn't have been breaching any of the human rights anyway. (Focus Group 4)

This narrative was connected to common sense, but was more subversive; indeed, it was one warned of early on in the reform process because of its potential to undermine human rights training (O'Rawe, 2005: 962–3). To suggest that respect for human rights was a new feature of policing, or something that TSG officers could proudly point to in completing their dirty tasks, was to miss the point: they had always respected people's rights, known the legal basis for their powers and acted properly. And yet their work was still sneered upon, their skills played down and their occupational image tainted. Furthermore, it was a strong challenge to the official police voice, which boasted of the great energy the organization had invested in far-reaching, world-leading human rights reforms.

The 'old guard' found themselves caught somewhere between the past and present of Northern Irish policing. Having spent half of their careers in the RUC (they each had between twenty and twenty-eight years of service), their socialization and experience as police officers began in the Northern Ireland of the late 1980s – a less violent, but nonetheless personally dangerous and politically turbulent period captured in Brewer and Magee's (1991) terrifically detailed ethnographic study of routine policing in Belfast around the time of the Anglo-Irish Agreement. In fact, one old-timer remembered Kathleen Magee's spell as a researcher in Belfast, joking about how she was always 'hanging about with the guys' in a station not far from his own. But at the same time, the officers voicing this narrative had out-served their erstwhile colleagues in the RUC. In what was highly turbulent period, these officers were experiencing first-hand the deeply divisive police reforms inspired by the Independent Commission on Policing. As described in Chapter 3, for a significant number of Unionists, the reforms amounted to a great betrayal of the bravery and sacrifice shown by the RUC throughout the conflict. For many in the policing community, RUC officers had loyally upheld the fundamental rights of law-abiding citizens in the face of terrorism and yet now, in peacetime Northern Ireland, as officers of the PSNI, the focus had shifted; for it was *they* who had to affirm a commitment to human rights, to sign up to the new rights-inspired code of ethics, oath of attestation and purposefully devised training courses.

As observed by Ravasi and Schultz (2006: 435), a rupture between past and present as experienced by the old guard can call into question members' beliefs about central and distinctive attributes of an organization, which can challenge collective self-perceptions and self-categorizations. It can amount to an identity threat that increases the likelihood members will engage in explicit recognition of identity issues. The 'need for continuity', as Whetten observes, can be 'so compelling that even profound organizational changes are typically portrayed as reaffirmations of higher-level identity claims' (Whetten quoted in Ravasi and Schultz, 2006: 453). It was an explicit, bold claim of consistency that lay at the heart of the old guards' narrative: as police officers in the RUC, they respected human rights just as much as they did now as PSNI officers; the pronounced vernacular of rights was really a rediscovery of the values and attitudes already embedded in the police. This is a hotly contested claim (see, e.g., the views of some Republican community members in Hearty, 2017: 224–5). A significant portion of Nationalist and Republican communities for a long time experienced the RUC as a sectarian organization, reliant on a paramilitary style of policing that showed a limited regard for the human rights of those in their communities.

The old guards' narrative of consistency is a hard one to assess concretely with respect to routine policing due to the relative dearth of research on the RUC; this is not, of course, to deny the various human rights abuses reported, spanning from police detention and interrogation, to police collusion with paramilitary groups and allegations of a 'shoot to kill' policy against terrorist suspects. What is clear from the Independent Commission's report, however, is that even in the late 1990s, human rights as a legal standard had a lowly, poorly recognized status in the RUC:

> In our contacts with the RUC, we found them broadly aware of [human rights] issues but at a very early stage of considering how to address them, and then mainly in the context of specific implications for policing of the Human Rights Act 1998. Human rights training in the RUC also lags behind other police organizations we have spoken to … of 700 sessions of training there are only 2 sessions dedicated to human rights, compared with 40 of drill and 63 of firearms training; the preponderance of these last two subjects reflects the security situation that has afflicted Northern Ireland and its distorting effect on policing, including the integration of human rights into policing culture. (ICP, 1999: 19)

Further insight of the reform period can be gleaned from an officer (outside of the TSG) I interviewed who was a member of the team responsible for implementing the HRA in the RUC and then the PSNI. The team's attempts to review training and policies for ECHR compliance in the late 1990s were, he admitted, 'a lot of guess work … we didn't have the guidance or anything, we were trying to make it as compliant as we could by our own studies … It was a lot of trial and error'. This viewpoint is supported by the Northern Ireland Human Rights Commission's evaluation of the initial post-Patten training for new recruits. Despite their efforts, trainers struggled to render human rights law and principles meaningful to student officers and admitted lacking sufficient knowledge of the law themselves (Kelly, 2002). So too, I was told, there was scepticism and obstructionism within police departments, including the training teams, which remained unconvinced of the merits of this human rights-inspired approach. As this officer explained, 'there was a perception that human rights is the criminal's charter, all that sort of nonsense, it's just going to make policing impossible. The old guard weren't happy'. However, with the appointment of human rights legal experts by the PSNI and the Policing Board since 2003, the same officer explained that understandings of the law improved, but that selling it internally to officers remained difficult.

The old guards' consistency narrative has, unsurprisingly, been critically received. Most notably, O'Rawe (2007: 223) has described this attitude as 'devaluing' the (seemingly proper) 'human rights message' through their 'insufficient knowledge' and reluctance to confront historic wrongdoing, thus 'shoring up unhelpful mind sets'. Frustration that some have failed to grasp the need for discontinuity with past practices and for critical re-appraisal of what went before is understandable, particularly for those who believe in the potential of human rights law to offer redress and transformation. Writing in the international context, Bronitt (2011: 17) similarly warns of rights rhetoric being detached from legal standards and operating 'only as a set of ethical imperatives'. To avoid 'window dressing', he insists on 'the importance of grounding police action in *compliance* with human rights *laws*' (Bronitt, 2011: 17; original emphasis). Human rights are capable of being picked up, recast and redirected for ends which those of us trained in its doctrinal purity may be both surprised at and uneasy with. Sensemaking is, after all, driven by plausibility rather than accuracy. Sensemaking takes what Fiske (cited in Weick, 1995: 57) has described as 'a relative approach to truth', in so far as people will believe what can account for not only sensory experience but what is also attractive, emotionally appealing and goal relevant. Once we accept that alternative human rights vernaculars *do* exist, the pressing question is how and why this 'nothing's changed' mentality was sustained by officers despite challenges to the veracity of its claim of consistency in human rights practices in the RUC and PSNI.

There were two discursive elements at work in officers' accounts of human rights consistency. The first was an acknowledgement of change in form, but not substance; that is, reference to human rights had just put a label on parts of training and practice that implicitly put individuals' interests first anyway. Officers frequently cited the Police and Criminal Evidence Act 1984 as an example of legislation that gave formal rights to suspects as evidence of a longer tradition of having to be cognizant of human rights. The sense that human rights had merely been a way of expressing old ideas in a more formalized manner was widely held by this group of officers. The view of Constable Nathan, a long-serving member of the TSG, is typical of his colleagues:

It's just pretty much been formalised now in the form of adopting the ECHR. Pretty much everything we did before, either consciously or unconsciously, is included in the ECHR. I mean, they talk now about Article 2. The first time I ever heard it used I thought 'What are they talking about?', somebody came on the [police] radio and said, 'If there's an Article 2 issues there, you know, intervene.' You know, okay, Article 2 is the right to life, and if there's a threat there in regards to that, well, deal with it. Well in the past somebody said, 'If somebody's life's in danger, deal with it'. You didn't have to know it was Article 2 ... Yes, it does have an impact, but it's more that it's been formalised, not so much that it's something new, you know.

It is significant that this narrative seems to have circulated in the PSNI since human rights reforms began (see also O'Rawe, 2007: 222). A number of officers recalled how their minds were set at ease by police trainers in the early 2000s who stressed that the HRA was nothing new or significant: 'people with big experience who'd policed through the 1970s and [19]80s – were saying this isn't any different from what you do anyway, it's just there's a label to it now' (TSG Constable Kevin) and 'trainers were saying we've nothing to fear about HRA because everything we do is human rights compliant, but it wasn't spelled out boldly in the RUC' (TSG Sergeant Adam). Hornberger (2011: 102–4) reports similar sentiments with police in Johannesburg. Officers from the apartheid era referenced legislation existing then as evidence of a longer-standing commitment to the law and regulatory procedures. This claim is one Hornberger debunks, but as I argue here, its significance lies less in its veracity than in its ability to foster a mind-set of consistency amongst officers. In striking similarity to their Northern Irish counterparts with respect to the HRA, this enabled South African officers to 'present the changes brought about by constitutional democracy as not particularly radical, and perhaps even negligible' (Hornberger, 2011: 104).

In trying to make some sense of the 'nothing's changed' narrative in Northern Irish policing, Brewer and Magee's (1991: 272–5) findings on the use of force policy in the RUC in the late 1980s is instructive. It does, at least, lend some credence to the idea that legal standards existed, formally, even though they were not couched in ECHR terms. Brewer and Magee report how the RUC's use of force had become more restrained in the wake of public outcry over an alleged 'shoot to kill' policy of suspected paramilitaries. New regulations were introduced by the late 1980s to limit officers' use of firearms and physical violence and a new code of conduct addressed these issues. For district policing, the bureaucratic regime governing the use of force was particularly strict, with officers recounting stories to Magee about policemen who had been demoted because of excessive use of force. Echoing this, a former legal trainer in the RUC and PSNI who I interviewed explained how principles like limited use of force were present in firearms training, but that processes and accountability were not framed around Article 2 of the ECHR. From the 1970s to 1990s, the criminal law was the primary legal basis; it was not until the late 1990s that human rights compliant lesson plans were devised (see also O'Rawe, 2007: 228).

The second element sustaining the narrative of consistency was one that bound human rights closely to officers' personal sense of self as ethical policemen and women. To talk about human rights reform as bringing a new style or philosophy to policing was interpreted by the old guard as a critique of the RUC, specifically the professionalism of its officers. This criticism did not resonate with this group's occupational experience; they were proud of having served in the RUC, not least because of the resilience and sacrifice of its officers. 'The way I police hasn't changed since I was in the RUC' insisted TSG Sergeant Adam, who had two decades of service. The sense of identity, ethos and belief that bridged the transition from RUC to PSNI was perhaps best summed up by TSG Sergeant Eric:

> Albeit there is a name change and a slight uniform change but the ethos to me remained the same. It didn't matter what I was wearing one day to the next, you know, I was there for the transition, I didn't get up the next day and go 'Right, I'm a member of the PSNI now, I'm a different person'. You're the same person, you have the same beliefs to go out and do the same job. And the expectation across Northern Ireland has always been that the police service provides this, to me, quite high level of a service.

When I presented this perspective to senior officers who had been proximate to the ICP-inspired reforms, they offered some explanation as to why TSG officers might plausibly hold this view. Superintendent Brian, for example, cited the non-fatal shooting of a suspect who had driven a car bomb into Belfast city centre in the early 2000s. Shots had been fired by experienced police officers:

> Those guys that pulled that trigger were exactly the same people who were in the RUC mobile support unit, not that long ago. In fact, most of them had been in it for twenty to twenty-five years. Exactly the same people, who were doing exactly the same jobs against the provisional IRA and not killing people ten years before that, fifteen years before that, twenty years before that. (Superintendent Brian)

His colleague, Superintendent Edwin, was more balanced. He understood the sentiments expressed by his rank-and-file colleagues from the RUC. Policing during the troubles was often about balancing the rights of colleagues, communities and suspects, but the expression of human rights as being fundamental was absent: 'and that was the critical terminology that came along with the codification of the Convention, these are fundamental'. Reflecting on this point, former Chief Constable Hugh Orde explained that it was the heavy emphasis the PSNI placed on rights that defined it: 'it was more explicit, and it was the golden thread throughout everything we did. Now that was different'.

These two discursive elements grounded what, I think, can be understood overall as a kind of 'stability narrative' (Sonenshein, 2010). This sense of 'nothing's changed' enabled the old guard to make sense of human rights as a core post-reform vernacular of policing while simultaneously preserving a legacy of the RUC that was of great personal and professional salience to the old guard but did not fit with the official narrative of the reforms or explicit findings of the Independent Commission on Policing. So what, if anything, might be the positive upshot of an incomplete, a redacted, a simplified retrospection of the past? Weick suggests that a reading of past that favours order and oversimplifies may make for more effective action, even if it is lousy history (Weick, 1995: 28–9). Similarly, Sutcliffe (1994: 1374) notes 'having an accurate environmental map may be less important than having some map that brings order to the world and prompts action'. An optimistic analysis, then, is that a 'nothing's changed' sensemaking has allowed the old guard to be more receptive to the rights paradigm than might otherwise have been the case. In fact, it might serve as an important means of fostering greater openness towards and engagement with human rights in training, briefings and routine practices. So too might it serve as a narrative that opens up the kind of 'common sense' thinking that, I think, helped to internalize rights-based 'theories of action'. But a more sceptical reading is possible too: the *feeling* of order, clarity and rationality that the 'nothing's changed' narrative expresses and affirms is one that, once achieved, may discourage further retrospective processing (Weick, 1995: 29). From a place of self-consistency and emotional stability, is there likely to be much incentive for critical self-reflection and an openness to alternate accounts of the role policing played in the conflict that transitional justice scholars have identified as key to a wider reconciliation process (O'Rawe, 2007; Lawther, 2014)?

Conclusion

In Hornberger's (2011) study of policing in Johannesburg she skilfully illustrates how the 'middle-classness' and 'techno-legalism' of international human rights law rendered it a remote, de-legitimate language for the officers she met. Formal manuals and standards simply did not resonate with many officers' social and cultural realities in Johannesburg. But as Hornberger argues, a failure to 'institutionalize' human rights is perhaps to misunderstand both what human rights are and the significance of the occupational settings into which they are introduced, and the complexity of emotions and experiences of those tasked with applying them. Police human rights training in Johannesburg was less of a 'failed' project and more of a lesson in translation; a process of construction of local rights vernaculars. Hornberger (2011: 85–94) describes how the techno-legalism of rights was translated into Christian terminology; that is, rights compliance was akin to a conversion, requiring commitment and self-discipline to achieve some higher morality. For lawyers trained in the integrity of human rights law concepts and the internal logic that accompanies legal reasoning, such re-imagination and re-interpretation might understandably be perceived as the bastardization of the very properties that give human rights its moral authority – properties like inalienability and universality, which are accompanied by its legal concepts of legality, necessity and proportionality. But crucially, for officers in Johannesburg, it was this re-imagined version of rights that offered the kind of moral authority that helped them to make sense of their power in a way the formal version did not.

The vernaculars of rights expressed by the TSG officers in Northern Ireland were also a product of an interpretative process, but the official version of human rights officers were presented with, the cultural resources they relied upon in the interpretive process and the narratives they produced each mark significant points of departure from Hornberger's findings in South Africa. Human rights were not presented to the TSG as the product of international law devised in the 'Global North', but rather as a local initiative, born out of the HRA and the ICP's reforms. Most significantly, however, human rights were now the language of the organization, spoken vocally by chief officers. Rank-and-file officers were being asked to share in it and adopt it. Training, policies and briefings were not aligned to alternative orientations, like Christian values, or even linked to the ethno-political colourings from Chapter 3; rather, the narratives were distinctly secular, formulaic and legalistic in tone. Officers knew of its organizational importance to the PSNI, and they could recite ECHR articles and the principles of legality, necessity and proportionality when asked to do so.

By detecting and interpreting the narratives TSG officers constructed within their routine work, we arrive at a fuller grasp of the how officers make sense of human rights. But such narratives are not only expressive or elucidatory, they are constitutive of the very material and discursive systems that structure future sensemaking and that enable and constrain future narratives and associated behaviours. As a result of their sensemaking, the very idea of human rights became more fluid for junior officers, less tethered to the legal properties of human rights echoed in the official police narrative. Adopting a social constructivist style of analysis, this chapter has shown how human rights came to be understood and experienced less as an external, imposed, distinct entity, and more as an 'embedded and emergent feature of social life' for officers (Ewick and Sibley, 1998: 22). This is not to say that the ideals and doctrines of the law are irrelevant in this realm of routine policing, but to suggest that they brush against and jostle alongside non-legal features of officers' own biographies, occupational settings and cultural sub-contexts. As a result of 'relying on ordinary social logics and local cultural categories and norms', Ewick and Sibley (1998: 18) argue, legal concepts, like human rights, reflect but also reproduce non-legal features of daily life.

Closely analysing the four narratives through the lens of sensemaking, a greater plurality of understandings and usages of human rights emerges. Some served to evidence and embed the official narrative, even if inadvertently. The narrative of '*ad nauseam*' depicts human rights as a *paradigm* used to regulate police powers. When it came to the deployment of AEP, for example, human rights brought relative order and coherence to ethical dilemmas arising from the use of potentially lethal baton rounds. So too were human rights understood as a *resource* for senior colleagues to use, an elaborate guide to decision-making and a vernacular through which to appeal to external audiences, including communities and oversight bodies. But other narratives contradicted core tenets of the official narrative. A commitment to human rights was a *legitimating* device for TSG officers in a more subtle, intimate and less choreographed way than for senior officers. In narrating rights as both 'common sense' and 'what we've always been doing', officers drew on their own images, identities and ideas of what good policing was about to create a narrative that embossed identity-laden values of efficacy, competence and humanity. Human rights, as a legitimating device, thus came to offer something of what Eisenberg (1984) has described as 'unified diversity'. Officers could deploy organization scripts transmitted in training sessions and policy manuals when called on to do so, but their internalization of human rights, as expressed in sensemaking narratives, was principally influenced by features of their occupational culture, the challenges arising from their routine work and the experiences belonging to their individual biographies.

For those most comfortable with, even committed to, a distinctly *legal* conception of human rights – as a body of external rules or instructions, emergent from legislatures and courts, and functioning as an instrument of policy or mode of regulation – such narratives that travel beyond it can be unsettling, disappointing, disruptive to these legal ones. A possible response might be to concede that human rights law, in practice, is confronted with the pressures of police culture, occupational pressures and situational exigencies officers encounter; that some doctrinal slippage or easing of normative weight is a sad but inevitable feature as law travels into operational contexts. But considerable solace, ought, I think, to be taken from the fact human rights law *was* operating, in some way, as a paradigm for the use of police powers and recognized as central guide for organizational training and operational planning. But a more sophisticated, sociological informed response is one that offers an answer to why, after well over a decade, human rights continues to operate as such a core idea and source of rich, identity-laden narratives for junior officers. It is precisely because understandings of human rights have taken on vibrant, varied and contradictory forms, extending beyond the legal, that it has been sustained in the collective conscience of the organization. If the official narrative was *the* single account of human rights in policing it would before long prove too brittle, too idealistic, too remote to make sense in the working lives of junior officers (cf. Ewick and Sibley, 1998: 225; Wahl, 2013). Rather, the official, more legal, narrative of rights is sustained because it is accompanied by a series of counter-narratives that not only enact and evidence it, but simultaneously enable officers to complicate and contradict it. Human rights, like legality, 'is enduring because it relies on and invokes commonplace schemas of everyday life' (Ewick and Sibley, 1998: 17).

5

Community Work

Neighbourhood Policing Teams

If the TSG are the 'pantomime villains' – a label used in jest by one senior officer – then the Neighbourhood Policing Teams are the friendly side-act trying to keep community audiences on-board with the performance of local policing. Neighbourhood Teams are the embodiment of the PSNI's 'policing with the community' strategy, an organizational ideal the ICP twinned with a 'human rights approach' to policing. However, as we will see in this chapter, the relationship between these two models remains poorly understood, both analytically and empirically. Whereas the TSG roamed the country in their heavy trucks, performing specific tasks, Neighbourhood Teams were wedded to their community 'patch', priding themselves on the detailed local knowledge they accrued. Despite being under the watchful eye of their sergeant, neighbourhood constables still enjoyed greater freedom than the TSG to shape their shift. Working in pairs, they drove out of the station gates in their yellow and blue 4x4s, able to decide which parts of their patch to visit, where to stop off on the way, when to erect a vehicle checkpoint or speed trap and whether to follow up on community complaints and those associated with them now, later or never.

Perhaps because of community policing's ill-defined terms and liberal connotations (Newburn and Reiner, 2012), it has proven easy for policymakers, as well as academics, to annex it to human rights in an uncritical fashion that does little to illuminate connections or expose disharmonies. Well-intentioned NGOs continue to promote community policing as the panacea to rights abuses in transitional societies (Brogden and Nijhar, 2005: 7). Kelling and Coles (1996: 158) assert that a function of community policing is 'protecting constitutional liberties'. Easton (2014: 22), writing on

Policing Human Rights. Richard Martin, Oxford University Press. © Richard Martin 2021.
DOI: 10.1093/oso/9780198855125.003.0006

community policing in Belgium, refers to an (undefined) 'right to security', working off the premise that: '[f]rom the point of view of community policing, the police are assumed to be guardians of human rights in democratic societies'. Though Easton hints at why this might not be so, the analysis is detached from human rights law and its discourse. Koci and Gjuraj's (2019) purported examination of the relationship between community policing and rights in Albania is similarly sparse. They restate the point that police have the capacity to both uphold and undermine democratic rights, at which point human rights fade out of their frame of analysis entirely.

This chapter addresses these shortcomings by engaging in a closer, more detailed examination of how neighbourhood officers made sense of human rights in everyday work with communities. I begin by introducing community policing in Northern Ireland, as well as in the two towns where the fieldwork took place. The analysis is then developed across three sections, drawing on neighbourhood officers' accounts, narratives and experiences. First, I critically test the two analytical bridges that have been constructed by the PSNI and the Policing Board to discursively connect human rights with community policing. Second, I examine how officers encountered, and responded to, the lay lexicons of rights that confronted them within communities, as juxtaposed with the official narrative of chief officers presented in Chapter 2. This analysis reveals how removed officers felt human rights were from their daily work; that is, rights could neither adequately account for, nor make sense of, their relationships or activities in communities. I conclude by asking what this distance means for the protection of certain groups in society.

Community Policing in Northern Ireland

It is hard to avoid clichés when introducing community policing. Most reviews recite its amorphous form – a 'semantic sponge' (Manning, 1977) – and its benevolent ideals – 'like cherry pie' (Brogden, 1999) – as well as the difficulties in its implementation and assessment (Tilley, 2003; Flanagan, 2008; Cordner, 2014). The genesis of community policing in England and Wales can be located in the reactions of police and policymakers to fears of waning police legitimacy in recent decades, compounded by bouts of protest and disorder as racial discrimination and class tensions simmered (Brogden and Nijhar 2005: chapter 2; Cordner, 2014). Its advocates speak of decentralized partnerships; shared ownership of crime control; police proactivity in addressing local needs; greater police discretion along with a more personal, welfare-orientated service. In theory, community policing is about officers being more integrated in the communities they purport to serve, and communities playing a greater role in identifying, prioritizing and addressing local crime issues (Skogan and Hartnett, 1999; Tilley, 2003). In practice, it is the reorientation of policing away from patrol and investigation, towards greater citizen involvement in police-community forums, joint crime prevention projects and neighbourhood watch schemes (Newburn and Reiner, 2012; O'Neill, 2019).

In Northern Ireland, the model of community policing was attractive to the RUC's senior officers, who saw it not only as fashionable, but a chance to appeal to disaffected Catholics, whilst also managing crime in Protestant areas (Brewer and Magee, 1991: 94). The RUC invested heavily in neighbourhood and community relations teams. They were assigned a small geographical area and were responsible for developing local knowledge, showing their presence and fostering informal community contacts (Brewer and Magee, 1991: 103–5). These were tasks neighbourhood constables enjoyed and performed well at – in predominantly Protestant 'Easton', at least. In west Belfast, however, the potential of beat patrols, outreach projects and school visits were greatly diminished. Many Catholics were distrustful of such 'ploys', while others were fearful of being seen to co-operate with police in case of reprisal from within their community, not least from the IRA (Brewer and Magee, 1991: 111–17). In these areas, neighbourhood patrols took the appearance of heavily armed convoys, stretching even the most generous interpretation of community policing.

The ICP-inspired reforms to policing in Northern Ireland came loaded with attempts to reinvigorate the community policing ethos in the hope it might stand a greater chance of success in a more settled, peacetime climate (Brogden and Nijhar, 2005: chapter 9). Branded organizationally as 'policing with the community' by the PSNI, its ideal was restated to me by one Assistant Chief Constable I interviewed: 'It's about the police being a key participant in policing but not the only participant, that communities are drawn into policing as an endeavour.' The responsibility of the police to foster local partnerships and collaborations, aimed at improving safety and reducing crime, was cemented in legislation by section 32(5) of the Police (Northern Ireland) Act 2000, which requires the PSNI 'as far as practicable, [to] carry out their functions in co-operation with, and with the aim of securing the support of, the local community'. The PSNI's bureaucratic machinery drove the 'policing with the community' strategy (known as 'PwC') forward, with mission statements, corporate guidelines and practices rolled out in 2002 and further revised in 2007 and 2011 (CJINI, 2012). Communities received dedicated Neighbourhood Teams,[1] and a multi-million-pound fund was created to support locally identified and managed projects.[2]

Community policing has been heavily researched in Northern Ireland, culminating in an insightful collection of works (e.g. Brewer and Magee, 1991; Topping, 2008; Ellison, Pino and Shirlow, 2012; Topping and Byrne, 2016). Almost without exception, Belfast has been the site of study – and the city's appeal is obvious: it serves as a microcosm of the country's inter-community tensions, legacies of the conflict, social segregation and enduring poverty. However, in consultation with a trusting district commander, I was offered a unique snapshot of community policing in a rural part of the country where researchers had yet to venture, to a place where the threat of paramilitary violence remains significant and police-community tensions still bubble at a high heat. Over the course of one month, I conducted interviews and focus groups with officers (fifteen in total) from the two Neighbourhood Teams working in 'Clantown' and 'Orangeville', and spent two weeks observing shifts in Clantown. The names of the two towns, like the officers' names, are pseudonyms to protect participants' identities. A longer period of observation would have been preferable in order to gain more than an impressionistic account, but

[1] Due to budget cuts in 2015, the number of Neighbourhood Police Teams was reduced from eighty to thirty-four. The communities retaining their Neighbourhood Teams are those which continue to experience high levels of crime and deprivation (McAleese, 2015).

[2] Between 2005 and 2009, for example, over 277 partnership projects received matched funds with other statutory and voluntary organizations (CJINI, 2009). Despite some successful reports (e.g. CJINI, 2012), the PSNI's implementation of community policing has not escaped the critical gaze of local criminologists (e.g. Topping, 2008; Ellison and O'Rawe, 2010; Topping and Byrne, 2016) or oversight bodies (CJINI, 2009, 2012).

time constraints, coupled with pressure to complete other parts of the fieldwork, made this unfeasible. Let us begin with a brief overview of Clantown and Orangeville to help situate this chapter's analysis.

The Research Sites: Clantown and Orangeville

Clantown is located several hours by car from Belfast. Once a market town that prospered from the linen trade, its economy booms no more. Turning off the motorway, you will soon reach the hairdressers, charity shops and fast-food outlets lining its short high street. Like many places, Clantown suffered its share of conflict-related tragedies: members of both communities were injured, maimed and killed by paramilitary groups and the RUC, while the fabric of the town itself was damaged by bombing. The RUC officers killed by the IRA in Clantown live on in the PSNI's organizational memory, as symbolized by the prominent plaque that hangs in the private quarters of the station, listing officers' names under the title, 'Our Murdered Colleagues'. The legacy of religious segregation also lingers on; to such an extent that you could trace a Protestant-Catholic transect over the town's map. Housing estates are distinctly Loyalist or Republican, with rows of terrace housing colourfully decorated with union jack or tricolour flags flying next to paramilitary modifications of each. Although some estates are just 100 metres from each other, their residents – in their politics, if not their poverty – are worlds apart. But you do not have to drive far again to reach Clantown's wealthier residential areas, situated between the town centre and the pleasing rural scenery.

Clantown's police station sits resolutely on a corner site near the main street. Its concrete facade rises to meet the sheets of metal caging that form a strong outer shield, protecting its buildings and their inhabitants from outside attack. Clantown's Neighbourhood Team has its own office on the main corridor, housing eight constables and four probationers. The constables are supervised by their sergeant, who regularly pops in to brief them, to check their progress or to just nudge them back out on patrol. Unlike the TSG or response teams who drive Land Rovers or darkened four-door saloons, neighbourhood officers usually patrol in liveried 4x4s. One constable reckoned their vehicle reflected neighbourhood policing: they were more approachable, even friendly looking. Each constable has their own area in which they are responsible for having a visible presence, maintaining contacts and managing local concerns that include anti-social behaviour, drug-dealing and burglaries. Clantown's sectarianism, deprivation and paramilitary presence ensured it kept its Neighbourhood Team despite the budget cuts to local policing in 2015.

However friendly the 4x4s look, their armour and bulletproof glass allude to the threats that police in Clantown face from Dissident Republicans – referred to by the policemen and women I met as the 'DRs'. Viscerally opposed to the peace process and Sinn Féin's political campaign, Dissident Republicanism is comprised of IRA splinter groups who continue to launch attacks against 'Crown forces', as well as administering rough justice within some Republican communities (Wilson, 2016: 43–6). Lethal plots against police are known to have been devised in Clantown, and house searches by the TSG continue to uncover weapons and terrorist paraphernalia in its estates. When responding to routine calls, officers follow protocols to ensure they are not lured into potentially lethal Dissident Republican ambushes (a threat referred to by officers as 'come-ons'). During house searches, local officers provide passing cover to ward off youths prone to petrol bombing police who hang around too long. The challenge Dissident Republicans pose to the PSNI's legitimacy is most apparent in one of Clantown's estates, where masked men march each year dressed in military regalia and dark sunglasses, reading out threats and firing live shots into the air. The murals in the background read: 'Oppose PSNI, M15' and 'RUC-PSNI, different name, same aim'.

The town of Orangeville is not too far away, but its story is slightly different. Unlike Clantown, its religious make-up is primarily Protestant and it is well-known as a politically engaged Unionist constituency that proudly displays its Orange heritage. In Orangeville there is a more peaceful, less dangerous Republican enclave lying behind a 'peace wall' separating it from its Protestant neighbours, with whom they have an antagonistic relationship. This was not always so. The town was less segregated in the 1980s but, before long, sectarian intimidation set in and estates soon became exclusively green or orange. Loyalist paramilitaries were responsible for most, but certainly not all, the deaths Orangeville endured during the conflict. This paramilitarism remains, whether its force is directed within communities (punishment beatings) or towards 'outsiders' (the immigrants trying to make Orangeville their home). Indeed, in the context of Northern Ireland, Orangeville is a fairly diverse town, with local shops selling a variety of Eastern European and North African foods and goods, reflecting the origins and cultures of newcomers.

The Neighbourhood Teams displayed a strong ownership over their 'patches'. As shifts began, officers searched incident logs for names and addresses that could alert them to local goings-on. They drove me by the trouble spots – drinking dens, notorious houses – taking pride in their ability to name local characters and recall recent issues. Such familiarity arose from chance encounters and small talk with residents, as well as planned initiatives like visits to schools or attendance at council meetings. Officers' sense of belonging in the communities they policed was affirmed by small but important signals, ranging from high-fives from school children (as I observed) to nicknames they had been given by teenagers. I was told that communities distinguished 'their' neighbourhood officers from officers in the TSG or response policing. In Orangeville's Republican enclave, for example, councillors complained when neighbourhood officers were spotted in a public order unit drafted in to tackle an outbreak of local disorder. This sat uncomfortably with the softer vision of policing this community had put their faith in: 'They were up in arms, "the neighbourhood teams shouldn't be in blue suits!"' (Neighbourhood Constable Andrew). It is within this local context that accounts, understandings and narratives of human rights and community policing ought to be understood.

Joining up the Dots: Human Rights and the Practice of Community Policing

Taking the official narrative presented in Chapter 2 as our starting point, it is apparent that the discursive bridge between human rights and community policing constructed by the PSNI and the Policing Board has two dimensions. The first links Neighbourhood Teams' familiarity with communities with an ability to best identify and protect the vulnerable groups within them:

> [C]ommunity consultation should identify and address the needs of vulnerable groups such as women, minority ethnic communities, the elderly,

children, members of the gay, lesbian and bisexual community and people with disabilities. (NIPB, 2006: 132)

This proximity to vulnerable groups ought to help the police fulfil their positive duty arising from certain articles of the ECHR that requires them to protect and properly investigate those at risk of serious harm. In the leading case of *Osman v UK*, the ECtHR held that Article 2 created a general duty on states to protect individuals' right to life.[3] This required not only criminal law provisions to deter offences against the person, but also law enforcement machinery capable of preventing, suppressing and sanctioning such violations. The specific obligation requires the state to take proactive 'preventative operational measures to protect an individual whose life is at risk from the criminal acts of another'.[4] But this obligation only arises where authorities knew, or ought to have known, of the existence of a real and immediate risk to the life of an identified individual and that they failed to take measures within their powers which they might reasonably have been expected to do to avoid the risk.[5] So too has the ECtHR held that failure to take pre-emptive protective measures,[6] or provide an adequate response to an initial complaint,[7] in the context of domestic abuse can constitute a violation of Articles 2 and 3, as well as Article 14, of the ECHR. The application of protective duties in domestic law in relation to vulnerable victims can be seen in cases such as *O v Commissioner of Police of the Metropolis*, concerning young Nigerian women who were victims of inhuman trafficking and forced labour, in which the High Court recognized a duty on police to carry out effective investigation into credible allegations of serious ill-treatment under Articles 3 and 4 of the ECHR.[8]

The second dimension that links the PSNI's commitment to human rights and community police is its role in generating the public trust needed for individuals to engage with police teams

[3] *Osman v UK* (App no 23452/94) ECHR 101 (28 October 1998).

[4] Ibid., at [115].

[5] Ibid., at [116].

[6] *Opuz v Turkey* (App no 34401/02) ECHR 870 (9 June 2009).

[7] *Kontrová v Slovakia* (App no 7510/04) ECHR (31 May 2007).

[8] *O v Commissioner of Police of the Metropolis* [2011] EWHC 1246. See also *Commissioner of Police of the Metropolis v DSD* [2018] UKSC 11 in which the Supreme Court held that 'egregious and significant' errors in investigation, even if not systemic in nature, could give rise to a breach of the positive duty arising from Article 3 of the ECHR, at [30]. See Rock (2004) and Starmer (2014) for insightful

and contribute to local security. Respect for rights ought to 'help integrate the police into the community' (NIPB, 2013: 153). In his keynote speech at the launch of the 2014 Annual Human Rights Report, former Policing Board legal advisor Sir Keir Starmer went further, insisting human rights promoted an 'intense focus' on victims, transparency and accountability, making it integral to public trust in police. So too has Alyson Kilpatrick, who took up the advisor role after Starmer, insisted that a human rights culture within the PSNI will impact 'either positively or negatively on the relationship between the police and the public and either makes the ultimate aim of policing by consent with the active participation and support of the community a reality or unhelpful rhetoric' (NIPB, 2019: 206). Striking a similar tone, the former Chief Constable (2014) himself stated: 'I believe that human rights are a core element of Policing with the Community and act as an enabler for the delivery of effective policing and community confidence'.

If this is how human rights and community policing were formally fused and promoted by official voices, how do these discursive connections unravel in the working lives of neighbourhood officers? In approaching this question, I was keen to get a sense of when, if at all, Neighbourhood Teams encountered organizational references to human rights in their daily work. The Teams I met – mostly made up of younger officers, earlier on in their years of service – did not voice such distinct rights narratives as officers in the TSG did. Neighbourhood officers articulated a broad, but less sharp, awareness of the legal principles (e.g. they could refer to the articles of the ECHR) and knew their importance to the organization (e.g. 'it's one of the core values' (Neighbourhood Constable Andrew) and 'the first thing you affirm to in your oath as a constable' (Neighbourhood Constable Gary). But when pushed to explain when they encountered human rights as a guide to instruct, inform or make sense of their work it was never linked to the tasks that defined community policing (e.g. fostering local partnerships, addressing vulnerability, tackling low-level criminality). Instead, rights norms were attached, almost exclusively, to typical police powers (arrest, stop and search, house searches) or

analyses of the emergence of 'victims' rights' from the ECHR and the implications of these in the UK.

the types of work often performed by the TSG (responding to disorder, conducting house searches).

A focus on these formal powers is certainly not a bad thing; in fact, as we shall see in Part IV, greater attention ought to be paid to the issues of arrest and detention. What is most interesting for the purposes of our immediate enquiry of the socialization of rights in community policing is how the two discursive connections promoted by the PSNI and the Policing Board were replaced by other narratives of community work inspired by officers' experiences, attitudes and identities. This analysis is best structured by taking each of the two official frames – first, human rights and vulnerability and second, human rights and community trust – in turn and illustrating the re-interpretive work associated with each.

When it came to responding to forms of vulnerability in communities, Neighbourhood Teams agreed that they had the additional time and resources necessary to go beyond the policing of the 'usual suspects' and better identify and respond to groups most in need. As Neighbourhood Constable Louise explains:

> We have a community surgery at the health centre every other week, so that people can come and report stuff to us who maybe wouldn't normally go into the police station or make a call, particularly older people, they will come over and chat ... We try to reassure them to pass on the relevant telephone numbers or put them in touch with other agencies that may be able to help with their problem.

This dimension of community work was not understood in human rights terminology though; no mention was made of positive duties to intervene where individuals were known to be at risk or the right of victims to an effective investigation. Instead, narratives centred around the more mundane, practical aspects of the job. The fiscal squeeze was a common trope as local success stories were qualified by concerns of diminishing budgets and staff shortages which divested officers of the resources to set up local projects. Another framing narrative, common to police culture (Banton, 1964: 85; Stenross and Kleinman, 1989), was the tedium and frustration of working with vulnerable groups. Constable Fiona complained of the rigmarole for getting a Police Information Notice in situations where allegations of harassment had been made – if it could really be called harassment in the first place. According to Fiona: 'Harassment these days is someone looking at you funny'. Even if the alleged harasser was found,

Fiona continued, 'you hear the whole story from his view and it's never ending, and all this for one wee bit of paper I'm going to submit, all this work that has to be done'. Constable Eddie, one of the few officers to mention hate crime, described working on an incident involving a woman from an ethnic minority group who was subject to abuse by local teenagers. Despite the fact that a criminal offence had been alleged and he had sought to reassure the complainant, the job was still 'a pain in the arse'. In Eddie's view, going to schools to educate youngsters about causing offence was hardly 'real' police work (see also van Maanen, 1973: 414–15; Ericson and Haggerty, 1997: 299).

The rare instance where explicit reference to human rights *was* made occurred when incidents involved a risk to a person's life. This type of incident was labelled an 'Article 2 issue', alluding to the positive duty imposed on public authorities by Article 2 of the ECHR, requiring them to take positive steps to protect threats to life, including where the threat or harm emanates from private actors. As Neighbourhood Constable Fiona describes:

> The odd time you'd maybe hear it mentioned in custody but it's never really mentioned out on the ground too much, it's never really mentioned in the station and I doubt that we'd be able to name all the human rights. The only one is Article 2 right to life, you'd hear it a lot on the radio: 'Is there an Article 2 issue here?' Am I putting on blue lights, basically ... If there's somebody in a house with a knife or whatever, is there an Article 2 issue here, and then you get supervision coming on giving the whole spiel about 'Oh, Article 2'. But you're so used to hearing that that you zone out.

This label added a formality to the police response because a commander was now overseeing the incident, especially where weapons or firearms were involved. At this point, the controller took over the radio, reciting their assessment of the situation and the precautions taken to protect the rights of officers, victims and the suspect. For some constables, this script was so familiar they 'zoned out'. But for the officers first on the scene, the framing of the event in terms of Article 2 duties could be anxiety inducing:

> Say you're told not to go into a house unless there's Article 2 issues, you hear that all the time, 'Contain unless there's Article 2 issues'. And we're sort of going okay, theoretically if you were to disobey that and go in, justifying in your head there's Article 2 issues, and it goes horribly wrong, they'll say you shouldn't have went in, you misread the situation.

By the same token, if you stand outside and don't go into the situation and it does go horribly wrong and somebody does get seriously injured or killed they'll use that same piece to say you should have went in, you had the personal responsibility that there was an Article 2 issue there. (Neighbourhood Constable Andrew)

Reference to Article 2 raised the stakes and concentrated officers' minds as to the possible interventions they might have to make to protect the person in grave danger. Yet the Article 2 duty to protect rarely gave frontline officers a clear guide to action; if anything, it posed a dilemma for which there was rarely a right answer but always a risk of 'in-the-job trouble' (Chatterton, 1979) if things went wrong. Unlike the account of the use of force described by baton gunners in the TSG, Article 2 here did not function as a 'theory of action' in sensemaking terms (Weick, 1995: 123). Rather, there was more room for ambiguity in reading the dynamics of a situation and the more direct role played by senior officers. The legalistic script commanders read out, which was triggered once an incident became an 'Article 2' issue, reinforced junior officers' suspicions that rights terminology was being used to guard against negative blowback. This concern is strikingly apparent in the experience recalled by Constable Andrew, following on from the extract above:

I had managed to get to a situation where the person who had contacted police was locked in a room but he was under the impression that the person with a machete was trying to get into the room. I had eyes on that door and I was happy enough that nothing was happening to the person that had phoned the police but while that script was going on about Article 2 issues and body armour and everything else, I heard somebody outside calling for the guy to climb out the window. I couldn't get on the radio to say there's nobody outside the door, he's safe, tell him to stay where he is until we get the other person. That person climbed out the window and jumped from the upper floor of the building! *Literally because I couldn't get space on the radio because of this script, which just strikes me as a tick box exercise: we've read out that script, therefore anything that happens we're covered, the organization is covered.* And it doesn't inspire confidence in the officers on the ground because we're all looking at each other going, get off the bloody radio so we can tell you what's happening. (emphasis added)

Here, once again, we can see how the human rights paradigm came to be made sense of according to centralized processes and procedures co-ordinated by senior officers in command roles. The construction and deployment of this 'scripting' of events in rights terminology is an important topic we will return to in detail in Part IV in the context of public order policing.

The PSNI and the Policing Board's second discursive connection between human rights and community policing is that respect for the former ought to engender trust in the latter. The basic intuition at the heart of this claim is well-supported by the burgeoning procedural justice research, which holds that people are more likely to trust institutions that treat them with respect, listen to their concerns and give them a voice in the process (e.g. Tyler and Blader, 2000; Martin and Bradford, 2019). And yet the same corpus of work alerts us to the social, cultural and economic factors that extend far beyond the police, but which remain critical to how the police are judged. The social characteristics of neighbourhoods – their cohesion, order, development or decay – are particularly important because they are symbolically associated with the police (Loader and Mulcahy, 2003; Jackson and Sunshine, 2007; Jackson and Bradford, 2009). Impressions of community breakdown 'undermine the narrative of policing – they suggest that there is a failure to maintain order and cohesion, and the police are implicated in this failure' (Bradford and Myhill, 2015: 27). In fact, recent research by Bradford et al. (2019) in Northern Ireland reveals how critical disorder and poverty, but also segregation and sectarianism, are in shaping public trust in the PSNI.

For the neighbourhood officers I met and observed, establishing semblances of order in their areas was core to their occupational self-understanding. In some housing estates, this was an order already enforced to a certain degree by community, including paramilitary groups (McAlister, Scraton and Haydon, 2009; Topping and Byrne, 2016). As such, the task was proving the PSNI's credentials as *the* security provider. At crucial times symbolism was enough. This was clear during a Monday morning shift I observed in Clantown. Over the weekend armed Dissident Republicans had walked through a Republican estate as a show of strength to residents and the PSNI. The Neighbourhood Sergeant, keen to re-assert the PSNI's status, sent her team out on a foot patrol through the estate. Usually the key signal police used to communicate their status as security-brokers within communities was an acute responsiveness to low-level complaints, especially anti-social behaviour. Constables eagerly pursued complaints of teenagers loitering, drinking or drug dealing in housing estates and actively patrolled the usual trouble spots. These policing activities chimed with officers' narratives of crime-fighting, as community meetings and youth groups were a chance to gather 'intelligence' about local crime (see also O'Neill, 2019: 21–3).

The relationships police described as having with communities were not framed in terms of individuals or groups as rights bearers, with the PSNI as the duty-bound public authority. Rather, relationships were characterized by a mixture of affectivity and instrumentality; there was an ongoing negotiation between police officers and community representatives who shared the goal of reaching agreement on matters of mutual interest with minimal fallout.[9] For Republican communities, this was consistent with what Hearty (2018: 158) has described as an approach of 'critical engagement' by which their endorsement of local policing is critical and strategic rather than one of wholesale acceptance. When it came to deadlines for state-funded projects, representatives were described as most helpful and communicative with police, but on other occasions, like when disorder broke out in estates or paramilitary attacks occurred, lines of communication were shut down as quickly as they had first appeared. Likewise, when communities wanted problematic tenants ousted from their estate's social housing, they worked closely with police and the Housing Executive. But when it came to reporting a spate of thefts, residents trusted informal (paramilitary) policing to resolve it. Officers made no reference to whose rights this kind of 'order' protected, or conversely, the groups whose rights might be negatively affected in targeting types of anti-social behaviour. This practice is something we will return to in the following section.

The transactional, give-and-take nature of police-community relationships was aptly illustrated by Neighbourhood Constable Callum (Orangeville), in an example of how it extended to Loyalist as well as Republican communities. As part of the Queen's Diamond Jubilee, a baton was due to pass alongside one of the Loyalist estates. However, in the preceding weeks, paramilitary flags still hung from the streetlamps. Wary that terrorist

[9] A transactional kind of relationship was also reported by O'Brien-Ollinger (2016: 220–4) in the context of ethnic minority interactions with An Garda Síochána at police-community forums, and by Koch (2018: chapter 5) with respect to residents of 'Park End' estate in England who used police as a means of managing personal disputes, tensions and problems that arose in their daily lives.

branded union jacks offered a rather embarrassing backdrop to the Orangeville leg of the procession, the PSNI wanted the flags taken down. The problem, Callum explained, was that 'you could guarantee if we'd taken those flags down 10,000 flags would have been up'. Instead, Callum liaised with his community contacts in the estate and, within two days, the flags had been replaced with plain, unbranded union jacks. The precise terms of this deal remained unclear. It was apparent, however, that the PSNI could offer their own services to communities when the time came. As Callum explained, the same community was very protective of their annual Twelfth of July bonfire – even more so after it was lit prematurely the previous year in an act of sabotage. Cautious of the inter-community tension this had caused, and keen to foster improved relationships with this local community representatives, the Neighbourhood Team made a point of keeping a watchful eye on the bonfire that year, reassuring the estate's bonfire builders and liaising with their Republican neighbours.

The lingering theme of mistrust was a defining feature that officers felt animated their relationships with communities. They described the slow but steady progress being made in fostering relationships within Republican and Loyalist estates that could elicit information about local criminality. The hallmarks of success were being able to conduct regular beat patrols with less security precautions and even take part in community meetings, perhaps the outworking of what Hearty (2017: 155–6) has described as Republicanism's new 'working relationship' with the PSNI based on 'critical engagement' – something officers described as impossible in Republican areas in Clantown as recently as five years previously. However, the end goal in the quest for trust was not thought to be found in greater human rights compliance, or the institutional transparency and accountability it was officially associated with in chief officers' narratives. Rather, neighbourhood officers preferred to credit their progress to high visibility policing and determined efforts to resolve the low-level issues reported to them. The imprisonment of paramilitary leaders was also cited as an important step in reaching out to what some interviewees termed the 'decent folk' living in estates who were fearful of contacting police because of paramilitary intimidation. A reluctance to openly engage with the PSNI remained within Republican, and to a lesser extent Loyalist, estates but residents were thought to be more forthcoming with minor complaints.

Just as communities were still establishing how far they could trust local police, officers themselves were scoping out the trustworthiness of the individuals and groups within their policing patch. They described how internal feuds and power-plays between characters claiming to represent communities made it difficult to identify the 'true influencers', let alone the sentiments or concerns held by the community at large. The serious crimes (e.g. drug dealing, punishment beatings, sectarian attacks) police were keen to hear more about tended to be heavily filtered, according to the officers I spoke to, by rumours, agendas and mistrust within communities, leaving officers with limited lines of enquiry (cf. Koch, 2018: chapter 5). Such uncertainty was compounded by a sense of insecurity within some Republican housing estates. Many officers managed the dangers of staying too long in certain parts of their towns in case they were attacked, with many attuned to the risk that a mundane call could, in fact, be a 'come-on' planted by Dissident Republicans. 'What about our rights, our safety?' one constable in Clantown asked.

For some officers, the simple fact was that Republican communities remained a relatively unknown entity. Suspicion remained. In the absence of a positive peace – a peaceful co-existence and ultimately reconciliation – police officers and former combatants tend to live in separate communities, inhabit their own social groups and maintain distinct political allegiances. Constable Callum, for example, described encountering an ardent Republican while going door-to-door as part of a Christmas crime prevention scheme in Orangeville's Catholic enclave:

> I'm well aware there's some community reps, and some of the [residents of one Republican housing estate], where I don't know whether I trust them. We have to work with them, but I don't know if I trust them or not. It may be a smiling assassin shall we say. I mean, we were in a house with this lady and she's got Portlaoise Republican Prisoner's Association posters on her wall and it's like, this is weird, this is surreal, we should not be in here and then she shakes your hand and stuff and it's like this is strange, I don't know what to make of this ...

Here, the legacy of the past confronted the promise of the present. Police were in the area to offer reassurance to residents and to help them to stay safe in their homes, yet, confronted by a culture alien, if not hostile, to his own, it was officers like Callum who soon felt unsafe. Such an account is rarely voiced in the local policing literature. But rather ironically, if not unsurprisingly, it has a remarkable familiarity to the concerns of Republican communities themselves. As demonstrated by Hearty (2017: 155), the appeal from Sinn Féin for Republicans to 'move on' and establish a new 'working relationship' can be a deeply personal challenge; it entails interacting closely with 'former enemies responsible for wrongs inflicted on the collective and individual levels'. As captured in the words of Constable Callum, this challenge is a shared one. Alongside organizational narratives of reform, officers retain their own personal accounts of bravery, but also sacrifice and trauma, that can make establishing trust and meaningful engagement with Republican communities difficult (Lawther, 2010). On returning to his station, Callum will have met another artefact that tells a competing tale of the conflict from the Portlaoise Republican Prisoner's Association: that list of names inscribed on the plaque titled 'Our Murdered Colleagues'.

Talking Rights in Communities

The adaptability of human rights to be interpreted and directed towards certain ends is an idea that was demonstrated in the context of police oversight in Part II of the book. In the official police voice, properties distilled from human rights – legality, ethics and accountability – were amplified and promoted as a language of legitimation directed at influential audiences. The local political parties responded to this human rights argumentation in different ways, revealing as much about the ethno-political fissures that remain today over the legacy of the conflict and the status of Northern Ireland as they did about the legitimacy of the PSNI and its policing practices. We have already begun to explore the processes of adaption and interpretation within the PSNI itself that TSG officers used to make sense of the official narratives of rights promoted by chief officers, management and trainers. In the context of community policing, it was striking, however, that these official narratives were juxtaposed with other, public narratives perhaps more prominent in their frequency and potency. In this section, I explore the 'rights talk' that Neighbourhood Teams heard expressed in the communities they policed – talk to which they had to respond in managing local order and which, in turn, offered further occasions, conversations and experiences from which officers could make sense of human rights beyond official narratives.

The primacy of human rights talk within Northern Ireland's grass-roots organizations and residents groups is well-documented. McEvoy (2003), for example, has demonstrated how rights vernaculars were adopted and applied by various actors in their respective efforts to promote (or resist) peace-making. Likewise, Curtis' (2014) rich ethnographic work has revealed how rights discourse was crafted into everyday advocacy by activists in Belfast to challenge the social, political and economic injustices communities faced. Human rights have also been thrust into political debates since the mid-2000s with the NIHRC's attempts to introduce a Bill of Rights (discussed in the Introduction). In Clantown and Orangeville, officers described how human rights seeped into local crime talk. This talk, as recounted by officers, resisted the official discourse of human rights. Prominent voices in communities wanted to see police responding to crime and antisocial behaviour in a tougher, swifter manner. Constable Andrew explained how negative reporting of rights in tabloid papers (e.g. 'the media just love having the big stories about somebody's breach of human rights') and anti-European sentiment (e.g. '"what's the EU law going to introduce next?" sort of thing') had given human rights a bad name (see also Rowbottom, 2019). As such, it was best to avoid entertaining this discourse where possible:

> It's actually sometimes more beneficial to avoid talking about human rights as such. People – and it's the media thing again – people hear human rights and it automatically gets their back up a lot of the time. Sometimes you're better to edge around an issue and talk about an issue – you might be talking about somebody's human rights but as long as you don't let them know you're talking their human rights, they take it on board a lot better. And it's a simple matter of maybe talking with them via example, you know, if this was your son or this was your cousin, and talking about it that way and trying to get them to picture it from another point of view ... People just hear human rights and they switch off, they don't want to know, they just automatically assume that somebody's getting something for nothing or getting one over on them and they just don't want to know, so I find it better not to use that language at all with them. (Neighbourhood Constable Andrew)

I witnessed a similar narrative in an encounter between officers and one of Clantown's middle-class residents. A builder's van had been stolen from the driveway of a house where extensive renovations were being done. The theft took place in broad daylight: two men had walked up the driveway and, within seconds, jumped into the van and sped away. The builder was bewildered. The home-owner, who had employed private security, was irate: 'Aw, it's a disgrace, absolute disgrace somebody could do this, that was his livelihood, they will be off down the border. You can't trust people these days, you couldn't have good faith in people, it was a matter of time before something was stolen'. The blame fell not on police, but the law itself: 'I know you'll do your best. It's not your fault, it's the law that's crooked'. The probationary constable was as curious as I regarding the home-owners' assessment:

> 'What do you mean crooked?' The answer was clear: 'It favours the offender, it's *for* the offender. I just want police to get him, to find the guy, lock him up and throw away the key'. You're that worried about telling someone to get off your land because they've all these civil rights, their rights, you know? And if you interview them they all refuse to speak, they shouldn't be allowed to do that, they should have to speak and tell the police where they were. (Field notes, 19 May 2015)

Neighbourhood officers had varying degrees of sympathy for this view of the law as having been bent – made crooked – because of an emphasis on the rights of the accused that came at the expense of seemingly virtuous, law-abiding folk. Constable Callum was obviously torn between the official police narrative, the counter-narrative he heard in communities and his own on-the-job experience:

> Human rights legislation protects everyone, but I honestly believe it does protect the perpetrator or offender more than the victim or more than even us. I mean, you know, examples. One night I was in custody, it had been a long day, I was well into my own time in terms of being beyond my shift, I had missed this and I had missed that. I was ready to interview someone and the sergeant went 'Wow, can't do that, it's going to be another half hour'. 'Why?' 'He's entitled to his meal break'. And I went, I haven't eaten in hours, right to private and family life, what about our family life? Being held on for hours simply because you're waiting for a solicitor or interpreter or some idiot is just being a complete tube and going on about 'I want to speak to this, I want to speak to that'. So yeah, I think it is stacked in the favour of the perpetrator or the offender, I do.

Callum's account marks a personal encounter with what Ewick and Sibley (1998: 247–8) have termed the 'imperfection' of legality, in which contradictions between its ideal and practice are sustained simultaneously. Callum insists human rights law protects everyone, from victims, to police officers like him to 'perpetrators', and readily draws upon the rights discourse to assert his own interests ('right to private and family life, what about our family life?'). But when confronted with grounded reality, the ideal he just endorsed is immediately acknowledged as a partial, if not flawed, one in practice. Callum exposed the contradictory qualities of human rights that complicated, yet also reflected, sentiments of the official police narrative of human rights as virtuous, inclusive and protective. Similarly, Neighbourhood Constable Andrew, reflecting on his own time in court in his role as a police officer, described how frustrating it was to see guilty defendants walk free or receive unduly lenient punishments. He found it hard to avoid agreeing with the criticisms he heard in communities, but feeling implicated in the apparent failings of the system, he tried to explain to critics in his patch that rights were for everyone and police did their best to bring offenders to justice – what the courts did was another matter.

Although officers were content to manoeuvre around or lend a sympathetic ear to the popular grievances just mentioned, the same could not be said where members of the public sought to deploy the vernacular of human rights themselves to challenge officers on the street. In such instances, rights talk shifted from understandable, even legitimate, grievances to what sounded like baseless moans of the ill-informed. In officers' accounts, I heard echoes of what Hornberger (2011) has coined human rights 'forgery' or 'fakery': improper claims to entitlement or protection cloaked in the language of rights. Whereas this language may draw its normative thrust from international conventions and treaties, such claims are loosely connected to the standards and prescriptions to which lawyers or judges would point. In contrast to law's 'authenticity', lay rights vernaculars are rarely clear or coherent but rather situational, improvised and momentary, crafted and deployed to affect change in the face of the circumstances or predicaments faced by their user (Hornberger, 2011: 10–12). To claim a right in such circumstances, a person's experience is condensed and concentrated in a 'set of abstractions that invoke connection and deference that have been empirically unavailable' (Ewick and Sibley, 1998: 232). Detached from questions of law, these rights claims tell us something about the relationship between the claim-makers and the power-holders who can validate or discredit them.

The ease with which 'fake' human rights claims slipped off the tongue of members of the public was a common feature of policing, according to officers. Several criteria were used by police to quickly assess the 'authenticity' of rights claims, the outcomes of which reinforced the role of officers as street adjudicators of 'right' or 'wrong' claims – but also, by implication of such efforts to police its use, the very status of human rights as a worthy ideal and one that belonged to the police as upholders of law and order. Each criterion represents a form of 'cultural knowledge' (Sackmann, 1991) reliant on categories and labels to define people and events, which, in turn, serve as behavioural guides as to what is or is not appropriate (see Chan, 1996; O'Neill, 2019). The first concerned the claims-maker themselves, and whether they were deemed either worthy or authoritative enough to substantiate their claim:

> Yeah. Kids are all 'My right to a solicitor' and 'You have no right to search me, you need an adult to search me'. Some of them can lay it on real thick and you're standing there going 'Why? What?' This is quite a simple job to do and they just make it more difficult. (Neighbourhood Constable Katrina)

This criterion, like the others below, form part of what Ericson (2007: 378) has described as the 'language game of police culture'. Unlike law, which formulates precedents as rules of conduct that bind future decisions, the language of police culture rather 'articulates a vocabulary of precedents in the form of anecdotes that provide a practical capacity to act' (Ericson, 2007: 378). We see the stock of experience that might inform future actions in the second criterion. This related to whether the kind of behaviour or circumstances associated with the rights claim indicated to the officer that failure to respect or validate the claims-maker could result in 'trouble'. In explaining this, Constable Katrina drew on a recent experience of hers:

> I was talking to a guy on Saturday night and I was telling him to go home because he was trying to start a fight, but he wasn't being disorderly enough [to be arrested], but he decided to take out his phone but he wanted to walk down the street past the guy he was trying to fight with and I was telling him to go the other way, so he said I was breaching his human rights because I was blocking him walking down the road, but I was trying to

prevent a fight happening, so he was recording me then because I told him he couldn't walk down the street. So, you get idiots like that.

The third arose in circumstances where officers sensed 'real' human rights claims were being made – claims which registered sufficiently with what they had been taught in training – but they were confident they still knew better than the suspect. In each case, rights were being deployed as a resistance narrative, deployed momentarily and opportunistically, which derives its normative weight from the very features of human rights contained in the official police narrative. As observed by Ewick and Sibley (1998: 235–6), those who are most subject to power – ethnic minorities, young people, the unemployed, the vulnerable – are most likely to be actually aware of its operation, but usually less well-placed to challenge meaningful abuses of it by asserting their rights. In these accounts of lay resistance, the rights claims formulated and deployed suggested both a sense of how legal power operated – whether subject to procedural rules or limited by individual rights – and also how it was sustained. Exploring how officers' criteria for authorizing rights claims are actually put to work in their daily practices with such groups would be an especially interesting avenue of future research.

A striking instance, however, where officers' power to validate or invalidate potentially 'fake' rights claims was obviously challenged concerned police encounters with the Dissident Republicans. The story told by officers was that Dissident Republicans were extremely well-versed and confident in the legal limits of police stop and search powers. Officers described acerbic encounters with Dissident Republicans who recited their rights and demanded police cite their own powers. As Neighbourhood Constable Fiona put it, Dissident Republicans:

Ask you what legislation are you using. They'll know that under Article 21 they can give you their name, their date of birth, the power to stop and question and they can walk on unless they are detaining them for a search under different legislation, like they're fully aware of all of this. And some of them would be quite blunt, that's all you're getting, and they'll walk on. And it is a bit of challenge because in the back of your head you're going what is that legislation, I can't think is that all I can do?

New recruits were warned to be alert to this type of challenge to authority. In a training session for new recruits that I observed, actors played suspected paramilitaries writing down vehicle registration plates. The task for the aspiring officers was to conduct a stop and search under terrorist legislation. The trainers were fierce in their criticism of what we observed: one officer cited the right article but the wrong legislation; the other cited the wrong article but the right legislation; and another ran after, and forcibly stopped, the suspect, something the trainer warned could amount to battery. The gravity of their mistakes was laid out in stark terms: 'We've got three suspects out there that we've let go with the registration numbers of my car, Sergeant A's car, your car, your car and your car [pointing at trainees], which they're going to take back to their bosses who are going to plant IEDs [Improvised Explosive Devices] under our cars' (field notes, 18 September 2015). The wily trainers reinforced the need to know the law, thus being able to out-smart rights 'forgery' by their adversaries: 'Don't let them walk away from you when you're speaking to them. You're police officers, no matter what people think of the terrorist legislation and powers, you've got that power to stop someone and search them, be confident using it' (field notes, 18 September 2015).

Whose Rights, Whose Order?

The disconnect between human rights and neighbourhood officers' accounts of their work offers insight into the extent to which they internalized human rights. Chapter 4 demonstrated how TSG officers could, if asked to do so, frame their 'dirty work' using the formal version of rights promoted by chief officers – even if this was made sense of in light of officers' own experiences, attitudes and identities. Neighbourhood officers, as discussed, policed 'fake' or 'forged' versions of human rights but, overall, found this language more difficult than TSG officers to apply readily to the types of task they performed. Neighbourhood Teams can be best characterized as displaying a partial form of human rights internalization characterized by an awareness of the 'proper' way to talk or act, and role playing in accordance with the official narrative when the situation required it, without embracing or endorsing it as a way of making sense of routine policing (Checkel, 2005: 84). But does a limited consciousness of human rights as articulated in the properties of the official voice, or a reluctance to meaningfully take into account the interests that lay vernaculars sought to convey, really matter?

To answer this question, it is necessary to return to the idea that human rights are a mode of regulating public authorities like police; that is, human rights frame how officers understand their work and guide the decisions they make. Some might argue, however, that provided officers endeavour to protect vulnerable groups and foster mutually beneficial community relationships, it is irrelevant whether they perceive such work as derived from the ECHR or their status as a public authority under the HRA. If outcomes seem broadly reasonable, we need not get too caught up as to whether the steer is, in fact, human rights. Taking this point head on, I want to pull the chapter's analysis together by considering the possible consequences of limited rights consciousness for the policing of certain groups. I suggest, as Hornberger (2011) has done in the South African context, that a lack of human rights consciousness might enable, even facilitate, practices which leave certain groups under- or over-policed. The practices discussed in the following paragraphs include the intersectional nature of vulnerability; the policing of young people and anti-social behaviour; and the socio-economic conditions that exist within marginalized communities.

The first – which I raise tentatively due to my short period of observation – is that vulnerability tends to be associated with an 'ideal-type' of victim, one that is usually white, female and perceived as innocent (cf. Christie, 1986). The following examples are illustrative. On patrol in Clantown, we pulled over to have a brief chat with an elderly woman walking her dog in a Republican housing estate. Constable Fiona explained that the lady had severe dementia and had been burgled by men she had let into her house after they asked to borrow her phone. Another rather sad encounter involved a widow whose garden gate had been marked with white chalk; the rumour was that this signalled her home had been targeted by burglars. Sitting in her small living room, the constable offered some crime prevention tips as a tear ran down her cheek. Her fear was that burglars would kill her dog, the only thing left since her husband's recent death. The following week, Clantown's officers gave an internet safety talk to children in social care. Constable Kirsty explained the dangers of speaking to strangers on social media, warning them not to send private pictures or agree to meetings. Kirsty told me how she worried about the young girls in the group, who had been in abusive relationships already and were victims of 'nasty' crimes.

The people just mentioned are, of course, deserving of support and protection. The point here is that there are many other groups, equally, if not more, vulnerable, who remain under-protected. It is thus necessary to acknowledge that gender, class, social isolation, ethnicity, visa status, sexuality and religion intersect to reproduce and reinforce types of vulnerability (Sokoloff and Pratt, 2010; Millings, 2013; Parmar, 2019). O'Brien-Ollinger's (2016) ethnographic study of policing ethnic minority groups in Dublin, for instance, offers a stark illustration of how police unfamiliarity with such groups, combined with Guards' 'neo-racism',[10] can lead to negative treatment and under-protection of ethnic minorities. Guards downplayed racially motivated hate crime as mere 'bullying', enabling police to dismiss such complaints as irrational (O'Brien-Ollinger, 2016: 218). I did not experience such practices during my short time in Clantown, but the kinds of knowledge gaps and parochial attitudes detected by O'Brien-Ollinger might begin to explain the strikingly low clearance rate for the catalogue of hate crimes in Northern Ireland.[11] Tolerance, cultural awareness and social capital cannot be bred by human rights reform alone, yet a greater rights consciousness in officers' daily work – especially the guiding principle of the universality of rights, regardless of one's race, creed, gender, ethnicity or sexuality[12] – might better alert them to the range of vulnerabilities across groups, particularly ethnic minorities.

The second practice concerns the over-policing of some marginalized groups. Approaching this issue of how police prioritize local issues, concerns and vulnerabilities from a different angle,

[10] Where the source of racism is not pseudo-biological inferiority, but rather attributes: 'individuals from ethnic minorities' difference, deviance and their criminality to some are assumed aspects of their cultural background' (O'Brien-Ollinger, 2016: 204).

[11] As reported in the 2016 Peace Monitoring Report, detection and outcome rates remain low for all forms of hate crime, especially when compared to general crime. As summarized by the author of the Report, '[t]his is a matter of concern, in that it raises the question of the adequacy with which crimes with a hate motivation are being pursued by the PSNI' (Wilson, 2016: 31).

[12] See Donnelly (2007: 282) on 'conceptual universal': 'human rights are ordinarily understood to be the rights that one has simply as a human. As such, they are equal rights, because we either are or are not human beings, equally.'

Goold (2016: 236) argues that improved knowledge of, and proximity to, communities might, in certain circumstances, undermine the human rights of particular groups:

> What may start as a well-intentioned effort to protect the rights of individuals living in these communities, can quickly evolve into a situation where the police become a constant factor in the life of the community, with the result that more and more individuals become subject to police power ... a greater focus on rights – as well intentioned as it may be – can lead the police to pursue law enforcement strategies that have negative effects on already vulnerable communities, which may exacerbate existing problems relating to class, gender and socio-economic status.

Goold's observation raises an issue that was rarely, if ever, made explicit in officers' self-accounts of their work; that is, who are the rights beneficiaries of the 'order' that police reproduce and whose rights are interfered with to achieve this 'order'? As Bradford and Loader (2016) note in their analysis of stop and search in England and Wales – a power they expose as a means of monitoring and controlling marginal populations – it is only when such practices are stripped of official rhetoric (safety, deterrence) and discussed in terms of their social reality (discrimination, coercion) that collateral harms implicated in police order maintenance become alarmingly clear.

The types of political, economic and cultural order police are crucial to maintaining in capitalist democracies is a topic of ongoing discussion (see, e.g., Loader and Mulcahy, 2003; Wacquant, 2009; Ellison and Pino, 2012; Koch, 2018). Many empirical studies of routine policing report the enforcement of laws and a vision of order 'particularly unfriendly to disempowered youth, minorities and those suffering from economic hardship and social and political disenfranchisement' (de Lint, 2017: 353). Such arguments are not intended to doubt the need for a service that enforces the criminal law – something the ECtHR itself has recognized as crucial to compliance with the effective protection of the rights of vulnerable groups[13]– but rather to underscore the point that the law, which has its own in-built biases, is often enforced

[13] See, e.g., *MC v Bulgaria* (App no 39272/98) ECHR 651 (4 December 2003) in the context of Article 8 and the criminalization of rape: 'Positive obligations on the State are inherent in the right to effective respect for private life under Article 8; these obligations may involve the adoption of measures even in the sphere of the relations of individuals between themselves' (at [150]).

asymmetrically, reflecting the outlooks, attitudes, prejudices, biases, pressures and mistakes of junior officers given the awesome responsibility of deciding what behaviour will be subject to the coercive state power (Ericson, 1981; Choongh, 1997; Hillyard and Gordon, 1999).

These debates over the values that motivate law enforcement find a resonance in recent human rights law scholarship. As argued by Lazarus (2012, 2020), the framing of protective operational obligations on policing arising from Articles 2 and 3 of the ECHR as an unqualified good – in so far as they serve to safeguard victims and protect an undefined right to 'security' – risks overlooking the 'coercive sting' that could accompany such obligations. Propelled by a rhetoric of public protection, Lazarus (2012) warns that protective duties arising from Articles 2 and 3 of the ECHR that fall on the police are rarely framed by the court, or in political discourse more generally, in such a way that adequately accounts for the forms of coercion directed at perpetrators, or potential perpetrators, of harm. It was recognized by the ECtHR in *Osman* of:

> the need to ensure that the police exercise their powers to control and prevent crime in a manner that fully respects the due process and other guarantees which legitimately place restraints on the scope of their action to investigate crime and bring offenders to justice, including the guarantees under Articles 5 and 8 of the Convention.[14]

But as illustrated by Lazarus (2020) in her critical analysis of the exemplary case law of the ECtHR, the recognition of countervailing interests, not least the negative rights of those subject to police investigatory and pre-emptive powers, are often lacking.[15] The danger that arises from such an emphasis on the rights of those who might be harmed, in operational terms, is a culture of risk aversion by law enforcement. To extend Lazarus' argument and to connect it with Goold's (2016) earlier observations, too sympathetic an account of collective security, motivated by a legitimate concern for particular forms of vulnerability in society, increases the likelihood of over-policing of certain groups in society perceived by police to be 'risky' – either to (other) vulnerable

[14] *Osman* (n 3), at [116].

[15] See, in particular, Lazarus' (2020) reference to the case of *Tagayeva and Others v Russia* (App no 26562/07) ECHR 354 (13 April 2017).

groups or to the reputation of police organizations themselves – in the form of surveillance, monitoring or active intervention.

In the micro-contexts of Clantown and Orangeville, young people's anti-social behaviour was, according to Neighbourhood Teams, a major challenge to communities' micro-orders. It was a hot topic animating local 'crime talk' (Loader et al., 1998: 389) as voiced in complaints made to officers, which usually involved young people 'hanging around', 'being a nuisance' or 'up to no good'. The anxiety anti-social behaviour provoked in communities is likely an expression of a host of social, economic and moral changes (Loader et al., 1998). In Republican and Loyalist communities, changes include the shifting provision of security from paramilitaries to the state, challenges to personal and communal identities cultivated during the conflict and fears that social controls are weakening and deference to authority is diminishing (McAlister, Scraton and Haydon, 2009). The concerns of adult residents and, by implication, local officers, were interwoven with visions of how youngsters ought to behave, socialize and interact with authority. Neighbourhood Constable Fiona captures this sentiment:

> Youths hanging around causing annoyance, we [are] definitely getting more people phoning that in. But they don't hang around their own estate, they go across the road to the old factory or they go up to the local school ... Probably within the estates they've still got that little bit of respect for elders, but then they move it across [outside the estate] and they just don't care that they're pissing up against somebody's fence or they don't care that the wee old lady has come out and shouts at them, but it's not where they live so it's nearly like nobody's going to find out – come over here and act the big lad and whenever I go down to my own estate I'll be fine. But a lot of stuff like eggs being thrown at windows. Like this morning, I was out at Green Park and a couple of new trees had been bent over and snapped last night and the local people don't take too kindly to that because that's their park, which is situated very much in their side of town ... it's a nice area and it's a complete bonus to have it on your doorstep but it's not used in the right way. I mean, there's football pitches there but there's stuff there that just isn't used.

In this account, Fiona is sympathetic to residents' concerns. Teenagers belonged in their estate where they were subject to informal social controls. When they strayed from there, they did not know how to 'use' the nicer area in the 'right way' or how to respect the places and spaces belonging to others.

In their efforts to protect against the threat of anti-social behaviour to communities' micro-orders, police have arguably upheld the interests of adult residents at the cost of one group in particular: young people. With a high premium placed on proactive intervention, I observed officers patrolling alleyways, street corners and parks where teenagers spent their evenings and weekends joking, drinking and making mischief. In interviews, officers described how they tried to divert teenagers away from certain areas before trouble arose and encouraged them to join local youth clubs instead of being a nuisance outside of them. Several officers had short shrift for teenagers annoying 'decent folk'. They contrasted this misbehaviour with their own, pro-social, behaviour as teenagers ('when I was their age, there was no youth clubs for me, but I used to kick a ball in the park and play cricket, climb trees and stuff'). Others explained local children's bad attitudes as a product of their upbringing, pointing the finger at parents. In one encounter I witnessed, the mutual distain was apparent: a teenager waved a stick at the police and shouted unsavoury words as we drove by. 'Wee dickhead!' was the response from inside the police car.

The impact this kind of police attention and intervention can have on young people's rights to freely assemble and enjoy public space is evidenced in McAlister, Scraton and Haydon's (2009) extensive research involving 196 8 to 25 year olds across Northern Ireland, including the districts containing Clantown and Orangeville. Young people complained of routine abuse, discrimination and a lack of respect from police. They considered themselves an 'easy target' and recounted experiences of officers constantly forcing them to move through their neighbourhoods, something they experienced as harassment and intimidation (McAlister, Scraton and Haydon, 2009: 67). In their eyes, age, rather than religion, was the most serious kind of discrimination they faced (McAlister, Scraton and Haydon, 2009: 78). The number of young people subject to police stop and search further hints at the over-policing of this group in many parts of the country. Between 2010 and 2017, almost 28,000 children (under 18 years of age) were stopped and searched by police, with an average of around 4.5 per cent of stops resulting in further police action (Topping and Bradford, 2020). Such alarming figures – much worse than elsewhere in the UK – have been both overlooked and facilitated, Topping and Bradford argue, by the keenness of chief officers and oversight bodies to present policing in Northern Ireland as rule-bound, highly regulated and widely endorsed. The use of stop and search powers under PACE can, however, be seen as a classificatory tool for PSNI to proactively police, even control, young, suspect, socially marginal populations (Topping and Bradford, 2020: 99).

This leads us to the third practice, best introduced as a question: if an organization like the police is committed to human rights, must it also confront, or at least be sensitive to, the challenges of the socio-economic rights of those living in deprived communities? After all, is the anti-social behaviour complained of, and which police actively respond to, not intimately linked to the exclusion, adversity and limited opportunities confronting young people in Clantown and Orangeville's housing estates? As expressed by one 16 to 25 year old participant in McAlister, Scraton and Haydon's (2009: 73) study:

> People aren't bothered with us. They just want us out of their area. But it's our area as well. It's not their place, we've been reared here too ... We should have more say. Most of the things they complain about we complain about as well. You know, like dog poo and the state of the estate. And there's nothing for us.

The reforms inspired by the Independent Commission on Policing focused exclusively on civil-political rights, but the groups over-policed – young, poor, minorities – are usually those whose basic socio-economic rights (to housing, education, healthcare) are least satisfactorily met by the state. The average rate of unemployment for 16 to 24 year olds in the most deprived parts of Northern Ireland is 34 per cent, compared with a national average of 18.5 per cent and the UK-wide youth unemployment rate of 11.9 per cent (Wilson, 2016: 93). Regarding educational attainment, just over 30 per cent of teenagers attending non-grammar schools (a proxy for lower social classes) and entitled to free school meals gain five 'good' GCSE grades, compared with over 90 per cent of grammar school pupils not entitled to free meals (Wilson, 2016: 100). For several neighbourhoods in Clantown in particular, the levels of social stress, community disengagement and local disorder experienced within them resulted in them being ranked in the top 3 per cent of the PSNI's Community Prioritization Index. The Index is used to identify and prioritize resources 'based on the experience of community harm and the potential risk from vulnerability and disengagement' (PSNI, 2011).

This socio-economic context raises a much bigger question about the utility of human rights discourse for those confronted with poverty and marginalization in their daily lives, and thus its value as a language for police engagement with communities. As Beirne and Knox (2014: 12) have remarked rather frankly, 'no one describes concerns about damp in flats (or the disparaging treatment of people with mental health issues, or racist attacks, or a failure to treat hospital patients with dignity) as a "human rights abuse", or cites chapter and verse from international law'. The connection between socio-economic rights and policing has been gestured at in the PSNI's official discourse, albeit in qualified fashion:

> Keeping communities safe requires a coordinated approach which increases the resilience of local communities and addresses concerns arising from a range of issues, such as isolation, a lack of opportunity, poor health and low educational attainment. *Many of these are human rights challenges which are beyond the remit of policing alone.* (PSNI, 2013a: 5; emphasis added)

Neighbourhood Teams were confronted daily with material deprivation and relative social disadvantage. During patrols they saw unemployed men and women nipping to the shops. At community meetings they heard complaints of dirty streets, broken lights, pavements in need of repair. Echoing the PSNI statement quoted above, officers generally understood these as issues far beyond their remit, instead the business of the local council or Housing Executive (cf. Miller, 1999: 211). Although this understanding may well be correct as a matter of civic administration, it is noteworthy that officers saw neither the connection between deprivation and rights, nor the link between socio-economic conditions and young people's misbehaviour. Socio-economic rights – such as the rights to adequate housing, education or healthcare, recognized in international human rights law, as well as a number of domestic constitutions – fell outside of officers' sense of what human rights captured. Officers maintained that their job was about law-enforcement – clearing up crime, not crumbling curb stones. The fact that living conditions were being brought to police attention was just another example of police being saddled with issues that other under-funded agencies were struggling to cope with.

Conclusion

Egon Bittner (1990: 131) classically described the role of the police as 'a mechanism for the distribution of non-negotiable coercive force employed in accordance with the dictates of an intuitive grasp of situational exigencies'. It is this capacity to use coercive force which has been the focal point of analysis in the few recent works on human rights and policing (Hornberger, 2011; Goold, 2016; McClanahan and Brisman, 2017). A common insight is the duality of this power; it can be used to fatally undermine rights or fundamentally protect them depending on how it is used. More interestingly, human rights can also serve as a powerful conceptual and semantic resource to convert illegal violence into legal force through ideas of 'proportionality' and 'necessity' (Hornberger, 2010). These valuable insights are given due attention in Part III, but before travelling there it is worth dwelling on Bittner's influential description of the police role a little further. As Bittner (1990) elaborates, the police mandate, rooted as it is in the potential to use coercive force, is an ongoing negotiation; a process of tacit bargaining between police and society as well as between individual officers and the people, behaviours and, we might add, communities, they encounter (see also Manning, 2013). An analysis of the role human rights play in policing surely ought to capture these dynamics of negotiation, audience and situational exigencies so core to the police role itself – and, I would argue, to how officers make sense of human rights in routine policing.

This chapter has taken some initial steps towards the situational dynamics that affect how Neighbourhood Policing Teams encounter, understand and interpret human rights in the context of community policing in Clantown and Orangeville. The discursive framing and primacy of human rights articulated by official police voices faded in relevance and meaning for the officers I met – even more so than had been the case with the TSG. While neighbourhood officers could repeat some of the core human rights references from their initial training, the distribution of policing as a resource was shaped neither by positive duties nor the recognition of rights, but by audience demands, often responsive to the specific needs within communities where trust was still being worked out. As Ewick and Sibley (1998: 51) observe, people express 'different understandings, values and expectations, depending on the situation in which they are speaking and what they imagine accomplishing through their talk'. Similarly, officers' understanding of human rights was embedded in, and emergent out of, their daily activities. Occupationally rooted in these neighbourhoods, officers had to maintain ongoing relationships with key influencers, make compromises and respond to local demands. Human rights were rarely helpful to officers in conveying messages or resolving local disputes. Similarly, when confronted on patrol with challenges framed in rights terms, officers described the same kind of pragmatic assessment Bittner's own work captured so well; that is, they quickly assessed the individual, their behaviour and the likelihood of trouble to decide whether to tolerate rights 'fakery'.

In sum, there is no doubt that chief officers would be proud to hear the ease with which their junior colleagues could recite lines from the official voice; aspects of the official narrative of human rights have clearly entered the lexicon of officers in these sites of routine policing. But juxtaposed with this legal conception of human rights promoted in the official narrative were 'residues of nonlegality' (Ewick and Sibley, 1998: 249) that heavily shaped how officers in both the TSG and Neighbourhood Policing Teams made sense of human rights. The official tropes of *legality*, *ethics* and *accountability* were mediated by officers' own experiences, outlooks and identities. Further still, the discursive bridges drawn by official voices between rights and policing had to jostle with the mundane realities of the tasks officers performed, the situational exigencies they faced and the cultural norms that animated their everyday experiences. In Parts IV and V, we continue the exploration of human rights and policing, taking with us Bittner's (1990) insights regarding the dynamics of negotiation, audience and situational exigencies. The emphasis now shifts away from officers' socialization in human rights and sensemaking narratives to critically examine the regulation of police decision-making on the basis of human rights – specifically how officers' performed as 'practitioners' responsible for interpreting and applying human rights standards and principles in two further sites of policing: the public order policing of parades and protests and police custody.

PART IV

Public Order Policing: The Rights of Protestors, Public and Police

6

Righting the Public Order Script

> There's a script the brass have and they want you to stay with it. They tell you to block this road so you just stand at that road and take abuse and take abuse and you can't do anything about it, and it's quite frustrating. (TSG Constable Larry)
>
> You're from this part of the world the same way I am, observer of this part of the world the same way I am, that's the nature of Northern Ireland, we're not politicians ... we're dealing with very sensitive, emotive, contentious issues, where there are absolutely competing views, if not rights, and I don't have it within my gift to bring a resolution to those competitions. I need to police in the middle of that and I suppose manage that. (Chief Superintendent Andrew)

Contentious parades and protests in Northern Ireland present a paradigm case of competing rights, requiring the PSNI to respond in ways that respect the human rights of the various parties involved. This is a weighty task. Parades and protests often take place in communities where police are working hard to establish or maintain trust and where the risk of rioting is real. In this operational context, the PSNI is equipped with formidable tactical options, albeit that their use comes with strict human rights law standards and exacting local oversight. The legal regime does not make the situation any more straightforward for the PSNI. Since 1998, the statutory responsibility for adjudicating upon notified parades, including the application of any restrictions on them, has been transferred from the police to a quasi-judicial body, the Parades Commission, which itself suffers from a legitimacy crisis and has been the subject of possible reform. The PSNI must enforce contested Commission determinations whilst upholding the rights of marchers, counter-protestors, nearby residents and police officers, and, in the case of parades about which the Commission is not notified, determine the appropriate response themselves.

Policing Human Rights. Richard Martin, Oxford University Press. © Richard Martin 2021.
DOI: 10.1093/oso/9780198855125.003.0007

The next two chapters explore how mid to senior ranking PSNI officers engage with, adapt to and interpret the very rules they promote so heavily in their official discourse. What appearance did human rights law take in the planning and carrying out of public order operations? To what extent did public order commanders understand the duties arising from the HRA? How did they interpret these duties, and, most interestingly, make them meaningful in an operational setting? Were there techniques or understandings that enabled officers to creatively use human rights law protections, perhaps enhancing or undermining its regulatory force? Did a rights-based approach make it easier for the PSNI to account for their decisions to communities and oversight bodies? The answers to these questions are addressed in the next two chapters and represent the views of a select sample of officers intimately involved in public order policing in Northern Ireland. In producing this account, I rely on interviews with twelve public order commanders (Chief Inspector to Assistant Chief Constable); interviews and focus groups with eleven sergeants and thirty constables from the TSG (the primary public order unit); four interviews with public order trainers/tactical advisors; and observations of public order training days and a week-long commander course.

To make sense of the firm institutionalization of human rights in this site of policing, I introduce and develop the idea of the PSNI's public order 'script'. The script can be thought of as the organization's carefully constructed template for managing public order events, especially contentious parades and protests. This script is written and promoted by public order commanders who are acutely aware of the political sensitivities of parades and protests and the formal oversight they face in policing them. In the material form of operational plans and briefing documents, the script is communicated to frontline officers – often the TSG – who are tasked with performing the police operation according to the script. In the first two sections of this chapter I provide the platform for the analysis of the police script by explaining the social and legal context within which it is written and performed. I then trace in detail the production, promotion and delivery of human rights law as an integral part of the police script, before analysing how public order commanders came to acquire the knowledge and expertise needed to become human rights script-writers and decision-makers. This hints at the movement away from the kinds of 'common sense' understandings described in Part III and towards a more legalistic, technical one reflecting the responsibilities commanders shouldered and the formal audiences they addressed.

Parades and Protests in Northern Ireland

Two centuries of Loyalist parades have provided rich subject matter for those eager to understand the rituals and changing dynamics of Ulster Loyalism (Bryan, 2000, 2015; Jarman 2000). A key question yet to be addressed, however, is what these cultural and political performances mean for policing; that is, how are we to make sense of parades and protests as *policed events*? In the last decade, only two studies of public order policing in Northern Ireland have been conducted, both produced after periods of particularly bad disorder. The first, commissioned by the PSNI in 2011, offers community perspectives of public order policing in Belfast (Byrne et al., 2013). The second, produced by Nolan et al. (2014), provides a detailed account of the 'Flag Protests' in Belfast (discussed below), tracing its origins as well as the experiences of those involved. Both reports are welcome additions to this significant yet poorly understood aspect of policing in Northern Ireland. Still, the need remains for conceptual scaffolding and empirical data so that we might begin to examine questions that have excited debate in other parts of the UK, where 'a considerable body of extant work' (Newburn, 2016: 141) on policing, disorder and protest stands in enviable contrast. Here, I take some initial steps in that direction by introducing parades and protests as events that are policed.

It has been said the 'great challenge' facing the reporter of parades in Northern Ireland rests in conveying their sheer scale and significance (Walley, 2013). For some, parades evoke images of bandsmen in sashes and bowler hats, proudly marching along traditional routes. For others, they are a symbol of Unionist domination, harking back to a time of discriminatory practices and repressive governance. Regardless of one's political outlook, for better or worse, parading is, in the words of the Chairman of the Parades Commission (2011: 7), '[p]art of the cultural fabric of our society, an inherent part of what is Northern Ireland'. Over the last decade, this fabric has become interwoven with a host of groups which enjoy membership and meaning regardless of one's creed, culture or nationality. As seen in Figure 6.1, created using data from the Parades Commission's annual reports, there are growing numbers of 'other' parades, a category featuring a kaleidoscope of events from the North Down Cycle Club to fairs and festivals, from Gay Pride to the Ford Anglia Owners Club. For other threads of the cultural fabric, however, meaning remains rooted in long-standing, deeply contested religious and cultural difference. This reflects the enduring presence of ritualized parades and protests organized by groups aligning themselves exclusively to Unionist/Loyalist or Nationalist/Republican communities.

The largest events in scale and frequency are the Loyalist marches punctuating the months of April to September, a period known locally as 'the marching season'. In the words of Jarman (2000: 159), '[t]he men march behind the Union Flag and the Ulster Flag, behind banners illustrating Biblical ideals, banners commemorating the Williamite wars and the Somme and other images of conflict or noble sacrifice for Faith, for the Crown and for Country'. The climax of the so-called marching season is the Twelfth of July, when Unionists celebrate the victory of Protestant King William III over Catholic King James II at the Battle of the Boyne in 1690. In 2015, for example, over 100,000 people took part in 800 Orange Order demonstrations across the country,

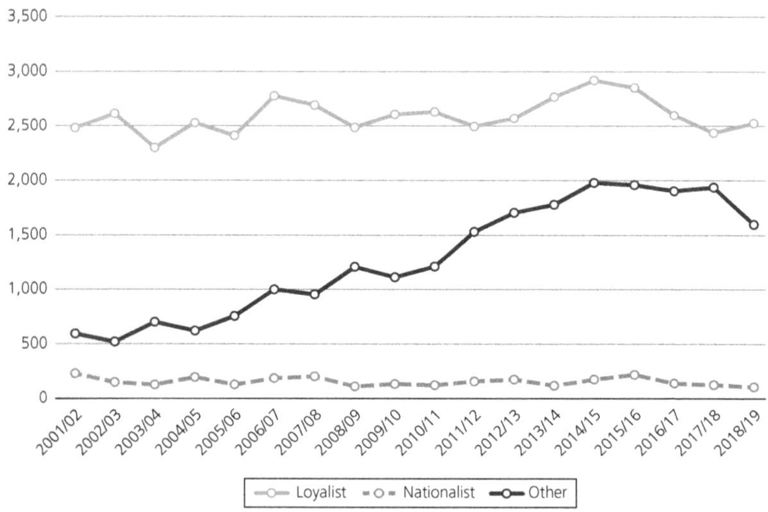

Figure 6.1 Notified Parades and Protests in Northern Ireland by Type

policed by 3,000 officers, including fifty-eight public order units (Black, 2015). Parades and related protests by Nationalist groups are much fewer, reflecting historical differences in tradition and treatment by the Unionist state (Bryan, 2000). Nationalist marches are also high-profile and politically significant, celebrating Republicanisms' own moments of victory and sacrifice, including the 1916 Easter Rising, the interment of terrorist suspects in 1971 and the hunger strikers of the early 1980s (Jarman and Bryan, 1998). The Republican Anti-Interment League march held each year in Belfast can attract especially large crowds, with up to 4,000 marchers and hundreds of counter-protestors (*BBC News*, 2014a).

A small but significant number of Loyalist parades are deemed 'contentious' by the Parades Commission, meaning they have the potential to raise concerns and community tensions (see Figure 6.2). These occur at well-known trouble spots where tensions are already high – usually interface areas of Belfast, where Republican and Loyalist communities share tight urban boundaries (Jarman, 2006). In their efforts to uphold Commission determinations, police officers have been badly injured by rioters armed with petrol bombs, heavy masonry and even firearms. One of the worst periods in the last two decades was 11–16 July 2011, when disorder erupted across Belfast and beyond, resulting

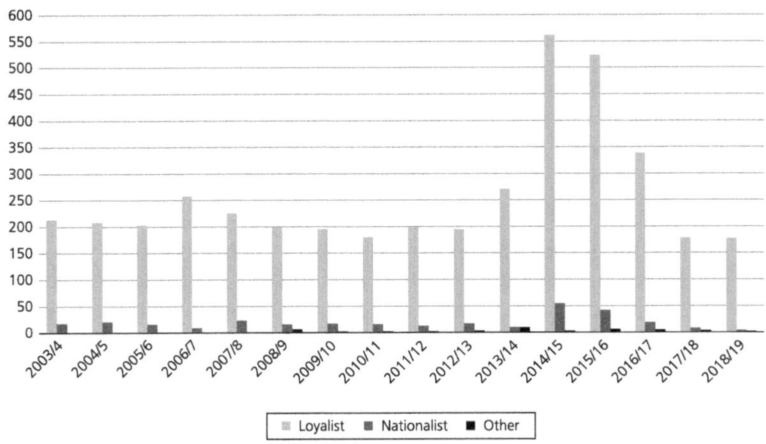

Figure 6.2 Contentious Parades and Protests in Northern Ireland by Type

in over fifty officers injured, extensive damage to property and 175 police baton rounds fired (NIPB, 2011: 58–63). The sharp spike in the number of contentious events and restrictions imposed between 2014 and 2016, illustrated in Figure 6.2 (compiled using data from the Parades Commission's annual reports.), was due to the nightly Loyalist protest held in North Belfast in response to the Commission's decision to reroute the return leg of an Orange Lodge parade away from Republican shop fronts in July 2012. Initially over 1,000 people strong, and marked by four consecutive nights of rioting, this protest was sustained for over three years by a small, nightly parade marching up to the point at which the original parade had been halted in July 2012 (*Belfast Telegraph*, 2016).

Growing Loyalist disenfranchisement with political parties, and the refusal of Republican groups to engage with the 'British state', has led groups from both communities to refuse to comply with the statutory notification scheme for public processions. The most significant period of un-notified parades erupted in December 2012 after Belfast City Council voted to limit the flying of the Union Jack at the City Hall to eighteen designated days. In grave despair, Loyalists rioted for several nights. Known locally as the 'Flag Protests', at its peak almost 10,000 people were involved in protests at eighty-four different locations, with a total of 2,980 crimes, incidents and information reported to police (Nolan et al., 2014). The so-called Flag Protests were followed by sustained protest marches in and out of Belfast City Centre on weekends from December 2012 until March 2013. The police operation is estimated to have cost £21.9 million, with over 214 arrests made and 160 police officers injured (PSNI, 2014b; Nolan et al., 2014). Albeit less high-profile, Republican groups have also refused to notify the Commission, in some instances trying to lure the PSNI into urban areas to provoke public disorder and injure police officers (Orde, 2009).

What binds these thousands of ethnically aligned parades and protests together is their political and cultural significance. They are performances and symbolic displays, projected at audiences within a society that continues to ache from bitter sectarian divisions. These performances reinforce in-group identities and, in interface areas, test the close urban boundaries opposing communities share (Jarman, 2006). In contrast to 'mere rioters' or 'wanton hooligans' who occupy positions outside of the moral community (Waddington, 2000: 157), many marchers and protestors involved in these events see themselves as championing a cause or identity, albeit a deeply divisive one. In their eyes, and in the eyes of many in their communities, they are actively participating in, and even contributing to, civic debate *within* the broader moral community (Barry, 2019). The belief held by those involved in contentious demonstrations, even when rioting occurs, is that these are acts done in defence of a culture and protection of an identity. As reported by Nolan et al. (2014), a metaphor used by the flag protestors was that the Council's decision was 'the straw that broke the camel's back'. The protest was a response to a whole series of issues: the inquiries which put the security forces in the dock; the role of former IRA members in government; increased visibility of the Irish culture; and the belief that Catholics were privileged in the jobs market. Loyalists described a sense of 'loss' and the 'threat' of the peace process.

We might think of such groups as taking part in a social phenomenon referred to by Charles Tilly and others as 'contentious politics'; that is, a mutually recognizable public interaction between competing claim-makers, in which the government acts as a mediator, target or claimant (Tarrow and Tilly, 2009). Applying Tilly's term to parades and protests in Northern Ireland, we can substitute government for the PSNI as the mediator (and occasionally target) of competing claims made by the two communities, Loyalism/Unionism and Republicanism/Nationalism. Police efforts to manage crowds and violent outbreaks are interpreted through the lens of identity, belonging and territoriality. The actions of the PSNI – how they deploy officers, the uniforms they wear, the tactics they use, the behaviours they tolerate – all convey signals to communities about their relationship with police, authority and the law. Groups are quick to compare experiences of how 'their' community has been policed with those of the 'other' community. Allegations of partisan or political policing are routinely levelled at police by both Loyalist and Nationalist communities (Byrne et al., 2013).

The Shifting Legal Landscape: Revisiting *Liberty and Order*

Having now sketched out this picture of parades and protests in Northern Ireland, I turn to further situate this chapter in the legal context that has emerged since Waddington's (1994) classic study. The most authoritative account of the role of law in policing political protests remains Waddington's (1994) *Liberty and Order*, which he conducted with the Metropolitan Police in the early 1990s (see also Waddington, 1995, 2000, 2003). His study was firmly anchored in the law and order debate that was unfolding in the 1970s and 1980s in Britain, amidst social change, political unrest and concerns that police were becoming more coercive, even paramilitary, in their style and appearance. The legal embodiment of these fears was the Public Order Act 1986, which criminalized forms of protest and assembly and empowered police to impose restrictions on demonstrations. Emerging from his fieldwork with the Metropolitan Police's public order commanders, Waddington produced a strong counter-narrative to the concerns of civil liberties groups. The most controversial provisions of the 1986 Act were barely used at all: no marches had been banned, few restrictions had been placed on protests and arrests were rare (Waddington, 1994: 37–9). More strikingly, the 1986 Act, and indeed, the law more generally, was largely absent on how senior officers discussed, understood and policed political protests and demonstrations.

Why was law confined to the margins? First, commanders were keen to avoid confrontation and manage 'trouble' in their precarious working environments by maximizing their control over events. This was best achieved through informal negotiations with parade organizers. Commanders used a combination of 'interactional ploys' and techniques of inducement to 'win over' organizers (Waddington, 1994: chapter 4). The law was of little assistance and was rarely mentioned because it risked alienating organizers and removing the air of friendliness and co-operation commanders consciously cultivated (Waddington, 1994: 87). Commanders' reluctance to engage with statutory powers also reflected their uncertainty over the precise meaning and application of the legislation. Ironically, this reluctance was compounded by a cultural expectation that experienced officers were cognizant of legal parameters. As Waddington (1994: 80) explains, '[r]eferring to the law was regarded by those [police officers] who deal with demonstrators on a regular basis as gauche and a sign of amateurism'. Second, law was confined to the margins because political protestors were themselves well-organized and receptive to these informal negotiations. In the eyes of the police, political protestors were 'professionals' that 'played the game'; use of legal powers were generally reserved for less 'institutionalized' groups, such as unruly youths or football hooligans (Waddington, 1995: 4). The result, Waddington (1994: 198) admitted, was that 'the interests of protesters are, at least, compromised. Protest is emasculated and induced to conform to the avoidance of trouble. In police argot, protest organizers are "had over".'

The loose commitment and strategic facilitation of civil liberties described by Waddington in *Liberty and Order* now falls well-short of what is required of the modern police commander under the ECHR.[1] As public authorities, police are under a legal obligation, by virtue of section 6(1) of the HRA, not to act in such a way that is incompatible with Convention rights. Article 11 of the ECHR is a qualified right that protects peaceful assembly, including public demonstrations and counter-protests.[2] While the precise ambit of this qualified right might remain fuzzy (Mead, 2010), its basic implications for policing are clear. Police have a negative duty to refrain from interfering with the rights of protestors to peacefully assemble, even if the views expressed cause annoyance or offence.[3] But further than this, and in contrast to common law's residual liberties in the era of *Liberty and Order*,[4] Article 11 places positive obligations on police to take reasonable and appropriate measures to facilitate peaceful protest, including the protection of a lawful demonstration against counter-demonstrations.[5] Any action limiting the right to peacefully protest must be justified by police according to the legitimate aims set out in Article 11(2) of the ECHR and standards of necessity and proportionality. Beyond the general duty on public authorities under section 6(1) of the HRA, there is dicta from the senior courts to suggest some form of procedural duty may,

[1] For a helpful overview of the development of police powers with respect to peaceful protest in the context of England and Wales more generally, and issues of compatibility with the ECHR specifically, see Mead (2018).

[2] *Kudrevičius and Others v Lithuania* (App no 37553/05) ECHR 1310 (26 November 2013), at [91].

[3] *Plattform 'Ärzte Für Das Leben' v Austria* (App no 10126/82) ECHR 15 (21 June 1998).

[4] As observed by Lord Bingham in *R(Laporte) v Chief Constable of Gloucestershire* [2006] UKHL 55, at [34]: 'The approach of the English common law to freedom of expression and assembly was hesitant and negative, permitting that which was not prohibited.'

[5] *Bukta and Others v Hungary* (App no 25691/04) ECHR 610 (17 July 2007), at [35].

in fact, arise under the HRA in protest scenarios. Lord Rodger in *R(Laporte) v Chief Constable of Gloucestershire Constabulary* stated:

> Under the Human Rights Act 1998 the police *must have regard* to the rights to freedom of expression and freedom of assembly which protesters, such as the claimant, are entitled to assert under articles 10 and 11 of the Convention.[6]

Just how onerous a duty to 'have regard' is remains to be determined. By analogy, 'have regard' would, linguistically, appear to impose a less onerous obligation than the public sector equality duty's '*due* regard' standard (section 149 of the Equality Act 2010) which has been interpreted as requiring authorities to undertake specific procedural steps. In *R(A) v Chief Constable of Kent Constabulary*, Beatson LJ suggested *Laporte* might belong to a select category of case in which 'substance and procedure are difficult to disentangle'.[7] In *Laporte*, the apparent 'entanglement' might be said to have arisen because the court assessment of the claimants' right to demonstrate at a lawful assembly (the substance of the decision) ran in conjunction with its assessment of whether the police commander had reasonable apprehension of an imminent breach of the peace (the decision-making process). What it does serve to emphasize, though, is the value of this chapter's empirical exploration of how police might respond to, and seek to fulfil, the kind of procedural duty alluded to by Lord Rodger.

The law, in sum, is no longer confined strictly to police powers, but also includes legally enforceable rights that must be respected, and proactively protected, by police. To this end, influential reports of statutory and parliamentary authorities now call for human rights to be at the core of how police respond to public processions and protests (Joint Committee on Human Rights (JCHR), 2009). These calls have helped give momentum to efforts to anchor human rights law more firmly in public order policies,

[6] *R(Laporte) v Chief Constable of Gloucestershire* [2006] UKHL 55, at [85] (my emphasis).

[7] *R(A) v Chief Constable of Kent Constabulary* [2013] EWCA Civ 1706, at [52]–[53]. See also *B v Chief Constable of Hampshire Constabulary* [2015] EWHC 1238 (Admin), at [86].

training and assessments (Stott et al., 2013; College of Policing, 2016a). This recognition of a fully fledged right to peaceful protest may have brought 'a sea-change in legal thought in the UK' (Mead, 2010: 25; cf. Gilmore, Jackson and Monk, 2019), but it was not until HMIC's fundamental review of public order policing – triggered by the policing of the G20 protests in London in 2009 – that the full ramifications of the HRA for policing were to be realized and acted upon. HMIC's (2009: 121) national review was particularly critical of 'the low level of understanding of the human rights obligations of the police in the public order context, particularly in relation to the use of force', concluding that it was 'of serious concern'. 'It is vital', HMIC (2009: 65) insisted, 'that police officers of all ranks properly understand the existing legal framework ... including their obligations under the Human Rights Act 1998'. The review prompted a national overhaul of public order training and assessment 'to ensure that relevant human rights principles are firmly embedded within the framework of Public Order policing' (HMIC, 2009: 65).

In Northern Ireland, duties under the HRA interact with another significant shift in the legal framework. The public order powers contained in the Public Order (Northern Ireland) Order 1987 – akin to those at the heart of Waddington's study – have been repealed. After violent bouts of disorder at Loyalist marches in the mid-1990s, and strong accusations of discriminatory use of force by the RUC, the North Report (1997) recommended the establishment of an independent body, the Parades Commission, to mediate, and ultimately adjudicate, on parades and protests. The North Report was implemented in part by the Public Processions (Northern Ireland) Act 1998, which requires organizers of a public procession or protest meeting to give advance notice to the police specifying the details of their proposed event (sections 6(4) and 7(4) of the Public Processions (Northern Ireland) Act 1998). The PSNI provides these details to the Parades Commission and it is then the Commission, not the PSNI, that issues a determination on any notified procession/protest. The Commission may impose such conditions as it considers 'necessary' on those organizing, taking part in or supporting the procession or protest, including restrictions on the parade route, the numbers involved and its duration (sections 8(1) and 9A(1)–(2) respectively of the Public Processions (Northern Ireland) Act 1998).

It might be thought this statutory regime would, if anything, lessen the significance of the law in policing. The PSNI, after all, is no longer the key 'negotiator' but merely the intermediary and enforcer of the Commission's determination. But this has not turned out to be the case; rather, police powers and human rights law have become central to the policing of parades. The most contentious parades and related protests are subject to Commission restrictions (Figure 6.3, created using data from the Parades Commission's annual reports), forcing to the surface questions about how rights of assembly and expression are balanced between marchers, residents, businesses and police officers. The Commission's determinations have proven divisive, highly contested and subject to routine derision by senior politicians and community leaders (*BBC News*, 2014b). PSNI commanders are challenged on how they will interpret and apply restrictions, respect competing rights and use police powers in an impartial manner (Public Session, NIPB, May 2014; CAJ, 2016). In voicing their concerns, a rights discourse has been adopted by community leaders to bluntly assert their preferred course of police action (Curtis, 2014). Caught between communities acutely attuned to their actions and decisions and the Commission's legally binding determinations,

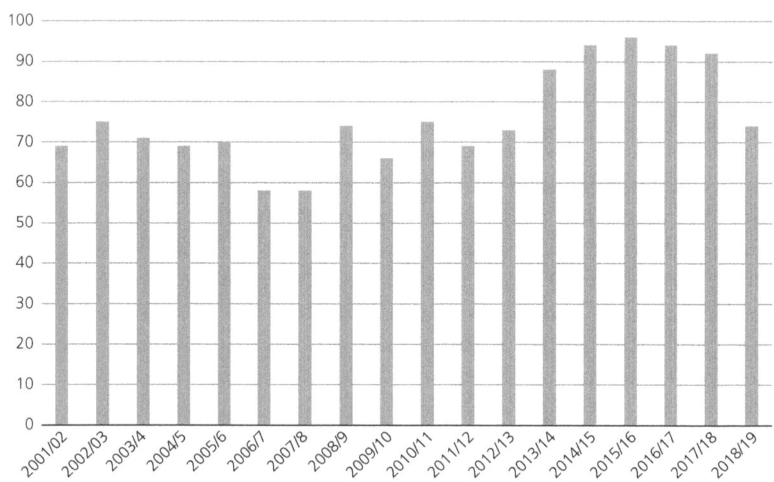

Figure 6.3 Percentage of Sensitive Parades/Protests on which the Commission Placed Restrictions

PSNI commanders described in our interviews this predicament as being 'piggy in the middle'.

In summary, the policing of parades and protests takes place in the crucible of contestation over how democratic rights ought to be politically respected and legally regulated. We will return to critically engage with Waddington's (1994) insights on the role law plays in policing political protests throughout this chapter and the next. For now, I want to delve into the internal workings of the PSNI to explore how human rights came to form such a prominent feature of commanders' responses to these events and the way that they ought to be policed. When describing how parades and protests were policed, officers likened them to tightly choreographed, staged performances. It was as if the police operation was 'scripted' by senior officers, who were keen to exert control, and performed by public order units, who were trained to stick within the script's parameters. In the following sections, I illustrate how human rights law has become an integral part of this script, reflecting the strong internalization of human rights amongst mid to senior ranking police commanders. In the next chapter, I proceed to explore why human rights have taken on such a prominent form, in light of the functions they serve for the senior officers responsible for this high-profile, contested part of Northern Irish policing.

Embedding Human Rights: The Organizational 'Script'

The 'script' took the material form of the strategic and operational plans devised by commanders. Its content was an amalgamation of PSNI formal policies and domestic human rights law, as well as relevant community intelligence gathered by the police. I begin this section by tracing how the script was written, promoted and delivered by commanders, revealing how human rights law was firmly institutionalized in the planning of contentious parades and protests. I then examine how references to human rights were understood and translated by police commanders and key 'bridgers' in the organization.

Writing the Script

Public order policing in Northern Ireland is regulated internally by a distinct operational command structure, based on the

College of Policing's guidelines. The 'Gold Commander' (an Assistant Chief Constable) is responsible for setting the strategic parameters for public order operations during the marching season. The 'Silver Commander' (usually a Superintendent) has the greatest operational duties, tasked with devising and overseeing the police approach and the tactics used. They are assisted by 'bronze commanders' (usually Inspectors) who are responsible for implementing the tactics on the ground. Based on their meetings with police departments and community groups, silver and bronze commanders must produce their own plans for each event, corresponding to their roles and responsibilities. We might think of commanders, quite literally, as writers who draft the organizational script. In so doing, they bring together hundreds of officers of different ranks, geographical districts and operational expertise: from roads policing and the intelligence branch, to the TSG and Neighbourhood Policing Teams.

Taking each rung of command in turn, we can see how the self-commitment to human rights by senior commanders ensured that human rights emerged as a central plot line in the scripts they produced for internal and external audiences. The injection of human rights was initiated by the gold commander, as former PSNI Deputy Chief Constable Duncan McCausland (2007: 216) describes:

> The key document, which underlies all planning and operational activities, is the Gold Strategy. This document is a comprehensive resource, containing detailed references to the HRA and other human rights standards, and addressing a range of potential operational scenarios. These scenarios range from benign, such as a parade proceeding peacefully, to scenarios involving credible threats of terrorist attacks ... A detailed analysis of the European Convention rights engaged is provided in relation to each scenario.

The Gold Strategy, devised months in advance of the marching season, sits at the apex of the PSNI's approach to public order. Providing the overarching principles for operations, it was described by one commander as 'setting out the stall and saying we will do it like this, these are the considerations you will undertake, and this is what you will do' (Silver Commander Charley). With the weight of an Assistant Chief Constable behind it, the early emphasis on human rights in the Gold Strategy served to embed it firmly into the script, requiring commanders at the next rung of the command ladder to pick up the baton and engage with human rights principles themselves. When devising their 'tactical plans', silver commanders' chief task was to evidence how they would 'get the job done' in light of the Gold Strategy. Having been talked through a plan by Silver Commander Derek in our interview, I saw how it included detailed, practical assessments of key components, including the history of the event, the intelligence assessment, the efforts being made to minimize disruption to the community, a brief description of the 'tipping point' at which commanders would intervene in a parade/protest, and the contingencies in place should disorder arise. The plan further replicated the ECHR, citing the human rights law and key principles engaged and, most obviously, the outer limits of peaceful protest per Articles 9 to 11 of the ECHR, the standards governing the use of force and how this linked with the 'style and tone' of the operation (discussed below).

Silver commanders emphasized that human rights were now part of their language, a 'touchstone' they would return to throughout their planning and strategy meetings. The tactical plan was passed down to the bronze commander, who was responsible for the task of devising a bespoke 'deployment plan'. Depending on the event, there could be multiple bronze commanders, from 'geographical bronze' (responsible for particular streets or locations), to 'functional bronze' (carrying out specific roles, such as a tactical option). With human rights law references flowing down through the tactical plan, the task of the bronze commanders was to try 'to evolve and roll out a plan which marries up with what the Silver Commander is trying to achieve' (Bronze Commander Cliff). We can see how continuity in rights-based thinking continued to be consciously replicated, here in relation to minimizing the recourse to the use of force, as described by Bronze Commander Daniel:

> There are silver tactical plans which are written by the Silver Commander where you would expect to see those – in terms of strategic intentions – you would expect to see those things [legality, proportionality, necessity] ... If the Silver Commander, as _____ frequently does, says 'I want to see a graduated response' then as a bronze commander I try and then demonstrate that within my deployment plan ... (Bronze Commander Daniel)

Once bronze commanders had produced a draft of their deployment plan, it was submitted to the silver commander for approval, serving as an example of the self-regulatory approach designed to ensure consistency across the public order script.

Great attention was placed on the importance of writing a comprehensive script that captured the various actors involved in policing parades and protests, including local community leaders and politicians, so as to minimize the likelihood of disorder arising.[8] Commanders were expected to embed the relevant aspects of the PSNI's Policy Directives and Service Procedures, specifically the Manual of Policy, Procedure and Guidance on Conflict Management, as well as the College of Policing's Authorized Professional Practice, each containing statements on the legal framework under the HRA. The format and language of commanders' plans were heavily dictated by these pre-written policies, which they had first encountered as part of their command training. By referencing these documents, specifically the sections on ECHR standards, commanders' plans formed part of the bureaucratic bind that embedded the discourse of human rights into the policing operation.

Significantly, the Policing Board's human rights legal advisor attends the major police planning meetings for the parading season. The advisor is present in their capacity to monitor the PSNI's compliance with the HRA and thus has no input into the police operations. The advisor observes meetings and pre-briefings before high-profile parades and takes notes, which then provide the basis for the advisor's assessment and is written up in the public order section of the Policing Board's Annual Human Rights Report. Attendance at these meetings has been described by the advisor as 'the most critical element of what I do' because it provides an insight into how police plan so as to comply with their positive duties under the HRA; most notably, Article 2 of the ECHR, which requires the police to plan in such a way that minimizes the likelihood of recourse to potentially lethal force (Kilpatrick, 2016). Consequently, the self-regulatory process of human rights script-writing takes place in the shadow of the Policing Board and its specialist human rights lawyer.

[8] The extensive planning meetings and the diverse range of police officers involved in them are well-documented in the Policing Board's human rights annual reports (e.g. NIPB, 2006: 60–72).

Promoting the Script: Reporting to the Parades Commission

Human rights are further institutionalized and actively promoted to attentive outside audiences through the reports the PSNI must submit to the Parades Commission. Following notice of a sensitive parade/protest, the Commission requests police evidence regarding the proposed event. In producing their report (known as the '11/9'), the PSNI has adopted a standardized form, completed by the district community planning team in conjunction with the silver commander.[9] Commanders must make a 'judged assessment' of how police strategies might affect the rights of individuals who may be involved by filling in a series of boxes assigned to articles of the ECHR. Commanders are instructed to pay special regard to: 'the effects police tactics have had in the past and may have in the future upon individual human rights. The author should in particular note the circumstances under which a human right can be restricted in furtherance of a legitimate aim by a public authority' (PSNI, 2008b: 10). Interestingly, the guide alerts commanders to the fact their reports are disclosable to public audiences and should be written with this in mind. In this way, the self-regulatory force of human rights was enhanced by the possibility of external scrutiny. Accurate completion of the form was made easier, though, by a detailed sample report issued to commanders, which stated the broad ECHR principles to be applied.

Although it is easy to dismiss the '11/9' form as a bureaucratic copy and paste exercise, commanders insisted it was part of a conscious process of trying to ensure the rights of different groups were actively considered. Silver Commander Andrew, for example, described it as an 'added element' to the planning process that helped to institutionalize rights-based awareness. He explained:

> [E]ven the way we report to the Parades Commission, yeah it's a template and that doesn't mean it's embedded in our culture and stuff but actually over a period of time it is. So, you know, we report our evidence to the Parades Commission along that spine of key human rights.

[9] Since 2007, the PSNI has made it policy to disclose 11/9 forms to interested parties. Copies can be found online courtesy of disclosures by the PSNI under the Freedom of Information Act 2000.

However, when reading the 11/9 reports made publicly available, some variation was evident in the detail with which commanders from different districts engaged with ECHR standards. Regarding Article 10 of the ECHR, for instance, one 11/9 report from an Apprentice Boys of Derry March in Lurgan explicitly acknowledged the rights of all individuals and groups to express themselves, set out the police aim to facilitate peaceful protest and the need to balance this against the overarching requirement to ensure that lawful activity can still take place (PSNI, 2015b: 7). In contrast, a form for the Orange Lodge parade in Dungiven simply stated 'it is not the police intention to restrict freedom of expression' and cited powers under the Public Order Act 1997 (PSNI, 2013b: 5). Further research that observes officers carrying out these tasks would be particularly valuable in an effort to capture the situational, even administrative, factors that might explain this kind of variation.

Delivering the Script: Briefings and Operational Orders

With the script written, the task for commanders was then to deliver it to its actors: the hundreds, and for major parades, thousands, of junior officers on the frontline of policing. This delivery was done in person at meetings and briefings in a systematic and detailed manner, especially for major parades/protests, as Bronze Commander Cliff explained:

> Briefings are vitally important … We have to be sure that people know what their task is. So, in terms of the levels Gold, Silver, Bronze, Silver Commander does his briefing, after his briefing's finished it's a breakout … 'All the TSG commanders who are in _____ Street, go over to the corner there and speak to the Bronze, he's going to tell you exactly what he wants and what he needs'. And then it's down to me, it's my responsibility as the Geographical Bronze to talk to my Inspectors who will be there on the ground.

A crucial part of commanders' efforts to control the event was ensuring junior officers performed their lines as planned (see also Waddington, 1994: 144–6) and, in this way, the self-regulatory format of human rights continued. Bronze Commander Cliff further explained that 'Practically speaking on a day-to-day basis that needs to be gripped by the Bronzes in the briefing room to tell the people: "Here's where we want you, here's the way we're doing it, now get that down to your people and make sure they understand".'

Junior officers could view a summary of the script in the 'Operational Order', emailed to TSG Inspectors and sergeants in advance of the event they were to police. I read some of these orders during my fieldwork. They cover an array of information, from the history of the event to the radio channels. References to human rights law were littered throughout and generally belonged to one of two categories. The first were organizational pronouncements, echoing the official voice by reaffirming the importance of human rights to the PSNI. These appeared in the opening lines of the Chief Constable's policy on public order:

> The human rights of all those affected by such events will be central to all stages of police preparations and subsequent actions. It is recognised that not all human rights are absolute rights and in some instance the rights of individuals must be balanced with those of others.

The second were more legalistic. Each order had a generic section dedicated to human rights that included a mission-style statement introducing the HRA, a brief reminder that it incorporated the ECHR into domestic law, followed by: 'It is imperative that all operational policing decisions are made against the background of the effects of this legislation.' This statement was preceded by a table listing articles of the HRA with an 'X' marking the rights engaged by the police operation. Greater detail was found in the page-long outline on the use of firearms, which repeated Article 2 of the ECHR in full and underscored the conditions where a negative and positive duty arose. In one operational order, these statements on human rights were supplemented by the gold commander's specific strategic aims, which included: 'Plan to reduce the likelihood of police recourse to the use of force particularly lethal or potentially lethal force. (This is in accordance with our positive obligations under Article 2 ECHR ref McCann v UK …).'

Appearances of human rights law in briefings and operational orders demonstrated the ability of commanders to drive the script down through the organization in bureaucratic form so as to regulate the behaviour of frontline officers. But how were these lines received by the actors tasked with delivering them on the ground, most commonly the TSG? As discussed in Chapter 4, officers in the TSG were broadly familiar with the format of briefing packs and operational orders and knew that, if they really wanted to, they could find references to the ECHR in a dedicated section. The extent to which this was 'briefed out', and the way in which it was done, varied depending on the individual briefing officers and the nature of the event. TSG officers described the concerted efforts made for major parades/protests, which involved multiple, detailed briefings given days in advance by bronze commanders and local Neighbourhood Inspectors. For low-key, less contentious parades, TSG officers described how only passing reference was made to human rights, with the briefing officer tending to 'just go through the motions'. The over-familiarity with human rights that officers described is summed up well by TSG Constable Jay:

> It becomes second nature because for ten years now that's how you operate, you have to take them [human rights] into consideration. You have to be aware of them, you have to work within them. So therefore, it's not a major problem to do that, it's in effect dipping your clutch to change gear. It comes as second nature now to take them into consideration.

Commanders were wary of this fatigue, expressed in the '*ad nauseam*' narrative examined in Chapter 4, and a related fear of human rights mindlessly 'rolling of the tongue' of officers, but they insisted, nonetheless, that the ECHR remained a central plot line that was communicated to the actors of the public order script.

For TSG sergeants, however, detailed briefings could not always be carried out because of the more pressing and immediate demands they faced. Reminding their unit about human rights sat alongside a range of other issues emerging from the 'whole slew of documents that come along' in the run up to operations. While technically the operational order should be read out, sergeants explained their primary concern was ascertaining the correct radio channels and ensuring their unit had eaten beforehand. As one Inspector similarly conceded during the bronze command course: 'You'll skip through the human rights stuff and you say you know it and then look for the meat and the bones – deployment of the unit, where you need to be'.

Besides, there was a strong suspicion that many orders were 'copy and paste jobs' (TSG Sergeant George) lifted off the shelf from the last operation. A common view amongst the TSG was that it was counter-effective to give a detailed briefing on human rights, either because it was patronizing or because it was simply done for the sake of it. As mentioned in Chapter 4, there was an even stronger suspicion that inclusion of the ECHR in the operational orders, especially references to case law, was a blatant 'ass covering exercise' by commanders should anything go wrong. TSG Sergeant George asked me rhetorically during a frank conversation, 'Do you think these were written for me or for an audit trail and the Ombudsman?' Similarly, TSG Sergeant Freya, having just printed off the operational order for the night's operation, quipped, 'Ten pages on human rights! A tree dies every day for this'. Many officers accepted that the inclusion of human rights law in operational orders was simply part and parcel of today's policing operations and had to be done by their commanders.

Understanding the Script: Translating Human Rights Law into Practice

According to Gold Commander Alex, human rights law had 'brought a consistency, a common language, a common understanding, a common way in which things are evaluated and interpreted'. Yet, as academics, we know little about how legal rules come to be a common language or commonly understood. As Dixon (1997: 277–8) observed two decades ago, the way police learn about the law, and how it is taught to officers in a way that transmits the necessary facts and their practical application, remains poorly understood. Manning and Hawkins (1989) describe officers' 'recipe knowledge' of the law, which is derived from oral traditions passed on by their colleagues or gleaned from exam material revised during promotion cycles. In Dixon's (1997: 277–8) research, officers were well-able to recite the law in 'parrot fashion', but when applying it to the facts, they fell back on generalized, normative statements about what people should or should not do. In this section, I want to look more closely at how officers came to know about and understand the human rights law standards that appeared in the police script, focusing on public order command training and the organizational actors who provide a 'bridge' between law and practice.

Public Order Command Training

The role of public order commander was just one of many responsibilities that kept senior officers busy. Their schedules were otherwise filled with a myriad of tasks connected to the district they oversaw or police units they were responsible for, from management meetings to community engagements. To acquire the skills and knowledge necessary to be a certified public order commander, officers had to attend and pass specialist bronze or silver command courses. These courses, run by the PSNI's Combined Operational Training department, are based on the College of Policing's standardized public order training curriculum and assessment used by police forces across England and Wales. With command training emerging as a key site of human rights law translation for the police, I eagerly took up the PSNI's offer to observe a bronze commander course in early summer 2015.

In Northern Ireland, these courses are a strong illustration of how the Policing Board's legal advisors have played a significant role in aligning the PSNI's organizational script with ECHR standards. The legal advisors have invested considerable energy in reviewing policies and observing a range of training courses. Between 2005 and 2007, the Policing Board made recommendations requiring the ECHR to be presented prominently, and explained more clearly, in the training lessons and materials (see, e.g., NIPB, 2006: 58; NIPB, 2007: 127).[10] Over the last ten years, the legal advisors have continued to monitor the content and delivery of public order training, reporting positive findings.[11] In the broader context of the UK, some of the most critical findings of HMIC have been commanders' poor understanding of, and inadequate training in, human rights law and public order powers,

[10] The PSNI implemented these, with the Policing Board approving the revised procedure and guidance as 'clear, comprehensive and carefully drafted' (NIPB, 2007: 120).

[11] It has been described as 'exemplary and a template for best practice' and 'an exceptional package of training which has at its core the duty to respect, protect and fulfil the human rights of all members of the community' (NIPB, 2009: 98).

as noted earlier. Having read the College of Policing's command course curriculum, it is apparent that efforts have also been made to remedy the knowledge deficit identified amongst commanders in England and Wales (College of Policing, 2014a, 2014b). Key learning outcomes for bronze and silver courses now include consideration of powers and policies relating to human rights, alongside an understanding of the human rights framework (College of Policing, 2014a, 2014b). In the guidance for trainers, the ECHR is described as 'an overarching theme' that must be 'delivered throughout all aspects of the public order training curriculum' as part of a 'pragmatic and lawful approach to human rights' (College of Policing, 2016a: 17).

The PSNI command course I observed was attended by nine Inspectors from police departments across the country, who assembled in a well air-conditioned and windowless training room. Equipped with PowerPoint, a whiteboard and the College of Policing lesson plans, a five-person team of accredited public order trainers delivered the course across six days. The goal was to train the Inspectors in becoming competent script-writers and decision-makers and to provide them with the knowledge to engage with ECHR principles. The officers were welcomed by a silver commander who made clear the organization's expectations: 'It is not enough to just say "It's an Article 2 issue" – we'll push you to deeper, what does that actually mean?' Likewise, as they were told early on by one trainer, 'Are all human rights the same? No, you've got balanced rights. You need to manage that – ask your silver in advance. It seems easy "protecting rights", but it's more difficult when they're qualified and you're balancing them.' It was apparent that some aspiring commanders were apprehensive about the depth of understanding required of them when the ECHR appeared on the 'needs and expectations' list they scribbled on the whiteboard on day 1.

Commanders were instructed, much like I was as an undergraduate law student, on the importance of being able to select and cite relevant case law, rather than 'just listing a whole load of cases' from the training material. They were taught to cite the principle for which the case was an authority and how it might apply to the police operation. Trainers told the Inspectors they had to learn 'to get into the weeds':

TRAINER: Don't give us McCann and Others but what you're going to do to make sure McCann and Others is covered – we're looking for the where's and the how's ... Can anyone give me a stated case?

INSP.: Is Osman one?

TRAINER: Yep, some info that could have brought to arrest, you need to know it. (Field notes, 11 June 2015)

Linking back to the presence of human rights in the public order script, one trainer remarked: 'There are loads of cases and you should be familiar with them, they're in [operational] orders now and again.' In choosing which cases to reference in their deployments plans, the training team helped by identifying the leading ECtHR cases in their presentations, such as *Bukta and Others v Hungary*[12] and *Handyside v UK*[13] for Article 11 of the ECHR (discussed in the next chapter), as well as the domestic authorities under the HRA, for example *Woods v Commissioner of Police for the Metropolis*[14] (regarding the retention of photographic evidence).

Providing a more legalistic, less 'common sense' understanding of human rights than officers were accustomed to in everyday police work posed a challenge for the trainers too, one joking to another 'No pressure!' when officers wrote 'Understanding of the ECHR' on the list of course needs. In most instances, trainers managed to summarize the law accurately.[15] The ambit of the right to peaceful protest (discussed below) – which, objectively speaking, is made up of clear core principles – proved straightforward to convey to trainee commanders:

After the right to freedom of assembly, the next slide was freedom of expression. The trainer was explaining how it applies to opinions and ideas. Speaking through rhetorical questions again, he asked 'Handyside v UK, tell me about it? I think he was an artist – anyway, the point is that freedom of expression includes ideas that offend, shock or disturb. If I hold an opinion that you find offensive, unlucky! If I'm not being obstructive or breaking the law, then we should be tolerant'. He then gave a local example of the protestors outside the Marie Stopes abortion clinic in Belfast, saying how the banners of the protestors outside

[12] *Bukta* (n 5).

[13] *Handyside v UK* (App no 5493/72) ECHR 5 (7 December 1976).

[14] *Wood v Commissioner of Police for the Metropolis* [2009] EWCA Civ 414.

[15] There were not, for example, any instances where trainers inaccurately adopted the dissenting minority judgment as the law or presented the lower courts' judgment, cf. Dixon (1997: 278–9).

might be shocking but they are still allowed to carry them. (Field notes, 11 June 2015)

For more technical aspects of the law, like the formula to be applied for qualified rights, trainers seemed less comfortable and relied heavily on the College of Policing curriculum. On the concept of proportionality, for instance, trainers explained the need for a link between the measures and the legitimate aim, reading out the considerations verbatim from the public order manual and bluntly telling the commanders: 'You must be cognisant of these when planning. It's in APP [Authorized Professional Practice]. Look for it.' In an effort to make this policy meaningful, officers were shown short video clips of public order scenarios. The responses of the Inspectors suggested, however, that the structured thinking and precise terminology trainers had just recited to them had already faded into the background. To be fair, clarity of understanding was not helped by encouraging trainees to make impressionistic judgments based on the police actions and decision-making they could glean from the short video clips.

Most interesting was how trainers presented cases that were both trickier to grasp and more contested. It is in these situations that we might think more deeply about what it means to translate human rights law for police as practitioners, applying principles 'on the ground'. Take, for example, the cases of *Austin v Commissioner of the Metropolis*[16] and *Austin v UK*,[17] which reached the Appellate Committee of the House of Lords and ECtHR respectively. The issue was whether the police containment of thousands of protestors and bystanders in a confined urban area for up to seven hours in cold conditions in order to prevent an imminent breach of the peace amounted to an unlawful deprivation of liberty under Article 5 of the ECHR. Ultimately, both courts held that the right to liberty was not engaged by the 'kettling' of the protestors. In command training, the points deduced were practical ones, stated plainly and without controversy by trainers: 'Containment is a Gold consideration. Provided the tactic is used in good faith, proportionate to the necessary situation and enforced no longer than necessary it's lawful'; 'The

[16] *Austin v Commissioner of Police for the Metropolis* [2009] UKHL 5.

[17] *Austin and Others v UK* (App nos 39692/09, 40713/09 and 41008/09) ECHR 459 (15 March 2012).

Bronze will have to be working with the Silver for this to work properly'; 'You should be thinking about things like access to toilets or the weather, it's a hot July, will there be water for them?'

Another case (discussed earlier in the chapter), *R (Laporte) v Chief Constable of Gloucester*,[18] concerned anti-war protestors intercepted by police on route to a military air base. Rigorously applying the standards of Article 11(2) of the ECHR, the House of Lords held that the police use of breach of the peace to send protestors back to London failed the standards of 'proscribed by law', 'necessity' and 'proportionality'. Central to the reasoning was temporal proximity. The breach of the peace had to be 'imminent' at the point of police intervention: that is, the violence had to be 'about to happen' (at [49]) and not just 'anticipated to be a real possibility' (at [47]). Yet, no clear view emerged from the judgment as to what these terms really meant. How did this ambiguity impact on the police translation? The trainers turned to the expertise of another 'translator', showing commanders an email from the PSNI's human rights lawyer, which identified factors police ought to consider in light of the House of Lords' discussion of 'imminence' – for example, whether it was the last opportunity police had to take preventative action. Officers were told to write down the lawyer's number: 'If you have any questions phone him and he'll get back to you, he's been very supportive in putting together the training. The advice of our legal advisor takes precedence over the cases we've mentioned'. The *R(Laporte)* case was soon followed by reference to *R (McClure and Moos) v Commissioner of the Metropolis*,[19] which concerned whether a Metropolitan Police Commander had reasonably apprehended an imminent breach of the peace and the proper approach of the court in making such an assessment. The case was summed up by the trainer: 'The case of Moos and McClure. The Met are at fault. Met appealed. All these fancy barristers paid loads of money to make the police look awful. But it was upheld on appeal that it was an honestly held belief by the police officer and that it was proportionate and in line with human rights' (field notes, 11 June 2015).

[18] *R(Laporte)* (n 6).

[19] *R (McClure and Moos) v Commissioner of Police of the Metropolis* [2012] EWCA Civ 12.

In translating these three leading authorities, police trainers prioritized their operational application and deemed finer points of law and broader concerns of constitutional principle academic (in both senses of the word). In academic scholarship, the *Austin* judgments provoked discussion over the court's premature assessment of proportionality and purpose of the interference to determine the very ambit of the right to liberty (Fenwick, 2009; Dickson, 2013; James and Pearson, 2015). Criticism has also been levelled at the excessive deference to the executive resulting from the court's reasoning. As argued by Fenwick (2009: 757), '[t]he impression given by all the judges involved in *Austin* is that they were seeking, after the event, and in reliance on doubtful and convoluted reasoning, to find a justification for the police action'. Similarly, in *McClure and Moos*, the Court of Appeal of England and Wales can be criticized for proving reluctant to meaningfully scrutinize decision-making, applying a test which is deferential to police and relying on a subjective assessment of decision-making considering what the officer knew and perceived at the time, provided their evidence seems honest and accurate. Consider, for instance, how the court approached the officer's assessment of possible disorder, such that the consequence works in the officer's favour regardless of whether the prospective outcome occurred:

> The mere fact that an anticipated or feared happening did not, in fact, occur, rarely can safely provide any support for the contention that it was not reasonable to anticipate or fear that the happening would occur; however, as we see it, the fact that the happening did, in fact, occur can properly be cited in support of the contention that it was reasonable so to anticipate or fear. (Lord Neuberger, at [89])

But does it matter that finer issues of law and broader points of principle were lost in translation? One police trainer acknowledged: 'On a command course we could spend days debating, and I'm sure if you went to Strasbourg you could spend the rest of your life discussing it, but when it comes down to the basics, for operational people, this is what you need to know.' Indeed, for training generally, the Policing Board's legal advisors have consistently promoted the practical delivery of legal tests and the value of applied, scenario-based learning (NIPB, 2009: 111; 2010: 57). Although such pedagogy undoubtedly has merit – most obviously, it makes rights meaningful and practically applicable for police as practitioners on the ground – from my observations, a more contextualized account (debated for minutes, not days) might be important for further promoting a positive culture of human rights. If a typical fear amongst officers is that human rights limit their ability to police effectively and firmly, then, if presented in terms of the role and extent of the court's oversight role, cases like *Austin* and *McClure and Moos* are an opportunity to reassure officers that the courts are interpreting human rights in a way that is sensitive to operational discretion. Conversely, *Laporte* could be taught as a rare reminder that breach of the peace, as the go-to police power of choice and as wide-ranging as it is, should be used with greater precision (Fenwick, 2009; Glover, 2018).

More critically, in the absence of a closer analysis of the substantive scope of human rights, the Inspectors seemed to be left relying on a 'gut feeling' of the ambit of ECHR articles. During a mock scenario, for instance, officers were considering if the stoning of a football supporters' bus raised human rights issues. Though the hypothetical situation concerned the acts of private parties, the Inspectors overlooked the possibility that a positive duty on the police to intervene could have arisen on the facts:

INSP. A: How about Article 3?
INSP. B: No, it's not torture! It's an Article 2 issue.
INSP. A: It's inhumane though!?
INSP. B: No, it's in relation to the state, not this sort of stuff where it's groups of people doing it to each other.
(Field notes, 13 June 2015)

In another scenario, officers were grappling with what to do about football supporters misbehaving on the way to the football stadium:

Officers were told that supporters were urinating and throwing litter in gardens of local residents. They were trying to decide whether or not to deploy uniform officers in the area to try and do something about it. Having decided to do so, they were faced with typing up the rationale for their decision on the computer. The officer typing explained he was going to record it as 'Protecting human rights of the residents' and in an easy manner spoke aloud 'Their right to private life … that's Article 8. Oh, and Freedom of Movement – the rights of both sets of football supporters too'.

(Field notes, 13 June 2015)

This kind of headline reading of the ECHR was apparent again in another group, when one officer got out their mobile phone to search the HRA online. In an effort to impress the trainers, and slightly in jest, the Inspector told his fellow trainees: 'Aye, Articles 9, 10, 11, put them down!' Although it is encouraging to see aspiring commanders attuned to ECHR considerations, the detachment from legal standards in these instances tended to result in a superficial, if not inappropriate, application of the broadly worded articles of the ECHR to the facts. This undermined the ability of the law to regulate the operational dilemmas thrown up by the scenario the trainee commanders faced.

The 'Bridgers'

Command training was, however, just the beginning for the Inspectors I observed. They would have to prove their mettle in the final course assessment, as well as future public order events, where their senior colleagues would determine who was up for the task. In interviews, the accredited bronze and silver commanders emphasized the importance of experience, especially when it came to the use of tactical options in periods of public disorder; it tended to be the seasoned, capable commanders that would be called on to police contentious parades and protests. In this way, the assessment and recruitment of commanders can be understood as another component of police self-regulation. With refreshers courses and operational exposure, commanders benefitted from the human rights law expertise of other actors in the PSNI, actors which a silver commander referred to as the PSNI's 'bridgers'. These were police staff and officers with knowledge and expertise of both human rights law and police practice and were able, therefore, to bridge the two.

The first 'bridger' was the PSNI's human rights lawyer, a solicitor with considerable experience in the field of policing and security, who provided the authoritative voice of translation of human rights law for the PSNI's commanders. Police legal departments, although rarely mentioned, are a significant source of legal knowledge and a conduit for informing officers of updates in case law and legislation (Dixon, 1997: 278–80). Throughout the early period of reform, the police lawyer played a direct role in providing training programmes rolled out for all officers involved in operational planning and command of public order events. These courses were a form of what Chayes and Chayes (1985: 280) have referred to as 'preventative law' whereby in-house lawyers attempt to insert legal standards and considerations into the earliest stages of decision-making. In 2005 and 2006, the lawyer led three days of training on the amendments introduced by the Public Processions (Amendment) (Northern Ireland) Order 2005[20] (NIPB, 2006: 58; NIPB, 2007: 117). Since 2008, short, intensive refresher courses have been delivered to up to sixty officers each year, outlining the legislative framework for parades and protests, the relevant human rights law standards and the key developments in public order cases (NIPB, 2008: 119). Officers were required to apply their knowledge of the legal framework and police powers to practical operational planning, and after completing each exercise, they were then debriefed and discussions were led by the human rights lawyer (NIPB, 2010: 55). These courses played a primary role in equipping the script-writers with up-to-date knowledge and expertise beyond that provided in the specialist command courses. Notably, the lawyer's legal translation was incorporated directly into the police script when a decision was made to replicate the course material in the Gold Strategy (NIPB, 2008: 120).

When it came to the gold and silver commanders' tactical and planning meetings, they stressed how the human rights lawyer would be 'a part of the furniture, part of the team – a trusted and well-liked member of the team, who's known to give sound advice regularly' (Bronze Commander Cliff).[21] Commanders explained that they would ultimately be the ones who would make the operational decisions, but the human rights lawyer would be an 'active player' whose advice 'certainly goes a long way' to informing the approach taken. Commanders expressed how useful it was to have someone who could help them get a sense of issues like the level of tolerance police were expected to show in facilitating protest activity or the legal powers they had to restrict protestors' movement (e.g. whether breach of the peace could be used, or more specific legislation was more appropriate): 'We've

[20] The Order amended the Public Order Processions (Northern Ireland) Act 1998 to enable, amongst other things, the Parades Commission to impose conditions on 'any persons supporting' a parade.

[21] The presence of PSNI's human rights lawyer at these meetings has also been recorded in the Policing Board's human rights annual reports (see, e.g., NIPB, 2007:123).

used him very practically. What is the terminology? What does it mean by imminence?' (Bronze Commander Cliff) and 'they would tell you the kind of out workings of case law, give you their interpretation … there's certainly room within that if you needed to go back and further debate the point or expand upon it' (Bronze Commander Daniel). This easy access to human rights legal advice, available 'on demand' throughout the strategic planning stages of operations, was heavily encouraged by the Policing Board's legal advisors as good practice for contentious parades (NIPB, 2006: 61).

In-house lawyers' familiarity, immediacy and continuity with the organization allows them to inject legal standards and opinion into routine decision-making, reinforcing pro-social aspects of workplace legalization (Edelman and Suchman, 1999: 970). Commanders emphasized that in planning meetings there was time and space to 'throw ideas round a bit' and seek clarification on particular ECHR standards. As Silver Commander Brian explains:

> Say we're going to put a block in at the exit of a roundabout or street, we're going to put a barrier in – we're thinking about the right to privacy of the nearby residents, blocking access to road users, are we blocking access to arterial route, are there other routes that we could block instead, what options and alternatives are there to that barrier? In the slower time of planning meeting we can think about all of this, we don't have the split second-decisions to make.

With a select few senior officers regularly performing silver command roles for big events in recent years, their continued exposure to legal advice led them to believe they had improved their understanding far beyond that taught in command courses. They described having had to confront many scenarios that required discussions with their human rights lawyer: 'We've been round the cycle in Northern Ireland, we've been right from that low-level sight and sound piece all the way round to serious disorder and all the way back round again, and we understand what each phase looks like and what the priorities are' (Silver Commander Brian). Consequently, although commanders admitted they would 'never feel entirely comfortable talking to anybody whose specific focus is human rights legislation' (Silver Commander Andrew), they were accustomed to, and comfortable with, hearing case law and detailed considerations of ECHR standards from their lawyer. Over time, this created a solid foundation that experienced commanders could draw upon and feel confident about when incorporating human rights law into the powers and policy section of their plans, rather than just copy and pasting the HRA.

The particular skill that commanders thought their lawyer had was the ability to take a 'pragmatic approach' that identified the legitimate police objective and walked officers through how they could reach it, bearing in mind potential challenges. As explained by Silver Commander Brian:

> I have become increasingly aware that perhaps the policing approach to human rights is very pragmatically based and that's where we would tend to differ from others in the legal profession who are much about a paper-based exercise and that where the likes of [Policing Board legal advisor] and [PSNI human rights lawyer], who can inhabit both sides of the world, are of such benefit, because they can *translate* both. I think the key element is that interaction.

Such interaction was necessary, Silver Commander Andrew reminded me, because 'we're cops, and cops have a broad knowledge of legislation, but we're not trained like lawyers'. Being 'trained like a lawyer', commanders thought, brought with it unique knowledge and expertise. They made reference, for instance, to documents sent by their lawyer offering specific commentary on the interpretation of 'lawful' and 'peaceful' protest under Article 11 of the ECHR and a condensed version of case law and legal opinion that was 'really effective, practical guidance'.

The working relationship between legal teams and organizations has been singled out as an area of concern. Edelman and Suchman (1999) argue that organizations are powerful engines of socialization and the more embedded lawyers become, the more likely they are to use their legal expertise to secure, rather than challenge, organizational goals. Legal teams can use their talents to make organizations more skilfully evasive and equip them with legal justifications that are skewed to satisfy the exigencies of the organization (Dixon, 1997; Edelman and Suchman, 1999). Suspicions of this kind of co-option have been voiced by outside observers of the PSNI, and commanders themselves did suggest, albeit in coded fashion, that they could draw upon legal advice to inform, if not realize, police goals. One example involved the assessment of proportionality made in the context of qualified rights. A commander explained how they had learnt to emphasize the seriousness of the police objective for big parading events. By suggesting, for instance, that 'the whole rule of law in Northern Ireland is at stake and if that falls to the wayside, here are the potential consequences, even demonstrating that rationale immediately changes the proportionality discussion and debate and lifts it up', police tactics could appear more proportionate, and therefore defensible, in the context provided by police.

In another example, commanders described being tasked with policing a Parades Commission determination that would have resulted in Loyalist marchers passing through a particularly contentious Republican area at a time when community tensions were already high. On the day of the event, rival factions gathered, and notorious characters were spotted within the crowd. Surveying their options, the command team realized the danger of violent clashes was so high that they might need to set aside the Commission's determination and stop the marchers from continuing down the route. Aware that this would be a controversial decision, they did not want to 'bluff it' and described how they searched for a strong legal basis that could justify contravention of the determination. In consultation with their human rights lawyer, the commanders worked through their options. Drawing on the legal advice, a decision was made (and the rationale written up) to restrict the march because of the fear of an imminent breach of the peace, with particular efforts made to demonstrate the factors that met the definition of 'imminence' as set out by their lawyer.

In the busyness of the command room, the PSNI's human rights lawyer was present alongside other actors, including firearm advisors, press officers, intelligence officers, staff officers, loggists and camera operators, as well as the Policing Board's human rights legal advisor. Based on the accounts of those present, the lawyer played a secondary role at this stage, and was there to answer any specific questions commanders had. When it came to giving advice and information, the second 'bridger' of law and practice seemed to be at the fore: a core team of accredited public order tactical advisors. These junior ranking officers (who were also public order command trainers) came equipped with a sharp knowledge of the capabilities of various tactical options, the legal authorizations and policy guidance for using them and the key public order legislation. The use of tactical advisors is encouraged by the PSNI's own policy, which requires commanders to consider the involvement of advisors at the outset of the planning stages for every operation that may present public order concerns, and where a decision is made *not* to use them, the rationale must be documented by the commander (PSNI, 2013c: para 13.116). Once a tactical advisor has been requested, they must be involved in all relevant planning meetings, including at gold and silver levels.

A tactical advisor I interviewed described their role as providing a safety net in the heat of the command room, pointing out any errors or encouraging commanders to fully flesh out their rationale for a decision. As they explained, this is because 'Commanders say "Get that done!" "Get them moved!" and it might be the job of the tactical advisor to say, "Well you've got this … legislation, you can close the road"'. I observed this first-hand in the Silver Command room at a multi-unit training day, which brought together TSG units, police dog units, AEP operators and water cannon teams to practise riot scenarios. In a room equipped with sixteen screens offering a live feed of the mock-up village (where disorder was scheduled to build and then erupt), a newly minted silver commander was watched carefully by a tactical advisor, who pushed the commander to verbalize his rationale for decisions and make more explicit reference to the ECHR. Pulling him aside at the end of the session, the tactical advisor reminded the commander that decisions were being recorded live and could not be amended later, so legal authorizations for the use of force needed to be verbalized accurately and contemporaneously with the decision. It was through this process of appraisal and tactical support that commanders became well-versed and rehearsed in managing trouble, something we turn to in the following chapter.

Conclusion

In the conclusion of *Liberty and Order*, Waddington (1994) weighed in on the debate at the time over whether democratic rights should be elevated to codified, constitutional principles. His answer was a firm 'no'. Public protest was, Waddington insisted, a political phenomenon, subject to political processes that were irreducible to a set of principles capable of universal application – and besides, the police had a widespread, albeit rarely articulated, commitment to liberal democratic values anyway (Waddington, 1994: 205). The last two decades have proven otherwise. Waddington's dismissal of codified rights now stands in stark contrast, firstly, to the introduction of HRA, and, secondly, to the influential reports of statutory and parliamentary authorities in recent years, which have continued to call for human rights law to be at the core of public order policing in the face of critical findings (ICP, 1999; HMIC, 2009, 2011; JCHR, 2009). This chapter has sought to begin to examine the impact of this shift towards human rights within the operational context of Northern Ireland's contentious parades and protests, looking specifically at how PSNI commanders come to engage with, and make sense of, human rights law.

Human rights have been heavily integrated into public order policing not through legislation or a regulatory scheme, but rather the PSNI's carefully crafted command structure and planning process, albeit closely monitored by the Policing Board's human rights legal advisors. Police commanders make a determined effort to write human rights law standards and principles into the police 'script' governing the policing of parades and protests. These standards and principles were interpreted with the help of the PSNI's trainers, legal advisors and tactical advisors, who bridge law and operational practice. It is significant that commanders, especially silver and gold commanders, were some of the best educated, well-resourced members of the organization and had learnt from their own experiences about the operational benefits of human rights. This learning process captures how senior ranking officers re-learnt human rights as a more technical regime of legal principles and authorities, moving beyond the 'common sense' narratives expressed so strongly by the TSG. Likewise, through their specialist role and sets of responsibilities, commanders enjoyed support, training and advice that helped them to understand the relevance of human rights law for the roles they performed, something notably absent in the roles and experiences of the junior officers in the Neighbourhood Teams we met in Chapter 5.

If this is how human rights came to be so embedded within the PSNI's approach to public order policing, with the police script being the material product of a structured police planning process, the question we might now ask ourselves is why. What function did a legalistic script, actively promoted through a distinct operational hierarchy, play in the context of policing Northern Ireland's contentious parades and protests? In other words, how did commanders use this script 'in action' and what kinds of institutional, political or cultural factors help to explain how decisions were made when it came to its performance? The answer to these questions lies in the following chapter, which explores how the script and its rights terminology were actively performed in public order operations and, most significantly, the audiences to which the script was presented to and the circumstances in which this took place.

7

The Script in Action

Participation and Performance

> John was tired. He had been the Gold Commander last night and was up early again this morning. He shrugged it off as we made our way down the back staircase and joined his staff officer, Nick, who would be driving the bulky five-door Skoda. We turned left out of Police HQ onto Knock Road. John checked Twitter for anymore chatter while directing Nick along his preferred route. We weaved our way across Belfast, then straight through the city centre. The sun began to fall. Streets were empty and few cars were on the roads. I didn't recognise the places I knew well. We crossed the Queen's Bridge towards the Short Strand, a Nationalist enclave in predominantly Loyalist East Belfast, driving alongside the barricades and metal fences police had erected earlier that day. TSG units were positioned along the strip of road marking the boundary between the two communities which had, for a long time, been at war. John put down the window and exchanged words with a few TSG officers, dressed in their jumpsuits. It sounded as if the operation was rolling out as planned. Once we finished surveying the route that thousands of Loyalist band members had been funnelled along hours earlier that day, we made a speedy return to Police HQ. Reports came in of growing tensions in the north of the city. I had never been in Belfast on the night of the Twelfth of July before. (Field notes, 12 July 2015)

Usually born and bred in Northern Ireland, the PSNI's public order commanders were acutely aware of the sensitivities surrounding parades and protests. So too were the ghosts of public disorder past lodged in the PSNI's organizational memory (Mulcahy, 2006). Commanders spent much of the year with one eye on the public order operations that well-known Loyalist or Republican events

Policing Human Rights. Richard Martin, Oxford University Press. © Richard Martin 2021.
DOI: 10.1093/oso/9780198855125.003.0008

would generate from Easter onwards. Scribbled down the side of a whiteboard that hung in Silver Commander Derek's office was a list of over twenty high-profile parades taking place in the coming months, next to which was a roughly sketched outline of the most contentious part of the parade route. He knew it took exactly twenty-seven minutes, at marching pace, to pass by this volatile strip. As he reminded me, such events were, after all, the PSNI's 'bread and butter stuff'. The aim was to police the Commission's determination with minimal disruption and casualties, all the while ensuring community expectations were carefully managed. As one Assistant Chief Constable publicly remarked: 'We define success on the night [of the parade] as nobody gets hurt, everybody gets home safely, no damage, and as limited disruption to the city as is humanely possible' (Public Session, NIPB, September 2014).

This chapter examines how the public order script, explored in Chapter 6, was performed by commanders. As we shall see, at certain junctures in this performance, the PSNI's script was exposed to the scrutiny of outside audiences. I begin by exploring how commanders sought to sell the script to one such audience: the parade and protest groups commanders sought to 'win over' (Waddington, 1994: 101). If such groups could be won over with the PSNI's pitch, the likelihood of disorder was greatly diminished, and commanders could better control the event. In some cases, however, the sales pitch proved unsuccessful; marchers and protestors proceeded with their own agendas. In such instances, commanders proved reluctant to intervene too forcefully, for reasons we will soon come to understand. In two high-profile cases, the police approach to disorder has led to legal challenges, both of which reached the UK's highest court. This introduces the second audience occasionally in receipt of the police script: the courts that must assess the internal self-application of human rights law by police. In their review of police decision-making in these cases, though, the senior judiciary have proven reluctant to interfere, showing deference to officers' relative expertise, their access to intelligence and the exigencies of operational situations. The final section asks what role human rights law has come to play in managing the kinds of 'trouble' that Waddington (1994) identified over two decades ago as crucial to commanders' decision-making. It is argued that human rights law, contained in the police script, has been skilfully deployed by commanders to manage 'in the job' trouble emanating from these external audiences.

Selling the Script: Community Engagement

The sales process is a year-round exercise in community engagement led by senior officers.[1] It was motivated by the same desire for control that the commanders in Waddington's (1994) study were so keen to exert over events that risked disorder or violence and the 'trouble' associated with it. The focus of the PSNI's commanders was on the local level, as they tried to identify and strengthen ties with the 'true voices' and 'key influencers' in communities (Silver Commander Charley). This outreach was extensive, strategic and resource intensive. As explained by Silver Commander Andrew: 'When I formally start to engage in formal planning meetings for that event, the starting point will be to look at all that information with a view to saying right who is that we need to engage with, what are the gaps?' Commanders described how a plethora of interests could be involved in just a single parade, requiring commanders to foster links with the Orange Order, local churches, community representatives and residents' groups. This was 'all about this rich picture of what are the actual views and dynamics within the community at that given time', said Bronze Commander Daniel. With input from community representatives, commanders sought to improve their knowledge of the groups involved, understand the groups' intentions and assess the likelihood of disorder erupting. All of this factored into a police assessment of the 'threat and risk' attached to the parade and how to best facilitate peaceful assembly and protest.

The relationship between the risk of serious violence and the exercise of democratic rights is an important one recognized by the ECtHR in its Article 11 jurisprudence. The likelihood that a demonstration will provoke a violent response in others does not prevent the demonstration from being 'peaceful' for the purposes of Article 11,[2] and demonstrators have the right to participate without fearing they will be subjected to physical violence by opponents.[3] Indeed, the ECtHR has stated that 'if every probability

[1] On the role of senior officers in holding discussions and consultations with parade organizers in the lead up to big events, see also NIPB (2007: 123–42) and HMIC (2009: 77–9).

[2] *Ziliberberg v Moldova* (App no 61821/00) ECHR 51 (1 February 2005).

[3] *Plattform 'Ärzte Für Das Leben' v Austria* (App no 10126/82) ECHR 15 (21 June 1998).

of tension and heated exchange between opposing groups during a demonstration was to warrant its prohibition, society would be faced with being deprived of the opportunity of hearing differing views'.[4] But if organizers or participants do have violent intent, then this is relevant in determining whether the assembly falls within Article 11 protections, which are limited to 'peaceful' assembly.[5] Of particular relevance for police commanders is the ECtHR's inclusion of a duty to communicate with the leaders of a protest demonstration as an essential part of the positive obligation on authorities to ensure the peaceful conduct of an assembly, to prevent disorder and to secure the safety of all involved.[6] Specifically, the ECtHR has emphasized the importance of 'taking preventative security measures in order to guarantee the smooth conduct of an event', including ensuring that first-aid providers are at the site of demonstrations.[7]

A central insight from research interviews was how the PSNI's commanders connected the right to peaceful assembly under Articles 9 to 11 with Article 2 of the ECHR. It will be recalled that Article 2 imposes a positive obligation on the police to take all reasonable steps to avoid a real and immediate risk to life and to plan operations in such a way as to minimize the likelihood of recourse to lethal force. This was articulated in a thoughtful, practical way by Gold Commander Alex:

> Whenever we're planning an operation, we try to plan it in such a way that force is minimised. Article 4.2 of our own Code of Ethics say about that, and then obviously Article 2 is foremost in our minds, so, around lethal force has to pass an absolute necessity test. So how you would plan it in such a way to do that might involve in the first instance the number of resources you have, the equipment those resources carry, are they in public order uniform, are they carrying long-barrelled weapons, what kind of vehicles are they in, can you use barriers instead of police officers, a whole range of tactics from vehicle tactics, dogs, down to putting humans – police officers, the use of the AEP system is a less lethal tactic – very controversial in Northern Ireland but nevertheless is a less lethal option.

[4] *Stankov and the United Macedonian Organization Ilinden v Bulgaria* (App nos 9221/95 and 29225/95) ECHR 563 (2 October 2001), at [107].

[5] *Kudrevičius and Others v Lithuania* (App no 37553/05) ECHR 1310 (26 November 2013), at [92].

[6] *Frumkin v Russia* (App no 74568/12) ECHR 64 (12 January 2016), at [129].

[7] *Oya Ataman v Turkey* (App no 74552/01) ECHR 493 (5 December 2006), at [39].

When it came to contentious parades where the risk of disorder loomed large, Silver Commander Brian explained that Articles 9–11 and 2 of the ECHR are 'two sides of the scales'. First, if police could help marchers/protestors to exercise their right to peacefully assemble (in accordance with the Parades Commission's determination) in a way that participants felt was appropriate and fair, then the likelihood of violence and disorder flaring up was greatly diminished. This, in turn, meant the positive obligation to intervene under Article 2 to protect marchers/protestors from seriously injuring or killing one another, or police officers, was less of a live issue. Second, on the other side of the scales, if there was intelligence suggesting a risk of serious violence at parades/protests (in some instances due to paramilitary involvement) then, again under Article 2, the police had to be prepared to intervene with tactical options to protect those marchers. In using these tactics and responding to the threat assessment, police might necessarily interfere with the democratic rights of marchers/protestors.

During Northern Ireland's most contentious parades/protests, violent clashes frequently occur between groups from each of the two communities intent on seriously injuring one another, as well as police officers. Commanders explained the best way to uphold their obligations under Article 11 – and the duties they perceived to arise under Article 2 – was through sustained engagement with parade/protest organizers in the months and days leading up to the demonstration. With these human rights law considerations written in the script, Commanders returned to communities to explain what the police operation would look like and to address community concerns or disagreement. In practical terms, commanders described meeting organizers with their iPads, showing them visual representations of where police units would be and explaining to them the thought process behind it. This approach, captured by the police mantra of 'no surprises', is in the spirit of procedural fairness and seeks to give organizers a voice (HMIC, 2009; Orde, 2009; Stott et al., 2013). A special concern of community groups was how the Parades Commission's determination had been interpreted.[8] In contrast to Waddington's (1994: 96) study, where the law was hardly ever mentioned for fear of

[8] The ambiguity in the wording of the Commission's determinations has been a major concern identified by the Policing Board's legal advisors for some time (NIPB, 2005, 2006).

alienating organizers, from PSNI commanders' accounts of their meetings, the issue of democratic rights and police powers was at the top of the agenda because of the restrictions often placed on parades/protests by the Parades Commission (see Chapter 6, Figure 6.3). Organizers were keen to know how police would respect and protect their right to march/protest:

> The Parades Commission's determination says basically the parade will not pass the end of that junction, so then you get right down into the microscopic detail of where exactly does the junction end ... We've sat down with the community and said, 'Well, actually, my view is that see this fencing, the line will run from there across this traffic island and then it will track the white line of the road to there, and that's where the police line is gonna be'... There's just a contest around where people think they're entitled to come to, and again, that has largely been avoided now because we've had that dialogue and engagement to say, 'Don't be surprised, we'll be on this line, we will give you as much as the determination says you're entitled to and we'll make sure you can see the parade', because that's actually what they're interested in. (Bronze Commander Daniel)

Event organizers generally understood the division of labour between the Commission and PSNI, according to commanders. The main issue, noted in Chapter 6, was that organizers' anger and frustration at any restrictions the Commission had placed on events was quickly redirected at the police as the organization tasked with enforcing the Commission's determination. A particular issue for commanders was how and when they ought to respond when breaches of determinations took place unexpectedly during the march or protest, especially when these involved participants known by police to have connections to paramilitary groups. In an attempt to reach a compromise, commanders had to weigh up whether to stop the march and make arrests to enforce the breach, but risk disorder in the process, or use 'soft skills' to negotiate with organizers and strike a compromise, such as returning to the parade route or removing the display of prohibited flags. As discussed in detail below, where possible, commanders described a preference for negotiation and compromise so as to avoid in- and on-the-job 'trouble'.

In operational planning and deployments, commanders' primary concern was whether the 'style and tone' of the police operation risked raising tensions or sparking disorder. Meetings with organizers provided important opportunities to test the water and see if police had got the 'optics' right. The first police priority was to 'appear neutral' in their deployment of resources. A common point raised by commanders was the direction that police Land Rovers or officers faced. Communities felt that if police officers or vehicles were facing them, then they had (unfairly) been identified as the trouble-makers. Based on this feedback and keen to avoid provocation, commanders deployed lines of police officers in alternate positions so they faced *both* communities. The second priority was to minimize the police 'footprint' or 'profile' so as to create the most benign environment possible. The mere appearance of water cannon or TSGs could be enough to enflame the situation. Efforts were made, therefore, to keep these tactical options close by, but out of sight. The situation was not always clear-cut, however. One year, police thought that deploying officers in ordinary, high-visibility uniform to marshal a group of marchers past a contentious flashpoint would de-escalate the situation. Yet, in the eyes of the parade organizers, this signalled that the PSNI was ill-prepared to protect their marchers and they asked to be accompanied by officers in protective public order uniform. There are strong resonances here with Waddington's own findings from public order policing in London in the 1990s. He described how the potential for violent clashes was minimized by careful control of the urban environment by police, 'transforming otherwise public space into "police property"', for example by removing items from the parade route that could be used as missiles and using traffic flows to keep protestors moving in a 'neat and tidy' fashion (Waddington, 1994: 153). Albeit in a very different operational context, a core motivation of public order commanders – to control the urban environment so as to thwart possible triggers of 'trouble' – seem just as, if not more, salient in the Northern Irish context today.

What about situations where the police were unable to sell the script to malcontent protestors? How did this impact on the police response given the link commanders drew between Articles 9 to 11 and 2 of the ECHR? The scenario commanders feared was one where protestors refused to engage with them. Ignorant of the protestors' intentions, the numbers involved or the likelihood of disorder, commanders feared 'running blind' and 'sailing into trouble'. An apt example is the Anti-Internment League parades in Belfast, which often involved groups suspected of being aligned to Dissident Republicanism who refused to liaise directly with police. In these situations, commanders felt forced from their default position: 'It is their event, we facilitate it. But if it becomes an unknown and from our intelligence we reckon it could lead to disorder, then we end up having to control it' (Silver Commander Derek). Not knowing what to expect, but fearing disorder, commanders prepared for the worst, often 'over-policing' the event by deploying large numbers of TSG units in protective uniform. PSNI Chief Constable Sir Hugh Orde (2009: Evidence 31) explained this well, in his typically pithy style: 'If they choose to engage: great. If they do not, then you know what you are dealing with and you police in a different way, and you would certainly see a harder edge to policing'. This explanation chimes with Waddington's (1994) account of policing 'the opposition': organizers who refused to 'play the game' and acted outside the boundaries of peaceful protest were less predictable, less controllable and, in turn, more likely to confront a coercive style of policing. For particular protest organizers hostile to the PSNI, non-engagement with commanders was, in fact, considered to be a point of principle, with the heavy police presence that resulted serving to fuel oppositional policing narratives in some Republican, but also Loyalist, localities.

Over-Facilitating (Un)Peaceful Protest?

The most operationally challenging situations for the PSNI have arisen where protest organizers have not only refused to negotiate with them but have then taken part in un-notified parades with significant impact on the rights of residents and, potentially, the wider community. There have been two important cases to reach the House of Lords/Supreme Court in recent years, brought by community members who alleged the PSNI had *over*-facilitated violent, unlawful protests and, in doing so, had violated the rights of those in the nearby vicinity by failing to uphold positive duties to protect individuals from the known acts of third parties. Both cases have thrown into sharp relief how the PSNI balance competing rights, but specifically just how far the police can justify a non-interventionist, or defensive, approach in the face of disorder affecting those in the vicinity. Conceptually, these legal challenges signal a shift in the site of human rights law interpretation and application from internal self-regulation by the police to external regulation by the judiciary. In this section, we explore how the courts have approached their review of the PSNI's performance of the police script, and how commanders experienced this external intervention by the courts.

In the first case, which reached the House of Lords in *Re E*,[9] and the ECtHR in *P.F. and E.F. v UK*,[10] Catholic pupils and their parents were subject to a 'barrage of intimidating clamour, insults, abuse and offensive missiles'[11] from Loyalist crowds as they walked to and from Holy Cross primary school in an interface area of North Belfast. This took place over a two-month period in 2001. Attempts by senior police and local politicians to negotiate an end to the protest failed. The police settled for an approach that contained protestors and provided a passageway/corridor for school goers to walk through with their parents. At its climax, 400 officers and 100 soldiers were deployed to protect the children and their families, using tall shields to deflect missiles lobbed by Loyalist protestors. A total of forty-one officers were injured. The mother of one pupil of Holy Cross School brought a judicial review of the police's defensive strategy, claiming, *inter alia*, the police had failed to fulfil their positive duty owed to the applicant under Article 3 of the ECHR (freedom from inhuman or degrading treatment). In operational terms, it was argued that the positive obligation required the police to forcefully move protestors back from the school and make more arrests. Such a response, the applicant submitted, would have quelled disorder, served as a deterrent and led to a speedier end to the disturbance. The police, meanwhile, submitted that the defensive approach they adopted was justified because a more robust approach to the Loyalist aggressors risked fomenting serious disorder elsewhere in Belfast which could have threatened the lives of those in the vicinity and wider community.

The issue before the House of Lords, and ultimately the ECtHR, was the scope of the positive duty under Article 3 of the ECHR, and, specifically, whether the risk to those in the wider community, as well as in the immediate vicinity, was a legitimate one that could be taken into account in determining the fulfilment of the positive duty under Article 3. Both courts concluded that the police were entitled to take such a consideration into account. The House of Lords emphasized that the positive duty arising under

[9] *Re E (a child) (AP) (Northern Ireland)* [2008] UKHL 66.

[10] *P.F. and E.F. v UK* (App no 28326/09) ECHR 2015 (23 November 2010).

[11] Baroness Hale, *Re E* (n 9), at [5].

Article 3 of the ECHR was not absolute, nor did the statutory duty to prevent crime require police to intervene on every occasion where an offence was committed.[12] Both the House of Lords and ECtHR extended to Article 3 the significant qualification of the positive duty first established in relation to Article 2 in *Osman*, in which the ECtHR stated:

> bearing in mind the difficulties involved in policing modern societies, the unpredictability of human conduct and the operational choices which must be made in terms of priorities and resources, such an obligation must be interpreted in a way which does not impose an impossible or disproportionate burden on the authorities.[13]

To have accepted an absolute positive duty under Article 3 would, Lord Carswell stated, 'place an intolerable burden on the state'. In its finding that the police had satisfied the qualified positive obligation under Article 3, the House of Lords held that the risks to those in the wider community and in the immediate vicinity were to be taken into account in the court's proportionality assessment and that there was 'clear evidence' of the risk of provoking sudden and violent disorder elsewhere in Belfast.[14] But in making their assessments, both the House of Lords and the ECtHR extended wide operational discretion to police, citing the special expertise, experience and the intelligence available to them.[15] This was, in fact, best captured in the dicta of Sir Brian Kerr LCJ, as he was then, in the Court of Appeal's judgment in *Re E*:

> It is not difficult to understand that an aggressive, uncompromising approach to the protest might have been the catalyst for widespread unrest elsewhere. It is precisely because the Police Service is better equipped to appreciate and evaluate the dangers of such secondary protests and disturbances that an area of discretionary judgment must be allowed them, particularly in the realm of operational decisions.[16]

Almost ten years later, the case of *Re DB* was a stark illustration of the unresolved tensions on the streets of Belfast, the competing human rights claims the PSNI must continue to engage with in

[12] Ibid., at [48].
[13] *Osman v UK* (App no 23452/94) ECHR 101 (28 October 1998), at [116].
[14] *Re E* (n 9), at [58].
[15] Ibid. For a helpful discussion of *Re E* in the wider context of the emergence of positive duties on the police in the UK, see Anthony (2009).
[16] *Re E* [2006] NICA 37, at [46].

public order policing and the weight that ought to be afforded to the police in determining the proportionality of their response to disorder. The applicant in *Re DB* was a resident of the Short Strand (a Nationalist enclave in a predominantly Loyalist area of East Belfast) whose house had been attacked by a Loyalist group involved in the un-notified Flag Protests (discussed in Chapter 6). PSNI commanders attempted to persuade protestors to use the notification scheme under the Public Processions (Northern Ireland) Act 1998 and even tried to encourage the Parades Commission to intervene and issue a determination (something they did not have the power to do). Both refused. It is an offence under section 6(7) of the Public Processions (Northern Ireland) Act 1998 for organizers and participants to knowingly organize or take part in an un-notified procession. Faced with un-notified, and thus unlawful, protests in which participants were potentially committing criminal offences,[17] the PSNI appeared unsure of the best course of action and whether they could, in law, prevent the parade from taking place or whether this was solely the preserve of the Parades Commission.[18] Ultimately, commanders decided to allow Loyalist protestors to travel in and out of the city centre via the Short Strand. Hundreds of officers were deployed to manage the protests and record evidence of offences taking place. The protest lasted three months, and on several occasions over several weekends protestors threw missiles at homes in the Short Strand as they returned from the City Hall. The applicant, a resident of the Short Strand, claimed, *inter alia*, that the failure of the police to actively intervene and stop the illegal protests violated their right to private and family life, protected by Article 8 of the ECHR, and which the PSNI was under a positive duty to protect.

The PSNI's legal arguments, in one respect, were similar to those advanced in *Re E*. Any positive duties owed to the applicant under Article 8, the PSNI argued, were protected on the basis that offenders were being identified and prosecuted under the

[17] See Mead (2018) on the significance of this requirement that, to commit an offence, organizers and participants must 'knowingly' take part in an un-notified procession and that any blanket dispersal of a procession might raise issues of compatibility with the ECHR given the individualized right to peaceful protest.

[18] As noted in Chapter 5, the police no longer have the power to impose restrictions on un-notified public processions or protests like those during the Flag Protests (see *Re DB* [2014] NICA 56, at [13]–[19]).

criminal law, and that in any respect, citing *Osman* and *Pf and Ef*, account must be taken of the difficulties involved in policing modern societies and the operational discretion of the police respected. But the operational response and legal justification differed from *Re E* in two significant respects, and which ultimately led the PSNI into difficulty. The first was the argument that they owed positive duties to the demonstrators under Article 11. An attempt was made to ground this in the ECtHR's jurisprudence which established that an unlawful situation, such as the staging of a demonstration without prior authorization, does not necessarily justify an infringement of a demonstrator's freedom of assembly.[19] The second was a rather hazy Article 2 justification for non-intervention. This argument was neither developed in full in the court's summary of counsel's arguments nor in the judgments of the courts.[20]

In developing our analysis of officers as a form of human rights 'practitioner' it is insightful at this point to pause for a moment to get beneath these legal arguments and grasp commanders' own practical understanding and operational application of these two legal submissions. With regards to Article 11, there was, it seemed, some confusion over just how far the positive duty to facilitate demonstrations went, as expressed by the Gold Commander of the Flags Protests in a public interview with the *Irish News* at the time:

> The European Convention makes it very clear that there is a right to peaceful assembly under Article 11 of the European Convention and the reasons it gets slightly confusing sometimes is that the European Convention is explicitly clear the Police Service has a responsibility to facilitate peaceful protests even if it is technically unlawful and that's where it takes us in to the space of confusing rights.

In a research interview with one silver commander, though, there was a sense that the positive duty was a strong one that could justify non-intervention in highly distributive, illegal protests that had endured for a matter of months:

> If there is no Article 2 risk, then in many ways there's absolutely no ability for us to restrict Articles 9–11. They are rights that can be restricted in

[19] *Bukta and Others v Hungary* (App no 25691/04) ECHR 610 (17 July 2007).

[20] *DB's Application* [2014] NIQB 55, at [95] and [112]; *DB's Application* (n 18), at [35]; *DB v Chief Constable of Police Service of Northern Ireland* [2017] UKSC 7, at [20].

certain cases, but broadly speaking it is going to be in cases of Article 2 risk or other risk of that nature. Therefore Articles 9–11 becomes fine.

...

They [Loyalist protestors] did it last week, they marched into the city centre and back out again and nothing happened and there was some disruption to the community in the City Centre, so back to *Bukta,* back to *Plattform* – minor inconvenience has been tolerated and will continue to be tolerated.

As a matter of law, the ECtHR has recognized the right to freedom of assembly as 'one of the foundations of a democratic society' which requires that any exceptions to it be 'narrowly construed' and any restrictions placed upon it 'convincingly established'.[21] As such, the ECtHR has held that Article 11 should extend to instances where a demonstration involves some level of minor disturbance and a certain level of disruption to ordinary life.[22] Crucially, though, the weight given to the positive duty by the PSNI in its operational response to the Flag Protests was considerable and downplayed the regard that must be had to the duration and extent of public disturbance caused by assemblies, as well as any demonstrated risk of insecurity or disturbance, in determining the tolerance that must be shown to demonstrators.[23]

As for the Article 2 arguments cited by the PSNI to justify for non-intervention in *Re DB*, greater clarity of thought emerged from the research interviews. The following account of a Silver Commander is again informative:

Okay, so what are our alternatives? Well, it is an illegal parade and there is an argument to say look we can, we can stop it.... Essentially your two options are: facilitate this march in the city centre or stop the march somewhere on the route. The primary place to stop it, bearing in mind your most likely conflict is likely to be around the Short Strand, was going to be in and around the Lower Newtownards Road area. The resources necessary to stop a march such as that, and I would suggest the likelihood of force meant that we would have had to have a significant justification to do that, because we would have ended up fighting, we would have ended up using a lot of force, arresting a lot of people, including police officers would have ended up getting injured. On the

[21] *Frumkin v Russia* (App no 74568/12) ECHR 64 (12 January 2016), at [93].

[22] *Bukta* (n 19), at [37]; *Kudrevičius and Others v Lithuania* (App no 37553/05) ECHR 1310 (26 November 2013), at [155].

[23] *Fáber v Hungary* (App no 40721/08) ECHR 2026 (24 July 2012), at [47].

basis that our primary consideration here, is not just Article 2 but the rights of those individuals to protest and the tolerance which society should show to that, which said, there is nothing horrendous about going into the City Centre here, clogging up the front of that City Centre for a few hours and then leaving again in isolation. And the only alternative to that is to risk officers and the lives of the public by blocking it. That to me is that rights-based approach to that and that's what was constantly reviewed ... How does that make a resident of the Short Strand feel? I can't imagine it makes them feel great and this comes back to this issue of even in an effective rights-based decision, it's always going to struggle because in Northern Ireland Article 2 is always going to be a factor on our paper.

What I think we can extract from this is an understanding that the duty under Article 2 to plan and control operations so as to minimize resort to lethal course justified police non-intervention in disorderly protests. In short, a passive approach was one that minimized the risk of sparking disorder or violence. The rationale is thus similar to the one advanced in *Re E* – the risk of police intervention sparking collateral disorder that could result in police then having to use potentially lethal force – but it was not formulated as a concern to be considered in relation to the scope of the positive obligation owed to the applicant under Article 8 either. Rather, it was repositioned within a negative obligation under Article 2 owed to the wider community; seemingly – as it was never expressly articulated – the requirement to plan and control police operations so as to minimize recourse to lethal force. But this negative duty was also considered alongside a positive duty to protect the lives of frontline officers who were in close proximity to potentially violent demonstrators. Although alluded to in the account above, this is expressed more explicitly by Bronze Commander Daniel:

Human rights obligations internally, in terms of Article 2 issues for the officers, I mean 44 officers injured last year and questions been asked about what plans, what was going to be put in place from a management and leadership perspective to be able to protect those officers going forward. And the commonality around this actually was both sides saying a situation where police officers and protestors or paraders end up in very close proximity to each other, like nose to nose, is not a good situation for anybody.

Taking a step back, what insights might we glean from these interpretations and applications of human rights law? They speak to a marked concern to avoid confrontation with demonstrators and possible injuries to officers, similar to that expressed by senior officers in their response to the Holy Cross dispute in *Re E*. But a decade on, what is striking about the response to the Flag Protests in comparison to the Holy Cross dispute is how the PSNI were now able and willing to rely upon and deploy human rights law – rooted in their interpretation of Articles 11 and 2 of the ECHR – to justify a passive approach to serious disruption involving a sectarian flashpoint in Belfast, notwithstanding positive duties owed to those in the vicinity. Article 2, in particular, played a defensive role, with its high threshold of risk to life or serious injury seeming to function as the minimum threshold for requiring intervention in public order situations. But if this pronounced use of rights-based justification is novel, the operational response it was used to justify seems less so. A central finding of Waddington's (1994) study of public order policing was that despite ample opportunities for frontline officers to make lawful arrests or use increased levels of force, senior officers carefully directed sub-commanders to avoid potential confrontation that might spark disorder or weaken police control of the event, wary of the 'in' and 'on' the job trouble that would ensue. This notion of 'trouble' is something we will return to shortly, but the immediate issue for now is how this understanding of human rights law fared before the courts.

The High Court was deeply critical of the PSNI's handling of the protest.[24] Justice Treacy held that the PSNI's passive approach was a result of their failure to grasp their powers. The un-notified status of the parade meant it was a criminal offence and thus police had the power to stop the protestors, a position senior commanders seemed unsure about.[25] The PSNI's failure to intervene undermined both the Public Procession Act 1998, which distinguished between legal and illegal parades, and the PSNI's general duty under section 32 of the Police (Northern Ireland) Act 2000 to prevent crime, and ultimately violated the applicant's Article 8 rights. While being unlawful does not necessarily take a parade outside of Article 11's protection, the PSNI had 'knowledge that those participating were likely to engage in serious public disorder, damage to property, disruption to life and behaviours which would impact adversely on relationships within the community', which

[24] *DB's Application* [2014] NIQB 55.
[25] Ibid., at [121].

thus took those involved outside of the protections of Article 11.[26] Treacy J was sceptical that fear of serious disorder was the true rationale for the police reluctance to intervene, suspecting it was rather to allow protestors to 'vent anger' outside the City Hall. Treacy J questioned whether there was sufficient evidence to substantiate the PSNI's claim that an Article 2 risk persisted at the time of the protests affecting the applicant, given that they took place a month after the worst of the disorder.[27]

The case provoked concern amongst the PSNI's chief officers. Shortly after the High Court delivered its judgment, the then Chief Constable Matt Baggott explained at a public session of the Policing Board that he would appeal it. This was 'essential', he insisted, because, if left to stand, 'it may constrain our operational flexibility in the future'. Baggott continued: 'We have to appeal this. I cannot have the expectation or implication that the police will always be able to take immediate and forceful action. It would require a far greater reliance on force and an uplift of resources to deal, there and then, with large crowds … it's not a merely technical matter' (Public Session, NIPB, May 2014). The PSNI was concerned about the practical implications of being required, as a matter of law, to forcefully intervene, disperse crowds and make arrests in future situations where the rights of local residents were engaged by those taking part in un-notified protests. But the question for the appellate courts was whether the PSNI's failure to act more assertively had unlawfully infringed the rights of others under Article 8 to peaceful existence in their home, free from violence and intimidation, and whether the Article 2 justification formulated by the PSNI was sound in law.

The Northern Ireland Court of Appeal allowed the PSNI's appeal.[28] Giving judgment for the court, Lord Morgan CJ relied heavily on the principles recognized in *Re E* and *Osman* regarding the wide discretion that ought to be afforded to the police in challenging operations situations like this.[29] Reference to the Article 2 argument was made in passing by the Court of Appeal, but remained unpacked as a basis for non-intervention. The issue quickly became an evidentiary one: in making decisions about

[26] Ibid., at [137].
[27] Ibid., at [122].
[28] *DB's Application* [2014] NICA 56.
[29] Ibid., at [35]–[37].

how to deal with the un-notified parades, had the PSNI actually taken into account the possibility of violence and disorder?[30] Lord Morgan CJ reviewed the transcript of the gold commander's *Irish News* interview, as well as the criminal justice strategy and the events policy book, apparently 'in the kind of detail which was not opened to the learned trial judge'.[31] The Court of Appeal was content that the PSNI had not, in fact, felt inhibited by the Public Procession (Northern Ireland) Act 1998; they were aware of the powers open to them to intervene in the illegal protests and had demonstrated a clear commitment to gathering evidence against the worst offenders. In a short conclusion, and without considering the extent of the positive duty arising under Article 8 of the ECHR, Lord Morgan CJ stated that in this 'difficult situation', which had 'left the police to manage such parades using public order powers rather than providing a tailored legislative scheme',[32] the PSNI had taken proportionate steps to protect the Article 8 rights of the applicant.

The Court of Appeal's judgment was handed down shortly before I began the fieldwork and was still fresh on commanders' minds. Some agreed that the Flag Protests could have been handled better, but in their eyes, the Court of Appeal had rightly overturned the High Court decision and endorsed the PSNI's pragmatic approach 'dictated by operational resilience and the realities' (Bronze Commander Daniel) in what was 'new territory for us' (Silver Commander Derek). They emphasized the importance of protecting their operational discretion to act in such difficult scenarios. The commanders I spoke with expressed in similar terms the importance of the successful appeal in protecting police discretion: 'Ultimately had we lost that appeal it would have put us in a very difficult position, practically in all sorts of ways' (Silver Commander Andrew) and '[w]e'll appeal it all the way to Europe if we have to, it's that important to us' (Silver Commander Edwin). This marked a similar finding in Waddington's study (1994), in which commanders feared legal challenges could result in rulings that would constrain their operational discretion or narrow police powers, thus tying their hands in future.

30 Ibid., at [34].
31 Ibid., at [52].
32 Ibid., at [54].

How did Commanders think the Court of Appeal's decision had impacted on their ability to sell the police script? Whilst relieved the court had safeguarded their operational discretion, they remained concerned that the legality of their defensive approach and the weight police attached to Article 2 meant little, if anything, to the groups they would have to negotiate with in the case of future un-notified parades. As Silver Commander Andrew explains:

> Yes, it [NICA in *Re DB*] did show that the way in which we go about things and make decisions set against human rights and all the rest of it, we weren't a million miles away and the judge [Lord Morgan CJ] bore that out ... So it was important we came out of that period and ultimately it was important that we won that appeal, but I think bottom line, practically, I'm dealing with some of the most sensitive parades in the country, issues which haven't gone away and issues which will continue to raise their head ... and that decision of the court ultimately won't mean much – it means something to me because at the end of the day it vindicated a certain approach which will come to the fore again no doubt, but in terms of the communities most involved that doesn't mean an awful lot. Policing is what they see and feel on the street at the time.

In response to the PSNI's heavy reliance on human rights law to explain their approach to the Flag Protests, the Committee on the Administration of Justice, a prominent local human rights NGO, published an information booklet (CAJ, 2016). Written for a general audience, it outlined the human rights standards relevant to public order policing and the PSNI's policies and procedures. But commanders were sceptical as to whether improved knowledge could overcome the cultural prejudices and divisions that had made agreement between the two communities so hard for so long. For instance, Silver Commander Brian contended that 'anybody can teach somebody human rights, what you can't teach is an understanding that human rights are universal, so I hear a lot from people about their rights, I don't hear a lot from people about their understanding of the rights of others'. In this way, commanders' efforts were not, it seemed, immune from the ethno-political dynamics of rights talk, examined in Chapter 3, which presented one community's interests as irreconcilable with the claims of their adversaries in the 'other' community.

The story, however, did not end with the Court of Appeal's judgment. In 2017, the applicant successfully appealed the decision before the Supreme Court, which found in favour of the resident, based on similar reasons as Treacy J in the High Court.[33] The argument before the Supreme Court shifted away from Article 2 and the interference with Article 8 and back to whether the PSNI really *had* grasped the scope of their legal powers under the Public Procession (Northern Ireland) Act 1998 in the first place. Giving judgment for the Supreme Court, Lord Kerr did not doubt that the PSNI sought to control the marches and minimize the disorder, or that commanders were concerned about the risk of greater disorder occurring with the consequent risk to life which might arise if they tried to prevent the parades from taking place.[34] However, the Supreme Court held that the gold commander had in fact failed to comprehend that, because of the illegality of the parade under the Public Procession Act 1998, police had the power to intervene and stop it from taking place. Indeed, they were under duty to do so by way of section 32 of the Police (Northern Ireland) Act 2000 to prevent the commission of offences – and it is an offence for organizers and participants to organize or take part in an un-notified procession unless they can prove they did not know and neither suspected or had reason to suspect it was un-notified (sections 6(7)–(8) of the Public Processions (Northern Ireland) Act 1998). As a result of this misapprehension, the PSNI never meaningfully considered stopping the parade. This misapprehension alone was sufficient grounds to allow the appeal.[35] The Supreme Court's judgment is significant in clarifying what precisely the police powers are to prevent parades where organizers fail to notify the Commission. However, in finding that the PSNI had misconstrued their statutory powers, this meant that the Supreme Court did not need to determine the human rights issue, that is, the proportionality of the PSNI's non-interventionist response, when it came to fulfilling their positive duty owed to the applicant under Article 8 of the ECHR and the introduction of a competing Article 2 ECHR claim by the PSNI.

If we conceptualize judges and police as two kinds of legal actor involved in the interpretation and application of human rights law, the court remains in no doubt who the authoritative

[33] *DB v Chief Constable of Police Service of Northern Ireland* (n 20).
[34] Ibid., at [2].
[35] Ibid., at [70].

voice on the law is. Lord Kerr corrected with ease the PSNI's inaccurate interpretation of the scope of Article 11. Senior PSNI commanders, despite their specialist training and advice from 'bridgers', misunderstood that although Article 11 requires police to facilitate un-notified protests, this was only in 'exceptional circumstances' such as spontaneous events, something the two-month period of demonstrations clearly was not.[36] In a firm rebuke to the police approach, '[t]here was no warrant for allowing Article 11 considerations to determine how these parades should be policed'.[37] But the Supreme Court was obviously sympathetic to what it described as the 'enormous, almost impossible, difficulties' the PSNI faced.[38] Lord Kerr shared the sentiments expressed by the House of Lords in *Re E* when his Lordship stated:

> A definite area of discretionary judgment must be allowed the police. And a judgment on what is proportionate should not be informed by hindsight. *Difficulties in making policing decisions should not be underestimated, especially since these frequently require to be made in fraught circumstances.*[39]

A question that remains only partially answered though, and one which commanders will no doubt confront in exercising their discretionary judgment in the future, is whether non-intervention in unlawful, sustained, disorderly demonstrations that engage positive duties owed to those nearby can be justified on the basis of an Article 2 duty to those in the vicinity and wider community to minimize the likelihood of recourse to potentially lethal force. This is, after all, a rationale that commanders were attracted to. A clue to the answer can be found in Lord Kerr's rejection of Article 2 as being the central issue in the case.[40] Having recognized there would be 'something of an air of unreality'[41] in discussing the proportionality of the PSNI's actions given it had wrongly construed its powers,[42] his Lordship continued by stating that the PSNI:

36 Ibid., at [58]–[61].
37 Ibid., at [61].
38 Ibid., at [1].
39 Ibid., at [76], my emphasis.
40 Ibid., at [37] and [68].
41 Ibid., at [74].
42 Ibid., at [74]–[75].

had an inescapable duty to prevent, where possible, what were plainly illegal parades from taking place and to protect those whose rights under article 8 of ECHR were in peril of being infringed. Meeting those obligations had to be tempered by operational constraints, of course. Stopping the parades without taking account of what further violence that might provoke was not an option.[43]

In its simplest terms, the issue is where these 'operational constraints' and risks of 'further violence' ought to be positioned in a human rights analysis. His Lordship's focus on the scope of the positive duty owed to the applicant under Article 8, rather than the negative duty under Article 2 to minimize recourse to lethal force, is in keeping with the style of analysis adopted in *Re E* in which fears of collateral violence were taken into account in determining the scope of the positive duty owed to the applicant. This seems preferable because it places the emphasis on the human right actually engaged on the facts, rather than on a prospective right, conditional on future action or inaction. So too does it place the onus on the police to justify the interference with the applicant's rights. Wherever the justification for non-intervention is located though – either the positive duty under Article 8 or the negative duty under Article 2 – it seems the courts will, quite rightly, require the risk of collateral disorder to be real and demonstrable.[44]

Performing the Script: Managing the Use of Force

The Holy Cross dispute and the Flag Protests offer a stark illustration of how commanders' efforts to devise and sell the police script did not always result in peaceful parades or protests. In such situations, where commanders feared provoking outbreaks of large-scale disorder they could not control, there was minimal intervention and use of force. However, when isolated incidents of rioting erupted in the immediate aftermath of

[43] Ibid., at [62].

[44] In *Re DB*, the High Court stated non-intervention when 'those participating were likely to engage in serious public disorder, damage to property, disruption to life and behaviours which would impact adversely on relationships within the community' would require 'the clearest possible explanation and justification for not taking appropriate measures' (at [137]).

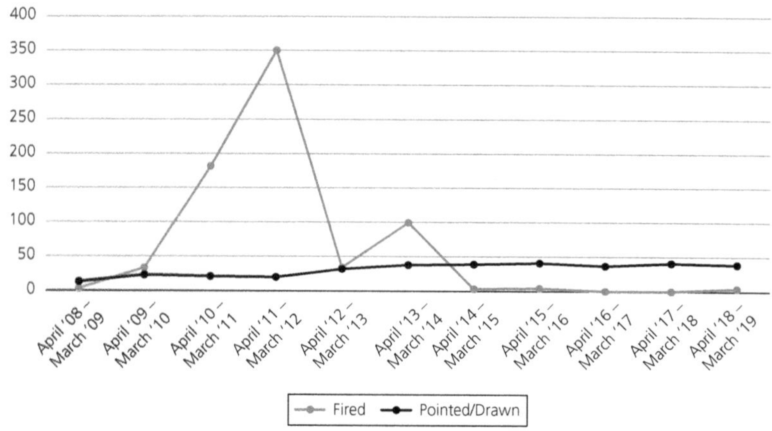

Figure 7.1 PSNI Use of Attenuated Energy Projectiles (AEP)

contentious parades and serious violence was directed at police, commanders have tended to resort more readily to force in order to push troublemakers away from police lines, back in the direction of their own neighbourhoods. Figures released by the PSNI give an example of the range of options used to quell public disorder during the 2009 marching season: batons were drawn and used ninety-one times, CS spray was drawn and sprayed on sixty-five occasions, police dogs were used on

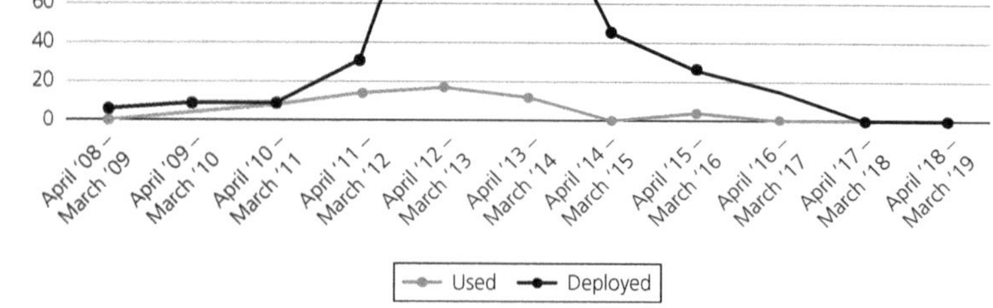

Figure 7.2 PSNI Use of Water Cannon

seven occasions, thirty AEPs (baton rounds) were fired, and water cannon were activated five times (NIPB, 2009: 101). The broader trend for the deployment and use of AEPs and water cannon – two tactics used almost exclusively for public disorder – are shown in Figures 7.1 and 7.2 (based on the PSNI's official figures), which illustrate how higher levels of force remain a central feature of the PSNI's operational response to contentious parades and protests.

Managing civil disorder poses a dilemma for police in liberal democracies because it challenges the twin bases of their legitimacy: impartiality and restrained use of force (Waddington, 1987). Forceful intervention against protestors invites allegations of police bias and brutality. Such complaints were levelled at the RUC throughout the conflict and remain a powerful oppositional discourse that adds to the sensitivity of police use of force today (Mulcahy, 2006). For commanders, the decision to use force also throws up risks of professional 'trouble' associated with accountability inside and outside the police (Waddington, 1994). One PSNI Commander remarked how it was 'the easiest thing in the world to make the decision to send in the troops and quell the violence'. He continued that a good commander would, however, opt for the 'tougher decision' and restore order in a way that did not alienate communities but instead respected protestors' rights and withstood scrutiny. In this section, I explore the operational and organizational tensions that commanders and frontline officers confronted in self-regulating the use of force and interpreting ECHR standards. In doing so, I critically engage with Waddington's (1994) analysis of the role of law in the policing of protests.

The Authorization Process

The authorization of higher levels of police force is subject to a strict hierarchy governed by the gold/silver/bronze command structure described in Chapter 6. Taking the use of AEP as an example, for the most contentious parades/protests, the gold commander exercised their power to authorize AEP to be carried by TSG units, meaning it would be locked in a secure compartment of the Land Rover ('authorization for carriage'). The police script on the use of potentially lethal tactical options was clear: although operationally available, AEP was not to be used unless it was absolutely necessary to protect life, as per the requirements under Article 2 of the ECHR. This criterion was explicitly stated in tactical and deployment plans, as well as the operational orders and use of force briefings. It was the job of silver (situated in a command room) and bronze (based with units on the ground) commanders to determine whether it *was* absolutely necessary, depending on the level of violence meted out by rival groups and the injuries sustained by officers.

In interviews, commanders explained their distinct roles in the authorization process, emphasizing their reliance on the input and assessment of one another. The bronze commander's role was to provide a first-hand account of the crowd dynamics and officers' wellbeing and, if they felt it necessary, initiate requests for AEP. Having done so, it was the job of the silver commander to decide firstly whether to permit officers to be armed with AEP ('authorization to deploy'), and secondly whether to allow them to fire AEP rounds ('authorization to use'). In essence, this was a process of self-regulation, whereby commanders asked more senior colleagues whether the legal threshold for use of force had been met. It was apparent that commanders could work together to make the authorization process smoother and less vulnerable to external scrutiny from official oversight bodies. This process is a vivid illustration of what Ericson (2007: 377) has termed as officers' skill in 'accountability', whereby they provide a record of activities that explains them in a credible rule-following manner. Bronze commanders described how they knew to use certain terms in their radio communications to 'paint a picture' that could provide the silver commander with the information needed to 'tick the boxes' of absolute necessity. In fact, three phrases had been taught to commanders after concerns authorizations were taking too long, something I experienced first-hand at the bronze command course:

[T]hese boxes are [clicks finger quickly several times] – we're not asking you to write it in triplicate and come along with a blood sample, we're asking you to justify the criteria ... the Bronze Commander is asking the Silver Commander to trust them but the Silver Commander can't trust them if they're not getting the information. So you might come on and say: 'Eh, Silver, *serious risk of injury*, *I cannot withdraw*, *no other tactical options available*, request for AEP immediately' 'AEP approved'. But if you come on and say: 'We're getting it a bit tight here, I need plastic,

I need plastic, I need plastic!' That's not giving you the picture. (Public Order Trainer; emphasis added)

From the relative calm of the control room, silver commanders underscored the need for this carefully sketched picture when devising their rationale for decision-making. Silver Commander Derek explained that if signs of disorder appeared on the monitors and their bronze commanders seemed to be under stress, they would sometimes prompt them to describe on the radio the most relevant information with the justification for use of force in mind: 'How do you feel? Are you taking missiles? How is it impacting on officers? How is it impacting on people's property? How big is the crowd?'

Given the well-known features of police culture – group solidarity, shared sense of mission, willingness to use force (Bowling, Reiner and Sheptycki, 2019: 171–80) – we might have expected a permissive approach to authorizations. That is to say, silver commanders would have trusted the assessments of their bronze commanders implicitly and been eager to arm junior colleagues under attack. Yet, despite the shared phraseology just mentioned, such solidarity was not something described as happening often in the context of authorizations for use of force. In fact, authorization was a bone of contention between the silver script-writer and public order units, like the TSG, on the shield line. There were rumblings of discontent from TSG officers over the 'marked reluctance' of their silver commanders to authorize bronzes' requests for AEP. Many recalled experiences of being attacked on shield lines by rioters armed with bricks, bottles, petrol bombs etc., but still the use of AEP was refused or only permitted after delay. As summed up by TSG Sergeant David:

> It comes down to the Silver Commander making a decision that woe behold a rioter getting injured or killed and it's the police's fault, then it all looks on him, all the inquiries look at him as to why he didn't make this decision or that decision. They're happy just to hold the line, let the police take a beating, get this parade past or whatever it is and then soak away, just sort of withdraw.

Some TSG officers even believed there was an acceptable level of injury to public order units that silver commanders would tolerate before granting authorizations for the use of force. In the aftermath of particularly violent disorder, such as in 2014 when one in four public order officers reportedly sustained injuries, the Police Federation was quick to criticize commanders, citing delayed authorization for AEP as a 'major reason' for the injury toll (McDonald, 2014). Interestingly, the TSG rarely felt confident enough to 'self-authorize' the use of AEP, batons or CS spray – an option available to them if they feared they or their colleagues were in serious danger. This option was described as 'career suicide' because of the difficulty of justifying using potentially lethal force to accountability bodies and their own bosses (field notes, 4 December 2015). As explained by TSG Sergeant Adam:

> Now you can under extreme circumstances self-authorize, which means if you believe that somebody's life is in danger you can fire, but in reality, for the officer standing in the line, and me as a supervisor behind them, it takes a lot of guts to self-authorize and fire. Normally you've to go through – and I can understand the commanders sitting in the stations, the famous picture has to be painted for them, as in why do you want to use this? Cause it is really a last resort, so you know that can be frustrating.

Silver commanders were aware of these concerns but explained that AEP was a significant use of force they would not authorize lightly or without going through the requisite checks. There were stories of silver commanders using CCTV cameras to zoom in on incidents to examine for themselves whether the situation described to them by bronze commanders really justified AEP. Silver commanders emphasized the importance of demonstrating a 'graduated response' that did not rise up the use of force continuum unless things 'really did go from flash-to-bang' (Silver Commander Derek). They were confident officers on shield lines were sufficiently equipped to absorb a degree of riotous behaviour before AEP was necessary. Likewise, from their planning meetings and briefings, bronze commanders ought to know the contingency plans before resorting to AEP. In the mock command room, I observed as part of training how the silver commander refused the bronze commander's requests for AEP on multiple occasions. It was explained to the bronze over the radio that police dogs and water cannon would be deployed first. Further requests for AEP were made after reports came in of masonry being thrown at officers, but it was only when the jets of the water cannon failed to quell the rioters that AEP was eventually authorized by the silver commander. This practice seemed to be the graduated response inspired by proportionality. For frontline officers, this style of approach was described in interviews as a 'very defensive role … We're basically providing a focus for the rioters to tire themselves out' (TSG Constable Kevin).

The situation described by officers raises the question of why, at different levels of the police hierarchy, officers faced with the same public disorder arrived at quite different conclusions on the justifiability of using higher levels of force. TSG officers and bronze commanders seemed to think the absolute necessity threshold for use of force per Article 2 had been met more often than silver commanders did. Indeed, they thought that requests for AEP were received by silver commanders with some hesitation, even scepticism. How might we explain these differing assessments? And what does it mean for the application and function of human rights law in such circumstances? Most obviously, frontline officers, squinting through their protective visors at angry mobs of rioters, might perceive a greater sense of threat and thus stress the need for the relief that AEP could provide. Silver commanders, after all, were in the comfort and safety of command rooms in police stations some miles away, or in the 'ivory towers of the control room', as one TSG Constable described it. But objectively, silver commanders had extensive access to CCTV, radio communications, helicopter overhead footage, dynamic intelligence assessments as well as legal and tactical advice, which allowed them to critically evaluate bronze commanders' own assessments. Although such explanations were noted by junior officers, I found that the clearest explanation for the differing assessments of junior officers and senior commanders lay in their perceptions of the 'trouble' associated with particular tactical decisions.

Avoiding 'Trouble'?

The avoidance of confrontation with protestors was a central finding of Waddington's (1994) study. Confrontation was to be avoided because it risked disorder and increased the likelihood of police use of force which, in turn, created considerable 'trouble'. Such trouble was 'on the job' (legal challenges, political pressure) but also 'in the job' (promotion prospects, disquiet from junior officers) (Chatterton, 1979). This insight – 'perhaps one of Waddington's most important contributions' (Stott,

2016: 116) – has been explored further in two small-scale studies by Cronin and Reicher (2006, 2009). These found that commanders were 'constantly aware of how, in a crowd event, others would judge their actions, and of the consequences these judgments would have for their future as police officers' (Cronin and Reicher, 2006: 190). It was only in situations of violent disorder that commanders perceived internal resistance and external critique of the use of force as sufficiently diminished to empower them to act. Furthermore, junior and senior officers were affected by audiences in different ways, depending on the real or imagined trouble they associated with them. Junior officers, less concerned with pressure from politicians, the media or lawyers, were eager to intervene against aggressive acts by crowd members and were sceptical of the restraint imposed by senior commanders, who were far warier of the consequences of intervention (Cronin and Reicher, 2009).

The picture that has emerged from my fieldwork provides strong support for these findings and offers insight into how officers perceived human rights law within the highly sensitive context of policing parades and protests. When it came to silver commanders' decision-making, TSG officers had a strongly held suspicion that two main sources of 'trouble' could explain the reluctance to authorize higher levels of force, neither of which were determined by human rights law. The first source was community leaders and local politicians, which could be costly for commanders because they were often the same 'key influencers' senior officers relied upon for co-operation and support with local policing issues in communities, from drug dealing to paramilitary attacks (see Chapter 5). The strongly felt views of TSG Constable Larry reflected those of many of his colleagues:

> They're [commanders] trying to appease communities from the past. They're trying to appease these scrutinising bodies rather than trying to get on with the job and you can just get on with the job within the guidelines set out by the human rights, but they're too busy worrying about how it's going to look on the media or how Sinn Féin or the DUP or whatever political department are going to come on the news and show footage of people getting hit with a public order baton.

According to officers, this situation was especially evident when it came to using AEP against Nationalist/Republican groups due to the extensive and disproportionate use of plastic bullets by the RUC against these communities during the conflict.

Convinced commanders were 'scared of upsetting the wrong people' (TSG Constable Pauline) and 'political backlash' (TSG Constable Owen), some officers described, with great frustration, how commanders were unduly influenced by requests, even demands, from community leaders. As TSG Constable Jay observed: 'There's obviously a lot of stuff that goes on behind the scenes ... "Well, if you move your line back to the junction of such and such a street, we'll get the boys to stop throwing stones and petrol bombs"'. Officers were giving voice to Waddington's (2012: 472) insight that 'the use of force in riot-control is as much a battle for legitimacy as it is for control of the streets'. There was a strong belief within the TSG that threats to their safety were the cost of maintaining relative peace in communities. This sentiment was commonly expressed as the elevation of others' rights at the expense of police officers'. During one focus group, an officer explained that '[i]t's all human rights going one way again. If anyone's human rights are being breached a lot, it comes down to ours. The conditions we have to work in and the big parades, that's the last thing on the bosses' minds, they don't care' (TSG Focus Group 4). Although undoubtedly annoyed by their sense that they were 'just small pawns in a big chess game' (TSG Focus Group 3), most officers acknowledged the pressure commanders faced in trying to appease communities, enforce Commission determinations and protect officers.

There was less understanding, however, when it came to the second source of trouble TSG officers felt commanders had succumbed to: professional self-interest. They explained how authorizing the use of force against rioters could be damaging for commanders in the eyes of their senior peers, especially when it came to promotion prospects. No commander wanted to be the one who authorized AEP or water cannon in case they injured, even killed, a protestor. This would attract notoriety and hamper career progression. Officers in one focus group were very praising of a bronze commander who had been especially good at 'painting the picture' and making firm requests for AEP when officers were coming under attack from rioters. The officers explained, however, that such proactivity meant the commander was 'Accused by community leaders of being heavy handed, breaching their human rights and all when he wasn't, he was acting well within the law, but the people in charge moved him aside ... the public didn't like him, which meant the bosses in turn didn't like him, which meant he got shifted out' (TSG Focus Group 2). In this instance, the two types of trouble – community perceptions and professional status – became intertwined, creating conditions which officers thought their senior commanders were keen to avoid.

How did the views of junior officers compare with their senior counterparts? Silver commanders did mention, albeit in more coded terms, that they were mindful of the impact their decisions had on communities. However, the primary source of trouble silver commanders sensed arose from being subject to the watchful eye of oversight bodies and legal authorities. At the top of the list was the Police Ombudsman. They knew that the use of AEP or water cannon would automatically trigger a formal Ombudsman investigation.[45] Commanders described how they would have to hand over their policy and decision logs to the Ombudsman after they clocked off in the command room, and could be interviewed months later about the authorizations they made. The Policing Board was the other external audience that commanders knew could create trouble. If AEP were discharged, the commander would have to submit a use of force form to the Policing Board, alongside a public disorder incident form providing an overview of the relevant details. This was not purely an academic exercise. In 2011 an increase in the use of AEP (in the face of widespread disorder in Belfast and the surrounding areas) provoked concern from some on the Policing Board. Notwithstanding the positive reports from the Ombudsman's investigations, the Board called for 'discrete and careful analysis' focusing on renewed training and briefing of the legal test for the lawful deployment and use of AEP, discussed earlier in the context of officers' reciting key authorization terms (NIPB, 2011: 64).

The wariness of external scrutiny was clear during the bronze commander course I observed. The tone was set by the silver commander who, opening the course, cautioned trainees about their new responsibilities and the need to be confident in their decision-making, all the while 'keeping one eye on the Ombudsman or, God forbid, the Coroner's inquest'. Throughout the course, aspiring commanders were reminded how a decision

[45] Section 55 of the Police (Northern Ireland) Act 1998 provides that any incident involving the use of force is subject to a Police Ombudsman investigation, regardless of whether a complaint is made.

might 'not look good in court' and asked: 'Will that option stand up to scrutiny if examined'. A stark warning came on the penultimate day, when a commander came to share their experiences of being subject to a lengthy investigation by the Health and Safety Executive after a rioter had been injured following the use of water cannon. The future bronze commanders were trained to anticipate and negotiate this sort of legal accountability during a session devoted to decision logs and audit trails. They were taught to produce clear, thorough rationales for their decision-making, which they could later rely on if they were subject to a formal investigation or inquiry. As Silver Commander Derek commented, 'If it's not written down, it didn't happen. Isn't that what MacPherson[46] said!?'

In previous courses, trainers went as far as to hire lawyers to create a mock scenario to test trainees in a fashion akin to a cross-examination in court, followed by a detailed debrief on their performance. As one trainer described: 'We had proper barristers coming in and saying this is what you will be asked in court, this is how you need to protect yourself, write down the key points why you authorized, when you authorized, for how long you authorized it for, any supporting rationale.' The potential chilling effect that fear of an impending investigation could have on commanders was acknowledged most explicitly by Gold Commander Alex:

> I would be wrong if I said that I didn't believe that across the service there are some people who are just completely and utterly fed up with the level and volume of scrutiny that takes place and that there is a sense amongst many that they're just out to get us, and that feeling can actually lead to some despondency and some morale problems but also could actually lead to some risk averse activity, when I would expect someone to put their foot forward, use force, take a course of action and they maybe are reticent of doing the right thing because they're frightened because 'The police ombudsman will come and investigate me' or 'I might be arrested or interviewed'.

This issue of risk aversion has been hinted at publicly by the former Chief Constable when speaking at the launch of the Policing Board's annual human rights report in 2016. Responding

[46] Referring to the public inquiry, conducted by Sir William MacPherson, into the Metropolitan Police's infamous handling of the murder of black teenager Stephen Lawrence in London in 1999.

to a question about how commanders approached public disorder, and why the public should have confidence in the police, he described how all senior commanders had, at some point, faced events that ended up 'looking really messy' and required 'impossible dilemmas' to be addressed as best they could (field notes, 7 September 2016). To do so, Chief Constable Hamilton explained, meant senior commanders needed to try to set aside their fears of accountability 'trouble': 'we will hold each other to account, we have the Ombudsman's investigations, we have the oversight of the Board, but actually I want to empower public order commanders to actually make decisions without looking over their shoulder' (field notes, 7 September 2016).

Human Rights Law in the Face of 'Trouble'

I want to pull together the strands of analysis to demonstrate the indirect, but nonetheless significant, impact of external legal audiences on the self-regulatory behaviours of commanders. In so doing, I draw a significant distinction from Waddington's (1994) findings and my own regarding the relationship between law and 'trouble'. It will be recalled that Waddington observed a marked reluctance on the part of commanders to engage with the Public Order Act 1986 because they lacked confidence in determining their actual powers. Officers feared interpreting the 1986 Act incorrectly and thus possibly attracting unfavourable judiciary commentary on top of the embarrassment of getting it wrong. This wariness of the law was, ironically, compounded by a cultural expectation that experienced officers were cognizant of legal parameters and that explicit reference to the law was 'gauche and a sign of amateurism' (Waddington, 1994: 80). In sharp contrast to Waddington, I found that (human rights) law was seen as a resource for managing trouble rather than a source of trouble itself.

It was strikingly apparent that commanders saw the application of human rights law, and careful reference to the ECHR throughout the script, as a most effective means of managing potential trouble arising from external accountability bodies. By engaging with human rights law, they could articulate police operational concerns in a way that was receptive, even convincing, to legal audiences like the courts and oversight bodies (see also Bullock and Johnson, 2012: 644–5). Human rights law provided an objective standard they could reference in support of decisions they had made. Silver Commander Andrew explained:

Because of the scrutiny and accountability we're under, for a large part of this we understand we need to be able to show, audit and reflect on our decision-making and thinking, so waiting for the challenge after the fact, not least the legal challenge, are you with me? So all that sort of [human rights] language, we capture that and we document it. As I say, my log, I can show you where I've taken legal advice from [human right lawyer] and factored that in, but that's there in many respects for the safety net after the fact.

As suggested by Ericson (2007), police *use the rules* not only to inform and justify decision-making, but also as a form of communication to persuade police audiences to endorse their decisions. Compliance with the law entails careful reference to formal legal rationality that is 'inscribed in formulaic phrases and forms' (Ericson, 2007: 377; Dixon, 1997: 273). Similarly, when it came to contentious events, decision-making could be 'copper fastened' by drawing on legal advice and terminology from the PSNI's human rights lawyer:

It just makes you feel like you're going to be more sure-footed in terms of the decision-making down the line. Because quite often you're thinking about the hypothetical situation that may or may not arise, and really, it is genuinely just about give them the kind of forethought and knowing what exactly your position is 'cause sometimes its, eh, there's no good decision, no good outcomes, it's just shades of bad. (Bronze Commander Daniel)

The self-regulatory nature of planning and decision-making remains in the shadow of the courts as the authoritative adjudicators. But that is not to say that this kind of detailed engagement with rights by commanders is irrelevant to how the court conducts its supervisory jurisdictions, far from it. In assessing proportionality, the court will examine the balance the decision-maker has struck, not just whether it is within the range of reasonable decisions, but also the relative weight the public authority has accorded to interests and considerations.[47] Where an authority is conscious of, or addresses its mind to, the Convention in arriving

[47] *R v Secretary of State, Ex parte Daly* [2001] UKHL 26, Lord Steyn, at [27].

at its decision, the court 'attribute due weight to that conclusion'.[48] Indeed, the court will be 'inherently less likely' to disagree with the public authority's decision where there has been 'proper consideration' of the Convention[49] and 'a challenger's task will be the harder' where the authority has 'conscientiously paid attention to all human rights considerations'.[50]

Human rights law was further referred to in the formal record of events through the live decision-making logs of silver and gold commanders. Silver Commander Charley gave an example: 'Say I need to move the crowd from A to B, that will be recorded as a decision in CLIO [the police management system]. I will then say to the loggist "That's because – ", and then I'll rattle off Articles 9, 10, 11. The longer entries [on CLIO] with regards to human rights will be around the planning piece that's been done in advance of the event.' This explicit framing of decision-making using the ECHR was a striking feature of the PSNI's public discourse and legal arguments during the Flag Protests. Commanders couched their concerns around public safety and high levels of force in the language of Article 2, while also aligning the tricky decision to facilitate the initial, unlawful protests with the positive duty to facilitate protest under Article 11 of the ECHR. Whilst this was received with scepticism by the High Court, which questioned whether such language could really account for police decision-making, the Article 2 explanation translated well in the Court of Appeal, opening up the wide area of operational discretion granted to police. Moreover, by refusing to endorse the High Court's suggestion that because the gold commander had sought legal advice, they must have misunderstood the legal position, the Court of Appeal safeguarded the 'copper fastening' potential of commanders' legal advice.

Although the courts and Ombudsman stood at the end of the line when it came to 'trouble', a different audience member, one whom commanders had grown keen to welcome aboard, was the Policing Board's human rights advisor. As mentioned in Chapter 6, the advisor is present throughout public order operations, after

[48] Lord Rodger, *Belfast City Council v Miss Behavin' Ltd* [2007] UKHL 19, at [26].

[49] Lord Neuburger, ibid., at [91].

[50] Lord Bingham, *R (SB) v Governors of Denbigh High School* [2006] UKHL 15, at [31].

the agreement first stuck between Sir Keir Starmer – then Policing Board's human rights advisor – and Chief Constable Sir Hugh Orde (see Chapter 3). The level of access granted has been extensive from the very beginning, as Starmer described in an early annual report:

> [W]e attended all planning meetings and briefings at all levels: Gold, Silver and Bronze ... On the 12th July, itself, we observed the policing operation on the ground, attending at the Ardoyne shop fronts when the parades passed through the area on the way out in the morning and when the police and military deployed in preparation for the return parades in the evening. The rest of the time, we either attended on-going planning meetings or observed events and decision-making in the Gold and Silver Command rooms. Subsequently, we examined the records made during the course of the policing operation, including the contemporaneous logs generated by Gold and Silver command. (NIPB, 2006: 60)

The arrival of Starmer in the PSNI's planning meetings and command rooms was something commanders remembered as rather unnerving. As noted by Waddington (1994: 118–20), lawyers pose a particular kind of threat by virtue of their knowledge of the law and ability to spot the working rules of police that might run contrary to it. Silver Commander Edwin recalled staffing the gold command room during one of the worst periods of disorder, just after Starmer began his role as advisor to the Board:

> That was first time anyone of us had really seen a QC in a command room. I mean, lawyers and police command rooms don't always go together whether they are working for you or not, and this one wasn't working for us, I mean, he was employed by the Board, he was there in an oversight capacity and he was able to see and listen to everything the Gold Commander is seeing and listening to. And sometimes that got really ugly, you had Gold Commanders showing less than perfect composure at times, you had stuff said on the radio that makes your toes curl a little bit and yet we exposed ourselves completely and utterly to someone of Keir Starmer's quality ... Lots in policing say 'Oh, it's a lonely place when you're in the witness box at the public inquiry' and of course very few of us get near a public fucking inquiry, they're that rare! But the reality is we have quasi-judicial interventions almost all the time, and it's not worrying about the public inquiry, it's worrying about what the Policing Board lawyers will say because they have unfettered access.

Some commanders thought such exposure helped them to ensure they were achieving the standards now expected of them as the police reform process unfolded. This was particularly so in 2004 and 2005, when Starmer undertook post-event examinations of commanders' decision-making, working through video footage, breaking it down frame by frame and asking commanders to account for their operational decisions (NIPB, 2004, 2005).

In the decade since, the Policing Board's human rights legal advisors have not been refused access to public order planning, briefings or command rooms, even for the highest profile events (Kilpatrick, 2018: 58; NIPB, 2019: 45). By now, commanders describe being un-phased by the presence of the advisors, most endorsing their work using the language of accountability heard in the official police voice (see also Waddington, 1994: 120). Several commanders even expressed the confidence they derived from having an independent advisor who could report back on their performance. Commanders knew if they successfully followed their training, tactical advice, policy and intelligence assessments, the Board's advisor could be an influential, impartial voice who could vouch for them in the annual human rights report and answer the concerns of certain Board members. Indeed, the legal advisors have consistently praised public order commanders, as reflected in one of many possible examples:

> Each operation was planned with an acute attention to detail with protection of the various ECHR rights providing a central component of all decisions made ... Those standards are so deeply embedded now within public order policing that decisions were instinctive and at times permitted a creative response aimed at keeping people safe while also protecting fundamental rights. (NIPB, 2019: 45–46)

Such accounts suggest the strong internalization of human rights amongst commanders, who proved able to apply legal standards to the situations before them. Given their command training, assistance from 'bridgers' and exposure to exacting oversight arrangements for over a decade, it is unsurprising that commanders were well-versed in rights standards and using them to make decisions. Moreover, in the face of pressing accountability, which they knew revolved around human rights law standards, commanders were undoubtedly aware it was in their professional interest to explicitly frame planning and tactical decisions in such terms. Even if rights-based considerations did inform their decision-making, to avoid accountability trouble, oversight bodies had to be able to see and hear it.

Conclusion

In Chapters 6 and 7 we have traversed the length of public order policing, from specialist training to officers' accounts of the planning stages to how operations were carried out. The police script was produced internally by commanders who strongly narrated the events they policed using ECHR terms and legal standards. Building on the preceding chapter's analysis of how human rights law is interpreted by commanders, the focus here has been on how the script was performed in action and what this tells us about the function of human rights law in this highly contested area of policing. Commanders exposed the script to different audiences, at different times, for different reasons. It was presented to parade and protest organizers in the run up to events for the same reasons public order commanders in Waddington's (1994) study invited protest organizers into their offices to 'win them over'. The aim of PSNI commanders was to convey to organizers that the police knew their responsibilities and would respect the democratic rights of those involved, within the limits set by the Parades Commission. In turn, commanders hoped that this 'no surprises' approach would improve relations with community leaders, reduce the likelihood of disorder and better enable the police to maintain control of the event. At times, however, reference to human rights law risked causing friction and misunderstanding, arising from the histories, agendas and associations discussed at length in Chapter 3.

If communities were an audience from which commanders actively sought endorsement, then so were the courts, albeit in a different way. Commanders were acutely aware of the ramifications their decision-making had for the parties involved, as well as their own professional standing. As illustrated by the Holy Cross dispute and Flag Protests, undoubtedly tricky decisions have to be made in determining how to balance between competing rights in fraught circumstances. In some situations, legal standards are prescriptive and make clear where the outer limits lie (as with Article 11 and un-notified protests), but in others, human rights law can structure, but not definitively answer, how competing interests should be resolved. In these cases, all that can be expected of decision-makers is that they are mindful of competing rights and apply the proportionality test in a structured and careful manner, drawing on reliable evidence to support their conclusions. The senior courts in *Re E*, and to an extent in *Re DB*, have affirmed that whilst the judiciary are the authoritative voice in determining how the balance must ultimately be struck, they will grant the police discretionary space to make these difficult, and often contested, operational decisions.

Within this discretionary space, commanders operated in the shadow of the courts: they took instruction from their human rights lawyer, they incorporated case law and ECHR standards into their script and they articulated the decisions they made in human rights law terminology. As *Re DB* demonstrates, the PSNI did not always get the law right within this space, but there can be no doubt they felt the regulatory force of human rights law. In understanding why this was so, Waddington's (1994) account of 'trouble' surely seems as salient now as it did two decades ago. In this chapter, the example of the police authorization of AEP revealed how self-regulation of police power was animated by a wariness of not just the political contestation over parades and protests, but also lawyers, oversight bodies and ultimately courts. These external audiences used human rights as the standard with which to assess police decision-making, and thus rights-based decision-making was the rubric that commanders knew they needed to operate within and appeal to. To be clear, then, human rights law was not seen as a source of trouble, but rather a way of talking, thinking about and justifying actions to avoid the trouble arising from negative reporting by the Policing Board's human rights legal advisor or the Police Ombudsman, and legal challenges brought before the courts. The Policing Board's legal advisor was thus a crucial ally – indeed, another kind of audience – who could vouch for the human rights-based decision-making of commanders and defend them from critique when this was deserved. Connected to the analysis in Chapter 3, though, the ability of the Policing Board's advisor to do so was premised on their perceived professionalism and independence, as well as access to the inner workings of public order operations and the sensitive intelligence assessments that contributed to them.

In sharp contrast to the publicly discussed, highly scripted and strictly enforced modes of policing just explored is the area of police custody. Tucked away, a world of its own, custody is animated by routine interactions between junior officers (constables and sergeants) responsible for making and receiving arrests. Holdaway (1983) describes this 'backstage' nature of custody, hidden from public view, while Hillyard and Gordon (1999: 516) refer to it as a 'closed site' with 'its own rules and procedures where justice cannot be seen to be done'. The types of senior officers we met in this chapter (Inspector rank and above) appeared in custody only infrequently. Custody Inspectors worked outside the suite, discovering its goings on remotely, either through CCTV feeds or over phone calls with staff. Custody Officers described it as 'their' suite: they controlled who came in and when, where officers should stand and how they should conduct themselves. It is this markedly different arena of policing to which we now turn to further examine the role human rights law and associated procedural safeguards in domestic law play in regulating officers' decision-making and self-conceptions of their work.

PART V

Police Custody: The Rights of Suspects

8

'Arrest, Arrest, Arrest'

Statutory Safeguards under Pressure

Most of us are fortunate enough not to have been the subject of police powers of arrest and detention, but for the hundreds of thousands of people each year in the UK who have been, it is no doubt a stressful and troubling experience, regardless of the offence they are suspected of committing (Gibbs and Ratcliffe, 2020). For some, arrest and detention may even be a regular feature of the lives or lifestyles they have come to lead or inherit. Hillyard and Gordon (1999: 505) remind us of how:

> arrest involves taking a person into custody, physically detaining him or her, and carrying out a range of detailed procedures. The person loses his or her freedom for a period of time, suffers varying degrees of public and private opprobrium, embarrassment, and perhaps significant direct and indirect costs.

The vast majority of people who are arrested are taken to custody suites located in local police stations. Many rights are at stake at this point, as the criminal justice process opens up and the coercive investigative powers of the police become acutely felt. Police custody, and the particular role of the custody officer as the statutory guardian of suspects' rights, thus emerges as an important avenue of enquiry for this book to deepen our understanding of the impact human rights law has on modern policing.

Police custody has long provided a rich arena in which to assess the regulatory potential of the law. The Police and Criminal Evidence Act 1984 (enacted in Northern Ireland as the Police and Criminal Evidence (Northern Ireland) Order (1989) (PACE) was a landmark piece of legislation designed to circumscribe police

Policing Human Rights. Richard Martin, Oxford University Press. © Richard Martin 2021.
DOI: 10.1093/oso/9780198855125.003.0009

discretion and protect suspects' rights. The enactment of PACE triggered an explosion of studies in the late 1980s and early 1990s that examined a number of issues including: the protection of suspects' rights in custody as well as the right to legal advice; the appropriate adult scheme; the authorization of detention; and the length of time suspects spent in custody (Maguire, 1988; Bottomley et al., 1991; Dixon et al., 1990; McConville, Sanders and Leng, 1991; Brown, 1997). By the late 1990s, however, interest in custody had dwindled. As Dixon (2012: 279) observes, there has been 'a long drought in empirical research on the detention of suspects in custody'. Some recent insight has been provided, however, by researchers who are venturing back into police custody to consider issues like legal advice (Skinns, 2009a, 2009b; Kemp, Pascoe and Balmer, 2011, vulnerability (Dehaghani, 2016), immigration (Parmar, 2019) and performance management (Kemp, 2014). Explaining this resurgence, Skinns (2011: 13–14) boldly asserts that '[u]ndeniably the socio-political context of police custody process has altered', with managerialism and privatization having left an 'indelible mark' that warrants reappraisal of earlier works.

For the purposes of this book's examination of human rights and policing, the attraction of custody as a research site is both old and new. This arena of policing remains significant for the same reason it always has. It is a frenetic but focused site of everyday interpretation and application of legal safeguards by rank-and-file officers that impacts heavily on individuals' rights. Its renewed attraction is twofold. First, the well-established PACE safeguards sit within the PSNI's culture that officially purports to place great value on human rights, as discussed in Chapter 2. Has this strengthened the PACE safeguards? Has this empowered custody officers to stand up for the rights of those arrested by their colleagues? Second, arrest powers underwent a significant overhaul in section 110 of the Serious Organized Crime and Police Act 2005 (SOCPA), which introduced a general power of arrest. The statutory safeguards designed to temper this power have been subject to recent judicial interpretation, including important cases decided by the Northern Irish courts. This case law raises pertinent questions regarding the suspect's right to liberty in light of routine police practices; whether the courts' statutory interpretation of domestic safeguards has been rigorous enough; and the scope of the protections granted under Article 5 of the ECHR – the right to liberty and security – in this context.

The focus of the empirical account of human rights in Part IV is on the suspect's right to liberty in the context of police custody. In keeping with the style adopted in Part III, the discussion that follows seeks to closely analyse how particular aspects of police practices and decision-making interact with human rights law standards. The data for this chapter and the next is marshalled from several sources. The primary source is qualitative data from interviews I conducted with PSNI custody officers (fifteen) and civilian detention officers (CDOs)[1] (eight), from six of the nine custody suites in Northern Ireland, as well as custody inspectors (two) and superintendents (two). Given the small proportion of policemen and women that perform the role of custody officer, this small interview sample does, in fact, constitute nearly one quarter of full-time custody officers in the PSNI. To compliment this interview material and corroborate officers' accounts, I draw upon nationwide custody data I obtained from the PSNI through freedom of information requests. The salient statistics and observations contained in recent reports produced by the Criminal Justice Inspectorate Northern Ireland and the Policing Board have also proven valuable.

The aim in this chapter is to explore how the three statutory safeguards established in PACE to protect the suspect's right to liberty have fared in the face of organizational pressure to detect and 'clear up' crime. This context requires an initial examination of the regulatory scheme and legal standards devised under PACE, including how it has been impacted by SOCPA. Using the three due process safeguards established in PACE to form a framework for this chapter's analysis, the chapter explores how officers apply, dismiss, interpret and reconstruct each of these safeguards in their everyday work. Once again, the richness of this analysis, specifically its appreciation for how law and practice do (or do not) interact, is enhanced by paying close attention to the development of lines of authority in the case law that have, it is argued, watered down the legal standards officers must apply. This analysis of the case law is based on recent judgments from the High Court and

[1] These members of staff perform what used to be the role of police gaoler. They are responsible for various tasks, including searching the detained person, obtaining evidential samples, monitoring their wellbeing whilst in custody, providing them with meals and transporting them around the custody suite.

Divisional Court of Northern Ireland, as well as from the Court of Appeal in England and Wales.

The story that emerges across this chapter and the next is as follows. Custody officers believed their supervisory role to be more expansive than it was, given how the courts have interpreted PACE. Officers described being routinely presented with arrests that fell short of the (judicially diluted) statutory standards designed to protect individuals' rights. This scenario caused custody officers considerable frustration. Whilst appreciating the daily pressures their colleagues faced to achieve performance targets, custody officers lamented their colleagues' limited knowledge of PACE. The management-led drive to, in the words of one custody officer, 'arrest, arrest, arrest', was cited as the greatest threat to individuals' rights. In the next chapter, these organizational pressures, especially the cultural allegiance amongst junior officers, are thrown into sharper relief, as we examine the custody officer's role in the 'booking-in' process as suspects arrive at the station. Recognizing that the authorized detentions that they earlier admitted were problematic, custody officers experienced a kind of cognitive dissonance. The next chapter explains how and why this dissonance arose by accounting for the cultural and organizational conditions described as animating social interactions between police, solicitors and lay visitors in custody.

Statutory Safeguards Protecting the Right to Liberty

Until as recently as the mid-twentieth century, arrest was merely a mechanism for bringing offenders to court at the end of an investigation, once the case for prosecution was ready to be brought before a magistrate (Sanders, Young and Burton, 2010: 137–8; Cape, 2017). But in today's practice, arrest has shifted to the early stages of the investigation, used as a tool to facilitate evidence gathering at the police station. Arrest, followed by detention in police custody, now marks the gateway into deeper parts of the criminal justice system. Its significance lies, most obviously, in the fact of a person's confinement in a small cell for up to thirty-six hours,[2] but also in the array of investigative powers that often

[2] Section 43(12) of PACE. Detention beyond twenty-four hours requires authorization by a magistrates' court that there are reasonable grounds for believing that the further detention of the person to whom the application relates

accompanies detention, and which interfere with the individual's right to private and family life and the right to property; for example, the power to search the suspect's home and seize relevant items of property (Part II of PACE), as well as the power to obtain and retain DNA profiles and fingerprints for up to three years for qualifying offences, regardless of whether the person is released without charge or acquitted (section 63F of PACE).

We should be suitably wary of such interferences with suspects' rights, especially because we know that arrest powers are often used for dubious purposes, such as securing evidence for offences unrelated to those for which the person is arrested (Sanders, Young and Burton, 2010: 132–40) and extracting deference from subordinated groups (Choongh, 1997; Hillyard and Gordon, 1999). Indeed, ill-founded prejudices and stereotypes that animate the 'working rules' that inform police use of discretion have long been recognized, and continue to be warned of (Ericson, 1981; Brewer and Magee, 1991; McConville, Sanders and Leng, 1991; Reiner, 2010; O'Brien-Olinger, 2016; Parmar, 2018). Yet there is, of course, a balance that must be struck in this area of policing, as in almost all others. Resting heavily on the other side of the scales is the importance of the power of arrest in ensuring the rights and freedoms of the general population in their everyday lives. The criminal law ought to be enforced in order to ensure a peaceful, prosperous and safe society. The use of arrest powers helps to detect and disrupt crime, maintain public order and protect individuals from intimidation, violence and theft.

The balance to be struck between the enforcement of the criminal law and the rights of the suspect who is confronted with the power of the state's criminal justice system is reflected in the qualified nature of Article 5 of the ECHR. This provision protects against arbitrary or unjustified arrest and detention, while still allowing police to lawfully detain those who they suspect of breaking the law by virtue of the list of exceptions set out in Article 5(1)(a)–(f). Most relevant for this chapter's discussion of police powers of arrest and detention is Article 5(1)(c) of the ECHR:

is justified. In the case of persons detained under section 41 of the Terrorist Act 2000, detention in custody can be for up to fourteen days based on an authorization from a district judge or resident magistrate (schedule 8 Part III of the Terrorism Act 2000).

1. Everyone has the right to liberty and security of person. No one shall be deprived of his liberty save in the following cases and in accordance with a procedure prescribed by law:

...

(c) The lawful arrest or detention of a person effected for the purpose of bringing him before the competent legal authority on reasonable suspicion of having committed an offence ...

Where deprivation of liberty is concerned, the ECtHR has emphasized that 'it is particularly important that the general principle of legal certainty be satisfied'.[3] As such, the ECtHR has held that it is 'essential' that the conditions for deprivation of liberty under domestic law be clearly defined and foreseeable in their application. The domestic courts' interpretation of what the protection from arbitrary arrest and detention requires of the police will be examined below as part of the exploration of custody officers' experience and understanding of being the guardian of rights in custody.

The proper starting point is the statutory safeguards in domestic law that govern the arrest and detention of suspects and which give effect to Article 5 of the ECHR. As a matter of practice, these safeguards ought to govern police decision-making in custody and, as a matter of law, provide the domestic legal standards that are assessed in accordance with Article 5(1)(c) of the ECHR, taking into account jurisprudence of the ECtHR where it is clear and consistent. The power of arrest in Northern Ireland, like England and Wales, was traditionally bifurcated by its distinction between 'arrestable' offences and residue 'non-arrestable' offences. After concerns were raised over the messiness and confusion this distinction caused, arrest powers were reformed by the Labour government in 2005. Parliament introduced a single code of arrest powers, thus extending the power of arrest to all offences, regardless of how trivial the offence might be.[4] As authorized by section 26 of PACE, a police constable now has the power to arrest anyone whom they have (i) reasonable suspicion has committed, is about to commit, or is in the acting of committing,

[3] *Khlaifia and Others v Italy* (App no 16483/12) ECHR 757 (15 December 2016), at [92].

[4] PACE (Amendment) (Northern Ireland) Order 2007, section 15.

an offence;[5] and (ii) reasonable grounds for believing it is necessary to arrest for at least one of a set list of reasons.[6]

The first safeguard in section 26 of PACE protecting the suspect's right to liberty comes in the form of the reasonableness standard attached to an officer's suspicion of the commission of an offence. The courts have made clear in their interpretation of earlier versions of this provision that reasonableness depends not only on the subjective, honestly held belief of the arresting officer, the officer must also demonstrate an objective, factual basis for their belief that the court too would consider reasonable.[7] As stated by Lord Hope in *O'Hara v CC of the RUC*, 'the protection of the subject lies in the nature of the [objective] test'.[8] Indeed, for the purposes of ensuring domestic law complies with Article 5(1)(c), the ECtHR has deemed this objective standard to be integral, as articulated in *Fox, Campbell and Hartley v UK*:

> The 'reasonableness' of the suspicion on which an arrest must be based forms an essential part of the safeguard against arbitrary arrest and detention which is laid down in article 5(1)(c) … [H]aving a 'reasonable suspicion' presupposes the existence of facts or information which would satisfy an objective observer that the person concerned may have committed the offence. What may be regarded as 'reasonable' will however depend upon all the circumstances.[9]

It follows from the requirement of 'reasonable suspicion' that a failure by police to make a genuine inquiry into the basic facts of a case in order to verify whether a complaint is well-founded will amount to a violation of Article 5(1)(c).[10] Likewise, the ECtHR has held that 'reasonable suspicion' requires that the facts an authority relies upon in arresting an individual can be 'reasonably considered' as constituting behaviour that amounts to criminal offence.[11]

[5] PACE (Northern Ireland) Order 1989, section 26(1).

[6] Ibid., section 26(4)–(5).

[7] *Castorina v Chief Constable of Surrey* [1998] WL 622865.

[8] *O'Hara v Chief Constable of the Royal Ulster Constabulary* [1997] AC 286.

[9] *Fox, Campbell & Hartley v UK* (App nos 12244/86, 12245/86 and 12383/86) ECHR 27 (30 August 1990), at [32].

[10] *Stepuleac v Moldova* (App no 8207/06) ECHR 897 (6 November 2007), at [73].

[11] *Kavala v Turkey* (App no 28749/18) ECHR 898 (10 December 2019), at [128].

This safeguard is bolstered by a second in section 26 of PACE: the officer must also have reasonable grounds for believing arrest is 'necessary' for at least one of reasons listed in section 26(5) of PACE.[12] Whereas this requirement formerly applied only to arrestable offences, by abolishing the arrestable/non-arrestable distinction, the Labour reforms extended the necessity criterion to all offences. This criterion was designed to maintain 'the crucial balance between the powers of the police and the rights of the individual' and 'places the emphasis on the need for arrest' (Home Office, 2004: 2, 5). The Court of Appeal of England and Wales has confirmed that the single code of arrest powers tightened officers' accountability and compliance with Article 5(1) because all arrests are now subject to the necessity criterion.[13] This criterion is a two-stage test: (i) the constable must actually believe the arrest is necessary (subjective); and (ii) based on the information known at the time, the decision was made on reasonable grounds (objective).[14] According to Lord Thomas CJ, the objective stage of the test[15] will attract 'careful scrutiny by the court' and 'therefore amply protects the liberty of the subject'.[16]

The third statutory provision protecting the suspect's right to liberty arises after arrest, when presented before the custody officer at the police station by the arresting officer. In an approach labelled 'authorize and regulate' (Dixon, 2008), the custody officer must adopt an impartial role and filter out arrests brought into custody by the arresting officer that fail the necessity to

[12] Including: to enable the name or address of the person to be ascertained; to prevent the person causing injury to themselves or others; to protect a child or other vulnerable person; to allow a prompt and effective investigation.

[13] *Shields v Chief Constable of Merseyside* [2010] EWCA Civ 1281.

[14] *Hayes v The Chief Constable of Merseyside Police* [2011] EWCA Civ 911, at [40]–[42].

[15] It remains unclear how the 'Wednesbury' review fits within this formulation. In *Fitzpatrick v Commissioner of Police of the Metropolis* [2012] EWHC 12 (Admin) and *B v Chief Constable of Northern Ireland* [2015] EWHC 3691 (Admin), the High Court stated Wednesbury is subsumed within the concept of 'reasonableness', but in the more recent case of *Parker v Chief Constable of Essex* [2017] EWHC 2140 (QB), the High Court re-identified Wednesbury as a distinct test that remains after consideration of the reasonableness of officers' suspicion and necessity.

[16] *B* (n 15), at [18].

detain standard. Unlike the power of arrest, the threshold for detention was unchanged by the statutory reforms of the Labour government in 2005. It remains the case that under section 38(1) of PACE, the custody officer must decide if there is sufficient evidence to charge the person. If there is, the charge decision must be made (i.e. the person must be charged or released); if not, the person must be released unless the custody sergeant has reasonable grounds for believing that detention is necessary to secure or preserve evidence or to obtain evidence by way of questioning.[17] Once again, the principle of necessity is at the core of this provision. As stated by the then Home Secretary Douglas Hurd during the legislative passage of what became PACE, the question is whether detention is 'necessary – not desirable, convenient or a good idea, but necessary' (quoted in Sanders, Young and Burton, 2010: 216).

Sanders, Young and Burton (2010: 143–4) argue that the arrest provisions in the 2005 reforms are merely enabling rules that prioritize police efficiency over suspects' interests and that 'eschews even rough context sensitivity in favour of naked crime control'. Given that police regularly arrest with a view to detaining suspects to secure evidence through questioning, Sanders, Young and Burton assert that the updated statutory safeguards likely play a purely presentational role, appearing to promote due process but failing to promote their substance. Moreover, they argue that a traditional reluctance on the part of the courts to interfere with the operational practices of officers makes it unlikely the court will interpret the statutory tests of reasonableness or necessity in such a manner as to strengthen suspects' rights. These two predictions are explored in the following sections, relying on accounts of police practice shared with me in research interviews by custody officers, alongside recent case law further fleshing out the scope of the statutory safeguards provided for in PACE. The story that emerges is one that largely supports Sanders, Young and Burton's scepticism of the statutory safeguards, interpreted by the courts and applied by police custody officers, to ensure detention really is the last resort, used only when other less intrusive options have been considered.

[17] PACE, section 38(2)–(3).

Processing Pressure: Receiving Arrests and Detaining Suspects

I asked custody officers and CDOs in interviews to guide me through what happens when arresting officers arrived in custody with arrestees and the types of exchanges that take place during this initial encounter. Officers described to me in detail the 'booking-in process' that the suspect's arrival triggered. This process was a highly formulaic, bureaucratic task performed by the custody officer. Their questioning of the arresting officer was tightly structured to provide answers to the pro forma custody log that was administered through a software package that flickered on the computer screens at the custody desk. The statutory safeguards had been subsumed within a digital format. Guided by each field that needed to be populated, custody officers described asking arresting officers for their grounds for arrest, including the offences the suspect had been arrested for, the relevant circumstances (e.g. time, location), and the necessity to arrest requirement that had been satisfied. Once the grounds for arrest had been recorded, the custody officer then completed their section of the form in which they documented their decision and supporting rationale as why it was – or, very rarely, was not – necessary to detain the suspect in custody.

The role of the custody officer has rightly been described as 'the linchpin of the whole system of safeguards' (Morgan et al., 1991 in Brown, 1997: 73). In addition to making the crucial decision as to whether to detain the person or not, the custody officer is responsible for looking after all aspects of the detained person's welfare, ensuring they are aware of their rights and that they receive the procedural protections afforded to them by PACE, including access to a solicitor and, where relevant, an appropriate adult, interpreter or doctor. This regulatory scheme places great trust in the custody officer to approach the task with independence and impartiality. It was apparent in interviews with custody officers that they were acutely aware of their role under PACE and the attitude they ought to adopt during the booking-in process. They described how they had to be 'impartial', 'neutral' and 'in the middle'. Ultimately, though, the custody officer's role as independent guardian of suspects' rights soon emerged as one that was heavily undermined by organizational pressures that manifested during the booking-in process. This processing pressure was felt most acutely, and is thus best analysed, in relation to the three statutory safeguards outlined above. Let us take each in turn.

Reasonable Suspicion of an Offence

It will be recalled that suspicion of whether an offence has been committed and the reasonable grounds for arrest must be formed by the arresting officer (*O'Hara*). The custody officer is there to receive the arrest at the police station and determine detention under the rules set out in section 37 of PACE. The issue of whether a custody officer must *also* satisfy themselves that the arrest is lawful before they can hold a person in lawful custody arose in *DPP v L and S*.[18] The High Court held that there was no express or implied requirement in either PACE or the Codes of Practice that places a duty on a custody officer to enquire into the legality of the arrest brought before them. This decision was confirmed by the Court of Appeal in *Al Fayed and Others v Commissioner of Police of the Metropolis*,[19] in which the applicant complained that the custody officer had simply 'booked in' the suspects without actively considering the grounds for arrest. The Court of Appeal held that while the custody officer's function is to introduce 'an independent filter' in determining whether detention is necessary, the custody officer 'is not required to inquire into the legality of the arrest and he is entitled to assume that it was lawful'.[20]

In contrast to this judicial interpretation of section 37 of PACE, almost all custody officers thought their role required them to not only review the necessity of detention, but also the legality of the arrest. In fact, several custody officers admitted refusing to authorize detention on the basis that they were not satisfied with the circumstances of the arrest. Given this (mis)understanding, it was understandable why custody officers complained at length about arresting officers' dubious grounds for arrest. Although plenty of their colleagues did 'book in well', many others, especially less experienced officers, struggled. Interviewees described, with frustration, situations in which officers arrived in police custody without

[18] *DPP v L and S* (Case no CO/3682/98) (unreported, 1998).

[19] *Al Fayed and Others v Commissioner of Police of the Metropolis* [2004] EWCA Civ 1579.

[20] Ibid., at [101].

a clear or convincing grasp of the grounds for which they had arrested a person, let alone the circumstances that could satisfy an objective observer that the arrest was reasonable. Custody officers detailed how arresting officers readily admitted that a complaint had not been made against the suspect either by the victim or a witness to the alleged offence, nor was a future complaint likely to arise. In other cases, arresting officers simply stated that they arrested a person for assault, without specifying which of the various categories of assault they suspected the person had committed. These rationales were in sharp contrast to what custody officers hoped to hear: a succinct set of circumstances clearly setting out the arresting officers' suspicion and grounds for arrest.

Several seasoned custody officers, who had policed for decades under the array of arrestable offences, explained that the new single arrest power introduced in SOCPA 2005 had, contrary to reformers' intentions, served to diminish officers' knowledge of the law and increase their over-eagerness to arrest. Under the previous arrest regime, officers explained how they were forced to think more carefully about the situations they were responding to in order to discern whether it was an offence that had an arrest power attached to it. As Custody Officer Mike explained:

> Before they brought in the latest version of PACE, offences like common assault, unless it happened in your view, you didn't have power of arrest for it, so you had to think: 'Now, that offence, do I actually have the power of arrest for it'. There was set offences that had powers of arrest and a lot of offences didn't.

Most custody officers, however, attributed the lack of demonstrable suspicion to arresting officers' assumption that custody staff would take a laissez-faire attitude to the booking-in process – a belief that enabled arresting officers' apparently poor knowledge of criminal offences and thus the types of behaviour that would amount to reasonable suspicion. Custody Officer Louise, for instance, expressed such concerns in the following way:

> I find that the younger officers coming in are arresting because they're frightened of making decisions. There's a number of options that are open to the officers ... [but] their knowledge of the legislation and law within the past ten years is very poor ... we're standing there and even though we're independent, we're telling the officer 'Do you know why you've arrested this person? Do you know the law? Do you know the legislation?' And whenever you're getting quite a substantial amount

coming through that don't even know what the offence is that begs the question of what is going wrong with this organization?

This lack of engagement with the elements of criminal offences was felt to be facilitated to some extent by the PSNI's volume crime team, which took over the case early on in its investigation so arresting officers could return to frontline response duties, similar to the 'police review teams' reported by Kemp (2014). In the eyes of some custody officers, this allowed arresting officers to abdicate responsibility and prevented them from better understanding the types of evidence required to process certain types of offences and offenders.

The requirement that the arresting officer specifically – not their supervisor or any other officer – must have formed the requisite suspicion to justify the person's arrest is a central issue that has arisen before the courts, as well as in my research interviews. The courts' willingness to grant significant operational leeway to police is apparent in the leading case of *O'Hara v RUC*.[21] Mr O'Hara is a prominent member of Sinn Féin; in fact, he was one of the political members on the Policing Board who we encountered in Chapter 3. In 1985, O'Hara was arrested by an RUC constable who had been briefed by a superior officer and instructed to arrest O'Hara for his suspected involvement in a murder. At trial, the constable stated his reasonable grounds for suspecting O'Hara's involvement were based on the briefing he had been given, the details of which were not subject to examination at trial, nor was the officer who gave the briefing called to give evidence. The trial judge held that although he had heard only 'scanty evidence' of the matters disclosed at the briefing, he was satisfied that a briefing officially given by a superior officer would provide reasonable grounds for suspicion for the purposes of section 26 of PACE.

On appeal to the House of Lords, the issue was whether the judge was entitled to hold that the constable had reasonable grounds for his suspicion based on such limited evidence given by the officer who briefed him. For 'obvious practical reasons', the House of Lords recognized that officers must rely upon each other in making decisions to arrest. Establishing a rather low threshold, the House of Lords held that powers of arrest do not require the

21 *O'Hara v Chief Constable of the Royal Ulster Constabulary* [1996] UKHL 6.

arresting officer to be in possession of all the information leading to a decision. A circular definition of the test was established. To satisfy reasonable grounds for suspicion Lord Hope stated the arresting officer 'must have equipped himself with sufficient information so that he has reasonable cause to suspect'.[22] Lord Steyn added that a mere request to arrest without further information would be incapable of amounting to reasonable suspicion, even if the request was made by a superior officer. Concerning the risk that the information briefed to the arresting offer may later prove to be inaccurate, Lord Hope made clear that this is not determinative of the reasonableness of the suspicion; more salient is the source of the information and the context in which it is given.[23]

This decision was challenged before the ECtHR in *O'Hara v UK* on the basis that the approach of the courts violated Article 5(1)(c) of the ECHR.[24] The ECtHR rejected the complaint 6–1. It held that it was compatible with Article 5(1)(c) for the trial judge to infer the existence of grounds of suspicion based on the sparse materials before him. O'Hara had been given the opportunity to cross-examine the arresting officer and make requests for discovery regarding the documentary evidence concerning the arrest. The approach adopted by the court in *O'Hara*, as approved by the ECtHR, offers considerable leeway to the arresting officer, with the court willing to accept only scant evidence from the arresting officer to evidence the briefing he had been given prior to arrest. In his strong dissent in *O'Hara v UK*, Judge Loucaides warned of the weakness of this approach. The trial court had not been searching enough in its assessment of the briefing given to the arresting officer. It had assumed too easily that the mere fact that a briefing took place meant that the substance of this briefing must have given further details to the arresting officer relating to the reasonableness of the suspicion.

The types of police behaviour that this lenient approach to objective scrutiny risks permitting have arisen in the recent case law. In *Alford v Chief Constable of Cambridgeshire*,[25] a senior police officer had failed to provide the arresting officer with a report

[22] Ibid., at [301H].
[23] Ibid., at [298C-e].
[24] *O'Hara v UK* (App no 37555/97) ECHR 598 (16 October 2001).
[25] *Alford v Chief Constable of Cambridgeshire* [2009] EWCA Civ 100.

salient to the case against the arrested person, which would have undermined the basis for the arrest. The Court of Appeal held that where the failure was not deliberate, the omission of relevant material could not render the briefing officer liable for wrongful arrest. Provided the arresting officer had genuine and reasonable grounds for suspicion, the arrest was not an unlawful decision that the briefing officer could be liable for.[26] Both cases, as noted by Stuart-Smith J in *Parker*, have 'very wide implications for the liberty of the subject', yet they must 'be taken as forming part of the balance struck and compromise that exists between the rights of the public and the rights of the individual'.[27] Whether this balance is struck appropriately in favour of the rights of the individual is questionable. In *Castorina*, the Court of Appeal held that the failure to follow an obvious course of action or line of enquiry may, in exceptional circumstances, be grounds for finding the exercise of discretion was 'Wednesbury unreasonable'.[28]

The reluctance of the courts to meaningfully scrutinize police briefing practices arose again in the more recent case of *Salmon v Chief Constable of PSNI*.[29] Salmon was struck across his head with a gun by Loyalist paramilitaries trying to intimidate him out of his home in a Protestant housing estate because he was Catholic. He reported the incident to the PSNI and made a formal complaint. Later that year, the same gun used to assault Salmon was discovered as part of a Loyalist arms dump. Salmon's hair was found on the gun and, for this reason, he was arrested and interviewed. The detective tasked with the pre-arrest research had failed to check the relevant police database that would have linked Salmon to the earlier assault. Salmon claimed his arrest was unlawful because the police had failed to diligently investigate information readily available on police databases before arresting him; had they done so, they would have discovered that his hair was on the gun because of the earlier assault on him. Relying on the principle that it is the source of the information that matters, the

26 Ibid., at [38].

27 *Parker* (n 15), at [24].

28 That is to say, it was so unreasonable that no reasonable person acting reasonably could have made it, *Associated Provincial Picture Houses Ltd v Wednesbury Corp* [1948] 1 KB 223.

29 *Salmon v Chief Constable of the Police Service of Northern Ireland* [2013] NIQB 10.

court held that 'reasonable suspicion' did not require the arresting officer to conduct the most basic review of the case themselves. Weatherup J affirmed 'the fact that there were other things that might have been done does not make that which was done an unreasonable exercise of power of arrest, provided the arrest was within the range of reasonable choices available'.[30] Ultimately, the careless briefing of an arresting officer that omits relevant information without malice is insufficient to render the arrest unlawful.[31] This sits uncomfortably, though, with the ECtHR's ruling that the failure to make a genuine inquiry into the basic facts of a case in order to verify whether a complaint is well-founded will amount to a violation of Article 5(1)(c).[32] As reiterated more recently in *Parker,* as a matter of domestic law, the fact that police have relevant information that would affect the reliability or balance of the arresting officer's ground for suspicion is incapable of affecting the lawfulness of the arrest.[33]

The relatively relaxed approach of the courts to briefings and prior investigations preceding arrest sits in notable contrast to custody officers' own concerns about how regularly their police colleagues made arrests based on inadequate briefings by other officers. In fact, custody officers were well aware of the standard set down in *O'Hara* (though none mentioned the case name itself) and described their first-hand experience of officers failing to fulfil even the 'sufficient information' standard:

> If the Inspector just came in and said, 'You go out and arrest that person' and you went out and said, 'Right you're under arrest', and then bring them into custody and I ask and say, 'Well, what did you arrest him for?' and you say, 'Well, the Inspector told me'. Take them away because that's not grounds for arrest. So, you have to be fully briefed and unfortunately the police are well stretched and they're doing things like that sometimes, where they're not fully briefed. You get a phone call from somebody saying, 'Can I email you the circumstances?' I would say okay, but then technically that's not right because the person coming in should

30 Ibid., at [19].

31 However, see *Chief Constable of West Yorkshire v Armstrong* [2008] EWCA Civ 1582 per Hallett LJ, at [14]: 'There may be circumstances, provided there is no urgency, which makes it incumbent upon an officer to make further enquiries before "suspicion could properly crystallise"'.

32 *Stepuleac* (n 10), at [73].

33 *Parker* (n 15), at [24].

be giving you the circumstances they have, not just, 'Oh, I was told they were going to email the circumstances and I've arrested this person'. (Custody Officer Ken)

Some response officers were even described as having called up a custody officer when they were outside a suspect's house to ask if they would accept the arrest if they brought the person into custody. At the most extreme, custody officers described how arresting officers had admitted to them that they did not think the arrest should have been made; they had been told to do so by their supervisor and were simply following orders. Such scenarios were compounded in some cases by arresting officers' over-reliance on pro-arrest policies to justify arrest decisions rather than determine the circumstances giving rise to reasonable suspicion that an offence was committed in that particular case. These stories recounted by custody officers reinforced their view that police lacked confidence in using their powers of arrest properly and relied on custody staff to remedy defects. Such practices sit uncomfortably with Code G of PACE which requires that the arresting officer record the reason why arrest was necessary, meaning that the arresting officer must be clear about the reasons why they believed arrest to be necessary from the outset (para 4.1).

The Necessity to Arrest

The second statutory safeguard is anchored in the requirement that the officer has reasonable grounds for believing arrest is 'necessary' for at least one of the grounds listed under section 26(5) of PACE. The interpretation of necessity, specifically the degree of consideration arresting officers must give to options other than arrest, has been at the centre of recent case law on the scope of the protections afforded to suspects. The first of these cases was *Re Alexander and Others* before the Northern Ireland Divisional Court.[34] The applicants claimed to have been wrongfully arrested because the arresting officer failed to consider whether it was necessary to arrest, or the arrest was made without sufficient grounds for necessity. In defining necessity, the Divisional Court heavily diluted the statutory safeguard, understanding necessity

[34] *Re Alexander and Others* [2009] NIQB 20.

to mean that arrest was merely 'the practical and sensible option'. Giving judgment for the court, Sir Brian Kerr LCJ continued:

> The decision whether a particular course is necessary involves, we believe, at least some thought about the different options. In many instances, this will require no more than a cursory consideration but it is difficult to envisage how it could be said that a constable has reasonable grounds for believing it necessary to arrest, if he does not make at least some evaluation as to whether voluntary attendance would achieve the objective that he wishes to secure.[35]

The interpretation of necessity arose again in *Hayes v CC of Merseyside*.[36] The applicant argued for a more rigorous interpretation of necessity, which would require the officer to actively consider all possible alternatives to arrest and take into account all relevant considerations and exclude all irrelevant ones. Giving judgment for the Court of Appeal of England and Wales, Hughes LJ endorsed the approach of the court in *Re Alexander*, but in clarifying Kerr LCJ's definition, weakened the criterion even further. Kerr LCJ clearly stated that the necessity criterion involves some thought of the alternatives to arrest, which would make it a pre-condition to the legality of arrest. Hughes LJ placed emphasis on the second sentence of Kerr LCJ's statement (above) to insist that consideration of other alternatives is *not* a pre-condition of the legality of the arrest but rather a feature that might be expected in demonstrating reasonable grounds for necessity: 'The officer ought to apply his mind to alternatives short of arrest, and if he does not do so he is open to challenge.'[37] Most recently in *B and others*,[38] Lord Thomas CJ referred to a slightly higher threshold, stating that necessity 'plainly requires more than merely desirable or more convenient to the arresting authority'.[39] How much more is unclear.

The court's interpretation of necessity has, I think, served to weaken the regulatory potential of this core standard which was elevated to greater importance as part of the 2005 statutory reforms that extended the power of arrest to all offences. The approach of the courts sits uncomfortably with the necessity

[35] Ibid., at [19].
[36] *Hayes* (n 14).
[37] Ibid., at [39].
[38] *B* (n 15) [2015] EWHC 3691 (Admin).
[39] Ibid., at [26].

standard as set out in Code G of PACE that requires consideration be given to whether 'necessary objectives can be met by other, less intrusive means' (para 1.3) and that 'the officer should consider that arrest is the practical, sensible and *proportionate* option in all the circumstances' (para 2C). But the court in *Hayes* had little difficulty playing down the Code's significance. Hughes LJ reiterated that failure to comply with the Code did not render the officer liable to criminal or civil proceedings, it simply provided officers with 'a sensible warning' that if they do not apply their minds to other options they are open to challenge. It was apparent that the Court of Appeal wanted to avoid imposing a 'full blown public law reasons challenge' on police for fear of the operational pressure it would place on officers:

> To require of a policeman that he pass through particular thought processes each time he considers an arrest, and in all circumstances no matter what urgency or danger may attend the decision, and to subject that decision to the test of whether he has considered every material matter and excluded every immaterial matter, is to impose an unrealistic and unattainable burden. Nor is it necessary. The liberty of the subject is amply safeguarded [by the requirement of honest and reasonable grounds for necessity].[40]

Anticipating some years ago that this approach might be adopted by the court, Cape (2008) argued that it would render worthless the due process protection the necessity criterion was designed to provide. Pearson, Rowe and Turner (2018: 204) rightly suggest a more demanding formulation: 'Is arrest the least restrictive way of achieving the lawful and proportionate aim of preventing harmful criminality or bringing an offender to justice, or are there alternative approaches which could achieve the same aim without restricting the liberty of the suspect?' The alternative in some cases will simply be a request for the person to voluntarily attend the police station for interview. Even if one does accept that the operational demands on policing make the standard of public law reasons simply unfeasible, there is, I would argue, a happy medium to be found in a slightly stricter version of the standard laid out in *Re Alexander*. This would require officers to give 'proper consideration' to options other than arrest as a pre-condition of necessity under section 24 of PACE, without imposing the

[40] *Hayes* (n 14) Hughes LJ, at [40].

burdensome duty to account for all relevant considerations and dismiss all irrelevant considerations, as required by a public law reasons requirement.[41]

What is significant, again, is how the courts in these cases seem to be detached from the routine practices of policing, which arguably call for a judicial interpretation that tightens the definition of necessity if this statutory safeguard is to achieve its purpose of protecting suspects' rights. Returning to the experiences of police practice recounted by custody officers in interviews, the consensus was that there were far too many arrests being made that were not necessary and that officers were failing to actively consider the necessity requirement or do so in a meaningful way. Custody Officer Alan went as far as to suggest that in seven-tenths of the cases he was seeing in custody the suspect could have been dealt with without arrest, while his colleague, Custody Officer Harold, thought this was true in about six-tenths of the cases he dealt with. In interviews, custody officers shared recent experiences of suspects who had been arrested in situations where it was difficult to see how arrest could possibly be deemed necessary, even under the broad list of factors listed in section 26 of PACE. Custody Officer Harold recounted a situation that for him epitomized constables' failure to grasp the necessity requirement:

> I've had people [constables], sending them [arrestees] to Omagh [custody suite]: Omagh's full. Then send them to Londonderry: full. And then they go, 'When will you be free?' and I go, 'Well, it'll not be until about 12 o'clock tomorrow' – and they don't make the arrest. And then they make the arrest at 12 o'clock and you're going 'Where's the necessity? If you needed to make the arrest it shouldn't have mattered if there was a custody suite available or not! Why did you not make the arrest last night?' 'Oh, you's were too busy last night, we'd have had to go to Musgrave Street [a custody suite some distance away]'. What! You've just said you made this arrest on Sunday afternoon because on Saturday night we were full and you would have had to go to Musgrave Street? And I'm going 'Where's your necessity?'

[41] This would replicate the heightened public law duty in section 38(1) of the Charter of Human Rights and Responsibilities Act 2006 to have 'proper consideration' to human rights. See generally, *Castles v Secretary to the Department of Justice* [2010] 28 VR 141, and in the context of policing specifically, *Bare v IBAC* [2015] 48 VR 129.

In another case, Custody Officer Eddie could not fathom the actions of officers who had caught a 14-year-old boy drinking in a forest with friends after he had tried to run away from police. The boy refused to tell officers his name and was, consequently, arrested. En route to custody, the boy did tell officers his name, yet the officers proceeded to custody to have him detained. Custody Officer Mike was equally baffled by actions whereby a lady in her late 70s, with a string of health problems, had been arrested and brought to custody on a minor assault charge. This arrest was justified on the basis that it was necessary to achieve a prompt and effective investigation and protect a vulnerable witness, but the arresting officers had not yet gotten CCTV evidence or even statements from the named witnesses. The lady ended up spending seven hours in custody, with the investigating officer having no evidence to put to her in interview; she was later released on bail, Custody Officer Mike recalled. Such accounts strongly support Pearson, Rowe and Turner's (2018) research with arresting officers which revealed significant confusion as to what arrest necessity means. Officers rarely engaged in meaningful contemplation of whether the arrest was more than merely desirable or convenient, indeed many did not appear to have considered the reasons for the arrest at all (Pearson, Rowe and Turner, 2018: 289–90).

In fact, it was striking how custody officers I interviewed held higher expectations of what necessity should require of arresting officers than the courts. Custody officers often interpreted necessity far more strictly than judges in the recent case law. Custody officers, for example, insisted that arrest ought to be 'absolutely necessary' (Custody Officer Barry), it 'should really be your last line of defence' (Custody Officer Owen) and the 'last option basically' (Custody Officer Dave). It was almost universally expected that arresting officers should have surveyed the range of options available to them, such as notebook interviews, on-the-spot fines or fixed penalty notices – or simply asking the person to attend the police station voluntarily for interview at an agreed place and time, a power provided for by section 31 of PACE. As such, custody officers seemed to desire much more than the 'cursory consideration' accepted by the court in *Re Alexander*. Arresting officers should have 'looked at every option not to detain this person, as there are a number of options that are open' (Custody Officer Louise) and be asking themselves, 'have we considered all our options?' (Custody Officer Barry).

What might explain the apparent over-use of arrest powers described in interviews? The main factor identified by custody officers was neither a strictly crime control mentality (McConville, Sanders and Leng, 1991) nor an eagerness to discipline certain social groups (Choongh, 1997; Hillyard and Gordon, 1999). Rather, the over-use of arrest was considered a direct response to the pressure placed on frontline colleagues to achieve police performance targets rigorously enforced by their supervisors. The rise of New Public Management in the public sector has tipped the calculus of administrative choice towards routinization, service rationing and incentive structures to maximize performance (Brodkin, 2008: 323–4). Custody officers described the prevalence of a 'figures driven mind-set' that led to 'target-orientated arrests'. Performance measurement crept into policing in the early 1990s through legislation that empowered government ministers to determine and enforce national police priorities (McLauglin et al., 2001; Loveday, 2006). The dovetailing of managerialism with the politics of law and order meant clearance rates became *the* indicator of police performance. A series of national targets were set, widened and narrowed from 2002 to 2010, before a single target to reduce crime was arrived at (Kemp, 2014). As argued by Dixon (2005), data analysis, computer mapping and management software served as new technologies that helped enable and promote the crime control logic of 'zero-tolerance policing' that emerged in the early 1990s and spread across western jurisdictions.

With over two decades of performance management now embedded in police command-and-control structures, organizational targets have been identified as a significant factor shaping police working rules (Sanders, Young and Burton, 2010; Kemp, 2014; Dehaghani, 2017). Rowe's (2007) observational research with response officers in an English constabulary offers a particularly good example of the impact of these developments. It reveals how live incident logs triggered by the call handler (and GPS trackers in police vehicles) have enabled supervisors to closely monitor how officers deal with incidents. The officers Rowe observed were motivated by an eagerness to avoid the trouble that was in store if they failed to follow the force's pro-arrest policy for domestic abuse incidents. Despite officers' ambivalence about the appropriateness and effectiveness of this policy, the force's IT system logged the type of incident they were responding to, meaning there was no way to hide from supervisors who could easily discern whether the policy was being implemented. In this context, 'policies may in some cases make arrest (or no arrest) so desirable, that for all practical purposes, the patrolman has no discretion: he is doing what the department wants done' (Wilson, 1968: 84 in Rowe, 2007: 285).

In Northern Ireland, an assessment of the PSNI's efficiency and effectiveness in 'delivering' policing is spearheaded by the Policing Board's exacting performance monitoring framework. This framework relies upon precise percentage point targets, with priority offences demanding special effort to improve detection and clear-up rates. Custody officers described how their colleagues were under the watchful eye of their target-minded supervisors. They recalled the daily morning meetings during which the performance of individual officers would be under the microscope. Likewise, stories were retold of emails flooding in from domestic abuse or volume crime units to ask whether arrests had been made in specific cases that had appeared in their in-trays. The situation was well-captured by Custody Officer Mike:

> Issues like road traffic stuff, the assault down the pub or the shoplifting issue, where the jumping in and arresting is for stats and if there was a serial [an incident logged in the police system requiring a response from officers] last night at twelve o'clock and someone was assaulted by someone who lives up the road or a known person that they've had an argument with or whatever it is and that person's named on a serial, if that officer didn't jump out and arrest last night when it was known, the duty inspector will get a rollicking [telling off] in the morning, the sergeant who didn't get his constable to do it will get a staver [a telling off] the next day and the constable will also get a staver. So it's forced upon them to run out, grab the person, get them arrested and throw them into custody and the bosses are all happy.

A significant problem this pressure gave rise to, when coupled with inadequate knowledge of the law, was that it prompted arresting officers to insist that because an offence was one that fell within the organization's pro-arrest policy or a Policing Plan priority, the necessity criterion must have been met (on the strong influence of force policies on arresting officers' decision-making, see also Pearson, Rowe and Turner, 2018: 293–6). This belief created tension as custody officers needed to ascertain the grounds for arrest in each specific case, which reference to a blanket arrest policy failed to satisfy. As such, some custody officers admitted to having to ignore pro-arrest policies in making their assessment of the evidence before them if they were to complete the digital booking-in form properly.

The use of performance targets has raised concerns about the over-criminalization of certain social groups as officers hunt for 'easy hits', in addition to the temptation it creates for officers to manipulate facts to fit within priority offences (Loveday, 2006; Kemp, 2014). The definition of what constitutes 'success' in terms of targets and priorities is, after all, not purely a matter of science but also a question of underlying policy choices that motivate what gets counted and what does not in devising targets and priorities (Dixon, 2005). In the context of custody, officers explained the pressure targets had in hardening their desire to get the suspect detained in custody and charged; a charge amounted to a clearance for the purpose of targets, regardless of the outcome at any eventual trial. The situation was summed up well by Custody Officer Nigel:

> If you're arrested and you're charged, it's a clearance. Now, irrespective of whether you're charged with a minor offence and it goes to court and you're not found guilty, it's already been dealt with as a charge so, it's still a clearance ... So, I know that the likes of the sergeants and the constables are under pressure to do things like arrest him, bring him in, get him charged, get him out, whatever and they are under pressure and I know they're under pressure to do something.

Custody officers complained of how performance targets unduly incentivized the use of custody to investigate crimes at the expense of more appropriate options like warnings, on-the-spot fines, or just a stern talking to. The performance culture was believed to be so engrained that several custody officers suggested the most effective way to reduce arrests was to amend the targets, so that officers were acknowledged or rewarded for their use of these alternative options. In a particularly frank interview, one sergeant noted the incongruity between the PSNI's performance target culture on the one hand, and their commitment to human rights on the other:

> TSG SERGEANT FREYA: In all this crap about human rights [PSNI's official narrative] they're [senior officers] pushing for figures and arrest figures and basically they want if somebody looks sideways at you to scoop [arrest] them. I ain't gonna do that! And then the next thing somebody's sayin' he hasn't got enough to arrest, well actually, there wasn't the justification to do it and they forget about that.

R.M.: And you think human rights is somehow part of that target driven mindset?

TSG SERGEANT FREYA: No, I think they [senior officers] forget about it when it suits them. When they want to prove to the public, so another smoke and mirrors standin' on TV 'Oh, we've arrest 130 people for the Flag protests' they want to be able to say that so they look good on TV but it's us who are actually on the coal face that have to provide those figures for them, you know. So they're all human rights, human rights but then when something happens they go 'Arrest! Go out and scoop them!'

In this extract, we can hear Sergeant Freya's frustration with the practices she saw and the police official narrative she heard. Whilst senior officers were proudly citing their arrest statistics on television, it was junior officers who were in police custody trying to negotiate the statutory safeguards to ensure the arrest and detention of suspects. Freya resented the pressure placed on her and her colleagues 'at the coal face' and questioned how this could be squared with the rights of suspects.

In light of custody officers' accounts, the relationship between organizational performance targets, the use of arrests powers and arresting officers' engagement with the statutory safeguards would be a fruitful line of enquiry for future research. In one of the few studies to do so, Pearson, Rowe and Turner's (2018) extensive ethnography with officers in the North of England revealed how the decision to make an arrest was influenced far less by the procedural safeguards in PACE than by a series of practical and policy pressures, alongside officers' own sense of their role and the situational dynamics of their interactions with colleagues and the public. Differential treatment was observed depending on whether the suspect fell into what the arresting officers deemed the category of 'criminal type' or 'decent person', which was influenced by the person's attitude towards the officer (Pearson, Rowe and Turner, 2018: 297–8). But so too was officers' behaviour shaped by practical issues discussed above. Similar to my own findings, circumstances where officers were more reluctant to make arrests included how long an officer had left on shift or the likelihood of having to wait around with the suspect at a busy custody suite (Pearson, Rowe and Turner, 2018: 301–3).

The Necessity to Detain

In the absence of sufficient evidence to charge the arrestee, the crucial decision the custody officer must make is whether there are reasonable grounds to believe that detention is necessary to secure or preserve evidence or to obtain evidence by way of questioning. If so, the custody officer may authorize detention. Given the legal formulation of the test for necessity to detain, most custody officers explained how easy it was to satisfy: there were few incidents where it would not be necessary to interview the suspect following their arrest. This test did, however, leave open the question – connected to the preceding analysis of necessity to arrest – of whether it was necessary to detain the arrestee in order to interview them. In the overwhelming majority of cases, custody officers deemed there to be reasonable grounds to believe detention was necessary. Yet, if custody officers were quizzing arresting officers as to why they needed to arrest suspects, especially if arresting officers had not considered voluntary attendance, then we might ask why custody officers deemed detention necessary in such circumstances. This is an issue we will consider in detail in the following chapter, but for now, let us examine the impact of performance management on this third statutory safeguard.

The pressure to achieve police targets was described as greatly affecting how higher-ranking officers treated custody officers. This culture of performance management was one custody officers struggled to reconcile with their role under PACE as the protector of the suspect's rights. Custody officers felt like a lonely breed of junior police officer. As Custody Officer Mike remarked, 'I always feel we're the block on the stat [performance statistic]. I'm between you and you getting your clearance on the other side of me and you have to pass a certain test, which is what I'm there for'. Tasked with this crucial filtering function, custody officers were an obvious target for ambitious middle-managers keen to achieve their monthly clearance rates. Strongly consistent with Kemp's (2014) findings in England, custody officers described how higher-ranking officers pressured them to accept charges in cases where there was insufficient evidence, or the investigation was still early on. If custody officers refused detention, they risked repercussions from Inspectors, or even Chief Inspectors, who would 'haul them up' to ask why. This sense of pressure over the decision to detain is expressed by Custody Officer Louise, who had been in the role for some time and was frustrated by the process:

The organization has got so figure-orientated that it is penalising the Custody Officers for making decisions which they themselves, when I say they themselves, I mean the higher authorities, believe that actions should be taken. More and more arrests are coming in that could have been dealt with by different means and as we question the officers, we feel that we are being pressurised by supervisors in order to 'We will take' rather than 'You won't take unless' ... We've also been called by some of our authorities as 'mini-judges' for doing our work to the best of our capability, so I feel that we're being undermined, our role and function is being seen as something which is interrupting the figures of the organization rather than what is right.

An issue that captured the pressure custody officers felt centred around the role of the 'gatekeeper', which was performed by Inspectors based centrally in Belfast (but latterly local District Inspectors). Their function was to advise arresting officers of the types of custody disposal they should seek. Custody officers felt that gatekeepers prioritized 'corporate level' concerns (i.e. police performance targets), were too far-removed from the particular case and usurped the custody officer's duty, prescribed by PACE, to determine whether there was sufficient evidence to charge the suspect and the appropriate disposal thereafter. Constables were under considerable pressure to follow the gatekeeper's 'recommendation', which meant custody officers ended up being the point of challenge when the gatekeeper's advice was under question. This situation, I was told, created 'a lot of friction' between Inspectors and custody officers, who could be at 'logger heads'. The gatekeepers were abolished as the research was being conducted, but for some custody officers their role had confirmed the 'very contemptuous attitude' senior officers were described as having towards custody. A recurring theme was that the higher ranks 'don't realise what we do down here', they were ignorant not only of custody officers' responsibilities under PACE and the procedures that had to be followed, but also of the deleterious impact that a 'charge culture' was having on the people being arrested.

Having now traced how the three statutory safeguards are formulated in law and performed in practice, it is instructive to incorporate into our analysis the actual criminal justice outcomes for cases where detention is authorized. There are two striking findings from the PSNI's official custody data over a five-year

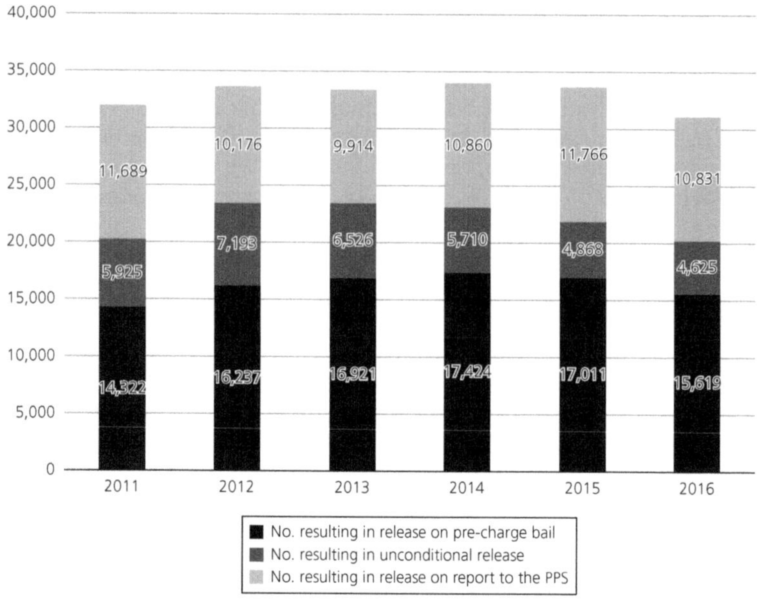

Figure 8.1 Most Common Outcomes Following Detention in Police Custody (at Offence Level)

period, reproduced in Figure 8.1.[42] The first is that the most common disposal, used in 41–53 per cent of cases, was release on pre-charge police bail,[43] applied in situations where there is insufficient evidence to charge but custody officers deem it necessary to continue the investigation (section 37 of PACE). This is an extensive power, especially given that, until this year, there was no limit on how long a person could be released on police bail.[44] At the most extreme, a PSNI Freedom of Information Act request

[42] I obtained this data by way of a Freedom of Information Act request (no F-2017-01265).

[43] This is referred to as 's.13.1.a' in the PSNI's Freedom of Information Act responses and is described in earlier requests to 'equate' to police bail (PSNI, 2014c).

[44] The Policing and Crime Act 2017 amends PACE to introduce: (i) authorization of conditions before bail (the custody officer must be satisfied it is 'necessary and proportionate in all the circumstances' and must be authorized by an inspector or above); (ii) a limit on the period of time that bail may be granted by police (initially twenty-eight days); and (iii) an extension procedure involving the magistrates' court. For a summary, see Cape (2017) and Martin (2020b).

revealed that a person had been on police bail for 804 days.[45] Although the number of people released on bail who were ultimately prosecuted is unknown in these figures, the available research in England and Wales by Hucklesby (2015) found that nearly half of those released on police bail were neither prosecuted nor dealt with by out-of-court disposals. My own research with a police constabulary in England and Wales found that over 72 per cent of offences released under investigation – which now accounts for the main pre-charge disposal type from police custody after the introduction of the Policing and Crime Act 2017 – resulted in No Further Action (Martin, 2020b). The second finding is that over the last five years, between 17 and 22 per cent of police detentions have resulted in unconditional release, the majority of which did not result in either a warning or an informal disposal. In sum, most detentions in police custody result in the person's release without charge.

How might we make sense of this data given what we now know about the courts' interpretation of the statutory safeguards and the experiences recounted by custody officers? The fact that the majority of detentions result in the person's release without charge surely seems unsurprising. If we return to the legal threshold for arrest, much will hinge on the officer's own subjective suspicion surrounding the alleged offence and the belief in the need to arrest the person. Although the reasonableness of this suspicion is a crucial means of review, it is one that will only ever be considered if the arrest is legally challenged. And even so, the domestic courts have consistently confirmed that the requisite level of suspicion is low, and they have proven reluctant to define 'necessity' (to arrest) in strong terms.[46] Similarly, the ECtHR has established that for the purposes of Article 5(1)(c), facts which raise a suspicion need not be of the same level as those necessary

[45] An exploratory study into pre-charge bail undertaken in nine police forces by the College of Policing (2016b) in anticipation of the reforms found that the average length of bail was forty-six days, with 9 per cent of cases bailed for over ninety days.

[46] See *Dumbell v Roberts* (1944) 1 All ER 326 per Scott LJ ('the requirement is very limited'), and *Castorina* (n 7) per Woolf LJ ('it is critical to note that [equivalent section to section 24(4) of PACE)] only requires suspicion of guilt, not belief or even prima facie proof of guilt').

to justify a conviction or even the bringing of a charge.[47] The law, therefore, permits arresting officers to act 'on the fog of suspicion', not certainty of proof; it is unsurprising, therefore, 'that inevitably hurriedly formulated belief is likely to turn out to be erroneous upon further investigation' (Waddington, 2015: 685). The statutory powers of arrest under section 26 of PACE thus serve as enabling powers, allowing wide interpretive latitude to officers to arrest those they suspect of wrongdoing (Ericson, 2007: 374). Even where an arrest seems dubious to the custody officer – a role specifically designed to protect suspects' rights – the courts have made clear it is not their responsibility under PACE to challenge it.

But as enabling as they are, the extent to which these standards really determine police behaviour remains questionable. Custody officers described arresting officers' lack of clarity surrounding the grounds for arrest and their limited consideration of the necessity to arrest. Some commentators are rightly sceptical that it is purely ignorance at work. In assessing the outcome of unconditional release, or 'no further action' as it is known in England and Wales, Young (2008: 151) argues that it is a likely response where officers lacked legal justification for use of power in the first place. By not pursuing the case any further, officers conveniently avoid the prospect of independent scrutiny by prosecutors or the courts. Sanders, Young and Burton (2010: 138–9) likewise refer to the 'unofficial purposes' of arrest, for example, where there is no intention to prosecute, but the arrest serves to secure evidence for unrelated offences. Such arguments alert us to the function police powers can serve beyond law enforcement – including the maintenance of social order, which can span from 'the drunk and disorderly' taken to custody to sober up overnight to more sinister practices of disciplining individuals who fail the 'attitude test' (Van Maneen, 1973; Brewer and Magee, 1991) and groups deemed suspicious because of stereotypes associated with their race, ethnicity, class or religion (Choongh, 1997; Warburton et al., 2005; Bradford and Loader, 2016).

Developing this further, does it really matter at all if officers do not know the criminal offence that they suspect has been committed and for which they are arresting an individual? Might it be enough that the officer is satisfied that the behaviour at issue is broadly that which could amount to *some* offence recognized in

[47] *Murray v UK* (App no 18731/91) ECHR 3 (8 February 1996), at [55]; *Kavala* (n 11), at [126].

law, even if they could not at the time of arrest or detention specify its title or the elements that comprise it?[48]

As a matter of law, what the protection from arbitrary arrest and detention under Article 5(1)(c) requires in this respect is not entirely clear. In *Kavala v Turkey*, the ECtHR established 'reasonable suspicion' requires that the facts relied on can be 'reasonably considered' as falling under one of the sections describing criminal behaviour in domestic law.[49] This maintains an objective standard of review, but given the sheer volume of criminal offences on the statute books (Chalmers and Leverick, 2013), it will likely not be hard to connect the behaviour to the *actus reus* of some offence or other. Where an administrative error results in a suspect being arrested and detained for the wrong offence, this is unlikely to amount to arbitrariness where the duration of the sentence is similar to that for the correct offence and the individual understood the nature and subject matter of what they were suspected of.[50] However, striking a significantly different tone, the ECtHR held in *S, V and A v Denmark* that lawful detention under the second limb of Article 5(1)(c) – to prevent a suspect from committing an offence or fleeing after having done so – requires authorities to 'show convincingly' that the suspect 'would in all likelihood' have been involved 'in the concrete and specific offence', had its commission not been prevented by the detention.[51] This calls on arresting officers to be much better versed in criminal law than was suggested in the stories from the frontline recalled by custody officers in research interviews.

This case law reflects a tension when it comes to what we ought to expect of an arresting officer between a pragmatic response and a more principled one. Informed by the policing literature revealing order maintenance as a core social function of policing, a desire to specify the *precise* offence can be perceived as secondary to officers' primary job of bringing an authoritative conclusion

[48] I am grateful to Jeremy Horder for a conversation that prompted me to reflect further on this.

[49] *Kavala* (n 11), at [128].

[50] *Douiyeb v Netherlands* (App no 31464/96) ECHR 67 (4 August 1999).

[51] *S, V and A v Denmark* [2018] (App nos 35553/12, 36678/12 and 36711/12) ECHR 353 (22 October 2018), at [91].

to '*something-that-ought-not-to-be-happening-and-about-which-someone-had-better-do-something-now*' (Bittner, 1990: 249). And this seems entirely reasonable. In the exigencies of the situation – the fight outside a pub, the dispute within the home, the car accident on the motorway – the central concern ought to be apprehending the suspect so as to minimize any harm caused and to protect those at risk; the minutiae of the offence itself can be presented post-arrest and detention. And yet account must still be taken of the risk of arbitrariness in the enforcement of the law, not least given the 'unofficial purposes' of arrest previously mentioned. Pushing this further, the rule of law, as a fundamental principle governing the relationship between the police and policed, requires the immense power of the state to be tempered by clear and precise rules that enable individuals to go about their daily lives, confident of when their behaviour will or will not attract the attention of the police. It follows, therefore, that to require officers to be able to cite, with a degree of specificity, the offence for which an individual is suspected of having committed in all but the most demanding or impractical of situations is an important means of guarding against discriminatory policing, reinforcing the value of rule of law and enabling those who have been arrested to mount a defence at the earliest stage possible.

Conclusion

Custody officers knew they were supposed to act as independent and impartial gatekeepers, but they felt their role was under threat from organizational pressures. This threat was described as arising from a culture of performance-driven behaviour that pushed officers to make arrests – an outcome made easier because officers had a poor grasp of the legal grounds for arrest in the first place. Custody officers described being presented with cases that had substantively weak, or at least poorly conveyed, grounds for arrest. But they were also confronted with cases which would be deemed lawful as per the court's interpretation of 'necessity' yet could still have been more appropriately dealt with outside of the police station. This frustrated custody officers. They felt people's liberty was being unfairly restricted by the practices of their target-driven colleagues, and in their eyes this was also just bad policing – it lacked 'craft' or 'investigative skills' as officers slipped into lazy practices or shortcuts. Some custody officers feared that cases sent to the Public Prosecution Service (PPS) were poorly evidenced, but that by this stage, senior officers had little interest as they had already got the case file passed on to the PPS and thus 'ticked the box'.

The routine practices of arresting officers recounted by custody officers – practices eroding the purported protections offered by PACE – have, however, taken place, if not been facilitated by, a permissive approach by the appellate courts in the last decade. The core standards of PACE require that arrests are only made where there is 'reasonable' suspicion of an offence, based on objective analysis, and where arrest is the 'necessary' response in the circumstances. In *O'Hara* and *Salmon*, the courts took a relaxed approach to the briefings and prior investigations officers must undertake before making arrests. So too have the courts proven reluctant to strengthen the 'necessity to arrest' criterion, interpreting it fairly loosely in *Hayes* and *Re Alexander*, which suggests a wariness of placing too great a demand on officers. To quote Hughes LJ in *Hayes*, there is a lurking fear of 'imposing an unrealistic and unattainable burden' on police. We can see a similar line of reasoning in the limits the courts have placed on positive duties, as demonstrated in the likes of *Osman* and *Re E*. Despite custody officers' own understanding of the important screening role they ought to play when suspects are brought to custody, the court in *Al Fayed* made clear that custody officers can lawfully authorize illegal arrests; it is not their duty to assess the actions of their colleagues. As a matter of statutory interpretation, it is hard to see how either a textual or purposive reading of PACE justifies the laxity the courts have granted police in defining the statutory safeguards that protect the right to liberty under Article 5 of the ECHR.

As a matter of practice, the chapter's empirical data has revealed how even these lower standards were reported as being routinely flouted by arresting officers burdened by management-directed performance targets. A pressing question this chapter raises is how did custody officers respond to the challenges they faced at the booking-in process? The answer is to be found in the following chapter.

9

Feeling the Pressure

Custody Officers' Decision to Detain

> Street-level bureaucrats often spend their work lives in a corrupted world of service. They believe themselves to be doing the best they can under adverse circumstances, and they develop techniques to salvage service and decision-making values within the limits imposed upon them by the structure of the work ... These work practices and orientations are maintained even while they contribute to perversion of the service ideal or put the worker in the position of manipulating citizens on behalf of the agencies from which citizens seek help. (Lipsky, 1980: xiii).

In his seminal account of 'street-level' bureaucrats in public services, Michael Lipsky (1980) describes the 'corrupted world' these workers come to face, whether in schools, hospitals, courts or police forces. This corruption arises, in large part, Lipsky suggests, because employees aspire to organizational, or working, lives that align with the very commitments, preferences and ideals that define them as individuals. And yet, the structures of their work – its administrative burdens, inadequate resourcing and pressures from colleagues or clients – make it near impossible for them to come close to achieving such commitments, preferences and ideals. For some, this dissonance is too strong; they move out and away. But for those who stay, Lipsky argues, their survival lies in adaption; they alter their workplace habits and attitudes, even if this means lowering their expectations of themselves, clients or public policy itself. This idea of managing occupational expectations, the adaption it can require and the cost it incurs by way of normative ideals (fairness, justice, efficacy), is one which helpfully

Policing Human Rights. Richard Martin, Oxford University Press. © Richard Martin 2021.
DOI: 10.1093/oso/9780198855125.003.0010

introduces this chapter's analysis of the tensions that animate the work of the PSNI's custody officers.

Similar to the street-level bureaucrats in Lipsky's (1980) study, the custody officers I met in the course of my fieldwork were faced with a dilemma emergent from competing occupational demands and police functions. On the one hand, they were conscious of their statutory duties under PACE to act as guardians of suspects' rights, and that the routine practices of their fellow officers could undermine the right to liberty. On the other, they were confronted with considerable organizational pressure to process arrests in custody and, in doing so, help their over-worked frontline colleagues who tirelessly bounced from one response call to another. The question emerging from the last chapter is the one I aim to answer here: how did custody officers respond to the pressure they faced to authorize the detention of suspects, especially where the arrest seemed to be on dubious grounds? Did they succumb to workplace demands and authorize detention, or did they feel able to push back and challenge arresting officers and their supervisors? By the end of this chapter, the reader will come to understand how and, more importantly, why, the former attitude prevailed and what this tells us about custody officers as human rights practitioners.

The Decision to Detain: Routine Authorization

Despite custody officers' concerns about the over-use of arrest powers and dubious grounds for the necessity to arrest, most admitted in interviews that they authorized detention in almost every case. Custody Officer Frank commented on how authorization 'very rarely wouldn't happen, to be honest, very rarely', and recalled refusing arrests on only two occasions in eleven years. Custody Officer Harold, who was newer to the job, mentioned turning down just four arrests that year; still several more than many of his colleagues, but a nominal figure, nonetheless. Refusal to detain was such an infrequent event that most could still remember the cases they had refused, even some years later. Indeed, refusals were so rare that when they did occur, they attracted some chatter in the police station, as this neighbourhood officer recalls:

> Generally speaking, by the time you get there [the custody suite] you've already decided yourself [if] it [the arrest] is required and at that point

the custody sergeant usually pretty much goes with it, it is always a bit of a surprise if you hear somebody getting refused and it becomes the talk of the station for a while: 'On what grounds?' and most people are shrugging their shoulders, but there's usually some reason. (Neighbourhood Constable Andrew)

This anecdotal evidence is well-supported by PSNI's official detention figures (see Figure 9.1), which I obtained through freedom of information requests. Between 2007 and 2016, just 3.2 per cent of arrests brought to custody suites in Northern Ireland were refused detention by custody officers.

These findings strongly support those from the first wave of PACE studies, which revealed that virtually all arrested suspects were detained in custody (Dixon et al., 1990; McConville, Sanders and Leng, 1991; Morgan et al., 1991). They raise a significant question about the rigour with which custody officers apply the statutory safeguard of necessity to detain and fulfil their filtering function in custody. Morgan et al. (1991), for example, referred to the authorization procedure as a 'presentational fig-leaf' that rarely attracted much scrutiny from custody officers. Similarly, Dixon et al.'s (1990: 130) observational research revealed how authorization of arrests had become an essentially routinized process: 'procedures are, generally, completed to the letter, but usually in a way which empties them of substance'. Only exceptionally

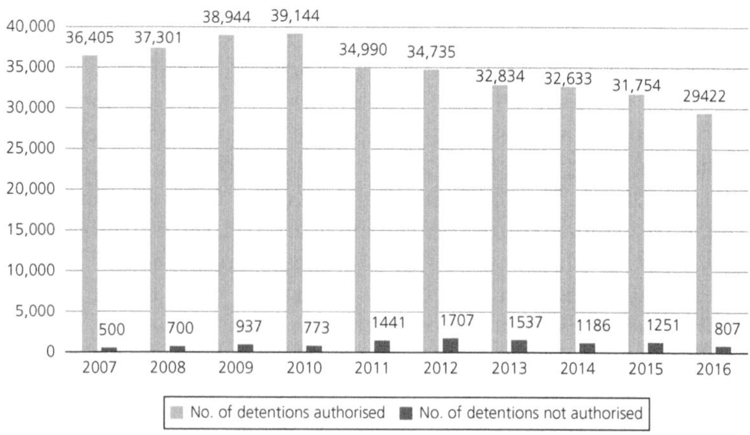

Figure 9.1 Rates of Authorization of Detention by PSNI Custody Officers

rarely would custody officers consider immediate charge or assess the weight of the evidence against the suspect on arrival in custody. Dixon et al. witnessed no instance in which a custody officer refused to accept a suspect into detention; in fact, a rubber stamp was used in one custody suite to record the statutory formula on each custody record.

A recurring finding confirmed in my own research, then, is that custody officers' criticism of, and sense of frustration with, arresting officers, described in the previous chapter, rarely affected their decision to detain. A form of cognitive dissonance was thus experienced by custody officers who knew that the target-driven, custody-reliant system was not fair to suspects and encouraged lazy, ineffective policing, yet they were crucial to propping it up. This finding is strongly supported by Kemp's (2014) study in 2010 across four police forces in England, which found that custody officers were rarely seen to challenge their colleagues when bringing suspects into custody, despite complaints of their misguided preference to arrest for minor incidents (see also Pearson, Rowe and Turner, 2018: 292). The findings of these studies and my own fieldwork raise two important questions worthy of closer inspection in this chapter's account of custody officers as human rights 'practitioners' tasked with interpreting and applying the PACE safeguards protecting the suspect's right to liberty. First, what were the techniques, and corresponding narratives, which enabled custody officers to book-in arrests they considered dubious and where the necessity to detain was questionable? Second, pushing this further, what factors explain why custody officers were so heavily swayed in the direction of pro-authorization of detention? Let us explore these questions in turn in the sections that follow.

Ploys and Narratives for Pro-Authorization of Suspects' Detention

There were several ploys custody officers described using, and CDOs confirmed seeing, when dubious arrests arrived in custody. The first was *evasion*; that is, they would simply avoid asking for much information from arresting officers about the circumstances of the arrest, especially if they sensed the more they asked, the weaker the grounds for arrest would appear. By preventing a 'can of worms' from being opened at the booking-in stage, the audio records could be kept clean. Rather than see arresting officers 'twist and turn', for example, Custody Officer Louise decided to stop asking her colleagues if they had considered options other than arrest. Similarly, Custody Officer Mike described how it was 'dangerous to start unrolling things' because he knew that on many occasions there was no good reason for the situation not to have been dealt with in another way. A narrative of futility accompanied this ploy: there was little that custody officers could do to change the target-driven culture their colleagues were responding to and which supervisors reinforced through the pressure they put on them. Furthermore, officers' lack of knowledge of the grounds of arrest, particularly the necessity standard, was deemed a training issue best tackled when officers joined the police.

This technique of non-enquiry is perfectly legal since the court has interpreted section 37 of PACE as not requiring custody officers to question the legality of the arrests brought to them in custody (see *Al Fayed*, discussed in the previous chapter). The curiosity, of course, is that custody officers *did* understand this to be a requirement of their role (see Chapter 8), yet in their everyday work, many described using this technique of non-enquiry. This approach was made easier due to the all-encompassing list of necessity grounds provided for in section 24(5)(a)–(f) of PACE. As Cape (2008: 200) argues, the list is 'so extensive that it is difficult to conceive of circumstances where an officer could not reasonably believe that at least one of them is satisfied'. Most striking is the necessity 'to allow the prompt and effective investigation of the offence or of the conduct of the person in question' as per section 24(5)(e) of PACE. Almost all custody officers stated this was the most common ground relied upon by arresting officers and was used in the overwhelming majority of cases. Aside from cases where the suspect has indicated a clear willingness to attend voluntarily (see, e.g. *Richardson*; *B and Others*), it is difficult to envisage how an arrest could ever fail to be in pursuit of a prompt and effective investigation if the aim is to interview the person or obtain evidential samples (Cape, 2008; cf. Pearson, Rowe and Turner, 2018: 291).

The second, more commonly reported ploy was to help arresting officers by *prompting* them. For example, some custody officers would hint at the missing elements of the offence or suggest possible grounds for why the arrest might be necessary.

As one custody inspector admitted, the custody officer was not supposed to put words into colleagues' mouths but, in his eyes, there was nothing wrong with 'feeding them' or 'pulling the necessity criterion out of them'. Custody Officer Nigel explained that whilst he was 'not allowed to coax' an answer out of the arresting officer, it was fine 'to ask for clarification'. Likewise, Custody Officer Harold admitted he would 'try and drag a wee bit out [of the arresting officer] and give a wee bit', and that 'although not strictly within the guidelines of PACE, I don't think it's wrong of me'. Unlike most, Harold worked in a custody suite yet to be equipped with video and audio recording, and because of this, he could be what he described as 'that wee bit more educational' by helping officers with their grounds for arrest. Indeed, he admitted to printing out the list of necessity criteria for arresting officers on several occasions, telling them to find a relevant factor from the list to strengthen their case. Several custody officers in suites with video and audio recording identified this technology as something that prevented them from going further in assisting officers.

Sometimes prompting could be as subtle as a facial expression or a gesture to hint to the officer that more information was required. In other cases, it was quite blatant, as described by Custody Officer Frank:

> We're supposed to be completely impartial but at the end of the day, if they've arrested someone for – I'll give an example: possession of an offensive weapon. Possession of an offensive weapon is only in a public place, so imagine they do that in a home. They've arrested them, but there is an offence for possession of an offensive weapon in a private place but it's called possession of an offensive weapon with intent to commit an indictable offence. So, in those sort of circumstances the person can say 'Listen, I've arrested them under this here'. You would then explain: 'Look, in this particular instance, is there anything that would make you think he or she was going to commit an indictable offence?' 'Well, of course, they were threatening me or – '. 'Okay, well that is alright then, there you go'. So wee things like that, just to keep people right.

This collaborative approach lifted some of the pressure from frontline officers when situations of uncertainty arose over how best to exercise their discretionary power of arrest (for a similar finding, see Pearson, Rowe and Turner, 2018: 290). The reassuring predictability that prior liaison with custody officers could bring, especially if they were willing to help fine-tune the grounds of arrest, is captured well by one response officer I interviewed:

> Sometimes you go to a call and you maybe don't have a suspect present there and you're sitting there going right, now what do we do? Do we go out and try and arrest them now or are we going to try and get them to come in voluntarily later? And quite often you would have discussions with custody sergeants and say 'Look, this is the situation I've got, these are the facts of the case, if I were to hypothetically bring this person in ... ' – because you don't want to bring someone to custody and have it refused. You can go and speak to them because they're quite happy to discuss their point of view on a particular case and say: 'I was thinking of going out and arresting this person'. And they might say: 'Yep, no problem, I'd have no issues with that'. Or they might say: 'Had you thought about another option?'... So there's always those kinds of discussions and even when you go in and you're giving your circumstances of arrest, quite often a [custody] sergeant might ask you further questions: 'I don't think you've given me enough, you need to explain more'. And you might then tell them a few more things and they might say: 'Right, perfect, you've covered everything I need.' (Response Officer Alexander)

In contrast with the first technique, custody officers justified this approach on the basis that they had greater knowledge of what the law required, so it was proper for them to educate and mentor junior colleagues. Some officers thought police custody to be a site of learning, where junior colleagues could improve knowledge and skills on how to 'book suspects in' properly. In fact, several custody officers thought more officers were 'now coming in pre-armed with their necessity criteria' because they knew certain custody officers would be firm in their requests for it. This is, of course, what officers should have been doing from the very outset; section 30(3) of PACE requires that for an arrest to be lawful, the officer must inform the person arrested of the ground for arrest at the time of the arrest, or as soon as is practicable after.

The third method was *diversion*. Custody officers navigated around potential tension at the booking-in stage by encouraging arresting officers to consult with colleagues or a supervisor when issues with the arrest arose. In such circumstances, several custody officers even allowed a supervising officer to contact them directly by phone or email. CDO Gavin, a former RUC officer, explained how he too would 'take officers to one side very quickly' to say, 'Mate, you need to just go back out there and take another deep breath, speak to someone, to your sergeant'. These interventions enabled arresting officers to obtain the advice they needed to pass the legal threshold for getting an arrest into custody. This approach was explained well by Custody Officer Mike in a situation where a constable was struggling to explain the 'driving whilst unfit' element of the drink-driving offence:

> I have stopped constables in the past where they're just not getting it, they're just not hitting it and I'm going, 'Right, I want you to go 'round the back, go into one of the briefing rooms, phone your sergeant and say that the custody sergeant says you ain't hittin' it and then come back to me with circumstances.' And I just sit there and twiddle my thumbs for ten minutes and then they come back and they go, 'Eh, by the way, sergeant, when I spoke to the guy his eyes were glazed, his speech was slurry, I got him out of the car to speak to him and he was unsteady on his feet'. Happy days. It's as stupid as that.

These apparently minor or 'stupid' routines, however, are not just crucial for keeping administrative processes running smoothly, they serve a social function as well. Such behaviour during the booking-in process allows officers to seek approval, learn or confirm standards for action and put problems into perspective with help from their fellow officers (McNulty, 1994: 289; Foster, 2003). But, again, this ploy sits uncomfortably with custody officers' concerns, discussed in Chapter 8, about their colleagues' over-use of arrest powers. Perhaps to reconcile this, a discourse of triviality was notably attached to this ploy of authorization by custody officers. Sometimes arresting officers had grasped the offence or necessity criterion but 'they just couldn't quite verbalise it', or it was so obvious the suspect should be in custody that it was just a matter of getting the phrasing right for the record.

Dynamics Affecting the Decision to Authorize

These ploys formed the primary means by which custody officers actively responded to the processing pressures outlined earlier. What motivated these kinds of responses is what I want to turn to now in considering more closely the factors that played on the minds of custody officers when determining whether to authorize detention under section 37 of PACE, based on their accounts described in our interviews. The reasons for nullity of the authorization procedure by custody officers attracted a 'substantial difference of view' after the first wave of PACE studies reported their respective findings (Brown, 1997: 58). Reviewing this debate in light of my own research findings, there are three key dynamics at work which, taken together, can help us better understand custody officers' decision-making: (i) cultural dynamics; (ii) organizational dynamics and (iii) dynamics of external accountability.

Cultural Dynamics of Legal Decision-Making

McConville, Sanders and Leng (1991: 43–7) are the principal advocates of the view that strong, and perhaps sinister, aspects of police culture best explain the ineffectiveness of the authorization process in custody. Alluding to the police 'mission' to safeguard social order and control crime, they argue that custody officers 'are unable to divorce themselves from the "needs" of policing', are 'emotionally committed' to believing fellow officers' versions of events, and 'share the instrumental goals of case clearance which underpins all police work' (McConville, Sanders and Leng, 1991: 42). Case-building demanded the suspect be detained; the custody officer became a functionary that assisted in the construction of cases (McConville, Sanders and Leng, 1991: 44). Their affinity to the police mission and institutional allegiances meant custody officers could not properly engage with, or apply, due process safeguards. Skinns (2011), in a more recent study, lends broad support to such sentiments, suggesting that a cultural commitment to crime control led officers to suppress suspects' rights to an appropriate adult or legal advice. In what is perhaps a more nuanced analysis, Dixon (1992) argues it can be easy to overstate these crime control attitudes at the expense of more practical or administrative features of decision-making. Based on my interviews with custody officers, there is good reason to share Dixon's apprehension of over-reliance on crime control ideology, but at the same time, cultural factors are key in accounting for custody officers' decision-making.

While McConville, Sanders and Leng (1991: 44) reported custody officers being 'baffled' by the researcher's questions about the decision to detain the suspect (because arrest meant detention), I found a rather different style of answer and sentiment expressed, even if the outcome remained the same (as Chapter 8, Figure 8.1 demonstrated, arrest still results in detention in the overwhelming majority of cases). For the custody officers I interviewed, arrests were driven less by a zeal for crime control and more by police targets, producing a culture of pro-arrest among constables who were keen to prove to their supervisors that they were 'performing'. This general sentiment is summed up well by Custody Officer Mike:

> It's a pressured job and sometimes we feel for the constables standing on the other side of the desk there – really you don't know if he's been pulled up this morning in relation to the sergeant saying 'I've had a wee word from the Inspector in relation to you, you've only had one arrest in the last six weeks, that's not good enough, you haven't had any clearances in the last two months, what's happening here? Under pressure, we're the lowest performing section'... So the point being there that the stats are so driven that if you were the lowest performing, you'd know about it, so I have to accept that the constable standing at the other side of the desk is under pressure and I'm looking at him going right, okay, why would I be difficult?

Far from endorsing this performance-driven culture, custody officers were frustrated by it and felt it had to change, but crucially, such concerns were outweighed by a deeper sense of solidarity with their junior colleagues. It was solidarity, not crime control, doing the cultural work when it came to police pro-authorization. Let us explore this some more.

Solidarity amongst officers, especially amongst junior officers, continues to be recognized as a defining feature of police culture (Loftus, 2009: 119–22; Westmarland and Rowe, 2018: 854–7). It is likely born out of the uniqueness of the danger, risk and uncertainty officers routinely experience in their work, as well as the power they wield and the associated pressures they face, both inside and outside the organization (van Maanen, 1973: 118; Brewer and Magee, 1991; Waddington, 1999). On numerous occasions officers in the TSG and neighbourhood policing alluded to what solidarity looked and felt like to them:

> I had to work with a guy there on Saturday, never worked with him in my life, but by end of the shift you'd have thought we were best mates, having a real laugh and getting on ... The camaraderie and the brothership of it ... There's nobody I've come across yet that I couldn't speak to or ask a question to, they're all there to help you. (Neighbourhood Constable Ben)

> Colleagues do help you out, colleagues with years of service really do carry your back, there is a great sense of comradery and sense that you're not on your own, we will help you through it. (Neighbourhood Constable Emma)

This kind of mutual support is said to be crucial in managing the in- and on-the-job 'trouble' mentioned in earlier chapters. In his observational research with a US police department, van Maanen (1973: 411) describes how new officers quickly grasped that it was their immediate peers, not senior officers, who would best support them in handling daily pressures, dilemmas and, of course, mistakes. This was certainly the case when it came to knowing the law: officers in the TSG and Neighbourhood Teams often joked that provided someone in the group knew the relevant legislation, there was no need to worry.

In interviews, participants explained to me that a good custody officer was one that 'looked after their constables on the ground'. Custody staff sympathized with the issues their colleagues in response policing faced, understood 'the angle they were coming from' and appreciated that mistakes would be made. Custody Officer Frank, for example, described how his own experience as a response officer shaped how he approached his role now:

> I can remember when I was young, and it was a very frightening thing [taking an arrest to custody] ... it would have been the talk of the station if someone had made an arrest and it was a very nerve racking thing to go in front of the custody sergeant and you could get some real tough custody sergeants and they would give you a real grilling and it was very stressful ... I always kept that in mind that I was the guy not 100% certain of my grounds for arrest ... and I would never really, I wouldn't want somebody to come in and be presenting a case and for me to make them feel very small because I notice whenever I was young and if I got criticised for working at something, I never really got criticised for not doing something but you get criticised for trying something.

The ability to relate to their colleagues' experiences encouraged custody officers to give them the benefit of the doubt when it came to questionable arrest. As Custody Officer Clive admitted, if he thought an arrest was '50/50' he tended to help out his colleagues by asking them for a bit more information that would justify the person's detention. This 'instructional attitude', as described by Cain (1973), was confirmed by several CDOs, who described how custody officers would extend a helping hand to their colleagues: 'they'll say before you bring them [the suspect] in, there's no problem just do it in slow time, chill out and relax … the relationships between them are very good'.

Closely related to this is the narrative of education that connected with the second ploy of authorization. Some custody officers had been 'tutor sergeants' (i.e. responsible for nurturing more junior officers) and, as a result, they described feeling a natural inclination to continue mentoring arresting officers in custody. Despite her frustration with officers' poor understanding of the law and necessity criteria, Custody Officer Louise conceded that 'it's a learning process. We go through, we help them as much as possible'. In situations where there had been a disagreement about the grounds of arrest or there were points for the officer to improve upon, some custody officers described how they would 'flag them up, but in the right manner'. Mirroring Morgan et al.'s (1991) research, 'the right manner' meant having quiet conversations after the booking-in process, away from the defence solicitors and the detained person to avoid the officer suffering any embarrassment or even reprimand. This practice reflected a feeling amongst some custody officers that they were there to protect the organization too. At times, this meant 'stepping in' to 'protect' young officers from 'failing' at the custody desk, either because they were unsure of their grounds of arrest or because suspects' solicitors were making arguments that the arresting officer was struggling with.

There were certain types of arrest, however, which tested the limits of this cultural affinity and custody officers' tolerance. One was the arrest of vulnerable groups seen by custody officers as undeserving of police attention. Several told the 'elderly lady' story, in which the thoughtless response officer had arrested an old lady (described with pathos: her husband had died recently, she was confused, she suffered from poor health) for shoplifting, when really, she had just forgotten to pay for her newspaper. The other group was the young teenagers in care homes who had breached their bail conditions by refusing to abide by care home rules, particularly curfews. Another type of arrest for which custody officers were less likely to authorize detention involved conduct deemed most trivial or harmless in nature. Custody Officer Jeremy, for example, described a man arrested and taken to custody for drunk and disorderly behaviour on a bus. The man was known to police and had sobered up by the time he was in custody. Jeremy refused detention and, like the elderly lady and young teenager cases, instructed the arresting officers to just issue a caution and take the person home. There was a misperception, said Custody Officer Barry, 'that all peelers are a big gang with guns, they all stick together', but he described how, to his colleagues' surprise, he would challenge them when he thought arrests were unfair or based on a suspicion of someone being a 'bad character' (see also Pearson, Rowe and Turner, 2018: 300).

Organizational Dynamics of Legal Decision-Making

The demands that come with running a busy, often chaotic, custody suite, inhabited by suspects with a myriad of needs and vulnerabilities, have been cited as an important factor making it impracticable to carry out enquiries during the 'booking-in process' (Bottomley et al., 1991; Dixon et al., 1990). From my interviews and observations, it was apparent that the custody officers' role was stressful, requiring constant alertness to the physical and mental wellbeing of the suspect, as well as keeping track of the actions of investigations officers, solicitors, forensic medical officers, appropriate adults, interpreters and so forth. When reflecting on their work in interviews however, custody officers and CDOs never connected the demands on their time and attention with the decision to detain; that is, none suggested they were simply too busy to engage in the kind of process PACE envisioned. Whether this factor would have emerged with greater time spent observing their work is an open question. During her short period of observational research, Skinns (2011: 129), for example, found that denial of rights or failure to fulfil the spirit of PACE was inadvertent and often a result of the sheer busyness and frantic nature of custody.

The most significant organizational factor linked to processing pressures was, in fact, the internal accountability of decision-making. Consistent with the analysis in Chapter 7, the avoidance of trouble was a central concern of custody officers. Echoing Dixon et al.'s (1990) findings, the custody officers I interviewed did not feel as if they had wide discretion or the freedom of control, describing being a custody officer as a 'very fallible' job with 'an awful lot of spotlight if anything goes wrong'. It was only a minority of custody officers who sensed accountability as arising from the law. In fact, Custody Officer Alan cited court decisions as the reason why he felt disempowered to challenge arresting officers. Without stating the case names, he understood the legal position as requiring custody officers 'not to interrogate arresting officers but take them at their word'. For the majority, though, the pressing source of trouble was their bosses who, as described in Chapter 8, were viewed as putting pressure on custody officers to accept detention and charges. In the eyes of custody officers, supervisors pushed frontline officers to achieve targets, all the while being ignorant of the rules and procedures that were supposed to act as procedural safeguards. Several custody officers described in frank terms how they had much more to fear from their bosses than judges, with one stating their fear of judicial review was just 30 per cent but fear from their own authorities would be closer to 90 per cent.

Taking a moment to reflect on this finding, custody officers were, legally speaking, right to be most concerned about internal trouble given the courts' weak standard of review. First, the exercise of discretion to authorize detention is subject to the administrative law test of 'Wednesbury unreasonableness', which sets a high threshold for illegality, asking: was the decision of the custody sergeant was unreasonable in the sense that no custody officer, acquainted with the ordinary use of language and applying his common sense to the competing considerations before him, could reasonably have reached that decision?[1] Second, even where an arrest is deemed unlawful because the arresting officer failed to comply with section 24 of PACE, this does not invalidate anything that the custody officer did thereafter in exercising their power of detention under section 37 of PACE.[2] Ultimately, receiving an unlawful arrest, continuing to process it and deciding to detain the person will not land custody officers in legal trouble.

As discussed in Chapter 8, and noted by commentators (Maguire, 1988; Sanders, 2008), record-keeping in policing can be understood as a memory aid and legitimating mechanism, as well as a mode of regulating behaviour. In rare instances of 'controversial decisions' (like refusing authorization), custody officers explained how they would make clear justifications on the custody record. Detailed record-keeping was considered a prudent exercise in managing blowback from senior officers, weeks or even months down the line. The custody record was especially

[1] *Wilding v Chief Constable of Lancashire* (CA, unreported, 1995).
[2] *DPP v L and S* (Case no CO/3682/98 (unreported 1998).

important because duty inspectors who disagreed with custody officers' decisions were known to document their dissatisfaction in their own records in an effort to ensure 'the buck stops with someone else'. As such, record-keeping is not only a way of producing an authoritative record of events (Dixon et al., 1990) or protecting against suspects' vexatious complaints (Maguire, 1988), it also serves to log competing decisions and associated rationales within the organization with a view to fending off internal challenges. As discussed below, rights discourse featured far less prominently in these rationales and justifications than in public order policing, where decisions were formally recorded with external human rights audiences firmly in mind.

There did, however, seem to be some exceptions to the norms of authorization at a larger custody suite equipped with forty cells and staffed by three to four custody officers. Here, custody staff had a reputation for taking the arrest grounds more seriously, being sterner with arresting officers and more likely to refuse detention. CDO Gavin, for example, described how there was 'no kind of pre-empting or giving them assistance with how their arrest should be worded' and that 'if your grounds for arrest aren't good enough for me to authorize detention, you're walking straight out the door'. An officer I met during my time in Clantown described how custody officers in the city station were 'like God down there', which was different compared to Clantown's custody suite, where this officer had only been refused detention twice in seven years. Some custody staff put it down to the 'big city culture' – a culture less friendly than in smaller or rural stations – or because custody officers were concerned that with such large capacity, if they authorized too many arrests the suite would quickly fill up and be harder to manage. In interviews with custody officers from the larger suite, it was apparent that they had a firmer expectation of police to demonstrate they had met the statutory requirements for arrest. One custody officer described how arresting officers had 'to fight their case', while another insisted custody was not a dumping ground for arrests and that officers would be challenged. This minority view was rooted in a sense of fairness to the suspect, as well as to a greater sense of being accountable to the courts, rather than senior officers. Interestingly, this custody suite is located just a stone's throw from the magistrates' and crown courts. It might also be the case that more confident, assertive custody officers had been selected to manage the busyness and pressure of this 'super suite'. More research at this site would be worthwhile, along with a breakdown of its authorization figures compared to other suites.

The Presence of Outsiders: Defence Solicitors and Lay Custody Visitors

By entering the closed, self-regulatory arenas of custody and 'chipping away at the traditional secretiveness and exclusivity of police stations' (Dixon et al., 1990: 116), third parties in custody have been described as one of the greatest checks on police power (Dixon, 2008; Sanders, 2008). Suspects enjoy rights of access and communication to family and friends, legal advisors, social workers, doctors, appropriate adults, interpreters and independent lay visitors. But the precise effect that these outside 'challengers' (Reiner, 2012: 613) have on police behaviour in custody remains a subject of debate. Some argue that the 'new archipelago' of multi-agency professionals and civilian staff in custody has the potential to have a 'profound impact' on police culture and reform in custody (Skinns, 2009b: 60), while others remain sceptical of how far such interventions really go in improving the treatment of detained persons, at least in their current form (Sanders, 2008). In this section, I focus on the impact that custody staff thought that two quite different types of external challengers had on police decision-making: defence solicitors and independent custody visitors.

The access to free legal advice has been identified as potentially the most significant safeguard for suspects under PACE. As was intended, the introduction of PACE brought about an increase in the number of detained persons requesting and receiving custodial legal advice. That said, research in two custody suites in England revealed that over one-third of detained persons still did not request legal advice (Skinns, 2009a). This figure is even higher in Northern Ireland, with 37 per cent of suspects not requesting advice in 2018–2019 (PSNI, 2019). The reasons why suspects remain reluctant to use their right to legal advice has been explored in detail elsewhere (Skinns, 2009a, 2009b). For the purposes of this chapter, most interesting is the fact that the defence solicitors were not generally considered by custody staff to pose much in the way of on-the-job accountability, nor did they inspire a commitment to the statutory safeguards. There were some 'wily old solicitors' and 'awkward ones', but overall defence lawyers were described by custody officers in favourable, friendly terms and, as in Dixon et al.'s (1990) findings, rarely caused an issue for custody staff by challenging their decisions.

The benign status of lawyers was connected in large part to a strong sense of familiarity, even collegiality, between custody staff and defence solicitors. CDO Gavin, for example, described how 'it's got to the stage now where I ring them and they know who it is on the phone, I don't even have to tell them my name'. Several custody officers similarly described how they knew almost all the solicitors in their station's town or city (see also Skinns, 2009a: 70). In a parochial jurisdiction like Northern Ireland, custody officers came to know the temperament and working ways of their local lawyers: 'you get to know their quirks. You get to know how they react, their buzzwords whenever they're going to start an argument, you can read them' (Custody Office Louise). Custody officers' ability to 'read' and 'learn' local solicitors worked to the mutual benefit of both by ensuring the process in custody went smoothly. In the rare instances of awkward solicitors, custody staff described how they would manage their behaviour by ensuring they 'went straight down the middle, by the book'. In most cases, however, custody staff described sharing gossip, gripes and football scores with solicitors over a cup of tea or a chat before the suspect appeared. This kind of rapport enabled some solicitors to whisper in the custody sergeant's ear to see if they could convince the investigating officer to drop a minor charge.

The primary concern of defence solicitors, according to custody staff, was not necessity for the arrest or the authorization of detention. This view, expressed in interviews, was broadly supported by PSNI data obtained through freedom of information requests, which revealed that just seven legal challenges to the necessity of detention were made in a four-year period from 2007 to 2011, over which time close to 100,000 detentions would have been authorized (PSNI, 2011). This figure can be partly explained by the absence of solicitors at the booking-in process – it is uncommon for solicitors to be in custody suites when clients arrive as most liaise with them over the phone and only attend when they are fit for interview (Skinns, 2009b; Sanders, Young and Burton, 2010). Custody staff recalled that the most heated exchanges with solicitors tended to arise over the suspect's disposal, especially pre-charge bail. As officers explained, detained persons were obviously keen to be released and this was an area where solicitors could make a strong case on behalf of their clients. Solicitors knew that if they failed to get lenient pre-charge bail conditions granted by the custody officer, it could be an uphill battle when it came to obtaining post-charge bail conditions at court.

There was, however, a strong sense amongst custody staff that there was a theatrical element to defence solicitors' work; they were performing in front of their clients and once the detained person had gone, the acting ended. Custody officers recounted how some solicitors would shout and scream, expressing their frustration and anger at police officers when their clients were present, and then later admit to the custody officer that they were right all along, or even ring up to apologize for the way they had behaved. This was described by custody officers as just part of the game, in which they were the referees. Solicitors wanted to portray a victory to their client by having charges dropped or bail conditions amended. Sometimes custody officers admitted they would play along, telling the suspect that they would have been staying in custody if their solicitor had not made such a strong case. This kind of behaviour underscored custody officers' sense that lawyers were not to be feared: their arguments were largely for show, not substance. As long as they put down solicitors' representations on the custody record (so they could refer to them later in court) solicitors were satisfied. The few lawyers who did hold a grudge or stir up a fuss in custody were well-remembered and considered naïve for misunderstanding how custody really worked.

A second group of outsiders of quite a different nature involved in overseeing the realization of the rights of the detained person are the independent lay visitors who make up the Independent Custody Visiting Scheme, administered by the Policing Board in accordance with section 73 of the Police (Northern Ireland) Act 2000. Lay visitors are volunteers drawn from across the community and are not associated with the police. The visitors make unannounced visits to custody suites and must be allowed access to inspect the facilities and, with consent, speak to detainees and check custody records. Noting their findings on a pro forma sheet, visitors report back to the Policing Board and PSNI on three key areas: the rights of the detainee; health and wellbeing in custody; and the conditions of detention. As illustrated in Figure 9.2

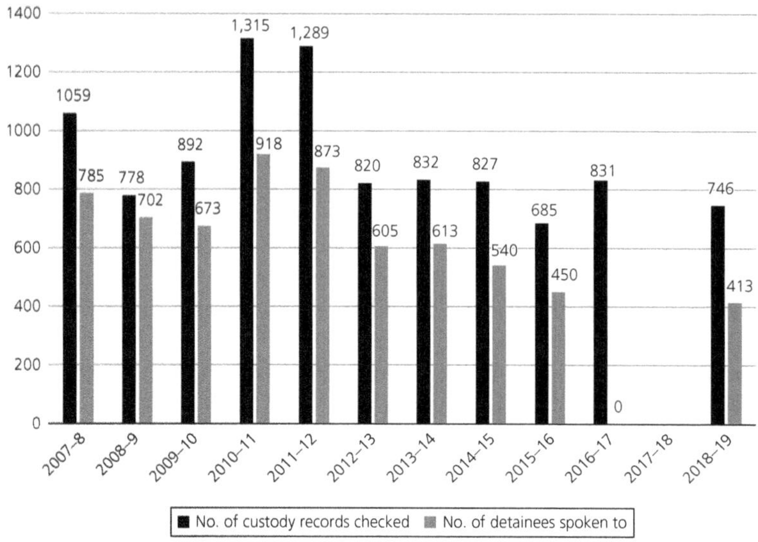

Figure 9.2 Annual Number of Custody Records Checked and Detainees Spoken to by Lay Visitors

(collated using the Policing Board's official figures (2017–2018 unavailable)), the extent of the lay visitors' coverage is impressive, especially for a voluntary scheme operating across the country. Between 800 to 1200 custody records are checked and 600 to 900 detained persons are spoken to each year.

The lay visitor scheme is described by the Policing Board as 'discharging a critical function in ensuring the protection of the human rights of detained suspects' (NIPB, 2015a: 199), with the Policing Board's human rights legal advisor relying heavily on their findings for the custody section of the annual human rights report. In interviews, custody officers and CDOs were broadly supportive of the scheme. Only a small number remained unconvinced of its benefits, with some suggesting visitors were 'liberal types' (Custody Officer Ken) and 'tree huggers' (Custody Officer Harold). According to this minority view, suspects were already well-treated, staff worked to strict guidelines and any issues could be dealt with via complaints to the Police Ombudsman. Most custody staff, however, thought the work of lay visitors was commendable and worthwhile. For instance, they could dispel myths about the mistreatment of suspects and injected independent oversight that could reassure the public and strengthen the PSNI's reputation. Some officers admitted if they ever ended up in custody as a suspect, they would like the idea of someone checking up to make sure they were being treated well.

This generally positive attitude towards lay visitors – who were, after all, outsiders with the power to demand access to the station as the 'home territory' of police (Holdaway, 1986: 148; Waddington, 1994) – reflected officers' sense that visitors were not a source of trouble. The inspections of custody visitors were described as benign events that attracted little interest for detained persons or custody staff. Lay visitors were not an audience police needed to be on show for, or appeal to, in carrying out their work. The core reason for this was likely one summed up by Kendall (2018: 108) in his valuable study of a lay custody visitor scheme in England and Wales: 'the practice adopted for the meeting [with detainees] was one which certainly suited the police: no notice, short, inconsequential, in the cell, the staff present, and no follow-up visit'. With custody visitors having to get their reports signed off by a member of custody staff, visitors were dependent on police, making them reluctant to include criticisms in the report that might result in confrontation with officers (Kendall, 2018: 111). Similar to their experience with solicitors, some custody officers I interviewed described having struck up a rapport with visitors, occasionally offering them a cup of tea. When asked what visitors did during their visits, almost all custody staff described the inspection as being primarily concerned with the material conditions of the custody suite itself, with very little mention made of their review of suspects' procedural rights. This perception accurately reflects the greater number of concerns raised by visitors about the conditions of custody than the treatment of suspects, as captured in Figure 9.3 (based on Policing Board figures (2017–2018 data unavailable)). Indeed, it is striking just how few concerns were raised about suspects' rights by visitors, with just eleven incidents of suspects not being read their rights between 2007 and 2019.[3]

[3] This contrasts, rather curiously, with the findings of two small-scale self-report surveys in 2009 and 2015, in which almost a quarter of detained persons reported not being read their rights (CJINI, 2016).

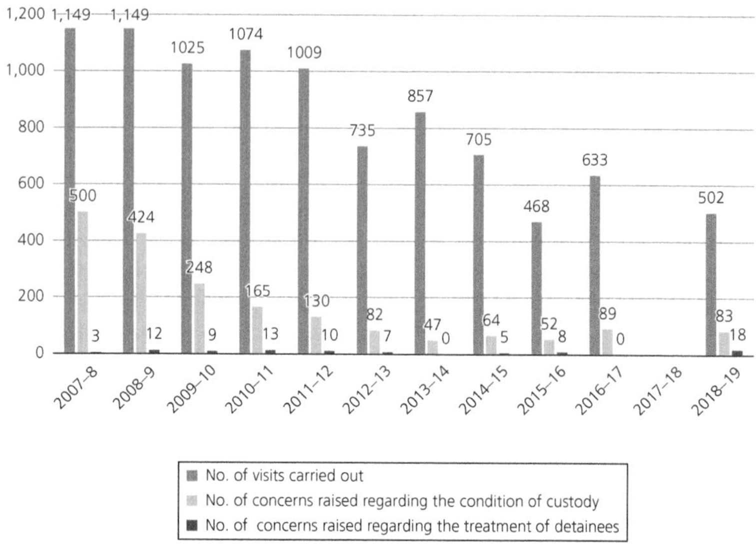

Figure 9.3 Concerns Reported by Lay Visitors by Type Relative to Total Annual Visits Made

By paying closer attention to lay visitors' assessments and the nature of the custody record, a significant regulatory gap emerges regarding the authorization of detention at the booking-in process which further explains officers' sense of having little to fear from lay visitors. In assessing the treatment of suspects, visitors must record whether procedural safeguards have been given, but all these relate to decisions and circumstances post-authorization (e.g. the right to legal advice, informed of their rights, appropriate adult called, reviews of detention). As Kendall (2018: 105) has revealed, visitors often lack a comprehensive knowledge of what rights detainees are entitled to in the first place and are susceptible to being misled by police about the extent of such entitlements. In fact, even if we assume lay visitors have the relevant legal expertise, it would be almost impossible for them to assess whether the statutory safeguards were adhered to in a specific case without observing the booking-in process live or interviewing the officers involved. Relying on the custody record alone to determine the legality of the arrest or detention is a blunt tool for two reasons. First, the record itself does not require custody officers to provide a sufficiently detailed account of their decision to authorize detention. Second, custody records can be manipulated or presented in such a way as to portray compliance (Ericson, 2007). Further still, many visitors lack the trust of detainees and the motivation required to probe further into any irregularities in a detention, with visitors' attitudes to detainees characterized by stereotypes, including that detainees must have done something wrong which is why they were in custody in the first place (Kendall, 2018: 107).

As mentioned above, visitors do speak with detained persons, but they are highly unlikely to have been present when police officers gave the grounds for arrest and detention – indeed, the detainee's absence at this initial stage was a practice I observed during fieldwork and heard recounted in interviews. And supposing the detained person was there, they may not have been in the state of mind (or sobriety) to fully appreciate, let alone critically assess, the situation. In an apparently typical month in custody, for example, one in three suspects were deemed to be drunk on arrival (CJINI, 2016: 17). For the 'frequent fliers' whose appearance in custody was a regular occurrence, the booking-in process and legal safeguards were described as a non-event. As Custody Officer Harold quipped, '[m]ost arrested people expect to be arrested, you know what I mean? You're not expecting the officer to explain the necessity criteria'. Indeed, in surveys carried out by the CJINI (2016), only one in two suspects recalled being told about the rights they were entitled to under PACE during their time in custody. But even if we assume suspects were alert to any misgivings over the legality of their arrest or detention, the prospects of conveying this in a meaningful way to a lay visitor were limited due to the sheer brevity of time visitors spend with suspects and the suspicion that many detainees have reported as having towards independent visitors (Kendall, 2018: 100–4). On average, custody visits last just twenty-three to twenty-eight minutes in total (based on the Policing Board's figures from 2008, 2013–2016, 2017–2019), offering very little time to carry out physical inspections and reviews of custody records, let alone establish rapport with detained persons.

Conclusion

Dixon (2008) argues that the 'authorize and regulate' strategy PACE embodied was typical of a period in the late twentieth century when liberal democracies prioritized individual rights, granting them constitutional protection. This time, he argues, has passed. Rights safeguards have since been weakened by changes in the socio-political climate. Neoliberal priorities captured in the rhetoric of 'security', 'competition' and 'responsibility' have pitted human rights against broader interests of the economy and of a capitalist community (see, e.g., Wacquant, 2009). To witness these sentiments, we need look no further than the political discourse that swirls around the HRA, routinely dismissed as a 'villain's charter' and an impediment to fighting crime, as well as European meddling in properly British affairs (Loader, 2007). Yet, the existence of HRA as a piece of legislation which officers are trained in and can be found in violation of leads Dixon (2008: 43) to suggest it might function as a rare and significant counterpoint to populist rights discourses that 'inevitably affect police implementation of PACE'. Similarly, de Lint (2017) writes of the 'modulating' or 'filtering' potential of human rights to temper an 'authoritarian neo-liberalism' that compels police to enforce laws indifferent to, if not actively hostile towards, socially disadvantaged groups.

An important finding from interviews was that custody officers' pro-authorization of detention occurred notwithstanding their consciousness of human rights. Custody officers were patently aware that protecting suspects' rights was their core function for as long as PACE had been around. Indeed, almost all referred to themselves as the 'guardian of rights', there 'to look after detained persons'. Their biggest concern was 'Article 2 issues' (right to life), a proxy they used to convey that a detained person was extremely vulnerable, even a suicide risk (cf. Chapter 5). Many custody officers, however, were equally able to cite the right to liberty and its relevance for authorizing detention, with some specifically linking it to the necessity criterion and the need to consider options other than arrest. Custody Officer Clive, for example, described detention as taking away a bit of a person's life – time that could otherwise be spent at home or with loved ones. The necessity criterion helped him to justify curtailing this freedom, but human rights were also, he insisted, about 'treating people with respect and not being judgmental. That's for the courts to do'.

Interestingly, human rights consciousness was rarely linked back to the HRA, which perhaps questions Dixon's (2008) optimism of its potential to reinforce the legal safeguards in custody. Most officers continued to see their obligations as arising from PACE, not the HRA, though the two were often linked. As Custody Officer Harold explained:

> PACE and human rights legislation are that interwoven now, you can't really separate them … if you do everything with the spirit of PACE, you'll not go far wrong with human rights, because PACE is written from a human rights perspective.

This was reinforced by custody officers' (objectively questionable) narrative that they had always completed their work with human rights in mind, even before the HRA: 'I've been in the police twenty years, looking back at it retrospectively, it's nothing we didn't already do. PACE is a really, really slick bit of regulation for managing prisoners' (Custody Officer Barry). Most curiously, several officers who had expressed concern about the infringement of suspects' rights due to dubious arrests and the target-focused culture proceeded to criticize the HRA. Custody Officer Nigel, for example, complained it 'was weighted far too heavily on the offender'. Likewise, despite her frustration with arresting officers' poor grasp of the law, Custody Officer Louise still complained that too much time was spent learning about the HRA and not enough time learning police craft and discretionary judgment; again, this suggests the disconnect between the PACE safeguards and the right to liberty enshrined in Article 5(1)(c) of the ECHR.

The peripheral status of the HRA might be further linked to the bureaucratic format of regulation in custody, especially when compared to public order policing. Organizational actors are governed not just by regulations, but also communication formats that require decisions to be accounted for in specific ways (Ericson, 2007: 380). The principles of necessity and proportionality may find form in PACE and its Codes of Practice, but the HRA itself is barely present in either the computer programmes that structure the booking-in process or the custody records it produces. Digital custody records seem to be populated in a mechanistic way, as Custody Officer Ken explained: 'You start at the top left and you read through it and ask all the questions and fill in the thing … you're just walking through all the pages and it basically prompts you what to do'. The necessity grounds were selected from a drop-down list and then moved to the next box; detainees' rights were rhymed off hundreds of times a month, following the on-screen prompts of their computer system. For regular suspects, some custody officers described populating the custody record before the suspect had even arrived at the custody suite. Such formats can embed regulations in a way that forces actors to make and report decisions so as to appear procedurally correct, while distracting from their human impact (Ericson, 2007). A further example of this in the context of police custody is Parmar's (2019: 946–8) illuminating study of the relationship between policing migration, technology and racism in police custody in England. This illustrated how data generated by computer software was presented to suspects as irreproachable; emboldened officers in challenging people's offending histories and immigration status; and served as a resource for officers to deflect human decision-making.

Research conducted before the HRA found that suspects already had strong awareness of their rights under PACE (Brown, 1997). A degree of rights consciousness existing amongst detainees was described by custody staff. What was most interesting in my interviews, though, was how the language of human rights was now being regularly deployed by detainees, animating the types of interactions that took place in custody. Similar to neighbourhood officers' response to rights 'forgery' (Hornberger, 2011) discussed in Chapter 5, custody officers were dismissive of this, perceiving it as a cynical, misguided appropriation of a concept suspects did not really understand, as the following quotes illustrate.

> All I get is 'I know my human rights'. 'Well, what exactly are your human rights?' I did actually say that to a boy recently, 'What do you mean? Quote me, what article are we talking about of the European Convention on Human Rights?' 'Doesn't matter, I know them, you have to do this.' 'Well, I actually I don't!' (Custody Officer Nigel)
>
> Oh aye, we're always getting human rights stuff, especially when they come in. I go to do a strip search, 'I have human rights!' You talk them out of it. You talk them out of it, you say 'You have your human rights, I have my rights as well, my right is to look after you and make sure you have nothing on you that could harm you or harm me.' (CDO Harry)

Empowered by their status and control of the rule book, custody staff belittled, even ridiculed, the vague and uninformed use of rights talk by suspects to convey their frustrations, anger or sense of unfairness (cf. Dixon, 1997: 293). The discourse of rights in custody would thus appear to serve as a less powerful bargaining tool for detainees than it did for the community representatives and protest organizers discussed in Chapter 6. Nonetheless, it was apparent that some detained persons (e.g. the middle-class drink-drivers) were talked about by custody officers in a manner that seemed to suggest their rights-claims would be taken more seriously than others (e.g. the drug dependent 'crazies').

Tying the threads of this chapter together, custody officers navigated their way through the pressures of their role using various modes of adaption – the ploys that enabled them to ease the pressures emergent from their awkward job. The rights of individuals were embossed in PACE, a statutory scheme of safeguards that the courts have been reluctant to interpret strongly and which arresting officers seem to have limited regard for. The eagerness of response officers to arrest and detain suspects was something custody officers could understand, even if they felt it was driven too often by performance targets and organizational demands rather than basic principles of fairness or the precept of necessity. Softened by a cultural affinity to their fellow junior officers and freed by a perceived absence of meaningful accountability from defence solicitors and lay visitors, custody officers succumbed to the pressure to detain. In law and in practice, the safeguards designed to protect the suspect's right to liberty at this entryway to the criminal justice system come to appear more fictional than real. To their dismay, many custody officers sensed this in their daily work. But as Lipsky's (1980) account of street-level bureaucrats revealed some decades ago, too often occupational survival lies in adaption.

Conclusion

Introduction

Human rights are a common feature of police reform, rhetoric and regulation in many jurisdictions. Yet how human rights law might serve to regulate policing, function as a discourse for describing what police 'do' or perform as a critical concept for engaging with what the police role is, or ought to be, has received limited attention. This book has endeavoured to produce one of the first sustained, interdisciplinary accounts of the empirical realities of human rights law in policing. The substantive insights are drawn from unprecedented access to the Police Service of Northern Ireland. As a police service 'made and imagined' to respect and protect human rights, and often cited as a world-leader in adopting a rights-based approach to policing, the PSNI is a most insightful case study to explore and examine the vernaculars and practices of human rights in contemporary policing. In the aftermath of the conflict, the PSNI underwent one of the most ambitious police reform programmes to have ever take place, including an accountability framework that is 'perhaps the most progressive and extensive model of oversight yet established' (Mulcahy, 2006: 193). The ICP's 'central proposition' is that human rights ought to inspire everything the police does and should be the very 'philosophy' of policing.

Two decades on from the landmark human rights reform of policing in Northern Ireland, this book has explored the presence of human rights law and critically engaged with how it is experienced, understood and applied by police. By way of its concepts, methods and style of analysis, the book has aspired to embrace criminology's interdisciplinary spirit to produce a sociological account that illuminates the empirical realities of human rights law. Part I began by introducing human rights as a sustained and prominent feature of police reform and regulation, and with the

Policing Human Rights. Richard Martin, Oxford University Press. © Richard Martin 2021.
DOI: 10.1093/oso/9780198855125.003.0011

case study of the PSNI, before fleshing out the book's sociological approach to human rights law. Applying this approach, Part II explored the official 'vernaculars' of human rights, Part III examined the 'sensemaking' efforts of officers conducting routine policing, and Parts IV–V analysed officers as 'practitioners' of human rights. Drawing the book to a close, I want to reflect upon the substantive findings from across the four sites of policing. In particular, I want to summarize the specific types of encounters officers had with human rights law and then to consider what lessons might be gleaned from the Northern Ireland case study. But before doing so, let us briefly recapitulate the type of sociological project the book has sought to advance across its chapters – and, in doing so, ask what this might offer in response to the 'clear legal fault line' that is said to crisscross academic criminology's engagement with human rights (Murphy and Whitty, 2013: 569–70).

Embracing a Sociological Approach to Human Rights Law

In thinking about how criminology might enrich a sociological approach to human law, an insightful parallel can be drawn, I think, with criminology's involvement with crime as a legal construct, specifically what this means for its proximity to government (Garland, 2011), or at least governance (Zedner, 2011). This proximity stems, in large part, from the subject matter of criminology often arising from legally defined entities and state-directed and managed practices: crime and its control (Garland, 2011). The state's legal categories and institutional power are very real in their consequences:

> They shape our world, they organize our lives, they determine the fates of millions of people. To reject these categories, to give them no place in our analyses, would be to opt out of an engagement with the real world – an engagement that has always been one of criminology's chief virtues. (Garland, 2011: 307)

One question this prompts, then, is whether academic criminology ought to derive its concepts, categories, questions and objects of study from state institutions – and, in doing so, must 'it accept the theories of action and responsibility in legal discourse and court decisions?' (Garland, 2011: 306). The solution Garland proposes lies in criminology's interdisciplinarity and the critical resources it can use to conceptualize the practices and consequences of such discourses and decisions. Doing so includes exposing and critically examining law's categories as social constructs, the outcomes of political processes, intellectual movements and historical moments across time and place. It is this same issue (how to engage with established, legitimated, state-defined concepts as an object of study) and interdisciplinary solution (a sociological approach to law) that Garland offers which ought to empower and embolden criminology's interaction not only with criminal law and its enforcement, but human rights law and its implementation. This entails acknowledging and engaging with the empirical reality of human rights law, including its doctrinal technicalities, while bringing to bear concepts and methods to expose how 'human rights are constituted through processes of negotiation, contestation, implementation, avoidance and neglect' (Murphy and Whitty, 2013: 580). The book has, in some small way, tried to embark upon this project using three conceptual foundations to ground a sociological approach to human rights law within criminology.

The first is engagement with human rights law as a *vernacular* adopted, made sense of and adapted by powerful actors within and surrounding policing. After some hesitation and disciplinary self-reflection, it is, by and large, legal anthropology which has turned its critical gaze to the 'vernacular' of human rights: that is, how the vocabulary of international human rights law is learnt, translated and adopted by local actors and within institutions. The book has exposed the capacity of human rights to be adopted by chief officers and political parties and imbued with a myriad of ideas, visions, priorities and principles that are directed to consolidate or challenge the legitimacy of police actions and conflict-related legacies. The second is the engagement with human rights law as a subject of 'sensemaking' by officers in their sites of formal and informal socialization. It has been argued that officers internalize human rights, with sensemaking providing the process by which this takes place, producing identity-rich, context-dependent narratives that foster self-enhancement, self-efficacy and self-consistency. Officers' interpretation and application of human rights are, it has been argued, influenced by their own values and experiences, workplace demands and associated sub-cultures. The third conceptual foundation is police officers as a class of *practitioner* of human rights, in the sense that they must bring a resolution to specific factual issues through understanding, engaging with and applying human rights law principles and standards. The book has revealed the legal, social and organizational factors that animate this practice, emphasizing the importance of officers' conceptions of their role and workplace oversight, but also internal processes and bureaucratic schemes used to safeguard human rights.

Human rights take on an especially pronounced form across Northern Ireland's civic society and local politics generally (Curtis, 2014) and the regulation and legitimation of the police specifically (Harvey, 2015). But looking beyond this specific locality, there remains an array of criminal justice and human rights law issues in other jurisdictions that would be greatly enriched through a more sociological approach to law. The emergence of international human rights law, the growth of associated organizations and institutions and the fleshing out of legal standards by supra-national and domestic courts has produced significant interactions and complex entanglements between human rights and the criminal process (Campbell, Ashworth and Redmayne, 2019). Just some of many possible examples include: the state's response to terrorism and 'emotive claims of insecurity' (Lazarus and Goold, 2019: 20); the treatment, detention and expulsion of non-nationals by states amidst the forces of nationalism and globalization (Bosworth, 2011); the relevance and application of ECHR in transitional justice contexts (Ní Aoláin, 2017); the use and reviewability of sentences of life imprisonment (van Zyl Smit and Appleton, 2019); the role and influence of the victim when it comes to policing, prosecution and sentencing (Manikis, 2017); and the democratic status of prisoners as this relates to voting rights and the appropriate constitutional decision-makers in this context (Lazarus, 2004). To attend to vernaculars, sensemaking and practices of human rights is to detect, situate and analyse the narratives of official, professional and lay actors intimately involved in the sites and struggles just listed. They offer a valuable way of eliciting actors' ideologies, sensibilities and motivations and thus tracing how legal and political campaigns, strategies and allegiances influence the content and presentation of human rights (e.g. McEvoy, 2000, 2003).

It is by paying attention to vernaculars, sensemaking and practices of human rights that we might better explain why ideas, projects and aspirations expressed through human rights are more or less likely to survive or falter, endure or fade. How is human rights discourse constructed and deployed by reformers to challenge abuse of power, historic injustices or the use of new technologies? In addition to providing the basis of legal campaigns, how might human rights discourse function to isolate and embarrass targets of reform? How do criminal justice actors make sense of, and respond to, human rights claims? How do they attempt to co-opt and transform rights-based argumentation? And as Risse and Sikkink (1999) suggest, might instrumental co-option by state actors be a crucial step in a longer process of internalizing human rights? Addressing such questions might offer some clues as to why human rights politics seems 'to assume an oppositional, defensive form – to be fighting a reargued action in hostile terrain' (Loader, 2007: 40). But so too can a sociological approach shed light on unexpected situations in which human rights law *is* mobilized to bring about change in policy and practice. An example is Rock's (2004: chapter 5) account of the emergence of victims' rights in England and Wales. Drawing on newspaper reports, policy documents, speeches and interviews, Rock captures how social forces, political alliances and legal cultures combined to advance the status and role of the victim. The emergence of victims' rights was swept up with 'rights talk' which was a 'product of the new coalitions being formed between Victim Support and the older civil liberties groups, the Act [HRA] creating the very social formations by which it was interpreted' (Rock, 2004: 261).

If some part of the criminologist's role lies in 'generating controversy, opening up and extending debate, challenging and provoking received public 'opinion and political postures' (Loader and Sparks, 2011: 23), then to consider the vernacular of human rights law in the context of crime and its control is also to play to criminology's strengths. Such strengths might be said to include its sustained attention to the power and paradoxes of official knowledge (see, in particular, Doyle, Chan and Haggerty, 2011 on Richard Ericson's legacy) and its critical exposition of the institutional apparatus and working practices that structure and formalize means of challenging power, including forums in which human rights are deliberated and determined (e.g. Britton, 2000; Bosworth, 2011). The power and effect of human rights law as a vernacular can depend on periods of 'hesitancy, self-doubt, vacillation and even crisis' that open up space of rights-based claims to receive official recognition (Bartholomew and Hunt, 1990: 58). And here, again, criminology is well-placed to detect and illuminate moments using qualitative methods to elicit narratives deployed by key players in the criminal process in times of strife or forced reflection. Take, for example, the use of ethno-methodology in research on police reform (Brewer and Magee, 1991; O'Brien-Ollinger, 2016), narrative analyses of self-legitimating accounts deployed by prosecutors (Mulcahy, 1994) and police organizations (Cote-Lussier, 2013), or the deconstructions of 'critical junctures' used by lawyers to sustain particular features of their institutional history in the midst of armed conflict (McEvoy, 2011).

In the context of routine policing in particular, more observational work examining how these narratives are (or are not) mobilized in police–public encounters, especially in communities where trust in police remains understandably fraught, would be invaluable (Hearty, 2017, 2018; Bradford et al., 2019). To observe which classes of people are given or deprived of rights at certain places and points in time is, as Douzinas (2012: 59–60) suggests, to reveal 'power's mode of operation'. It would be intriguing, for example, to situate and examine the kinds of interactions recounted by TSG Larry in our interview:

> The layman on the street would sorta start shouting 'My human rights, my human rights', I think there's a common misconception with people saying their human rights says they can do whatever the bloody hell they want ... That's probably where the hindrance comes in because these people think we can't enforce the law because it impinges upon their human rights and their civil liberties when that's a load of bullshit.

Such a pursuit might be understood as taking up Loader's (2007: 29) invitation to examine what he refers to as 'the cultural life of human rights'. That is to say, 'a style of enquiry comprised of close observation and in-depth interpretation best conducted *in situ* ... the fine-grained interpretive analysis of the political and lay vernacular of rights and security' (Loader, 2007: 29). What kinds of lay vernaculars of human rights are in circulation? When and why are they used – and by whom? Do officers deploy similar rights narratives in response to lay rights discourse as they do in research interviews? How do officers negotiate the rights 'fakery' reported in parts of this book? These are questions that would begin to expose rights narratives circulating within communities and brought to public–police encounters.

Finally, a central concern of the book has been to illuminate some of the qualities that animate police as 'practitioners' of human rights, and the legal, social and organizational factors that structure and inform such practices. Criminological insights into police culture, working rules and self-regulation can enrich a sociological approach to human rights law. Police scholarship, of course, has a proud history of engagement with these themes in the empirical studies that the introduction of PACE stimulated (see Dixon, 1997: chapter 1). The task that remains even some decades on is to capture 'the diversity of forms of regulations and exploring a variety of settings and methods of creation, interpretation and application' (Cotterrell, 1997: 310). Going beyond street policing to examine under-explored regulatory spaces, sub-cultures and routine practices has the potential to offer new insights to policing and human rights scholarship (see, e.g., Loftus and Goold, 2012; Bacon, 2016). The possible frontiers include the blend of internal and external human rights-based regulation that now governs pre-charge bail powers, involving senior officers and magistrates; the deployment and use of Automated Facial Recognition technologies by police, specifically how this engages with privacy rights and equality law protections; and how police respond to the positive duties with respect to the protection of third parties from harm and the investigative standards police now owe to complainants (see *Osman* and *DSD*).

Encounters with Human Rights Law in Policing

This book demonstrates in the context of human rights specifically Dixon's (1997: 318) claim that law is best understood 'as an adaptable set of practices, discourses, techniques and modes of regulation'. The book has explored the circumstances and forms in which human rights law appears by touring four sites of police work: the public forums host to 'official' police narratives, routine policing, public order policing and police custody. A central finding is the persistent tension between the 'lightness' and 'weight' of human rights (McCann, 2014). The 'weight' of human rights derives from its potential to direct and regulate state power to better protect, respect and fulfil special features of our common humanity that should not be easily traded off in favour of utilitarian interests. The weight is felt when formal human rights guarantees are brought to life by way of a culture of justification, constructive oversight of state actors by independent bodies and the mainstreaming of human rights-based principles in frontline decision-making. In the book's case study, the weight of human rights has arisen from the PSNI's implementation of hundreds of recommendations and sustained external human rights oversight. However, the material presence and discursive accounts of human rights law in policing speak to what McCann (2014: 248) has described as the 'lightness' of rights – their indeterminacy and malleability, their susceptibility to be reworked and reformed by ideas, attitudes and agendas, especially when experienced and invoked in commonplace schemes of everyday life. The various vernaculars, sensemaking and practices that make up the empirical realities of human rights law in policing can be helpfully recapitulated using Sibley and Ewick's (1998) framework of law in everyday life that is expressed through people's accounts of being '*before*', '*with*' and '*against*' the law.

'Before the Law'

To be '*before the law*' is to receive and experience human rights law as an objective, disinterested, institutionalized doctrine, sitting at a distance from everyday life, functioning through distinct rules in delimited spheres, brought to bear to resolve disputes (see Ewick and Sibley, 1998: 28). Objectively, the PSNI are 'before' an array of manifestations of the law: statutory oversight bodies, reviewers of counter-terrorism legislation and covert policing powers, local and national criminal justice inspectorates and, ultimately, the courts. Indeed, the courts have made clear that for the purposes of section 6(1) of the HRA – which makes it unlawful for a public authority to act in a way which is incompatible with a Convention right – the court will conduct its assessment of whether the appropriate balance has been struck by the decision-maker. Throughout the book, we have seen how section 6(1) of the HRA has been used as a legal basis upon which to bring the PSNI 'before' the courts. Challenges have required the PSNI to account for the legality of arrests (e.g. *Salmon* and *Re Alexander*), and, in high-profile cases, justify and evidence their operational approach to sustained disorder (*Re E*) and un-notified protests (*Re DB*). As discussed in Chapter 7, the PSNI was forthright in its concern about the implications of being required, as a matter of law, to forcefully intervene, disperse crowds and make arrests in future situations where the human rights of local residents were engaged by those taking part in un-notified protests.

Especially significant, though, is the immense responsibility that has fallen on the PSNI to investigate conflict-related deaths in order to fulfil the positive obligation on the state arising under Article 2 of the ECHR. For the families of those who died at the hands of state actors, the standards established under Article 2 have been at the heart of their legal challenges to the official state response to their deaths (Bell and Keenan, 2005). The success of these families' cases before the ECtHR has injected detailed legal standards into how the state – and, accordingly, the PSNI in fulfilling the state's obligations under Article 2 – must respond to deaths involving state forces and those killed after allegations of collusion (Bell and Keenan, 2005). As discussed in Part I in the context of the official narratives of human rights, the PSNI has been subject to judicial review concerning the independence and rigour of specific police investigations into conflict-related deaths that must comply with the standards of Article 2 (e.g. *Re McQuillan*), as well as probing reviews by Her Majesty's Inspectorate of Constabulary into the management, staffing and oversight of the PSNI's Historical Enquiries Team and, latterly, the Legacy Investigation Branch.

However, another, particularly novel, way in which the PSNI are 'before the law' has arisen from how the Policing Board has carried out its statutory duty to monitor, and annually report on, the PSNI's compliance with the HRA. As observed at various points in the book, the Board's legal advisors have been key to fulfilling this monitoring duty. Crucially, they supply the Board with the necessary legal advice to properly question, scrutinize and report upon the PSNI's rights compliance; this is enabled by the extensive access the PSNI has granted advisors to observe live policing operations (including public order command rooms), police training (new recruits and annual refresher training) and review internal policies and procedures. So too has the advisor been central to the task of compiling and drafting the Board's annual human rights report. The report relies on ECHR standards to assess fourteen core aspects of policing, based on the advisors' own assessments of empirical data and legal analysis. This monitoring framework places the PSNI 'before the law' without the cost, delays and adversarialism associated with being before the courts and, quite rightly, has been described by Bayley (2008: 237) as 'a model of its kind ... It is the most complete on-going assessment of police adherence to human rights anywhere in the world'.

The book has explored, though, officers' subjective sense of being 'before' human rights in their working lives. Human rights law, at specific times and places, had a material presence in their everyday work. Many officers described their first encounter with human rights law as being in the examinations they sat as police recruits and in the oath of attestation they signed soon after, where its authoritative principles and standards carried normative weight. There was a consensus that the drum of the PSNI's official rights discourse beat loudly in their training sessions and official communications and in the operational orders they received. In authorizing detention and overseeing detained suspects, for example, custody officers were acutely aware that protecting suspects' rights was their core function. Almost all referred to themselves as the 'guardian of rights', there 'to look after detained persons'. This was reinforced by statutory safeguards forming an integral part of their discussions with arresting officers and the pride they took in 'knowing the rules' better than many of their colleagues. The public order commanders we encountered in Chapter 7 described the PSNI's human rights lawyer and the Policing Board legal advisors as 'the embodiment of the law' in their planning meetings and command rooms. In their own way, officers performing routine policing described working in the shadow of the law. Junior officers, in emotive remarks, expressed concern about the ease with which the Code of Ethics could be brought to bear on the unsuspecting officers who, inadvertently, put a foot wrong. References were often made to the injustice of being potentially subject to a Police Ombudsman's Office due to a spurious complaint made by an aggrieved member of the public. This captures a more subtle, affective sense of being 'before the law' for the officers who serve in a service surrounded by 'vast accountability machinery that acts as a general guarantor to PSNI's status as the most overseen human rights compliant service in the western world' (Topping and Bradford, 2020: 94).

Yet, at the same time, and in contradictory ways, officers described being distant from human rights law. For neighbourhood officers, the primacy of human rights articulated in the official police voices faded in relevance and meaning. The distribution of policing as a resource was shaped neither by positive duties nor community confidence indicators but local demands for security in circumstances where trust in the police was fragile. Turning to human rights was rarely helpful to officers in resolving local disputes, legitimating their power or making sense of their work. For officers in the Tactical Support Group meanwhile, sustained exposure to, and internalization of, human rights was now accompanied with a degree of fatigue – tempting them to tune out of the discussion when it appeared in briefings, documents or training – rather than blind ignorance or a latent hostility towards human rights. Officers actively drew on their experiences to generate a narrative of human rights that recast it as a resource belonging to senior officers who first dealt in its technicalities, and second played in its rhetoric. Indeed, the common sense narrative of human rights law, deconstructed in Chapter 4, revealed how, in contrast to the official voice, officers' understandings of the significance of human rights was not allied to the HRA or the ICP's reforms, but to officers' own humanity, to their decency as individuals and as colleagues. For most officers, respect for human rights was a core but unremarkable part of policing; neither interesting nor of great concern to them. The cumulative effect of these 'common sense' properties was to downplay the elevated status of human rights in the official voice, casting human rights as something ordinary, typical, not worthy of making such a big deal about.

'With the Law'

Human rights law and reform initiatives also came to operate as a way of legitimating the police and policing practices, easing workplace pressures and satisfying organizational goals. It is in this sense that police can be understood as being '*with the law*' in so far as human rights, as interpreted and applied in occupational settings, are a resource for managing 'tactical encounters' (Sibley and Ewing, 1998: 28). As argued in Chapter 2, the construction and deployment of three distinct features of human rights by the PSNI – legality, ethics and accountability – are part of police legitimation. Through their public remarks, statements, speeches, forewords to reports and responses to criticism, chief officers articulate the 'police voice' to enhance and cultivate their moral authority. In enacting landmark rights reforms and the verve with which they have gone about it – human rights being 'part of their

DNA' and 'how they think' (Chapter 2) – chief officers reclaimed the 'police voice', that is, 'the power to "name", diagnose and classify social problems' (Loader and Mulcahy, 2003: 226). In the wake of highly contested and emotive reforms, the PSNI have sought to regain the legitimacy to comment on matters of crime control, social order and dealing with the past. By constantly invoking its commitment to human rights, using sub-narratives of legality, ethics and accountability before powerful 'authorizers' or 'carriers', chief officers are striving to prove to others, as well as themselves, that the PSNI *is* the legitimate provider of order and security in Northern Ireland.

When faced with accusations of partisan policing, especially by politicians at the Policing Board's meetings, chief officers have, more defensively, routinely sought refuge in the notion of legality. This is combined with authoritative 'sources' deployed to proffer a definitive answer to community concerns and complaints of partisan policing. Senior officers' individual motivations are likely to be a mixture of a genuine commitment to human rights, professional pragmatism needed to manage in- and on-the-job 'trouble', and career-minded adaption in order to progress in an organization that expects a degree of rights fluency. Nor is there any doubt that significant human rights law duties arise with respect to politicized aspects of policing – coronial disclosure, public order policing, protection of informers – that the PSNI are acutely aware of and do take seriously. But the heavy recourse to legal discourse through the official voice, especially in public arenas and democratic deliberation, risks crowding out other ways of understanding harm and recompense arising from the conflict. The resort to legality risks distracting from the wider societal and budgetary debates that surround information retrieval, access to justice and the need for a more institutionally joined-up process for dealing with legacy issues. Most significant in this respect are the conflict-related investigations where there are very real concerns raised, and disappointment expressed, by victims' families and community groups.

When it came to various aspects of police practices, we have also seen how officers move closer to be 'with' human rights law to manage public encounters and workplace pressures. In the highly pressured public order situations, for example, commanders were also trained in, and adept at, thinking about and justifying actions using human rights law and, in doing so, helping to avoid in- and on-the-job 'trouble' from oversight bodies or even challenges before the courts. They described, for example, working 'with the law' by using certain terms in their radio communications to 'paint a picture' in order to provide silver commanders with the information they needed to 'tick the boxes' of Article 2's absolute necessity standard governing the use of potentially lethal force. This close reference to Convention standards can, it has been argued, assist commanders to work 'with' the law, while being simultaneously 'before' it, because the courts have proven to show deference to police when conducting its proportionality assessment. Where decision-makers turn their mind to Convention rights in arriving at their decision, the court will give due weight to such judgments.[1] Indeed, the court will be 'inherently less likely' to disagree with the public authority's decision where there has been 'proper consideration' of the Convention.[2]

The book has further sought to reveal how the doctrinal features of human rights law, and how its standards are fleshed out through judicial interpretation, can enable officers to work with the law to achieve police priorities. In some areas, the case law is prescriptive (e.g. what qualifies as 'peaceful protest' under Article 11 of the ECHR), but in the context of qualified rights, police are granted what Bell (1992: 99) has described as 'technical discretion' that goes beyond mere evaluation of means alone. In working 'with' qualified rights, the concept of proportionality enables police to determine whether their action is in pursuit of a legitimate aim, how feasible particular tactics or deployments will be in achieving that, the possible side-effects or collateral intrusion on other rights that might arise, and ultimately the desirability of pursuing the proposed action in so far as it achieves a fair balance being struck between the right of the individual and the right of the community. Where multiple, if not competing, rights are engaged, the proportionality assessment will not pre-determine a specific course of action but will provide a framework for police to work *within* the law. That human rights can function as a moderating framework, capable of accommodating security pursuits, is an important message to relay in the face of direct challenges to the human rights paradigm as insufficiently responsive to security

[1] *Belfast City Council v Miss Behavin' Ltd* [2007] UKHL 19.
[2] Lord Neuburger, ibid., at [91].

claims (Lazarus and Goold, 2019: 8). Much hinges, though, on individuals' values and priorities, but also, as demonstrated in Parts III–V of the book, on the influence on decision-making of workplace pressures, organizational incentives and cultural affinities (see also Loftus, Goold and Mac Giollabhuí, 2016; Pearson, Rowe and Turner, 2018). How law enforcement agencies use proportionality as a framework for guiding and legitimating decision-making, especially when issues like security and privacy are at stake, is a fertile site for further empirical research (see e.g. Stubbins Bates, 2020).

The court's interpretation of the law can also enable police to work 'with' human rights law by making the very legal standards themselves responsive to the practical concerns, operational dilemmas and limited resources of police. Often this reflects a sensible approach to what can be practically expected of police. As observed by the Supreme Court in *Re DB*, some weighty assessments of conflicting rights will be made in 'fraught circumstances', relying on inevitably partial knowledge of the circumstances, which are often too easy to scrutinize with the benefit of hindsight. So too are the courts wary of imposing disproportionate burdens on the police authorities when it comes to positive obligations due to limited police budgets and staffing. In *Osman*, for example, the positive duty under Article 2 only arises where there is a *real and immediate* risk to the life of an *identified* individual and authorities failed to take measures that were *reasonable* and *within their powers*. But, in certain instances, the court's interpretation of legal safeguards has legitimated troubling practice: here police have come to work 'with' legal safeguards because the very substance of these safeguards has come to reflect dubious police practice. As argued in Chapter 8, the courts have proven reluctant to strengthen the 'necessity to arrest' criterion, interpreting it to mean 'the practical and sensible option' (*Hayes*) and 'more than merely desirable or more convenient' (*B and Others*). So too has there been a relatively relaxed approach by the courts to the role of pre-arrest briefings and preliminary investigations that would render the arrest either unnecessary or unlawful to pursue (see *Alford* and *Salmon*).

But beyond the instrumental ways in which officers could be 'with' the law, the book has also sought to draw attention to the power of 'sensemaking' as a way in which officers come to work *within*, not outside of, or against, the human rights as a vernacular. Officers were well-able to deploy formal scripts from training sessions and policy manuals when called on to do so, but so too was their internalization of human rights, expressed in sensemaking narratives, influenced by features of their occupational culture, the challenges of routine work and their personal experiences. In making sense of human rights, officers drew on their own identities and ideas of what good policing was about, thus conveying identity-laden values of efficacy, competence and humanity. In the 'common sense' narrative, for example, officers attached human rights to a taken-for-granted morality through which they were able to speak of the maturity and discipline they saw regularly in their colleagues. Sensemaking was bound up with officers' experiences of performing 'dirty work' together, specifically the human qualities they inferred from each other's behaviour that served to counter external claims that challenged their self-legitimacy. It has been argued that the official account of human rights law as legality, ethics and accountability that appeared in training, policies and procedures, was sustained in part because it is accompanied by a series of counter-narratives that not only enact and evidence it, but simultaneously enable officers to complicate and contradict it. Human rights, like legality, 'is enduring because it relies on and invokes commonplace schemas of everyday life' (Ewick and Sibley, 1998: 17).

'Against the Law'

Finally, and less frequently, officers described being in situations where human rights was being used 'against' them in going about their everyday work. This was different from being 'before the law' because such encounters were not in legal forums but rather experienced through interactions with the public and colleagues. As discussed in Chapter 5, for example, neighbourhood officers recalled experiences with drunken revellers and young people who attempted to articulate complaints, concerns or contempt using human rights 'talk' which officers learnt how to negotiate or dismiss. A critically engaged account of human rights and policing should not lose sight of the wider inequalities of the social order the police help to uphold. This order is itself marked by inequalities of wealth and privilege and institutional structures that disempower and discriminate against certain groups due to their class, race, gender, ethnicity or religion. Indeed, much police work does not entail law enforcement, but rather is about providing an authoritative response to a panoply of complaints and concerns and in mediating disputes between individuals and communities. In such circumstances, the affective ideas of security, safety, confidence and crime control are often addressed by police drawing on their soft, or symbolic, power, albeit with the potential to use coercive means to achieve resolution of the issue at hand or compliance. In addition to being positioned 'against' human rights by members of the public, junior officers recounted how more senior colleagues could also engender a feeling that human rights worked 'against' the rank-and-file because their *own rights* were not being given sufficient weight by commanders. This was especially so in the context of sustained public disorder that resulted in injuries to frontline officers. As one officer quoted in Chapter 7 remarked, 'It's all human rights going one way again. If anyone's human rights are being breached a lot, it comes down to ours!'

As an organization, however, the PSNI has been cast as being 'against' the spirit, if not the letter, of human rights law in the political skirmishes and discursive stances that have played out publicly at the Policing Board. SF has mobilized Article 2 of the ECHR to critique police disclosure of material to coronial inquests and Police Ombudsman investigations into conflict deaths, as well as to condemn the practices and staffing of the Historical Enquiries Team. In public sessions of the Policing Board, the PSNI's very commitment to human rights has been questioned by Republicans. Chief officers' use of Article 2 as a justification for non-disclosure has been directly challenged, including questions as to whether the PSNI are fully aware of the agreement reached between the British government and Committee of Ministers regarding the package of measures to satisfy the Article 2 obligation concerning conflict-related deaths. Reference to Article 2 was used by SF to propel the idea that the law was on the side of the Republican families who were seeking justice, and as such, the PSNI must have something to hide if they were not prepared to be faithful to the law by being transparent about the officers involved in reviewing the inquest or investigation material. SF's commitment to human rights oversight of the police reflects what Hearty (2017) has described as Republicans' 'critical engagement' with the PSNI. This proximity to, and familiarity with, a legalistic human rights vernacular further reflects the political campaigning and legal challenges so central to Republicanism during the conflict itself. In contemporary public forums, Republicans continue to draw upon their involvement with victims' groups and rights-based advocacy to reassert themselves as custodians of human rights.

The fact that human rights law was deployed in public forums by chief officers and SF to justify or defend the very same activities speaks to its capacity, when deployed by social actors, to convey competing sets of claims (Tushnet, 1984; Wilson, 2006). This reflects the open-textured formulation of human rights in so far as 'rights conflict with one another, rights are vague, rights have exceptions, many situations fall between rights' (Kennedy, 2002: 116). But in the political forums, in the absence of definitive judgments of the courts, human rights – including reference to its legal formulations and sources – are susceptible to be reworked and reformed through their interaction with other discourses, traditions and institutions. Yet human rights discourse is not open to all actors as a language to make sense of the police as an institution. For Unionist members of the Policing Board the sense remains that human rights discourse had been used 'against' their political community during the conflict and once again in peacetime. Scepticism towards the idea of levelling claims against the state using human rights discourse remains, allied to a fresh cynicism of how human rights law was being interpreted and applied by Republicans to 'unfairly discredit' police officers and the PSNI's efforts to investigate conflict-related deaths. Yet despite their aversion to a human rights critique of the state generally and policing specifically, Unionist accounts suggest they have, to an extent, come to contribute to, and implicitly endorse, a rights-based approach to police oversight, though they do not frame it as such. But Unionism's reluctance to adopt their own human rights-based discourse has left them poorly equipped to articulate their own communities' experiences and understandings of conflict-related deaths in a political arena in which human rights is the lingua franca. Indeed, the PSNI's strong endorsement of human rights, articulated by chief officers who served in the RUC, has served to place Unionists at odds with a core tenet of an organization they remain loyal to and seek identity in (Lawther, 2010).

Within local politics, then, human rights harbours much deeper sentiments and concerns, at the heart of which are competing histories of the conflict, legacies of policing and understandings of the country's imperfect peace. Rather than bringing 'a fresh sense of urgency or moral obligation to the debate' (Gearty, 2006: 2), as human rights have done in other contexts, rights talk can, at times, stick onto, if not further entrench, ethno-political vantage points. This underscores Ignatieff's (2001) call for deliberations to be premised on a broad evaluative consensus of the general significance of human rights to the matter at hand but also a willingness to listen respectfully to opponents' particular inflection of rights claims. But the Northern Ireland case study also serves as a vivid reminder of the symbolic power of the police as an institution that conveys rich, affective signals of identity, status and belonging to individuals and groups within a political community (Loader and Mulcahy, 2003). The legacy of the conflict remains a part of many people's lives, especially those who grew up under the spectre of 'trauma or bereavement, displacement and violence' (McAlister, Scraton and Haydon, 2009: 11). This collective trauma finds expression in community murals and commemorations, but also quieter accounts of loss and suffering, as well as forgiveness and friendship (Carruthers, 2013; Henderson and Little, 2018). To assess police 'performance', even when grounded in human rights discourse, is to open up 'a complex, contradictory, and differentially felt range of emotions ranging from anger, fear and resentment, to guilt, empathy, even pleasure' that swirl around the police and policing (Loader and Mulcahy, 2003: 322). In Northern Ireland, these emotions are filtered through personal experiences and collective memories of the conflict (Lawther, 2014; Hearty, 2017) and are brought to bear on issues of trust and confidence in the police in the context of both 'high' and 'low' policing (Brodeur, 1983), as argued in Chapter 3.

Especially significant are questions of how investigations into conflict-related deaths are prioritized, by whom and for what purposes. How these are answered raise fundamental issues of victimhood, blameworthiness, trust and reconciliation with which post-conflict societies must grapple. There has been a surge 'from below' as victims' groups, NGOs, lawyers and politicians have worked tirelessly for answers about the circumstances of particular deaths during the conflict and greater accountability for the paramilitary groups or state actors involved (McEvoy and Bryson 2016). But in the absence of an overarching approach to dealing with the legacy of the conflict, the immense responsibility for investigating conflict-related incidents remains with the PSNI and orientated towards a criminal justice response. Much could change if the Stormont House Agreement, signed in December 2014, and recommitted to (in part) in November 2015, is finally realized. If implemented as it was originally proposed – something that at the time of writing seems far from certain (O'Neill, 2019) – it would create the Historical Investigations Unit (HIU) as one of a number of bodies tasked with addressing the legacy of the past. The HIU would be an independent investigative body responsible for conflict-related work currently being done by the PSNI and Police Ombudsman. Significantly, the HIU would be equipped with powers of arrest, stop, search and question and would be accountable to the Policing Board. The HIU is an opportunity for an independent review of historic cases, conducted by a body with a specific mandate and dedicated resources to produce victim-centred reports for the families of those killed, as well as contributing to new prosecutions where evidence allows. If the HIU should ever emerge from the political mire, and if the PSNI would engage transparently and constructively with its investigations, especially on disclosure, its creation could herald a true opportunity for the police, organizationally and operationally, to emerge out of the shadow of the conflict.

Lessons from the Local?

The potential of the law to regulate police decision-making has, for good reason, been subject to sustained scepticism in policing scholarship (Bittner, 1990; Ericson 2007; Manning, 2013; Bradford and Jackson, 2016). Yet legal regulation of police powers continues to play a major role in reform initiatives, not only in post-conflict societies but also in established democracies where police misconduct, brutality and discrimination remain all too frequent. In discussions of such initiatives, the PSNI is an oft-cited example of mainstreaming human rights, with the former Chairperson of the Policing Board memorably describing that the ICP's report offered a 'blueprint for modern policing worldwide' (Mulcahy, 2006: 191–3; see also Bayley, 2008; Topping 2016). Northern Irish policing continues to attract the attention of police forces, accountability bodies and policymakers from all over the world, who are keen to learn lessons from its experience. The transfer of law and policy from one jurisdiction to another, even when well-intentioned, is, of course, a notoriously complex business. Indeed, Northern Ireland has had particular advantages in its reform of the police that many post-conflict societies lack, including a political settlement that foresaw the centrality of police, human rights and the rule of law for sustained peace, as well as a vibrant civil society and advanced regulatory schemes to help implement and oversee the reforms (Bayley, 2008: 239–40). But for scholars, policymakers, governments, police leaders and community groups – the 'host of actors, old and new, concerned with human rights practice' (Gready and Phillips, 2009: 3) – in search of ideas, what broad lessons might be gleaned from the Northern Irish experience? What conditions might facilitate, encourage and contribute to human rights reform of policing? And what role might legal regulation play in fostering compliance with human rights?

For readers at the coalface of police reform, eager to know what programmatic steps might be taken to implement human rights law in policing based on the Northern Irish experience, Kilpatrick's (2018) authoritative report published by the Irish Council for Civil Liberties is a most valuable resource. This guidance identifies a number of core recommendations that chime with the book's findings, including a willingness by senior officers to meaningfully engage with accountability mechanisms and promote the virtues of a rights-based approach within the police; the provision of expert human rights legal advice for live operational decision-making, but also for accountability bodies in their oversight of police practices; police training that conveys legal principles in a clear, consistent and practical manner; the collection and analysis of data on police powers, especially use of force and public order tactics; and a reporting regime that encourages a dialogue about human rights compliance between the police, accountability bodies and community groups. Drawing on the book's findings, though, I want to reinforce three factors that are especially important in encouraging officers to be 'before' and 'with' human rights law: (i) the interaction of human rights law within officers' socialization in specific areas of police work; (ii) the situational dynamics of decision-making, especially constructive scrutiny; and (iii) human rights as guiding principles for legal regulation.

First, much is made of dominant characteristics of police culture that function as barriers to organizational reform: cynicism, machismo, racism, commitment to ends over means etc. But references to police culture too often underplay significant differences within policing, neglecting the complexity and variety of sub-cultures, as well as the potential for the legal environment to influence these (Dixon, 1996: 287; Sklansky and Marks, 2008). This book has illustrated the importance of the subtle and variable dynamics of socialization across sites of policing that affect how human rights is made sense of and practised by officers. Socialization, it will be recalled, is the process by which officers are inducted into the norms of police work through social interactions that convey expected ways of thinking, feeling and acting. Socialization is a combination of *formal* sources – human rights law in training, policies, operational orders and briefings – and *informal* sources – social encounters, interactions, cues, adaptions etc. arising from the performance of police work and involving colleagues, bosses, suspects, victims and communities. In sum, how officers make sense of human rights will inevitably be a blend of the formal and informal features of the workplace. In striving for the institutionalization of human rights it is thus important to recognize that the non-legal will inevitable surround and inform the legal; rights narratives will 'overlap, interweave, distance and disassociate' (Humphreys and Brown, 2002: 439) with distinctly official, formal or legal pronouncements of human rights. This has practical implications.

One implication is that formalities of training, policies, briefings etc. *do* matter. They provide a core expectation of formally acceptable practices and serve to impart values that influence perceptions of appropriateness, the roles to be played and the tasks to be performed (Feldman, 1992: 176). A particularly noteworthy finding of the book was that the majority of constables could list, with considerable accuracy, the Convention rights engaged in their work and then impart, in practical terminology, the efforts made to respect these rights and reduce their interference, with the terminology of necessity and proportionality frequently cited. But so too can features of informal socialization function to embed, sustain and energize human rights in policing. The challenge for reformers is to detect, engage with and channel features of informal socialization so that these might serve to promote rights-based principles relevant to such sites, whether these features take the form of proud professionalism, common sense knowledge or insistence that remarkable change is a result of no change at all. There is value in harnessing elements of officers' 'stances' to human rights, rather than belittling or condemning them, because informal narratives such as 'common sense' and 'nothing's changed' can serve to maintain the significance of human rights, sustain discussion of its principles and reinforce officers' sense of responsibility for how they use their powers.

The second general lesson the book offers is the importance of paying close attention to how officers' engagement with human rights law is influenced by organizational processes and bureaucratic procedures. There is often a tendency for academics and police reformers to 'persist in stressing the group psychology of the police and in treating the internal organization of police departments as largely irrelevant' (Sklansky, 2007: 7). Decisions are affected by the time, place and complexity of decisions to be made, and how differing priorities, resource constraints and values arise in particular sites of policing. Those who make decisions relatively infrequently are more likely to approach them in a complex way, taking more time and considering more information (e.g. public order commanders) whereas those having to make regular and repetitive decisions (e.g. custody officers) turn to adaptive techniques involving shorthand ways of 'classifying cases and appraising each one by focusing on the extent to which it presents typical features' (Hawkins, 1992: 39). In both situations, decision-making 'horizons' are also at play and can be put to work in prompting and rewarding rights-based considerations. Applied to policing, horizons refer to officers' background knowledge of the organizational sources, meanings and parameters of the case that requires a decision (Emerson and Paley, 1992: 234). The subject of the decision – for example, whether to arrest or authorize detention; which public order tactic to deploy; whether 'absolute necessity' to use potentially lethal force is satisfied – are made in the context of *retrospective* and *prospective* horizons. The former refers to the organizational history of the issue at hand, including where, how and why it has come to the present point and the judgments and practices of fellow officers that propelled it to this stage. The latter refers to the organizational futures, such as the known or likely organizational consequences, that inform choices between future alternative courses of action (Emerson and Paley, 1992: 235–6).

The contribution of organizational 'routines' and 'horizons' to decision-making is a helpful way of making some sense of the contrast in human rights law practices by officers in Parts IV and V of the book. Human rights came alive in public order policing through the police 'script' that was the outworking of a hierarchical, co-ordinated and resource-intensive process. Senior officers were appointed to key roles as gold, silver and bronze commanders, and were specifically trained and supported with dedicated legal and tactical advice. This was a process the PSNI spent years devising and over a decade improving, drawing on local and national reforms to public order policies, training and tactical advice. This prompted a sub-culture in which a grasp of human rights law was seen by commanders as a mark of professionalism, progress and skill. There is resonance here between the commanders and the HRA and Dixon's (1996: 290) much earlier findings in the context of PACE. Detectives came to perceive PACE as a significant resource to create a new police 'professionalism', accompanied with a sense that their work could be done within the rules. The PSNI commanders' proximity to their in-house human rights lawyer, as well as the Policing Board's legal advisor, in planning meetings and command rooms reinforced the need to meaningfully consider and rationalize decisions. As analysed in Chapter 7, prospects of 'trouble' were a marked feature of officers' prospective decision-making 'horizon'. Commanders, for example, must submit to the Policing Board, as soon as possible after a major public disorder incident, a record detailing the nature of the disorder, any force used, any injuries sustained by police officers or members of the public and any damage caused to property (see Kilpatrick, 2018: 58). As powerfully illustrated by *Re DB*, commanders did not always get the decision right on the scope of their powers or positive duties, but as the annual reports of the Policing Board suggest, overall, commanders did pay close and careful attention to the kinds of human rights considerations analysed in detail in Part IV.

In police custody, by contrast, the bureaucratic format of human rights law was a checklist on a computer screen, where the grounds for detention were selected from a drop-down list. Detainees' rights were rhymed off by custody officers hundreds of times a month, following the on-screen prompts of their computer system, with some officers populating the custody record before the suspect had actually arrived. Individuals' procedural rights were sourced from PACE, rights the courts have been reluctant to interpret strongly and which arresting officers seem to have limited regard for. In their retrospective decision-making 'horizon', custody officers saw the police service's target-driven ethos as contributing, in part, to officers' making dubious arrests in the first place. Formally enacted policies and endorsed practices can thus make it harder, operationally and culturally, to make rights-based decisions in individual cases if this requires officers to collectively push back against wider organizational trends. Seemingly routine, automatic decision-making ought to be subject to disruption by regular reviews drawing on the insights and experiences of a diversity of community groups which can expose how routine police practices are reifying social injustices or perpetuating inequalities (Lacey, 1992: 386). But so too were custody officers' prospective decision-making horizons influenced by a cultural affinity to fellow officers and a subjective sense that neither solicitors nor lay visitors were sufficient sources of 'trouble' to affect decisions to detain. Officers knew how to manage potential trouble, using ploys to process problematic cases, and had learnt the limits of what they could get away with when prompting arresting officers on grounds for arrest. The task is to channel officers' wariness of trouble by promoting oversight where practices or procedures that risk violating rights are likely to attract the attention of proactive and constructive forms of accountability.

This leads neatly to the third and final lesson to be drawn from the Northern Ireland case study: the value of human rights as regulatory *principles*. As the book has demonstrated, the human rights reporting system in Northern Ireland involves the Policing Board and PSNI, and functions as an institutional dialogue centred around human rights principles. Participation and deliberation over how the police have struck the balance between competing rights or fulfilled their negative and positive duties is promoted at the annual launch of the Policing Board's human rights report, and is continued in the live-streamed public sessions of the Board, as well as within the PSNI as part of their own planning, training and debriefings sessions. This avoids a regulatory approach to human rights adherence that stifles officers' meaningful engagement with it and instead encourages officers to draw on their expertise and knowledge of the likely consequences and risks associated with tactical, operational or investigative decisions. Importantly, though, by tethering human rights oversight to the HRA, the monitoring and reporting processes in Northern Ireland ensure the core human rights law concepts – legality, necessity and proportionality; absolute, strong and qualified rights; the development of negative and positive duties – find expression with sufficient specificity to positively regulate police action. The value of these principles, after all, lies in their 'subtle weighting of different rights, and … [their] structuring for making exceptions to rights' (Campbell, Ashworth and Redmayne, 2019: 46).

A principles-based approach to human rights oversight ought to be accompanied by external stimulus, oversight and assistance that promotes consultation, justification and persuasion. The appeal of principles, after all, is their ability to create 'opportunities for police officers to become participants in, rather than simply the object of, regulatory dialogue and activity' (Loader, 2016: 433; see also Oberleitner, 2012: 257). The adherence to substantive human rights protections is promoted when officers articulate and explain their decision-making to colleagues, communities, oversight bodies and other criminal justice actors using rights-based principles because this will clarify thinking, prompt alternative approaches not initially considered and make it harder to overlook rights abuses (Schneider, 1992: 86). This can be achieved by sending authoritative regulatory signals that prompt, encourage and reward police for meaningfully engaging with rights principles in sites of police decision-making. In Northern Ireland, such signals are sent through a bespoke reporting and monitoring scheme, but they might also be sent using administrative law mechanisms too. In three Australian states, for example, there is now an innovative procedural duty to give 'proper consideration' to the rights contained in their particular state's bill of rights.[3] The courts in Victoria have interpreted this duty in such a way as to promote human rights as regulatory principles and dissuade public authorities from reverting to a defensive approach of 'tick-box' decision-making.[4] The Northern Ireland case demonstrates, however, that

[3] See Charter of Human Rights and Responsibilities Act 2006 (Victoria), section 38(1); Human Rights Act 2019 (Queensland), section 58(1)(b); and the Human Rights Act 2004 (ACT), section 40B(1)(b).

[4] What is required of public authorities in giving 'proper consideration' to human rights is that they: (i) understand in general terms which of the rights of the person affected by the decision may be relevant and whether, and if so how, those rights will be interfered with by the decision; (ii) seriously turn their mind to the possible impact of the decision on a person's human rights and the implications thereof for the affected person; (iii) identify the countervailing interests or obligations; and (iv) balance competing private and public interests as part of the exercise of justification (*Bare v IBAC* [2015] VSCA 197, per Tate JA, at [288]). For a formulation more closely aligned to proportionality in the context of the ECHR, see Mead (2012: 73), who proposes the following questions that

to foster a culture of justification on the basis of human rights, such duties must be complemented by organizational leadership, training and legal advice, as well as the influence of outside bodies capable of encouraging and challenging police to deliver on their obligations long before litigation arises.

However, the political ambition, ethical ideals and material resources that it took to reform the PSNI was itself the outworking of a special socio-political – and indeed constitutional – moment in Northern Ireland. At the turn of the millennium, the air was thick with human rights. The ink was still wet on the GFA, which was replete with references to human rights, and the Council of Europe was promoting an ambitious human rights programme. The introduction of the HRA spurred remarkable efforts to raise awareness of, and competence in, human rights law. This included a human rights audit of a vast number of policies, the drafting of guidance for public authorities and departments, a huge training programme for advocates, judges and officials, new appointments to the High Court, and liaison with NGOs and the legal profession (see Rock, 2004: 223–32). The air has a different quality today. Extensive efforts to introduce a Bill of Rights specific to Northern Ireland have stalled, while a co-ordinated approach to dealing with the past remains elusive. In an attempt to regain sovereignty, 'restore common sense' and 'tackle the misuse of rights contained in the Convention', Conservative governments have threatened replacing the HRA with a 'British Bill of Rights'. And across liberal democracies there seems to be a growing assault on the values of human rights, constitutionalism and tolerance, fuelled by populist policies, nationalist rhetoric and security concerns (Lazarus and Goold, 2019: 20; Klug, 2019: 364–6).

Let us end by returning to that morning at Belfast's Crumlin Road Gaol with which the book began. When asked what he thought of the possible repeal of the Human Rights Act 1998, the PSNI's then Chief Constable turned to the audience and stated

decision-makers might ask: 'What are we trying to achieve in taking this decision? Is that objective sufficiently important to us to warrant this likely restriction on rights? If so, will this decision actually help us achieve that objective? If so, what alternative decisions are open to us – what will their effect be? Is this decision the least restrictive decision we can take while still achieving our objective? If not, are the negative effects of this decision, in our opinion, outweighed by the greater, wider social benefit?'

unequivocally: 'All of these rights and freedoms are things that I struggle to understand how people could argue with in a progressive, liberal, democratic society'. The civil society actors, statutory oversight bodies, academics, lawyers, policymakers and police officers, amidst the ghosts of Crumlin Gaol's past, were involved in an annual conversation about human rights, debating a series of topics at the heart of which was what intrusions the police should be permitted, or required, to make into our lives. This kind of inclusive debate, directed towards the realization of human rights, is something those of us in liberal democracies have never been so well-placed to meaningfully engage with. But as this book has demonstrated, we must recognize that human rights law and discourse, is not, as some may hope, a refuge from political rough and tumble, a panacea for police reform or a clear-cut regulatory ideal. Human rights are open-textured in formulation, contested in interpretation and conditional in application. They offer a set of powerful norms for challenging state power but, at the same time, rely upon that same power to realize them in practice. In seeking to promote human rights reform and regulation of criminal justice actors, we must be prepared for its principles and standards to be interpreted and applied, and possibly appropriated and transformed, by such actors. This calls for scholarly curiosity as much as it does for vigilance. Exploring human rights law and criminal justice systems using a sociological approach that attends to the vernaculars, sensemaking and practices of frontline decision-makers offers an opportunity to identify, understand and critique these new members of human rights law's interpretive community.

Bibliography

Adams, G. (2007) Fein Ardfheis: Gerry Adams's speech. *Irish Times*. 29 January.

Amatrudo, A. and Blake, L. (2014) *Human Rights and the Criminal Justice System*. (Abingdon: Routledge).

An-Na'im, A. (2012) The Interdisciplinarity of Human Rights. In C. Gearty and C. Douzinas (eds), *The Cambridge Companion to Human Rights Law*. (Cambridge: Cambridge University Press).

Andreassen, B., Sano, H-O and McInerney-Lankford, S. (2018) Human Rights Research Methods. In B Andreassen, H-O Sano and S McInerney-Lankford (eds), *Research Methods in Human Rights: A Handbook*. (Cheltenham, UK: Edward Elgar).

Anthony, G. (2009) Positive Obligations and Policing in the House of Lords. *European Human Rights Law Review*. 538–51.

Anthony, G. and Mageean, P. (2007) Habits of Mind and 'Truth Telling': Article 2 ECHR in Post-Conflict Northern Ireland. In J Morrison, K McEvoy and G Anthony (eds), *Judges, Transition, and Human Rights*. (Oxford: Oxford University Press), 181–200.

Ashforth, E. and Kreiner, G. (1999) 'How Can You Do It?' Dirty Work and the Challenges of Constructing a Positive Identity. *Academy of Management Review*. 24(3): 413–34.

Ashworth, A. (2014) A Decade of Human Rights in Criminal Justice. *Criminal Law Review*. 5: 325–37.

Ashworth, A. and Horder, J. (2013) *Principles of Criminal Law*. (7th ed.) (Oxford: Oxford University Press).

Attwood, A. (2004) Attwood Wants Rights Based PSNI. *News Letter*, 20 April.

Aughey, A. (1989) *Under Siege: Ulster Unionism and the Anglo-Irish Agreement*. (Belfast: Blackstaff).

Bacon, M. (2016) *Taking Care of Business: Police Detectives, Drug Law Enforcement and Proactive Investigation*. (Oxford: Oxford University Press).

Baldwin, R. and Kinsey, R. (1982) *Police Powers and Politics*. (London: Quartet).

Baggott, M. (2012) Key Budgetary and Resourcing Challenges / Human Rights and Policing in Northern Ireland, Northern Ireland Assembly Committee for Justice, 16 February. http://www.niassembly.gov.uk/globalassets/documents/official-reports/justice/2011-2012/120216_psnikeybudgetingchallenges.pdf (accessed 5 December 2017).

Baggott, M. (2014) *Launch of the Annual Human Rights Report*. Titanic Belfast, Belfast, 25 March.

Banton, M. (1964) *The Policeman in the Community*. (London: Tavistock).

Bardon, J. (2012) *The Plantation of Ulster*. (Dublin: Gill Books).

Barak, A. (2012) *Proportionality: Constitutional Rights and Their Limitations*. (Cambridge: Cambridge University Press).

Barker, R. (2001) *Legitimating Identities: Self-Presentation of Rulers and Subjects*. (Cambridge: Cambridge University Press).

Barry, J. (2019) Class, Political Economy and Loyalist Political Disaffection: Agonistic Politics and the Flag Protests. *Global Discourse*. 9(3): 457–77.

Bartholomew, A. and Hunt, A. (1990) What's Wrong With Rights? *Law and Inequality*. 9(1): 1–58.

Bayley, D. (2008) Post-conflict Police Reform: Is Northern Ireland a Model? *Policing: A Journal of Policy and Practice*. 2(2): 233–40.

BBC News (2009) 50% increase in police DNA files. 21 July. http://news.bbc.co.uk/1/hi/northern_ireland/8160493.stm (accessed 7 April 2015).

BBC News (2014a) Anti-internment march: Minor trouble amid tight security in Belfast. 10 August. http://www.bbc.co.uk/news/uk-northern-ireland-28728651 (accessed 19 March 2021).

BBC News (2014b) Peter Robinson: Parades Commission ruling is threat to institutions. 3 July. http://www.bbc.co.uk/news/uk-northern-ireland-28138927 (accessed 19 March 2021).

BBC News (2015a) Sean Brown murder: Chief constable denies PSNI is 'shielding murderers. 5 February. http://www.bbc.co.uk/news/uk-northern-ireland-foyle-west-31144235 (accessed 19 March 2021).

BBC News (2015b) Human Rights Act: Gerry Adams criticises 'attack' on NI peace deal. 13 May. http://www.bbc.co.uk/news/uk-northern-ireland-32721851 (accessed 19 March 2021).

Beckley, A. (2017) Human Rights and Police Training: Democratizing Policing Systems. In L Weber, E Fishwick and M Marmo (eds.), *The Routledge International Handbook of Criminology and Human Rights*. (Abingdon: Routledge).

Beetham, D. (1991) *The Legitimation of Power*. (London: Macmillan).

Beirne, M. and Knox, C. (2014) Reconciliation and Human Rights in Northern Ireland: A False Dichotomy? *Journal of Human Rights Practice*. 6(1): 26–50.

Belfast Telegraph (2006) Ulster's policing goes global. 1 December.

Belfast Telegraph (2007) Why we still need touts. 8 February.

Belfast Telegraph (2009) Can Matt rip up the paperwork? 28 August.

Belfast Telegraph (2011a) Is publication of this picture a breach of his human rights … and do we care? 27 January.

Belfast Telegraph (2011b) Human rights lawyer's £10,000 a month for human rights advice. 19 February.

Belfast Telegraph (2010) End of random stop and search powers welcomed. 21 July.

Belfast Telegraph (2013) Fury as fresh probe ordered into police's human rights compliance. 9 February. http://www.belfasttelegraph.co.uk/news/northern-ireland/fury-as-fresh-probe-ordered-into-polices-human-rights-compliance-29056012.html (accessed 5 December 2017).

Belfast Telegraph (2015) SDLP annual conference: Party 'will not tolerate a vacuum on human rights'. 14 November. https://www.belfasttelegraph.co.uk/news/politics/sdlp-annual-conference-party-will-not-tolerate-a-vacuum-on-human-rights-34200342.html (accessed 8 December 2017).

Belfast Telegraph (2016) Twaddell camp dismantled as Orange parade past Ardoyne shops in north Belfast passes off peacefully. 1 October. https://www.belfasttelegraph.co.uk/news/northern-ireland/twaddell-camp-dismantled-as-orange-parade-past-ardoyne-shops-in-north-belfast-passes-off-peacefully-35092282.html (accessed 9 December 2017).

Belfast Telegraph (2017a) DUP's Jim Shannon in tearful plea for justice for murdered cousin, 23 February. http://www.belfasttelegraph.co.uk/news/northern-ireland/dups-jim-shannon-in-tearful-plea-for-justice-for-murdered-cousin-35476451.html (accessed 7 December 2017).

Belfast Telegraph (2017b) Pursuit of Troubles-era soldiers a bid to re-write history, says Foster. 9 February. http://www.belfasttelegraph.co.uk/news/northern-ireland/pursuit-of-troublesera-soldiers-a-bid-to-rewrite-history-says-foster-35435868.html (accessed 7 December 2017).

Belfast Telegraph (2017c) PSNI Chief shares frustration over political impasse in meeting with Sinn Fein. 8 August. https://www.belfasttelegraph.co.uk/news/northern-ireland/psni-chief-shares-frustration-over-political-impasse-in-meeting-with-sinn-fein-36013494.html (accessed 9 December 2017).

Bell, C. (2002) Dealing with the Past in Northern Ireland. *Fordham International Law Journal*. 26(4): 1095–147.

Bell, C. (2012) Human Rights and the Struggle for Change: A Study in Self-Critical Legal Thought. In R. Dickinson et al. (eds), *Examining Critical Perspectives on Human Rights*. (Cambridge: Cambridge University Press, 2012).

Bell, C. and Keenan, J. (2005) Lost on the Way Home? The Right to Life in Northern Ireland. *Journal of Law and Society*. 32(1): 68–89.

Bell, J. (1992) Discretionary Decision-Making: A Jurisprudential View. In K. Hawkins (ed.), *The Uses of Discretion* (Oxford: Oxford University Press).

Berger, J. and Zelditch, M. (1998) *Status, Power and Legitimacy*. (New Brunswick, NJ: Transaction).

Bittner, E. (1974). Florence Nightingale in Pursuit of Willie Sutton: A Theory of the Police. In. H. Jacob (ed.), *Potential for Reform of Criminal Justice*. (Beverley Hills, CA: Sage).

Bittner, E. (1990) *Aspects of Police Work*. (Boston: Northeastern University Press).

Black, R. (2015) Twelfth 2015: Smiles and aching feet as 100,000 defy rain. *Belfast Telegraph*, 14 July. https://www.belfasttelegraph.co.uk/news/twelfth/twelfth-2015-smiles-and-aching-feet-as-100000-defy-rain-31374549.html (accessed 8 December 2017).

Blaustein, J. (2015) *Speaking Truths to Power: Policy Ethnography and Police Reform in Bosnia and Herzegovina*. (Oxford: Oxford University Press).

Bosworth, M. (2011) Human Rights and Immigration Detention. In M.-B. Dembour and T. Kelly (eds), *Are Human Rights for Migrants? Critical Reflections on the Status of Irregular Migrants in Europe and the United States*. (Abingdon: Routledge).

Bosworth, M. and Hoyle, C. (2011) *What is Criminology?* (Oxford: Oxford University Press).

Bottomley, K., et al. (1991) The Detention of Suspects in Police Custody. *British Journal of Criminology*. 31(4): 347–64.

Bottoms, A. and Tankebe, J. (2012) Beyond Procedural Justice: A Dialogic Approach to Legitimacy in Criminal Justice. *Journal of Criminal Law and Criminology*. 102(1): 119–70.

Bottoms, A. and Tankebe, J. (2013) 'A Voice Within': Power-Holders' Perspectives on Authority and Legitimacy. In J. Tankebe and A. Liebling (eds), *Legitimacy and Criminal Justice: An International Exploration*. (Oxford: Oxford University Press), 60–82.

Bowling, B., and Phillips, C. (2007) Disproportionate and Discriminatory: Reviewing the Evidence on Police Stop and Search. *Modern Law Review*. 70(6): 936–61.

Bowling, B., Reiner, R. and Sheptycki, J. (2019) *The Politics of Policing*. (5th ed.) (Oxford: Oxford University Press).

Bradford, B. (2017) *Stop and Search and Police Legitimacy*. (Abingdon: Routledge).

Bradford, B. and Jackson, J. (2016) Enabling and constraining police power. In J. Jacobs and J. Jackson (eds), *The Routledge Handbook of Criminal Justice Ethics*. (Abingdon: Routledge).

Bradford, B. and Myhill, A. (2015) Triggers of Change to Public Confidence in the Police and Criminal Justice System: Findings from the Crime Survey for England and Wales Panel Experiment. *Criminology and Criminal Justice*. 15(1): 23–43.

Bradford, B. and Loader, I. (2016) Police, Crime and Order: The Case of Stop and Search. In B. Bradford et al. (eds), *The SAGE Handbook of Global Policing*. (London: Sage), 241–60.

Bradford, B. et al. (2019) Can Diversity Promote Trust? Neighbourhood Context and Trust in the Police in Northern Ireland. *Policing and Society*. 29(9): 1022–41.

Bradley, D. (2002) Memory is still the reason why Sinn Fein is boycotting the PSNI. *Irish Times*. 6 July.

Bradley, M. (2001) Flanagan does not expect to remain at helm of North's new police service for long. *Irish Times*. 3 November.

Brewer, J. (1984) Competing Understandings of Common Sense Understanding: A Brief Comment on 'Common Sense Racism'. *British Journal of Sociology*. 35(1): 66–74.

Brewer, J. and K. Magee (1991) *Inside the RUC: Routine Policing in a Divided Society*. (Oxford: Clarendon Press).

Britton, N.J. (2000) Race and Policing: A Study of Police Custody. *British Journal of Criminology*. 40(4): 639–58.

Brodeur, J-P. (1983). High Policing and Low Policing: Remarks about the Policing of Political Activities. *Social Problems*. 30(5): 507–20.

Brodeur, J.-P. (2010) *The Policing Web*. (New York: Oxford University Press).

Brodkin, E. 2008. Accountability in Street-Level Organizations. *International Journal of Public Administration*. 31(3): 317–36.

Brogden, M. (1999) Community Policing as Cherry Pie. In Mawby, R. (ed.), *Policing Across the World: Issues for the Twenty-first Century*. (Abingdon: Routledge).

Brogden, M., and Nijhar, P. (2005) *Community Policing National and International Models and Approaches*. (Portland, OR: Willan Publishing).

Bronitt, S. (2011) Reconciling policing mandates and human rights. Paper presented at 2011 Peter Allan Memorial Lecture at the University of Hong Kong. (On file with author).

Bronitt, S., O'Brien, M. and Bull, M. (2014) Linking Policing and Human rights: A Recent Invention or an Enduring Legacy? *Australian Journal of Human Rights*. 20(2): 1–7.

Bronitt, S. and Stenning, P. (2011) Understanding Discretion in Modern Policing. *Criminal Law Journal*. 35: 319–32.

Brown, D. (1997) *PACE Ten Years On: A Review of the Research Home Office Research Study No. 155*. (London: Home Office).

Brown, A. D., Stacey, P. and Nandhakumar, J. (2008) Making Sense of Sensemaking Narratives. *Human Relations*. 61(8): 1035–62.

Bruner, J. (1991) The Narrative Construction of Reality. *Critical Inquiry*. 18(Autumn): 1–21.

Bryan, D. (2000) *Orange Parades: The Politics of Ritual, Tradition and Control*. (London: Pluto Press).

Bryan, D. (2015). Parades, Flags, Carnivals, and Riots: Public Space, Contestation, and Transformation in Northern Ireland. *Peace and Conflict: Journal of Peace Psychology*. 21(4): 565–73.

Bullock, K. and Johnson, P. (2012) The Impact of the Human Rights Act on Policing in England and Wales. *British Journal of Criminology*. 52(3): 630–50.

Bushe, A. (2006) Getting PSNI's take on human rights. *News Letter*. 3 August.

Byrne, J., Jarman, N. and Topping, J. (2013) *Community Perspectives on Public Order Policing in Northern Ireland*. [On file with author].

Cain, M. (1973) *Society and the Policeman's Role*. (London: Routledge and Keegan).

Çali, B. and Meckled-García, S. (2006) Lost in Translation: the human rights ideal and international human rights law. In S Meckled-García and B Çali (eds), *The Legalization of Human Rights: Multidisciplinary Perspectives on Human Rights and Human Rights Law*. (Abingdon: Routledge).

Campeau, H. (2015) 'Police Culture' at Work: Making Sense of Police Oversight. *British Journal of Criminology*. 55(4): 669–87.

Campbell, L., Ashworth, A. and Redmayne, M. (2019) *The Criminal Process*. (Oxford: Oxford University Press).

Cape, E. (2008) PACE Then and Now: Twenty-one Years of 'Re-balancing'. In E. Cape and R. Young (eds), *Regulating Policing: The Police and Criminal Evidence Act 1984 Past, Present and Future*. (Oxford: Hart Publishing), 191–221.

Cape, E. (2017) The police bail provisions of the Policing and Crime Act 2017. *Criminal Law Review*. 8: 587–600.

Carruthers, M. (2013) *Alternative Ulsters: Conversations on Identity*. (Dublin: Liberties Press).

Chalmers, J. and Leverick, F. (2013) Tracking the Creation of Criminal Offences. *Criminal Law Review*. 543–60.

Chan, J. (1996) Changing Police Culture. *British Journal of Criminology*. 36(1): 109–34.

Chan, J. (2007) Making Sense of Police Reforms. *Theoretical Criminology*. 11(3): 325–45.

Chayes, A. and Chayes, A. (1985) Corporate Counsel and the Elite Law Firm. *Stanford Law Review*. 37(2): 277–300.

Chatterton, M. (1979) The Supervision of Patrol Work Under the Fixed Points System. In S. Holdaway (ed.), *The British Police*. (London: Edward Arnold).

Checkel, J. (2005). International Institutions and Socialization in Europe: Introduction and Framework. *International Organization*. 59(4): 801–26.

Chibnall, S. (1975) The Crime Reporter: A Study in the Production of Commercial Knowledge. *Sociology*. 9(1): 49–66.

Cohen, S. (1993) Human Rights and the Crimes of the State: The Culture of Denial. *Australia and New Zealand Journal of Criminology* 26(2): 97–115.

Cohen, S. (2001) *States of Denial: Knowing about Atrocities and Suffering*. (Cambridge: Polity)

Choongh, S. (1997) *Policing as Social Discipline*. (Oxford: Clarendon).

Christie, N. (1986) The Ideal Victim. In Fattah, E. (ed.), *From Crime Policy to Victim Policy*. (Basingstoke: Palgrave Macmillan).

Cobain, I. (2014) Delay, delay, delay: Northern Ireland Troubles inquests still outstanding. *The Guardian*. 13 April. https://www.theguardian.com/uk-news/2014/apr/13/delay-northern-ireland-troubles-inquests-outstanding (accessed 5 December 2017).

Cohen, S. (1996) Government Responses to Human Rights Reports: Claims, Denials, and Counterclaims. *Human Rights Quarterly*. 18(3): 517–43.

Cohen-Eliya, M. and Porat, I. (2011) Proportionality and the Culture of Justification. *American Journal of Comparative Law*. 59(2): 463–90.

Collantes-Celador, G. and Schwandner-Sievers, S. (2019) Introduction to Special Section on 'Police Reform and Human rights in the Western Balkans'. *International Journal of Human Rights*. 23(4): 447–53.

College of Policing (2014a) National Policing Curriculum, C3 Public Order: Bronze Commander, Version 2.01. (Coventry: College of Policing).

College of Policing (2014b) National Policing Curriculum, C2 Public Order: Silver Commander, Version 2.01. (Coventry: College of Policing).

College of Policing (2016a) National Police Public Order Training Curriculum, Guidance for Trainers, Module A2—Underpinning Public Order Knowledge Version 1.2. (Coventry: College of Policing).

College of Policing (2016b) *Bail Report: Pre-Charge Bail—An Exploratory Study*. (Coventry: College of Policing).

Committee on the Administration of Justice (1988) *The Stalker Affair: More Questions Than Answers Pamphlet No.10*. (Belfast: CAJ).

Committee on the Administration of Justice (1991) *Allegations of Ill-Treatment in Castlereagh*. (Belfast: CAJ).

Committee on the Administration of Justice (2015) *What is Going on at the Policing Board?* (Belfast: CAJ).

Committee on the Administration of Justice (2016) *How Public Order Policing Works in Northern Ireland: Standards and Accountability*. (Belfast: CAJ).

Connolly, A. (2013) Human rights no impediment to policing riots. *Belfast Telegraph*. 17 September.

Cordner, G. (2014) Community Policing. In M. Reisig and R. Kane (eds), *The Oxford Handbook of Police and Policing*. (Oxford: Oxford University Press).

Cory, P. (2004) *Cory Collusion Inquiry Report: Patrick Finucane*. (London: The Stationery Office).

Cote-Lussier, C. (2013) Narratives of Legitimacy: Police Expansionism and the Contest Over Policing. *Policing and Society*. 23(2): 183–203.

Cotterrell, R. (1997) *Law's Community: Legal Theory in Sociological Perspective*. (Oxford: Clarendon Press).

Cotterrell, R. (1998) Why Must Legal Ideas Be Interpreted Sociologically? *Journal of Law and Society*. 25(2): 171–92.

Cotterrell, R. (2006) *Law, Culture and Society: Legal Ideas in the Mirror of Social Theory*. (Aldershot: Ashgate).

Cowell, D. and Cowell, K. (1999) Human Rights as Conflict Management: The Unionist use of Human Rights Language in Northern Ireland. *Nationalism and Ethnic Politics*. 5(1): 1–28.

Cramphorn, C. (2001) Human Rights and Policing – Accountability. *Police Research and Management*. 5(3): 29–36.

Crawford, A. (2008) Dispersal Power and the Symbolic Role of Anti-Social Behaviour Legislation. *Modern Law Review*. 71(5):753–84.

Crawshaw, R., Cullen, S. and Williamson, T. (2007) *Human Rights and Policing*. (2nd ed.) (Leiden/Boston: Martinus Nijhoff).

Criminal Justice Inspectorate of Northern Ireland (2009) *Policing with the Community: An inspection of the Policing with the Community in Northern Ireland*. (Belfast: CJINI).

Criminal Justice Inspectorate of Northern Ireland (2012) *Policing with the Community: A follow-up review of inspection recommendations*. (Belfast: CJINI).

Criminal Justice Inspection for Northern Ireland (2013) *A Review of the Cost and Impact of Dealing with the Past on Criminal Justice Organizations in Northern Ireland*. (Belfast: CJINI).

Criminal Justice Inspection for Northern Ireland (2016) *Coronial Processes: An inspection of the arrangements in place in the Police Service of Northern Ireland to manage and disclose information in support of the Coronial process in Northern Ireland*. (Belfast: CJINI).

Cronin, P. and Reicher, S. (2006) A Study of the Factors that Influence how Senior Officers Police Crowd Events: On SIDE Outside the Laboratory. *British Journal of Social Psychology*. 45(1): 175–96.

Cronin, P. and Reicher, S. (2009) Accountability Processes and Group Dynamics: A SIDE Perspective on the Policing of an Anti-Capitalist Riot. *European Journal of Social Psychology*. 39(2): 237–54.

Cunningham, C. (1992) The Lawyer as Translator, Representation as Text: Towards an Ethnography of Legal Discourse. *Cornell Law Review*. 77: 1298–387.

Curtis, J. (2014) *Human Rights as War by Other Means*. (Pennsylvania: University of Pennsylvania Press).

de Lint, W. (2017) Bent to Good Authorities? Human Rights, Authoritarian Neoliberalism and Consent Policing. In L Weber, E Fishwick and M Marmo (eds), *The Routledge International Handbook of Criminology and Human Rights*. (Abingdon: Routledge).

de Londras, F. (2017) The DUP's Worrying Human Rights Record. *Oxford Human Rights Hub Blog*. 13 June. http://ohrh.law.ox.ac.uk/the-dups-worrying-human-rights-record/ (accessed 14 December 2017).

de Silva, D. (2012) *The Report of the Patrick Finucane Review: Volumes I and II*. (London: The Stationery Office).

de Witte, B. (2012) New Institutions for Promoting Equality in Europe: Legal Transfers, National Bricolage and European Governance. *American Journal of Comparative Law*. 60(1): 49–74 .

Dehaghani, R. (2016) 'He's Just Not That Vulnerable': Exploring the Implementation of the Appropriate Adult Safeguard in Police Custody. *Howard Journal of Crime and Justice*. 55(4): 396–413.

Dehaghani, R. (2017) Automatic Authorisation: An Exploration of the Decision to Detain in Police Custody. *Criminal Law Review*. 3: 187–202.

Dembour, M. (2010) What are Human Rights? Four Schools of Thought. *Human Rights Quarterly*. 32(1): 1–20.

Democratic Unionist Party (2018) Response to Government Consultation on 'Addressing the Legacy of Northern Ireland's Past'. 5 October. http://www.mydup.com/images/uploads/publications/DUP_Response_to_NIO_Legacy_Consultation.pdf (accessed 5 July 2020).

Dempster, S. (2001) New Chapter for Policing in Ulster. *News Letter*. 8 November.

Dick, P. (2005) Dirty Work Designations: How Police Officers Account for their Use of Coercive Force. *Human Relations*. 58(11): 1363–90.

Dickson, B. (2000) The Protection of Human Rights: Lesson from Northern Ireland, *The Paul Sieghart Memorial Lecture 2000*. British Institute of Human Rights, King's College, London. 6 April.

Dickson, B. (2009) Counter-Insurgency and Human Rights in Northern Ireland. *Journal of Strategic Studies*. 32(3): 475–93.

Dickson, B. (2010) *The European Convention on Human Rights and the Conflict in Northern Ireland*. (Oxford: University Press).

Dickson, B. (2013) *Human Rights and the United Kingdom Supreme Court*. (Oxford: Oxford University Press).

Dickson, D. and Osborne, R. (2007) Equality and Human Rights since the Agreement. In P. Carmichael, C. Knox and R. Osborne (eds), *Devolution and Constitutional Change in Northern Ireland* (Manchester: Manchester University Press).

Dixon, D. (1996) Reform of Policing by Legal Regulation: International Experience in Criminal Investigation. *Current Issues in Criminal Justice*. 7(3): 287–301.

Dixon, D. (1992) Legal Regulation and Policing Practice. *Social & Legal Studies*. 1(4): 515–41.

Dixon, D. (1997) *Law in Policing*. (Oxford: Oxford University Press).

Dixon, D. (2005) Beyond Zero Tolerance. In T Newburn (ed), *Policing: Key Readings*. (1st ed.) (Cullompton: Willan Publishing), 483–507.

Dixon, D. (2007) Changing Law, Changing Policing. In M. Mitchell and J. Casey (eds), *Police Leadership and Management*. (Sydney: The Federation Press).

Dixon, D. (2008) Authorise and Regulate: A Comparative Perspective on the Rise and Fall of a Regulatory Strategy. In E. Cape and R. Young (eds), *Regulating Policing: The Police and Criminal Evidence Act 1984 Past, Present and Future*. (Oxford: Hart Publishing), 21–45.

Dixon, D. (2012) Book Review: Layla Skinns, Police Custody: Governance, Legitimacy and Reform in the Criminal Justice Process. *Australian and New Zealand Journal of Criminology*. 45(2): 279–81.

Dixon, D. et al. (1990) Safeguarding the Rights of Suspects in Police Custody. *Policing and Society*. 1(2): 115–40.

Donnelly, J. (2006) The Virtues of Legalization. In S. Meckled-García and B. Çali (eds), *The Legalization of Human Rights: Multidisciplinary Perspectives on Human Rights and Human Rights Law*. (Abingdon: Routledge).

Donnelly, J. (2007) The Relative Universality of Human Rights. *Human Rights Quarterly*. 29(2): 281–306.

Douzinas, C. (2012) The Poverty of (Rights) Jurisprudence. In C. Gearty and C. Douzinas (eds), *The Cambridge Companion to Human Rights Law*. (Cambridge: Cambridge University Press).

Douzinas, C. and Gearty, C. (2012) Introduction. In C. Gearty and C. Douzinas (eds), *The Cambridge Companion to Human Rights Law*. (Cambridge: Cambridge University Press).

Doyle, A., Chan, J. and Haggery, K. D. (2011) Transcending the Boundaries of Criminology: The Example of Richard Ericson. In M Bosworth and C Hoyle (eds), *What is Criminology?* (Oxford: Oxford University Press).

Drisko, J. and Maschi, T. (2016) *Content Analysis*. (New York: Oxford University Press).

Dudai, R. (2017) Entryism, Mimicry and Victimhood Work: The Adoption of Human Rights Discourse by Right-Wing Groups in Israel. *International Journal of Human Rights*. 21(7): 866–88.

Durkan, M. (2003) Policing is key to breaking the deadlock in Northern Ireland. *The Guardian*. 18 August. https://www.theguardian.com/politics/2003/aug/18/northernireland.northernireland (accessed 5 December 2017).

Easton, M. (2014) 'Blind Spot' Policing in Belgian Multicultural Neighbourhoods and the Implications for Human Rights. *Australian Journal of Human Rights*. 20(2): 19–38.

Edelman, L. and Suchman, M. (1999) When the 'Haves' Hold Court: Speculations on the Organizational Internalization of Law. *Law and Society Review*. 33(4): 941–92.

Eisenberg, E. M. (1984) Ambiguity as Strategy in Organizational Communication. *Communication Monographs*. 51: 227–42.

Elliot, T. (2017) Tom Elliott: For balance over the past, we need new legacy processes that include the inquests. *News Letter*. 24 February.

http://www.newsletter.co.uk/news/opinion/tom-elliott-for-balance-over-the-past-we-need-new-legacy-processes-that-include-the-inquests-1-7837384 (accessed 8 December 2017).

Ellison, G. (2010) Police-Community Relations in Northern Ireland: Towards an Ecological Analysis. In J Doyle (ed), *Policing the Narrow Ground: Lessons for the transformation of policing in Northern Ireland*. (Dublin: Royal Irish Academy) 242–76.

Ellison, G. and Mulcahy, A. (2001) Policing and Social Conflict in Northern Ireland. *Policing and Society*. 11: 243–58.

Ellison, G. and O'Rawe, M. (2010) Security Governance in Transition: The Compartmentalising, Crowding Out and Corralling of Policing and Security in Northern Ireland. *Theoretical Criminology*. 14(1): 31–57.

Ellison, G. and O'Reilly, C. (2008) 'Ulster's Policing Goes Global': The Police Reform Process in Northern Ireland and the Creation of a Global Brand. *Crime, Law and Social Change*. 50(4): 331–51.

Ellison, G. and Pino, N. (2012) *Globalization, Police Reform and Development: Doing it the Western Way?* (London: Palgrave Macmillan).

Ellison, G. and Smyth, J. (2000) *The Crowned Harp: Policing Northern Ireland*. (London: Pluto).

Ellison, G., Pino, W. and Shirlow, P. (2012) Assessing the Determinants of Public Confidence in the Police: A Case Study of a Post-Conflict Community in Northern Ireland. *Criminology and Criminal Justice* 13(5): 552–76.

Emerson, B., Ashworth, A. and Macdonald, A. (2012) *Human Rights and Criminal Justice*. (3rd ed.) (London: Sweet and Maxwell).

Emerson, N. (2014) Opinion – Grotesque Reading of Human Rights Law. *Irish News*. 12 June.

Emerson, R. and Paley, B. (1992) Organizational Horizons and Complaint-Filing. In K Hawkins (ed.), *The Uses of Discretion*. (Oxford: Oxford University Press).

Engle, K. (2001) From Scepticism to Embrace: Human Rights and the American Anthropological Association from 1947—1999. *Human Rights Quarterly*. 23(3): 536–59.

English, R. (2016) Keynote speech, Reflecting and Refocusing: 15 years on. Queen's University Belfast. 3 November.

Ericson, R. (1981) *Making Crime: A Study of Detective Work*. (London: Butterworths).

Ericson, R. (1996) Why Law is Like News. In D Nelken (ed), *Law as Communication*. (Aldershot: Dartmouth), 195–231.

Ericson, R. (2007). Rules in Policing. *Theoretical Criminology*. 11(3): 367–401.

Ericson, R. and Haggerty, K. (1997) *Policing the Risk Society*. (Oxford: Clarendon Press).

Ericson, R., Baranek, P. and Chan, J. (1989) *Negotiating Control: A Study of New Sources*. (Milton Keynes: Open University Press).
Evans, C and Evans, S. (2011) Messages from the Front Line: Parliamentarians' Perspectives on Rights Protection. In T. Campbell, K. Ewing and A. Tomkins, (eds), *The Legal Protection of Human Rights; Sceptical Essays*. (Oxford: Oxford University Press).
Ewick, P. and Sibley, S. S. (1998) *The Common Place of Law: Stories from Everyday Life*. (Chicago and London: University of Chicago Press).
Feldman, M. (1992) Social Limits to Discretion: An Organizational Perspective. In K Hawkins (ed.), *The Uses of Discretion*. (Oxford: Oxford University Press).
Felner, E. (2012) Human Rights Leaders in Conflict Situations: A Case Study of the Politics of 'Moral Entrepreneurs'. *Journal of Human Rights Practice*. 4(1): 57–81.
Fenwick, H. (2009) Marginalising Human rights: Breach of the Peace, 'Kettling', the Human Rights Act and Public Protest. *Public Law*. (Oct): 737–65.
Flanagan, R. (2008) *The Review of Policing: Final Report*. (London: Home Office).
Foster, J. (2003) Police Cultures. In Newburn, T. (ed.), *Handbook of Policing*. (Cullompton: Willan Publishing).
Fredman, S. (2012) Breaking the Mold: Equality as a Proactive Duty. *American Journal of Comparative Law* 60(1): 265–87.
Fredman, S. (2013) From Dialogue to Deliberation: Human Rights Adjudication and Prisoners' Rights to Vote. *Public Law*. 292–311.
Freeman, M. (2011) *Human Rights: An Interdisciplinary Approach*. (2nd ed.) (Cambridge: Polity Press).
Fudge, J. and Glasbeek, H. (1992) The Politics of Rights: A Politics with Little Class. *Social and Legal Studies*. 1(1): 45–70.
Garland, D. (1997) Of Crimes and Criminals: The Development of Criminology in Britain. In M. Maguire et al. (eds), *The Oxford Handbook of Criminology*. (2nd ed.) (Oxford: Oxford University Press).
Garland, D. (2011) Criminology's Place in the Academic Field. In M Bosworth and C Hoyle (eds), *What is Criminology?* (Oxford: Oxford University Press).
Gearty, C. (2006) *Can Human Rights Survive?* (Cambridge: Cambridge University Press).
Gearty, C. (2016) Neo-democracy: 'Useful Idiot' of Neo-liberalism? *British Journal of Criminology*. 56(6): 1087–106.
Geertz, C. (1975) Common Sense as a Cultural System. *Antioch Review*. 33(1): 5–26.
Gerth, H. and Mills, C. (1946) *From Max Weber: Essays in Sociology*. (New York: Oxford University Press).
Gewirth, A. (1982) *Human Rights: Essays on Justification and Applications*. (Chicago: University of Chicago Press).

Gibbs, P. and Ratcliffe, F. (2020) *24 Hours in Police Custody – is Police Detention Overused?* (London: Transform Justice).

Gilbert, P. (2018) *Human Dignity and Human Rights*. (Oxford: Oxford University Press).

Gilmore, J., Jackson, W. and Monk, H. (2019) 'That is Not Facilitating Peaceful Protest. That is Dismantling the Protest': Anti-Fracking Protesters' Experiences of Dialogue Policing and Mass Arrest.' *Policing and Society*. 29(1): 36–51.

Glover, R. (2018) Keeping the Peace and Preventive Justice – A New Test for Breach of the Peace? *Public Law* 444–460.

Goffman, E. (1959) *The Presentation of Self in Everyday Life*. (London: Penguin).

Goldberg, S. (2015) Obergefell at the Intersection of Civil Rights and Social Movements. *California Law Review Circuit*. 6 157–65.

Gomez and Tonge, J. (2016) New Members as Party Modernisers: The Case of the Democratic Unionist Party in Northern Ireland. *Electoral Studies*. 42: 65–74.

Goodale, M. (2006) Toward a Critical Anthropology of Human Rights. *Current Anthropology*. 47(3): 485–511.

Goodale, M. (2007) Locating Rights, Envisioning Law Between the Global and the Local. In M. Goodale and S. Engle (eds), *The Practice of Human Rights: Tracking Law Between the Global and the Local*. (New York: Cambridge).

Goodman-Delahunty, J., Beckley, A. and Martin, M. (2014) Complaints Against the New South Wales Police Force: Analysis of Risks and Rights in Reported Police Conduct. *Australian Journal of Human Rights*. 20(2): 81–105.

Goold, B. (2016) Policing and Human Rights. In B. Bradford et al. (eds), *The SAGE Handbook of Global Policing*. (London: Sage), 226–40.

Goodman, A. (2018) *How Judges Decide Cases* (London. Wildy, Simmonds and Hill Publishing).

Goodale, M. and Merry, S. (eds) (2007) *Transnationalism and the New Legal Order: Tracking Rights between the Global and the Local*. (Cambridge: Cambridge University Press).

Gorringe, H., Rosie, M., Waddingon, D. and Kominou, M. (2012) Facilitating Ineffective Protest? The Policing of the 2009 Edinburgh NATO. *Policing and Society*. 22(2): 115–32.

Gready, P. and Phillips, B. (2009) An Unfinished Enterprise: Visions, Reflections, and an Invitation. *Journal of Human Rights Practice*. 1(1): 1–13.

Grear, A. (2012) 'Framing the Project' of International Human Rights Law. In C. Gearty and C. Douzinas (eds), *The Cambridge Companion to Human Rights Law*. (Cambridge: Cambridge University Press).

Greer, S. (2009) Being 'Realistic' About Human Rights. *Northern Ireland Legal Quarterly*. 60(2): 147–61.

Grewal, K. and Munasinghe, V. (2016) Human Rights and Everyday Practices of Policing in Post-War Sri Lanka. In L. Weber, E. Fishwick and M. Marmo (eds), *The Routledge International Handbook of Criminology and Human Rights*. (Abingdon: Routledge).

Habermas, J. (1992) *Between Facts and Norms: Contributions to a discourse theory of law and democracy*. (Cambridge, MA: MIT Press).

Hadden, T. (2012) War and Peace in Northern Ireland: Reflections on the Contribution of Academic and Human Rights Communities. In G. Gilbert, F. Hampson and C. Sandoval (eds), *Strategic Visions for Human Rights: Essays in Honour of Professor Kevin Boyle*. (Oxford: Routledge).

Hall, S. et al. (1978) *Policing the Crisis: Mugging, the State and Law and Order*. (London: Macmillan).

Halliday, D. and Ferguson, N. (2016) When Peace is Not Enough: The Flag Protests, the Politics of Identity & Belonging in East Belfast. *Irish Political Studies*. 31(4): 525–40.

Hambly, D. (2014) Police and Human Rights: 1963 and 2013. *Australian Journal of Human Rights*. 20(2): 9–17.

Hamilton, G. (2014a) *Human dignity in a rights-based decision-making framework*. Dignity and Rights: A Framework for the Future, 4 December 2014. (Belfast, Human Rights Consortium) https://audioboom.com/posts/2704208-dignityandrights-chiefconpsni-human-dignity-in-a-rights-based-decision-making-framework (accessed 5 December 2017).

Hamilton, G. (2014b) *Pubic Session, Monthly Meeting, Northern Ireland Policing Board*, December.

Hamilton, G. (2015a) *Public Session, Northern Ireland Policing Board*, March.

Hamilton, G. (2015b) *Public Session, Northern Ireland Policing Board*, December.

Hamilton, G. (2015c) *Public Session, Northern Ireland Policing Board*, April.

Hamilton, G. (2016a) *100th Graduation Ceremony*. Belfast: Police Service of Northern Ireland. https://www.psni.police.uk/globalassets/news-and-appeals/latest-news/news-stories/2016/april/010416-100th-graduation/cc-speech-100th-graduation.pdf (accessed 5 December 2017).

Hamilton, G. (2016b) *The Role of the Human Rights Act in policing in Northern Ireland*. Northern Ireland Human Rights Consortium Conference. 26 February (Belfast: Police Service of Northern Ireland).

Hamilton, G. (2016c) *Launch of the Annual Human Rights Report*. Crumlin Road Gaol, Belfast. 7 September.

Harris, D. (2016) *Police Service of Northern Ireland Budget and Funding Issues: Police Service of Northern Ireland*. Oral Comments, Committee for Justice, Northern Ireland Assembly, 25 February.

Hart, H. L. A. (1961) *The Concept of Law*. (Oxford: Oxford University Press).

Harvey, C. (2000) Governing after the Rights Revolution. *Journal of Law and Society*. 27 (1) 61–97.

Harvey, C (2001) Building Bridges? Protecting Human Rights in Northern Ireland. *Human Rights Law Review*. 1(2): 243–64.

Harvey, C. (2012) Contextualised Equality and the Politics of Legal Mobilisation: Affirmative Action in Northern Ireland. *Social & Legal Studies*. 21(1): 23–50.

Harvey, C. (2015) Bringing Humanity Home: A Transformational Human Rights Culture for Northern Ireland? In A.-M. McAlinden and C. Dwyer (eds), *Criminal Justice in Transition: The Northern Ireland Context*. (Oxford: Hart Publishing).

Harvey, C. (2017) What Price Human Rights and Equality in Northern Ireland? *Oxford Human Rights Hub Blog*. 16 June. http://ohrh.law.ox.ac.uk/what-price-human-rights-and-equality-in-northern-ireland/ (accessed 14 December 2017).

Harvey, C. and Schwartz, A. (2009) Designing a Bill of Rights for Northern Ireland. *Northern Ireland Legal Quarterly*. 60(2): 181–99.

Hastrup, K. (2003) Representing the Common Good: The Limits of Legal Language. In R. Wilson and J. Mitchell (eds), *Human Rights in Global Perspective: Anthropological Studies*. (Oxford: Routledge), 16–33.

Hatch. M.J and Schultz, M. (2002) The Dynamics of Organizational Identity. *Human Relations*. 55(8): 989–1018.

Hawkins, K. (1992) The Use of Legal Discretion: Perspectives from Law and Social Science. In K. Hawkins (eds), *The Uses of Discretion*. (Oxford: Oxford University Press).

Hawkins, K. (2002) *Law as Last Resort*. (Oxford: Oxford University Press).

HC Deb (2014–2015) 30 June 2015. c417WH. https://www.publications.parliament.uk/pa/cm201516/cmhansrd/cm150630/halltext/150630h0002.htm (accessed 8 December 2017).

Hearty, K. (2014) A Shared Narrative? A Case Study of the Contested Legacy of Policing in the North of Ireland. *British Journal of Criminology*. 54(6): 1047–66.

Hearty, K. (2015) The Great Awakening? The Belfast Flag Protests and Protestant/Unionist/Loyalist Counter-Memory in Northern Ireland. *Irish Political Studies*. 157–77.

Hearty, K. (2016) Legislating Hierarchies of Victimhood and Perpetrators: The Civil Service (Special Advisers) Act (Northern Ireland) 2013 and the Meta-Conflict. 25(3) *Socio-Legal Studies*. 333–53.

Hearty, K. (2017) *Critical Engagement: Irish Republicanism, Memory Politics and Policing*. (Liverpool: Liverpool University Press).

Hearty, K. (2018) Discourses of Political Policing in Post-Patten Northern Ireland. *Critical Criminology*. 26: 129–43.

Hedberg, B. (1981) How Organizations Learn and Unlearn. In P. C. Nystrom and W. H. Starbuck (eds), *Handbook of Organizational Design*. (New York: Oxford University Press).

Henderson, D. and Little, I. (2018) *Reporting the Troubles: Journalists tell their stories of the Northern Ireland conflict*. (Newtownards: Blackstaff Press).

Her Majesty's Inspectorate of Constabulary (2009) *Adapting to Protest – Nurturing the British Model of Policing*. (London: HMIC).

Her Majesty's Inspectorate of Constabulary (2011) *Policing Public Order, An Overview and Review of Progress Against the Recommendations of Adapting to Protest and Nurturing the British Model of Policing*. (London: HMIC).

Her Majesty's Inspectorate of Constabulary (2013) *Inspection of the Police Service of Northern Ireland Historical Enquiries Team*. (London: HMIC).

Her Majesty's Inspectorate of Constabulary (2015) *A Follow-Up Inspection of the Police Service of Northern Ireland Historical Enquiries Team*.

Hillyard, P. (1988) Political and Social Dimensions of Emergency Law in Northern Ireland. In A Jennings (ed), *Justice Under Fire: The Abuse of Civil Liberties in Northern Ireland*. (London: Pluto Press), 191–212.

Hillyard, P. (1993) *Suspect Community*. (London: Pluto Press).

Hillyard, P. and Gordon, D. (1999) Arresting Statistics: The Drift to Informal Justice in England and Wales. *Journal of Law and Society*. 26(4): 502–22.

Hillyard, P. and Tomlinson, M. (2000) Patterns of Policing and Policing Patten. *Journal of Law and Society*. 27(3): 394–415.

Hoffmann, F. (2012) Foundations Beyond Law. In C. Gearty and C. Douzinas (eds), *The Cambridge Companion to Human Rights Law*. (Cambridge: Cambridge University Press).

Holdaway, S. (1983) *Inside the British Police: A Force at Work*. (Oxford: Basil Blackwell).

Holdaway, S. (1986). Police and Social Work Relations – Problems and Possibilities. *British Journal of Social Work*. 16(2): 137–160.

Hopkins, S. (2015) Sinn Féin, the Past and Political Strategy: The Provisional Irish Republican Movement and the Politics of Reconciliation. *Irish Political Studies*. 30(1): 79–97.

Hornberger, J. (2010) Human Rights and Policing: Exigency or Incongruence? *Annual Review of Law and Social Science*. 6: 259–83.

Hornberger, J. (2011) *Policing and Human Rights: The Meaning of Violence and Justice in the Everyday Policing of Johannesburg*. (Abingdon: Routledge).

Home Office (1999) *The Stephen Lawrence Inquiry: Report of an Inquiry by Sir William Macpherson of Cluny*, Cm 4262-I.

Home Office (2004) *Policing: Modernising Police Powers to Meet Community Needs*. (London: Home Office).

House of Commons Defence Committee (2017) *Investigations into Fatalities in Northern Ireland Involving British Military Personnel*. Seventh Report of Session 2016–2017 (London: House of Commons).

Hughes, E. (1951). Work and the Self. In J Rohrer and M Sherif (eds) *Social Psychology at the Crossroads*. (New York: Harper and Brothers), 313–23.

Hughes, E. (1958). *Men and their Work*. (Glencoe, IL: Free Press).

Hucklesby, A. (2015) *Pre-charge Bail: A Response to a Consultation on the Introduction of Statutory Time Limits and Related Changes*.

Human Rights Watch (1997) *To Serve Without Favor: Policing, Human Rights, and Accountability in Northern Ireland*. (Helsinki: Human Rights Watch).

Humphreys, B. and Brown, A. D. (2002) Narratives of Organizational Identity and Identification: A Case Study of Hegemony and Resistance. *Organization Studies* 23(3): 421–47.

Hunt, M. (1999) The Human Rights Act and Legal Culture: The Judiciary and the Legal Profession. *Journal of Law and Society*. 26(1): 86–102.

Hunt, M. (2010) The Impact of the Human Rights Act on the Legislature: A Diminution of Democracy or a New Voice for Parliament? *European Human Rights Law Review*. 6: 601–8

Ignatieff, M. (2001) *Human Rights as Politics and Idolatry*. (Princeton, Princeton University Press).

Independent Commission on Policing in Northern Ireland (ICP) (1999) *A New Beginning: Policing in Northern Ireland—The Report of the Independent Commission on Policing in Northern Ireland*.

Irish News (2005) PSNI hosts human rights conference. 28 February.

Irish News (2008a) Religion was never an issue for retiring top Catholic policeman Assistant Chief Constable Peter Sheridan, the PSNI's most senior Catholic officer, is preparing to leave policing after more than 30 years. He spoke to Allison Morris. 29 July.

Irish News (2008b) Police under Fire over Tasers, 11 January.

Irvine, A. (1998) The Development of Human Rights in Britain under an Incorporated Convention on Human Rights. *Public Law* 221–36.

Jackson, J. (2007) Rights to Indigenous Culture in Colombia. In M. Goodale and S. Merry (eds), *Transnationalism and the New Legal Order: Tracking Rights between the Global and the Local*. (Cambridge: Cambridge University Press), 204–41.

Jackson, J. and Bradford, B. (2009) Crime, Policing and Social Order: On the Expressive Nature of Public Confidence in Policing. *British Journal of Sociology*. 60(3): 493–521.

Jackson, J. and Bradford, B. (2010) What is Trust and Confidence in the Police? *Policing: A Journal of Policy and Practice*. 4(3): 241–48.

Jackson, J. and Sunshine, J. (2007) Public Confidence in Policing: A Neo-Durkheimian Perspective. *British Journal of Criminology*. 47(2): 214–233.

James, M. and Pearson, G. (2015) Public Order and the Rebalancing of Football Fans' Rights: Legal Problems with Pre-emptive Policing Strategies and Banning Orders. *Public Law*. (Jul) 458–75.

Jarman, N. (1997) *Material Conflicts: Parades and Visual Displays in Northern Ireland*. (Oxford: Berg Publishers).

Jarman, N. (2000) For God and Ulster: Blood and Thunder Bands and Loyalist Political Culture. In T. Fraser (ed), *The Irish Parading Tradition: Following the Drum*. (Basingstoke: Palgrave Macmillan), 158–72.

Jarman, N. (2006) Policing, Policy and Practice: Responding to Disorder in North Belfast. *Anthropology in Action*. 13(1–2): 11–21.

Jarman, N. and Bryan, D. (1998) *From Riots to Rights: Nationalist Parades in North of Ireland*. (University of Ulster).

Johnston, A. (2001). Treating International Institutions as Social Environments. *International Studies Quarterly*. 45(4): 487–515.

Joint Committee on Human Rights (2009) *Demonstrating Respect for Rights? Follow–up*. 22nd Report of 2008–2009. (London: The Stationary Office).

Joint Committee on Human Rights (2015) *Human Rights Judgments*. 7th Report (London: The Stationary Office).

Kalberg, S. (2002) *The Protestant Ethic and the Spirit of Capitalism, Max Weber*. (Los Angeles: Roxbury Publishing Company).

Kavanagh, A. (2004) The Role of a Bill of Rights in Reconstructing Northern Ireland. *Human Rights Quarterly*. 26(4): 956–82.

Kavanagh, A. (2015) The Joint Committee on Human Rights: A Hybrid Breed of Constitutional Watchdog. In M. Hunt, H. Hooper and P. Yowell (eds), *Parliaments and Human Rights: Redressing the Democratic Deficit* (London: Hart Publishing).

Kearney, V. (2014) NI's chief constable accused of obstructing Troubles' investigations, 3 June. *BBC News*. http://www.bbc.co.uk/news/uk-northern-ireland-27682154 (accessed 7 December 2017).

Kelling, G. L. and Coles, C. M. (1996) *Fixing Broken Windows: Restoring Order and Reducing Crime in Our Communities*. (New York: Free Press).

Kelly, M. (2002) *An Evaluation of Human Rights Training for Student Police Officers in the Police Service of Northern Ireland*. (Belfast: NIHRC).

Kelly, G. (2017) Contract of Policing Board Human Rights Advisor should not be terminated – Kelly. http://www.sinnfein.ie/contents/46327 (accessed 6 February 2018).

Kemp, V. (2014) PACE, Performance Targets and Legal Protections. *Criminal Law Review*. 4: 278–97.

Kemp, V., Pascoe, P. and Balmer, N. (2011) Children, Young People and Requests for Police Station Legal Advice: 25 years after PACE. *Youth Justice*. 11(1): 28–46.

Kendall, J. (2018) *Regulating Police Detention: Voices from behind Closed Doors*. (Bristol: Bristol University Press).

Kennedy, D. (1991) A Semiotics of Legal Argument. *Syracuse Law Review*. 42: 75–116.

Kennedy, D. (2002) The International Human Rights Movement: Part of the Problem? *Harvard Human Rights Journal*. 15: 101–25.

Kilpatrick, C. (2014) Baptism of fire as PSNI's new Chief Constable to take up post at marching season's peak. *Belfast Telegraph*. 3 June.

Kilpatrick, A. (2016) Launch of Human Rights Annual Report, Crumlin Road Gaol. Belfast. Speech. 7 September.

Kilpatrick, A. (2018) *A Human Rights-Based Approach to Policing in Ireland*. (Dublin: Irish Council for Civil Liberties).

Kinkaid, S. (2001) Is Your Police Service a Human Rights Champion? *Police Research and Management*. 5(3): 13–18.

Klug, F. (2000) *Values for a Godless Age: The Story of the United Kingdom's New Bill of Rights*. (London: Penguin).

Klug, F. (2019) The Universal Declaration of Human Rights at Seventy: Rejuvenate or Retire? *Political Quarterly* 90(3): 356–67.

Klug, F. and Starmer, K. (2005) Standing Back from the Human Rights Act: How Effective is it Five Years on? *Public Law* 716–28.

Koch, I. (2018) *Personalizing the State: An Anthropology of Law, Politics, and Welfare in Austerity Britain*. (Oxford: Oxford University Press).

Koci, A. and Gjuraj, T. (2019) The Relationship between Community Policing and Human Rights in Albania's Police Reform. *International Journal of Human Rights* 23(4): 512–530.

Kreiner, E., Ashforth, B. and Sluss, D. (2006). Identity Dynamics in Occupational Dirty Work: Integrating Social Identity and System Justification Perspectives. *Organization Science*. 17(5): 619–36.

Lacey, N. (1992) The Jurisprudence of Discretion: Escaping the Legal Paradigm. In K Hawkins (ed), *The Uses of Discretion*. (Oxford: Oxford University Press).

Lamb, M. (2013) Ethno-nationalist Conflict, Participation and Human Rights-based Solidarity in Northern Ireland. *International Journal of Human Rights*. 17 (7–8): 723–38.

Lawther, C. (2010) 'Securing' the Past: Policing and the Contest over Truth in Northern Ireland. *British Journal of Criminology*. 50(3): 455–73.

Lawther, C. (2013) Denial, Silence and the Politics of the Past: Unpicking the Opposition to Truth Recovery in Northern Ireland. *International Journal of Transitional Justice*. 7(1): 157–77.

Lawther, C. (2014) *Truth, Denial and Transition: Northern Ireland and The Contested Past*. (Abingdon: Routledge).

Lazarus, L. (2004) *Contrasting Prisoners' Rights: A Comparative Examination of England and Germany*. (Oxford: Oxford University Press).

Lazarus, L. (2012) Positive Obligations and Criminal Justice: Duties to Protect or Coerce? In L. Zedner and J. V. Roberts (eds), *Principles and Values in Criminal Law and Criminal Justice: Essays in Honour of Andrew Ashworth*. (Oxford: Oxford University Press).

Lazarus, L. (2017) Human Rights and Counterterrorism. *Oxford Human Rights Hub Blog*, 19 June. http://ohrh.law.ox.ac.uk/human-rights-and-counterterrorism/ (accessed 9 December 2017).

Lazarus, L. (2020) Preventive Obligations, Risk and Coercive Overreach. In L. Lavrysen and N. Mavronicola (eds), *Coercive Human Rights*. (Oxford: Hart Publishing).

Lazarus, L. and Goold, B. (2007) *Security and Human Rights*. (1st ed.) (Portland: Hart Publishing).

Lazarus, L. and Goold, B. (2019) *Security and Human Rights*. (2nd ed.) (Oxford: Hart Publishing).

Lee, M. and McGovern, A. (2013) Force to Sell: Policing the Image and Manufacturing Public Confidence. *Policing and Society*. 23(2): 103–24.

Lindholt, L. et al. (eds) (2003) *Human Rights and the Police in Transitional Countries*. (The Hague: Kluwer Law International).

Lipsky, M. (1980) *Street-Level Bureaucracy: Dilemmas of the Individual in Public Services*. (New York, Russell Sage Foundation).

Little, L. (1996) Characterization and Legal Discourse. *Journal of Legal Education*. 46(3): 372–406.

Livingstone, S. and Murray, R. (2005) *Evaluating the Effectiveness of National Human Rights Institutions*. http://uir.ulster.ac.uk/31721/1/NHRI_report.pdf (accessed 8 December 2017).

Loader, I. (2007) The Cultural Lives of Security and Rights. In B. Goold and L. Lazarus (eds), *Security and Human Rights*. (Portland: Hart Publishing).

Loader, I. (2016) In Search of Civic Policing: Recasting the 'Peelian' Principles. *Criminal Law and Philosophy*. 10(3): 427–40.

Loader, I., Girling, E. and Sparks, R. (1998) Narratives of Decline: Youth, Dis/order and Community in an English 'Middletown'. *British Journal of Criminology* 38(3): 388–403.

Loader, I. and Mulcahy, A. (2001) The Power of Legitimate Naming. *British Journal of Criminology*. 41(1): 41–55.

Loader, I. and Mulcahy, A. (2003) *Policing and the Condition of England*. (Oxford: Clarendon).

Loader, I. and Sparks, R. (2011) *Public Criminology*. (Abingdon: Routledge).

Löfstrand, C., Loftus, B. and Loader, I. (2016) Doing 'Dirty Work': Stigma and Esteem in the Private Security Industry. *European Journal of Criminology*. 13(3): 297–314.

Loftus, B. (2009) *Police Culture in a Changing World*. (Oxford: Oxford University Press).

Loftus, B. and Goold. B. (2012) Covert Surveillance and the Invisibilities of Policing. *Criminology and Criminal Justice* 12(3): 275–388.

Loftus, B., Goold, B. and Mac Giollabhuí, S. (2016) From a Visible Spectacle to an Invisible Presence: The Working Culture of Covert Policing. *British Journal of Criminology*. 56(4): 629–45.

Loveday, B. (2006) Policing Performance: The impact of Performance Measures and Targets on Police Forces in England and Wales. *International Journal of Police Service and Management*. 8(4): 282–93.

Lovell, G. (2012) *This is Not Civil Rights: Discovering Rights Talk in 1939 America*. (New York, Cambridge University Press).

Luhmann N. (2004) *Law as a Social System*. (Oxford: Oxford University Press).

Lundy, P. (2009) Can the Past be Policed? Lessons from the Historical Enquiries Team Northern Ireland. *Journal of Law and Social Challenges*. 11(Spring/Summer): 109–56.

Lundy, P. (2011) Paradoxes and Challenges of Transitional Justice at the 'Local' Level: Historical Enquiries in Northern Ireland. *Contemporary Social Science: Journal of the Academy of Social Sciences*. 6(1): 89–106.

Lundy, P. and McGovern, M. (2008) A Trojan Horse? Unionism, Trust and Truth-telling in Northern Ireland. *International Journal of Transitional Justice*. 2(1): 42–62.

McBarnet, D. (1981) *Conviction: The Law, the State and the Construction of Justice*. (London: Macmillan).

Mageean, P and O'Brien, M. (1998) From the Margins to the Mainstream: Human Rights and the Good Friday Agreement. *Fordham International Law Journal*. 22(4): 1499–1538.

Maguire, M. (1988) Effects of the 'P.A.C.E' Provisions on Detention and Questioning: Some Preliminary Findings. *British Journal of Criminology*. 28(1): 19–43.

Manikis, M. (2017) Expanding Participation: Victims as Agents of Accountability in the Criminal Justice Process. *Public Law* 1: 63–80.

Manning, P. (1977) *Police Work: The Social Organization of Policing*. (Cambridge, MA: MIT Press).

Manning, P. (1986) The Social Reality and Social Organization of Natural Decision-Making. *Washington and Lee Law Review*. 43(4): 1291–311.

Manning, P. (1989). Occupational Culture. In W. Bailey (ed.), *The Encyclopedia of Police Science*. (New York and London: Garland).

Manning, P. (2013) The Work of Egon Bittner. *Ethnographic Studies*. 13: 51–66.

Manning, P and Hawkins, J. (1989) Police Decision-making. In M. Weatheritt (ed.), *Police Research: Some Future Prospects*. (Avebury: Aldershot), 139–56.

Martin, R. (2019) A 'Culture of Justification'? Police Interpretation and Application of the Human Rights Act 1998. In Varuhas, J. and Stark, S. (eds), *The Frontiers of Public Law*. (Oxford: Hart Publishing).

Martin, R. (2020a) Ethno-National Narratives of Human Rights: The Northern Ireland Policing Board. *Modern Law Review*. 83(1): 91–127.

Martin, R. (2020b) Pre-Charge Bail Research Project: Summary of Descriptive Findings (on file with author).

Martin, R. and Bradford, B. (2019) The Anatomy of Legitimacy: Dialogic, Power and Procedural Justice *Theoretical Criminology*. 19 December. https://doi.org/10.1177/1362480619890605 (accessed 5 July 2020).

Maruna, S. and Copes, H. (2005) What Have We Learned from Five Decades of Neutralization Research? *Crime and Justice*. 32: 221–320.

Mawby, R. (2002) *Policing Images*. (Collumpton: Willan Publishing).

Mawby, R. (2010) Police Corporate Communications, Crime reporting and the Shaping of Policing News. *Policing and Society*. 20(1): 124–39.

Mawby, R. (2014) The Presentation of Police in Everyday Life : Police–Press Relations, Impression Management and the Leveson Inquiry. *Crime, Media, Culture: An International Journal*. 10(3): 239–57.

McAuley, J. (2003) Unionism's Last Stand? Contemporary Unionist Politics and Identity in Northern Ireland. *Global Review of Ethnopolitics*. 3(1): 60–74.

McAuley, J. (2004) Fantasy Politics? Restructuring Unionism after the Good Friday Agreement. *Eire-Ireland*. 39(1–2): 189–214.

McAleese (2015) Police to axe beat officers in 40 towns and villages in Northern Ireland. *Belfast Telegraph*, 29 June. http://www.belfasttelegraph.co.uk/news/northern-ireland/police-to-axe-beat-officers-in-40-towns-and-villages-in-northern-ireland-31336151.html (accessed 8 December 2017).

McAlister, S., Scraton, P. and Haydon, D. (2009) *Childhood in Transition: Experiencing Marginalization and Conflict in Northern Ireland*. Childhood, Transition and Social Justice Initiative, School of Law Queen's University. (Belfast: Queen's University Belfast).

McClanahan, B. and Brisman, A. (2017) Police Violence and the Failed Promise of Human Rights. In L. Weber, E. Fishwick and M. Marmo (eds), *The Routledge International Handbook of Criminology and Human Rights*. (Abingdon: Routledge).

McCambridge, J. (2007) World police top brass set to meet in Ulster summit. *Belfast Telegraph*. 19 January.

McCann, M. (2014) The Unbearable Lightness of Rights: On Sociolegal Inquiry in the Global Era. *Law and Society Review*. 48(2): 245–73.

McCausland, D. (2007) Policing Parades and Protest in Northern Ireland. *European Human Rights Law Review*. 3: 211–19.

McCausland, N. (2017) Where was Sinn Fein's concern for human rights on Bloody Friday, at Claudy, La Mon or Enniskillen? *Belfast Telegraph*. 6 July. https://www.belfasttelegraph.co.uk/opinion/columnists/nelson-mccausland/where-was-sinn-feins-concern-for-human-rights-on-bloody-friday-at-claudy-la-mon-or-enniskillen-35900315.html (accessed 9 December 2017).

McConville, M., Sanders, A. and Leng, R. (1991) *The Case for the Prosecution*. (London: Routledge).

McCrudden, C. (2005) Mainstreaming Human Rights. In C. Harvey (ed.), *Human Rights in the Community: Rights as Agents for Change*. (Oxford: Hart Publishing).

McCrudden, C. (2006) Legal Research and the Social Sciences. *Law Quarterly Review*. 122: 632.

McDevitt, C. (2011) Denying rights is nothing more than a cop out. *Belfast Telegraph*. 11 November. http://www.belfasttelegraph.co.uk/opinion/news-analysis/denying-rights-is-nothing-more-than-a-copout-28681327.html#ixzz1fq4XLiO8. (accessed 8 December 2017).

McDevitt, C. (2013) How police are having cards marked on human rights; Protecting the rights of the public and PSNI officers is an essential element of making the service work to its best, says Conall McDevitt. *Belfast Telegraph*, 8 February.

McDonald, H. (2012) Northern Ireland police service 'rehired 20% of retired RUC officers'. *The Guardian*, 3 October. https://www.theguardian.com/uk/2012/oct/03/northern-ireland-police-rehired (accessed 9 December 2017).

McDonald, H. (2014) 25% of Northern Ireland riot police hurt in loyalist clashes in one year. *The Guardian*. 28 May. https://www.theguardian.com/uk-news/2014/may/28/25percent-northern-ireland-police-injured-sectarian-clashes (accessed 9 December 2017).

McDonald, H. (2015) IRA's 'army council' still exists and influences Sinn Féin strategy – report. *The Guardian*, 20 October. https://www.theguardian.com/uk-news/2015/oct/20/ira-still-exists-but-in-much-reduced-form-says-official-report (accessed 8 December 2017).

McEvoy, K. (2000) Law, Struggle, and Political Transformation in Northern Ireland. *Journal of Law and Society*. 27(4): 542–71.

McEvoy, K. (2003) Beyond the Metaphor: Political Violence, Human rights and 'New' Peacemaking Criminology. *Theoretical Criminology*. 7(3): 319–46.

McEvoy, K (2007) Beyond Legalism: Towards a Thicker Understanding of Transitional Justice. *Journal of Law and Society*. 34(4): 411–40.

McEvoy, K. (2011) What Did the Lawyers Do During the 'War'? Neutrality, Conflict and the Culture of Quietism. *Modern Law Review*. 74(3): 350–84.

McEvoy, K. (2017) Amnesties, Prosecutions and the Rule of Law in Northern Ireland. Briefing Paper, Defence Select Committee, House of Commons. 7 March.

McEvoy, K. and Bryson, A. (2016) Justice, Truth and Oral History: Legislating the Past 'From Below' in Northern Ireland. *Northern Ireland Legal Quarterly*. 67(1): 67–90.

McEvoy, K. and Schwartz, A. (2015) Judges, Conflict, and the Past. *Journal of Law and Society*. 42(4): 528–55.

McEvoy, K. and White, C. Loyalty, Redress and Citizenship: Security Vetting in Northern Ireland (1998) *Modern Law Review*. 61(3): 341–61.

McGlynn, C. Tonge, J. and J. McAuley (2014), The Party Politics of Post-Devolution Identity in Northern Ireland. *British Journal of Politics and International Relations*. 16(2): 273–90.

McGovern, A. and Lee, M. (2010) 'Cop[ying] it sweet': police media units and the making of news. *Australian and New Zealand Journal of Criminology*. 43(3) 444–64.

McInerney-Lankford, S. (2009) Human Rights and Development: A Comment on Challenges and Opportunities from a Legal Perspective. *Journal of Human Rights Practice*. 1(1): 51–82.

McInerney-Lankford, S. (2018) Legal Methodologies and Human Rights Research: Challenges and Opportunities. In B. Andreassen, H.-O. Sano and S. McInerney-Lankford (eds), *Research Methods in Human Rights: A Handbook*. (Cheltenham, UK: Edward Elgar).

McKinnon, A. (2010) Elective Affinities of the Protestant Ethic: Weber and the Chemistry. *Sociological Theory*. 28(1): 108–26.

McKittrick, D. and McVea, D. (2012) *Making Sense of the Troubles: A History of the Northern Ireland Conflict*. (London: Penguin).

McLaughlin, E. and Murji, K. (1998) Resistance through Representation: 'Storylines', Advertising and Police Federation Campaigns. *Policing and Society*. 8(4): 367–99.

McLaughlin, E., Muncie, J. and Hughes, D. (2001) The Permanent Revolution: New Labour, New Public Management and the Modernization of Criminal justice. *Criminal Justice*. 1(3): 301–18.

McNulty, E. (1994). Generating Common Sense Knowledge Among Police Officers. *Symbolic Interaction*. 17(3): 281–94.

McPhillips, R. (2016) Private Members' Business: International Human Rights Day. Northern Ireland Assembly. 5 December. 118(1): 17.

Mead, D. (2007) The Right to Peaceful Protest under the European Convention on Human Rights – A Content Study of Strasbourg Case Law. *European Human Rights Law Review*. 4: 345–84.

Mead, D. (2009) Of kettles, Cordons and Crowd Control – Austin v Commissioner of Police for the Metropolis and the Meaning of

'Deprivation of Liberty'. *European Human Rights Law Review*. 3: 376–94.

Mead, D. (2010) *The New Law of Peaceful Protest: Rights and Regulation in the Human Rights Act Era*. (Oxford: Hart Publishing).

Mead, D. (2012) Outcomes Aren't All: Defending Process-Based Review of Public Authority Decisions under the Human Rights Act. *Public Law*. 63–87.

Mead, D. (2018) A Seven (or so) Year Hitch: How has the Coalition's Pledge to Restore the Right to Non-Violent Protest Fared? *King's Law Journal*. 29(2): 242–74.

Mead, D. (2019) 'They Offer You a Feature on Stockings and Suspenders Next to a Call for Stiffer Penalties for Sex Offenders': Do We Learn More About the Media Than about Human Rights from Tabloid Coverage of Human Rights Stories? In M Farrell, E Drywood and E Hughes (eds), *Human Rights in the Media: Fear and Fetish*. (Abingdon: Routledge).

Meckled-García, S. and Çali, B. (eds), (2006) *The Legalization of Human Rights: Multidisciplinary Perspectives on Human Rights and Human Rights Law*. (Abingdon: Routledge).

Merry, S. E. (2006a) Transnational Human Rights and Local Activism: Mapping the Middle. *American Anthropologist*. 108(1): 38–51.

Merry, S. E. (2006b) *Human Rights and Gender Violence: Translating International Law into Local Justice*. (Chicago: University of Chicago Press).

Merry, S. E. (2017) The Potential of Ethnographic Methods for Human Rights Research. In B. Andreassen, H.-O. Sano and S. McInerney-Lankford (eds), *Research Methods in Human Rights: A Handbook*. (Cheltenham, UK: Edward Elgar).

Mesko, G. and Tankebe, J. (eds) (2015) *Trust and Legitimacy in Criminal Justice: European Perspectives*. (Switzerland: Springer).

Miller, S. (1999) *Gender and Community Policing: Walking the Talk*. (Boston, MA: North Eastern University Press).

Millings, M. (2013) Policing British Asian Identities: The Enduring Role of the Police in Young British Asian Men's Situated Negotiation of Identity and Belonging. *British Journal of Criminology*. 53(6): 1075–92.

Moffett, L. (2016) A Pension for Injured Victims of the Troubles: Reparations or Reifying Victim Hierarchy? *Northern Ireland Legal Quarterly*. 66(4): 297–319.

Morgan, R., Reiner, R. and McKenzie, I. (1991) *Police Powers and Police: a study of the work of custody officers*. Final report to the ESRC (unpublished).

Muir, K. (1977). *Police: Streetcorner Politicians*. (Chicago, IL.: Chicago University Press).

Mulcahy, A. (1994) The Justifications of 'Justice': Legal Practitioners' Accounts of Negotiated Case Settlements in the Magistrates' Courts. *British Journal of Criminology*. 34(4): 411–30.

Mulcahy, A. (1999) Visions of Normality: Peace and the Reconstruction of Policing in Northern Ireland. *Social and Legal Studies*. 8(2) 277–95.

Mulcahy, A. (2000) Policing History: The Official Discourse and Organizational Memory of the Royal Ulster Constabulary. *British Journal of Criminology*. 40(1): 68–87.

Mulcahy, A. (2006) *Policing in Northern Ireland: Conflict, Legitimacy and Reform*. (Collumpton: Willan Publishing).

Mulcahy, A. (2008) The Police Service of Northern Ireland. In T. Newburn (ed.), *Handbook of Policing* (2nd ed.) (Collumpton: Willan Publishing), 204–23.

Mulcahy, A. (2016) Keynote speech, The Policing Authority Code of Ethics Public Consultation, Dublin. 8 September.

Mulcahy, A. and Ellison, G. (2001) The Language of Policing and the Struggle for Legitimacy in Northern Ireland. *Policing and Society*. 11 (3–4): 383–404.

Munce, P. (2014) Unionism and the Northern Ireland Human Rights Commission 1999–2005: Hostility, Hubris and Hesitancy. *Irish Political Studies*. 29(2): 194–214.

Mureinik, E. (1994) A Bridge to Where? Introducing the Interim Bill of Rights. *South African Journal of Human Rights*. 10(1): 31–48.

Murdoch, J. and Roche, R. (2013) *The European Convention on Human Rights and Policing: A Handbook for Police Officers and Other Law Enforcement Officials Manual*. (Strasbourg: Council of Europe).

Murphy, J. (2013) *Policing for Peace in Northern Ireland*. (Basingstoke: Palgrave Macmillan).

Murphy, T. and Whitty, N. (2013) Making History: Academic Criminology and Human Rights. *British Journal of Criminology*. 53(4): 568–87.

Murray, G. (2013).Human Rights of all Highlighted in Guide, *News letter,* 16 December.

Murray, K. and Harkin, D. (2017) Policing in Cool and Hot Climates: Legitimacy, Power and the Rise and Fall of Mass Stop and Search in Scotland. *British Journal of Criminology*. 57(4): 885–905.

Neyroud, P. and Beckley, A. (2013) *Policing, Ethics and Human Rights*. (Abingdon: Routledge).

Newburn, T. (2016) Reflections on Why Riots Don't Happen. *Theoretical Criminology* 20(2): 125–44.

Newburn, T. and Reiner, R. (2012) Policing and the Police. In M. Maguire, R. Morgan and R. Reiner (eds), *The Oxford Handbook of Criminology*. (Oxford: Oxford University Press).

News Letter (2001) Patten 'legacy of destruction'. 10 November.

News Letter (2004) Attwood wants rights based PSNI. 20 April.

News Letter (2007) DUP and Sinn Fein clash over new report. 25 September.

News Letter (2010) Matt Baggott Interview – in full. 6 April.

News Letter (2017a) Call for judge to lead probe into soldiers' prosecutions welcomed, 25 January. http://www.newsletter.co.uk/news/call-for-judge-to-lead-probe-into-soldiers-prosecutions-welcomed-1-7791150 (accessed 7 December 2017).

News Letter (2017b) Foster and O'Neill clash over Stormont House Agreement and legacy plans. 2 February. https://www.newsletter.co.uk/news/politics/foster-and-oneill-clash-over-stormont-house-agreement-and-legacy-plans-1382841 (accessed 14 July 2020).

Ní Aoláin, F. (2001) The Evolving Jurisprudence of the European Convention Concerning the Right to Life. *Netherlands Quarterly of Human Rights*. 19(1): 21–42.

Ní Aoláin, F. (2002) Truth Telling, Accountability and the Right to Life in Northern Ireland. *European Human Rights Law Review*. (5): 572–90.

Ní Aoláin, F. (2017) *Transitional Justice and The European Convention on Human Rights*. (Geneva: Geneva Academy of International Humanitarian Law and Human Rights).

Nolan, P. et al. (2014) *The Flag Dispute: Anatomy of a Protest*. (Belfast: Queen's University Belfast).

North Report on Parades (1997) *The Full Text, Review of Parades and Marches in Northern Ireland, Executive Summary*. http://cain.ulst.ac.uk/issues/parade/docs/north97sum.pdf (accessed 14 December 2017).

Northern Ireland Affairs Committee (NIAC) (2005) *The Functions of the Northern Ireland Policing Board: 7th Report of Session 2004-5*. (London: The Stationery Office).

Norther Ireland Affairs Committee (NIAC) (2015) *The Administrative Scheme for 'On-the-Runs': Second Report of Session 2014–2015*.

Northern Ireland Committee for Justice (2012) Police Service of Northern Ireland Budget and Funding Issues: Police Service of Northern Ireland. In *Police Service of Northern Ireland Budget and Funding Issues: Police Service of Northern Ireland*. (Belfast, Northern Ireland Assembly, Committee for Justice).

Northern Ireland Committee for Justice (2013) Committee for Justice, Official Report (Hansard), HMIC Report on Historical Enquiries Team, 26 September.

Northern Ireland Executive (2013) *An Agreement Among the Parties of the Northern Ireland Executive on Parades, Select Commemorations and Related Problems; Flags and Emblems; and Contending With The Past*, 13 December.

Northern Ireland Policing Board (2004) *A Report on the Policing of the Ardoyne Parades*. 12 July.

Northern Ireland Policing Board (2005) *Report on the Policing of the Ardoyne Parades. 12th July 2005 and the Whiterock Parade 10th September 2005*.

Northern Ireland Policing Board (2006) *Human Rights Annual Report 2006*. (Belfast: NIPB).
Northern Ireland Policing Board (2007) *Human Rights Annual Report 2007*. (Belfast: NIPB).
Northern Ireland Policing Board (2008) *Human Rights Annual Report 2008*. (Belfast: NIPB).
Northern Ireland Policing Board) (2009) *Human Rights Annual Report 2009*. (Belfast: NIPB).
Northern Ireland Policing Board (2010) *Human Rights Annual Report 2010* (Belfast: NIPB).
Northern Ireland Policing Board (2011) *Human Rights Annual Report 2011* (Belfast: NIPB).
Northern Ireland Policing Board (NIPB) (2013) *Human Rights Annual Report 2013* (Belfast: NIPB).
Northern Ireland Policing Board (2014) Position Paper, Northern Ireland Policing Board Historical Enquiries Team Working Group. 27 April. (Belfast: NIPB), 23. https://www.nipolicingboard.org.uk/sites/nipb/files/media-files/het-position-paper.pdf (accessed 5 July 2020).
Northern Ireland Policing Board (2015a) *Human Rights Annual Report 2015* (Belfast: NIPB).
Northern Ireland Policing Board (NIPB) (2015b) *Freedom of Information Request 44/2015*. https://www.nipolicingboard.org.uk/sites/nipb/files/media-files/foi-442015.pdf. (accessed 9 December 2017).
Northern Ireland Policing Board (2019) *Human Rights Annual Report 2016–2017*. Belfast: NIPB).
Nussbaum, M.C. (1997) Capabilities and Human Rights. *Fordham Law Review*. 66(2): 273–300.
Oberleitner, G. (2012) Does Enforcement Matter? In C. Gearty and C. Douzinas (eds), *The Cambridge Companion to Human Rights Law*. (Cambridge: Cambridge University Press).
O'Brien-Ollinger, S. (2016) *Police, Race and Culture in the 'New Ireland': An Ethnography*. (Basingstoke: Palgrave Macmillan).
O'Byrne, D. (2012) On the Sociology of Human Rights: Theorising the Language-structure of Rights. *Sociology*. 46(5): 829–43.
O'Hara, G. (2015) Sinn Féin welcomes PSNI Human Rights Report. 20 February. http://www.sinnfein.ie/contents/33508 (accessed 8 February 2018).
O'Neill, M. (2019) *Police Community Support Officers: Cultures and Identities within Pluralised Policing*. (Oxford: Oxford University Press).
O'Rawe, M. (2005) Human Rights and Police Training in Transitional Societies: Exporting the Lessons of Northern Ireland. *Human Rights Quarterly*. 27(3): 943–68.

O'Rawe, M. (2007) Human rights, Transitional Societies and Police Training: Legitimating Strategies and Delegitimating Legacies *St. John's Journal of Legal Commentary*. 22(2): 199–259.

Orde, H. (2009) *Oral Evidence to Policing of the G20 Protests, Eighth Report of Session 2008–09. Report, together with formal minutes, oral and written evidence.* https://publications.parliament.uk/pa/cm200809/cmselect/cmhaff/418/418.pdf (accessed 9 December 2017).

Parades Commission (2011) *Annual Report and Financial Statements Parades Commission for Northern Ireland for the year ended 31st March 2010.*

Parmar, A. (2019) Policing, Migration and Racial Technologies. *British Journal of Criminology*. 59(4): 938–57.

Payne, L. (2008) *Unsettling Accounts: Neither Truth nor Reconciliation in Confessions of State Violence.* (Durham, NC and London: Duke University Press).

Pearson, G., Rowe, M. and Turner, L. (2018) Policy, Practicalities and PACE s. 24: The Subsuming of the Necessity Criteria in Arrest Decision Making by Frontline Police Officers. *Journal of Law and Society.* 45(2): 282–308.

Pegram, T. (2010) Diffusion Across Political Systems: The Global Spread of National Human Rights Institutions. *Human Rights Quarterly.* 32(3): 729–60.

Police Ombudsman of Northern Ireland (2007) *Statement by the Police Ombudsman for Northern Ireland on her investigation into the circumstances surrounding the death of Raymond McCord Junior and related matters.* (Belfast: PONI).

Police Ombudsman of Northern Ireland (2016) *Statutory Report Public Statement by the Police Ombudsman in accordance with Section 62 of the Police (Northern Ireland) Act 1998. Relating to a complaint by the victims and survivors of the murders at the Heights Bar, Loughinisland, 18 June 1994.* (Belfast: PONI).

Police Service of Northern Ireland (2002) *Report of the Chief Constable 2001/02* (Belfast: Police Service of Northern Ireland).

Police Service of Northern Ireland (2006) Human Rights Programme of Action 2005–2006 (Belfast: PSNI).

Police Service of Northern Ireland (2007) Human Rights Programme of Action 2006–2007 (Belfast: PSNI).

Police Service of Northern Ireland (2008a) Human Rights Programme of Action 2007–2008 (Belfast: PSNI).

Police Service of Northern Ireland (2008b) *Service Procedure SP 14/2008* (Belfast: PSNI). http://library.college.police.uk/docs/APPref/service-procedures-processions-2008.pdf (accessed 10 December 2017).

Police Service of Northern Ireland (2009) Human Rights Programme of Action 2008–2009 (Belfast: PSNI).

Police Service of Northern Ireland (2010) Human Rights Programme of Action 2009–2010 (Belfast: PSNI).
Police Service of Northern Ireland (2011) Human Rights Programme of Action 2010–2011 (Belfast: PSNI).
Police Service of Northern Ireland (2012) Human Rights Programme of Action 2011–2012 (Belfast: PSNI).
Police Service of Northern Ireland (2013a) Human Rights Programme of Action 2012–2013 (Belfast: PSNI).
Police Service of Northern Ireland (2013b) *Freedom of Information Request F-2013-04578*. (Belfast: PSNI). https://www.psni.police.uk/globalassets/advice--information/our-publications/disclosure-logs/2013/operational-policing/annual_orange_parade_in_dungiven.pdf (accessed 9 December 2017).
Police Service of Northern Ireland (2013c) *PSNI Manual of Policy, Procedure and Guidance on Conflict Management, Chapter 13, Public Order*. (Belfast: PSNI). https://www.psni.police.uk/globalassets/advice--information/our-publications/conflict-management-manual/chapter_13_-_public_order.pdf (accessed 14 December 2017).
Police Service of Northern Ireland (2014a) Human Rights Programme of Action 2013–2014 (Belfast: PSNI).
Police Service of Northern Ireland (2014b) *Freedom of Information Request F-2014-01314*. (Belfast: PSNI). https://www.whatdotheyknow.com/request/cost_of_clean_up_operation_after (accessed 9 December 2017).
Police Service of Northern Ireland (2014c) *Freedom of Information Request F-2017-01265*. (Belfast: PSNI). (On file with author).
Police Service of Northern Ireland (2015a) Human Rights Programme of Action 2014–2015. (Belfast: PSNI).
Police Service of Northern Ireland (2015b) *Freedom of Information Request F-2015-02573*. (Belfast: PSNI). https://www.psni.police.uk/globalassets/advice--information/our-publications/disclosure-logs/2015/operational-policing/apprentice_boys_derry_day_parade_lurgan_2015.pdf (accessed 7 December 2017).
Police Service of Northern Ireland (2016a) Human Rights Programme of Action 2015–2016. (Belfast: PSNI).
Police Service of Northern Ireland (2016b) *Freedom of Information Request F-2016-00188*. (Belfast: PSNI). https://www.psni.police.uk/globalassets/advice--information/our-publications/disclosure-logs/2016/crime/historical_enquiries_team_investgations.pdf (accessed 8 December 2017).
Police Service of Northern Ireland (2017) *Police and Criminal Evidence (PACE) Order Statistics, Covering the 12 month period 1st April 2016 - 31st March 2017*. https://www.psni.police.uk/globalassets/inside-the-psni/our-statistics/police-and-criminal-evidence/pace-statistics-report-2016.17.pdf (accessed 9 December 2017).

Police Service of Northern Ireland (2019) *Police and Criminal Evidence (PACE) Order Statistics 1st April 2018 – 31st March 2019* (Belfast: PSNI).

Quigley, G. (2002), Review of the Parades Commission, 27 September 2002 (Belfast: Northern Ireland Office). http://cain.ulst.ac.uk/issues/parade/docs/quigley270902.pdf (accessed 14 December 2017).

Raine, J. and Walker, C. (2004) Implementing the Human Rights Act into the Courts in England and Wales: Culture Shift or Damp Squid. In S. Halliday and P. Schmidt (eds), *Human Rights Brought Home: Socio-Legal Perspectives of Human Rights in the Domestic Context.* (Oregon, USA: Hart Publishing), 111–36.

Ravasi, D. and Schultz, M. (2006) Responding to Organizational Identity Threats: Exploring the Role of Organizational Culture. *The Academy of Management Journal.* 49(3): 433–58.

Raz, J. (2009) *Between Authority and Interpretation: On the Theory of Law and Practical Reason.* (Oxford: Oxford University Press).

Rea, D. and Masefield, R. (2014) *Policing in Northern Ireland: Delivering the new Beginning?* (Liverpool: Liverpool University Press).

Reiner, R. (2010) *The Politics of the Police.* (4th ed.) (Oxford: Oxford University Press).

Reiner, R. (2012) Book review: Layla Skinns, Police Custody: Governance, Legitimacy and Reform in the Criminal Justice Process. *Criminology and Criminal Justice.* 12(5): 613–15.

Richards, S. (2015) Unearthing Bureaucratic Legal Consciousness: Government Officials' Legal Identification and Moral Ideals. *International Journal of Law in Context.* 11(3): 299–319.

Riles, A. (2006) Anthropology, Human Rights and Legal Knowledge: Culture in the Iron Cage. *American Anthropologist* 108(1): 52–65.

Risse, T. and Sikkink, K. (1999) The Socialization of International Human Rights Norms into Domestic Practices: Introduction. In T. Risse, S. Ropp and K. Sikkink (eds), *The Power of Human Rights: International Norms and Domestic Change.* (Cambridge: Cambridge University Press).

Rock, P. (2004) *Constructing Victims' Rights: The Home Office, New Labour, and Victims.* (Oxford: Oxford University Press).

Rowbottom, J. (2019) Careful What You Wish For: Press Criticism of the Legal Protection of Human Rights. In M. Farrell, E. Hughes and E. Drywood (eds), *Human Rights in the Media: Fear and Fetish.* (Abingdon: Routledge).

Rowe, M. (2007) Rendering Visible the Invisible: Police Discretion, Professionalism and Decision-making. *Policing and Society.* 17(3): 279–294.

Royal Ulster Constabulary (1999) *Report of the Chief Constable 1998/9.* (Belfast: Royal Ulster Constabulary).

Sackmann, S. (1991) *Cultural Knowledge in Organizations.* (Newbury Park, CA: Sage).

Sanders, A. (2008) Can Coercive Powers be Effectively Controlled or Regulated? The Case for Anchored Pluralism. In E. Cape and R. Young (eds), *Regulating Policing: The Police and Criminal Evidence Act 1984 Past, Present and Future*. (Oxford: Hart Publishing), 45–75.

Sanders, A., Young, R. and Burton, M. (2010) *Criminal Justice*. (Oxford: Oxford University Press).

Sibley, S.S (2005) Everyday Life and the Constitution of Legality. In M. Jacobs and N. Hanrahan (eds), *The Blackwell Companion to the Sociology of Culture*. (Malden, MA: Blackwell Publishing).

Scheinin, M. (2017) The Art and Science of Interpretation in Human Rights Law. In B. Andreassen, H.-O. Sano and S. McInerney-Lankford (eds), *Research Methods in Human Rights: A Handbook*. (Cheltenham, UK: Edward Elgar).

Schmidt, P. and Halliday, S. (2004) Introduction: Socio-Legal Perspectives on Human Rights in the National Context. In S. Halliday and P. Schmidt (eds), *Human Rights Brought Home: Socio-Legal Perspectives of Human Rights in the Domestic Context*. (Oregon, USA: Hart Publishing), 1–22.

Schneider, C.E. (1992) Discretion and Rules: A Lawyer's View. In K. Hawkins (ed.), *The Uses of Discretion*. (Oxford: Oxford University Press).

Schulz, D. (1998) *Leveraging the Law: Using Courts to Achieve Social Change*. (New York: Peter Lang).

Schütz, A. (1953). Common-Sense and Scientific Interpretation of Human Action. *Philosophy and Phenomenological Research*. 14(1): 1–38.

Shearing, C. (2000) A New Beginning' for Policing. *Journal of Law and Society*. 27(3): 386–393.

Shearing, C. and Ericson, R.V. (1991) Culture as Figurative Action. *British Journal of Sociology*. 42(4): 481–506.

Sheridan, P. (2006) Platform – PSNI Cannot Stop Crime without Use of Informers. *Irish News*. 30 June.

Sheridan, P. (2007) Why We Still Need Touts. *Irish News*. 8 February.

Shiner, M. (2010) Post-Lawrence Policing in England and Wales: Guilt, Innocence and the Defence of Organizational Ego. *British Journal of Criminology*. 50(5): 935–53.

Simpson, K. (2013) Political Strategies of Engagement: Unionists and Dealing With the Past in Northern Ireland. *British Politics*. 8(1): 2–27.

Sinn Féin (1991) Freedom: A Sinn Féin Education Publication. http://www.sinnfein.org/documents/freedom.html#civ (accessed 8 December 2017).

Sinn Féin (2004) Rights for All: A Sinn Féin Discussion Document. http://www.sinnfein.ie/files/2009/FinalRightsForAll1.pdf (accessed 8 December 2017).

Skinns, L. (2009a) I'm a Detainee; Get Me out of Here. *British Journal of Criminology*. 49(3): 399–417.

Skinns, L. (2009b) 'Let's Get it Over With': Early Findings on the Factors Affecting Detainees' Access to Custodial Legal Advice. *Policing and Society*. 19(1): 58–78.

Skinns, L. (2011) *Police Custody: Governance, Legitimacy and Reform in the Criminal Justice Process*. (Abingdon: Routledge).

Skinns, L. and Wooff, A. (2020) Pain in Police Detention: A Critical Point in the 'Penal Painscape'? *Policing and Society.* 15 January. https://doi.org/10.1080/10439463.2019.1706506.

Sklansky, D.A. (2007) Seeing Blue: Police Reform, Occupational Culture and Cognitive Burn-in. In M. O'Neill, M. Marks and A.-M. Singh (eds), *Police Occupational Culture*. (Oxford: Elsevier JAI).

Sklansky, D.A., and Marks, M. (2008) The Role of the Rank and File in Police Reform, *Policing and Society*. 18(1): 1–6.

Skogan, W. and Hartnett, S. (1999) *Community Policing, Chicago Style*. (New York: Oxford University Press).

Smith, D. (1998) Reform or Moral Outrage – The Choice is Yours. *British Journal of Criminology*. 38(4): 616–22.

Smith, A., McWilliams, M. and Yarnell, P. (2014) *Political Capacity Building: Advancing a Bill of Rights for Northern Ireland*. (Transitional Justice Institute: University of Ulster).

Smith, A., McWilliams, M. and Yarnell, P. (2016) Does Every Cloud Have a Silver Lining? Brexit, Repeal of the Human Rights Act and the Northern Ireland Bill of Rights. *Fordham International Law Journal*. 40(1): 1–51.

Snow, D. (2004) Framing Processes, Ideology, and Discursive Fields. In D. Snow, S. Soule and H. Kriesi (eds), *The Blackwell Companion to Social Movements*. (Malden, MA: Blackwell).

Sokoloff, N. J. and Pratt, C. (2010) *Domestic Violence at the Margins: Readings on Race, Class, Gender and Culture*. (Piscataway, NJ: Rutgers University Press).

Sonenshein, S. (2010) We're Changing or Are We? Untangling the Role of Progressive, Regressive, and Stability Narratives During Strategic Change Implementation. *Academy of Management Journal*. 53(3): 477–512.

Starmer, K. (2007) Monitoring the Performance of the Police Service in Northern Ireland in Complying with the Human Rights Act 1998. *Policing*. 1(1): 94–101.

Starmer, K. (2014) Human Rights, Victims and the Prosecution of Crime in the 21st Century. *Criminal Law Review*. 11: 777–87.

Starmer, K. and Gordon, J. (2005) Monitoring the Performance of the Police Service in Northern Ireland for Compliance with the Human Rights Act 1998. *European Human Rights Law Review*. (3): 233–9.

Starmer, K., Strange, M. and Whitaker, Q. (2002) *Criminal Justice, Police Powers and Human Rights*. (Oxford: Oxford University Press).

Stenross, E. and Kleinman, S. (1989) The Highs and Lows of Emotional Labor: Detectives' Encounters with Criminals and Victims. *Journal of Contemporary Ethnography*. 17(4): 435–52.

Stott, C. (2016) Revisiting the Classics: Policing Coercion and Liberty: A Review of P.A.J. Waddington's Liberty and Order (1994) and Policing Citizens (1999). *Policing and Society*. 26(1): 114–19.

Stott, C., Scothern, M. and Gorringe, H. (2013) Advances in Liaison-Based Public Order Policing in England: Human Rights and Negotiating the Management of Protest? *Policing: A Journal of Policy and Practice*. 7(2): 212–26.

Stott, C., West, O. and Radburn, M. (2018) Policing Football 'Risk'? A Participant Action Research Case Study of a Liaison-Based Approach to 'Public Order' *Policing and Society*. 28(1): 1–16.

Strategic Review of Parading in Northern Ireland (2008) *Interim Consultative Report*. (Belfast: Strategic Review of Parading). http://cain.ulst.ac.uk/issues/parade/srp/srp290408interim.pdf (accessed 11 December 2017).

Stubbins Bates, E. (2020) The British Army's Training in International Humanitarian Law. *Journal of Conflict and Security Law*. 25(2): 291–315.

Sutcliffe, K. M. (1994) What Executives Notice: Accurate Perceptions in Top Management Teams. *Academy of Management Journal*. 37(5): 1360–78.

Sykes, G. and Matza, D. (1957) Techniques of Neutralization: A Theory of Delinquency. *American Sociological Review*. 22(6): 664–70.

Tankebe, J. and A. Liebling (eds.) (2013) *Legitimacy and Criminal Justice: An International Exploration*. (Oxford: Oxford University Press).

Tarrow, S. and Tilly, C. (2009) Contentious Politics and Social Movements. In C. Boix and S. C. Stokes (eds), in *The Oxford Handbook of Comparative Politics* (Oxford: Oxford University Press).

Teubner, G. (1988) *Autopoietic Law: A New Approach to Law and Society*. (Berlin: Walter de Gruyter).

Tilley, N. (2003) Community Policing, Problem-Oriented Policing and Intelligence-led Policing. In T. Newburn (ed.), *A Handbook of Policing*. (Collumpton: Willan Publishing).

Topping, J. (2008) Diversifying From Within: Community Policing and the Governance of Security in Northern Ireland. *British Journal of Criminology*. 48(6): 778–97.

Topping, J. (2015) Policing in Transition. In A McAlinden and C Dwyer (eds), *Criminal Justice in Transition: The Northern Ireland Context*. (Oxford: Hart Publishing).

Topping, J. and Byrne, J. (2016) Shadow Policing: The Boundaries of Community-Based 'Policing' in Northern Ireland. *Policing and Society*. 26(5): 522–43.

Topping, J. and Bradford, B. (2020) Now You See It, Now You Don't: On the (In)Visibility of Police Stop and Search in Northern Ireland *Criminology and Criminal Justice*. 20(1): 93–110.

Trinkner, R., Jackson, J. and Tyler, T (2017) Expanding 'Appropriate' Police Behavior Beyond Procedural Justice: Bounded Authority and Legal Legitimation, unpublished. https://ssrn.com/abstract=2846659 (accessed 2 December 2015).

Tsoukas, H. and Chia, R. (2002) An Organizational Becoming: Rethinking Organizational Change. *Organization Science*. 13(5): 567–82.

Turner, C. (2017) *Violence, Law and the Impossibility of Transitional Justice*. (Abingdon: Routledge).

Tushnet, M. (1984) An Essay on Rights. *Texas Law Review*. 62(8): 1371–5.

Tyler, T. and Blader, S. (2000). *Cooperation in Groups: Procedural Justice, Social Identity, and Behavioral Engagement*. (Philadelphia: Psychology Press).

Tyler, T. and Jackson, J. (2014) Popular Legitimacy and the Exercise of Legal Authority: Motivating Compliance, Cooperation and Engagement. *Psychology, Public Policy and Law* 20(1) 78–95.

Uildriks, N. (2005) *Police Reform and Human Rights: Opportunities and Impediments in Post-Communist Societies*. (Antwerpen-Oxford: Intersentia).

Unger, R.M. (1987) *Social Theory: Its Situation and Tasks* (Cambridge: Cambridge University Press).

van Hulst, M. (2013) Storytelling at the Police Station: The Canteen Culture Revisited. *British Journal of Criminology*. 53(4): 624–42.

van Hulst, M. (2020) Ethnography and Narrative. *Policing and Society*. 30(1): 98–115.

van Hulst, M., and Ybema, S. (2020) From What to Where: A Setting-Sensitive Approach to Organizational Storytelling. *Organization Studies*. 41(3): 365–91.

van Maanen, J. (1973). Observations on the Making of Policemen. *Human Organization*. 32(4): 407–18.

van Zyl Smit, D. and Appleton, C. (2019) *Life Imprisonment: A Global Human Rights Analysis*. (Cambridge, MA: Harvard University Press).

Verschraegen, G. (2002) Human Rights and Modern Society: A Sociological Analysis from the Perspective of Systems Theory. 29(2) *Journal of Law and Society*. 258–81.

Wacquant, L. (2009) *Punishing the Poor: The Neoliberal Government of Social Insecurity*. (Durham, NC: Duke University Press).

Waddington, P. A. J. (1987) Towards Paramilitarism? Dilemmas in Policing Civil Disorder. *British Journal of Criminology*. 27(1): 37–46.

Waddington, P.A.J. (1993) The Case Against Paramilitary Policing Considered. *British Journal of Criminology*. 33(3): 353–73.

Waddington, P. A. J. (1994) *Liberty and Order, Public Order Policing in a Capital City*. (London: UCL Press).

Waddington, P. A. J. (1995) Both Arms of the Law: Institutionalised Protest and the Policing of Public Order. In J. Vagg and T. Newburn (eds.). *The British Society of Criminology Conferences: Selected Proceedings. Volume 1: Emerging Themes in Criminology*.

Waddington, P. A. J. (1999) Police (Canteen) Sub-Culture. *British Journal of Criminology*. 39(2): 287–309.

Waddington, P. A. J. (2000) Public Order Policing: Citizenship and Moral Ambiguity. In L. Leishman, B. Loveday and S. Savage (eds), *Core Issues in Policing*. (London: Longman), 114–30.

Waddington, P. A. J. (2003) Policing Public order and Political Contention. In T. Newburn (ed.), *A Handbook of Policing*. (Collumpton: Willan Publishing).

Waddington, P. A. J. (2012) Police Use of Deadly Force. *Policing and Society*. 22(4): 538–45.

Waddington, P.A.J. (2015) Revisiting the Classics: Police: Streetcorner Politicians: William K. Muir. *Policing and Society*. 25(6): 681–86.

Waddington, P. A. J. and Wright, M. (2012) Police Use of Force, Firearms and Riot-Control. In T Newburn (ed), *Handbook of Policing*. (2nd ed) (Collumpton: Willan Publishing), 465–97.

Wahl, R. (2013) Policing, Values, and Violence: Human Rights Education with Law Enforcers in India. *Journal of Human Rights Practice*. 5(2): 220–42.

Wallach, J. (2005) Human Rights as an Ethics of Power. In R. A. Wilson (ed.), *Human Rights in the 'War on Terror'*. (New York: Cambridge University Press).

Walley, R. (2013) 6th Annual Report of Independent Reviewer of Justice and Security (London: The Stationery Office).

Walsh, R. (2018) Adapting the Police Authority Concept to a Centralised National Police Service: Appearance over Substance in the Republic of Ireland? *Modern Law Review*. 81(4): 622–45.

Warburton et al. (2005) Looking the Other Way: The Impact of Reclassifying Cannabis on Police Warnings, Arrests and Informal Action in England and Wales. *British Journal of Criminology*. 45(2): 113–28.

Weber, M. (1968) *Economy and Society: An Outline of Interpretive Sociology*. G Roth and C Wittich (eds), (Berkeley and Los Angeles, CA: University of California Press).

Weber, K. and Glynn, M. A. (2006) Making Sense with Institutions: Context, Thought and Action in Karl Weick's Theory. *Organization Studies*. 27(11): 1639–60.

Weick, K. E. (1995) *Sensemaking in Organizations*. (California: Sage Publications).

Westmarland, L. and Rowe, M. (2018) Police Ethics and Integrity: Can a New Code Overturn the Blue Code? *Policing and Society*. 28(7): 854–70.

Whitaker, D. (2010) Debating Rights in the New Northern Ireland. *Irish Political Studies*. 25(1): 23–45.

Whitty, N. (2011) Human Rights as Risk: UK Prisons and the Management of Risk and Rights. *Punishment and Society*. 13(2): 123–48.

Wildbore, H. (2010) Human Rights Act Reporting in the Media: Corrections and Clarifications. *UK Bill of Rights Commission, Political and Constitutional Reform Committee*. (London: Stationary office). https://www.publications.parliament.uk/pa/cm201012/cmselect/cmpolcon/writev/1049/m2.htm (accessed 6 December 2017).

Wilson, R. A. (2006) Afterword to 'Anthropology and Human Rights in a New Key': The Social Life of Human Rights. *American Anthropologist*. 108(1): 77–83.

Wilson, R. A. (2007) Tyrannosaurus Lex: The Anthropology of Human Rights and Transnational Law. In M. Goodale and S. Merry (eds), *Transnationalism and the New Legal Order: Tracking Rights between the Global and the Local*. (Cambridge: Cambridge University Press), 342–69.

Wilson, R. A. (2016) *Northern Ireland Peace Monitoring Report (Number Four)*. (Belfast: Community Relations Council).

Young, R. (2008), Street Policing After PACE: The Drift to Summary Justice. In E. Cape and R. Young (eds), *Regulating Policing: The Police and Criminal Evidence Act 1984 Past, Present and Future*. (Oxford: Hart Publishing).

Zedner, L. (2011) Putting Crime Back on the Criminological Agenda. In M. Bosworth and C. Hoyle (eds), *What is Criminology?* (Oxford: Oxford University Press).

Index

For the benefit of digital users, indexed terms that span two pages (e.g., 52–53) may, on occasion, appear on only one of those pages.